VAN NOSTRAND POLITICAL SCIENCE SERIES

Editor

FRANKLIN L. BURDETTE
University of Maryland

GODSHALL, W. L. (Editor)—*Principles and Functions of Government in the United States*

LONDON, K.—*How Foreign Policy Is Made*

PLISCHKE, E.—*Conduct of American Diplomacy*

DIXON, R. G., JR. and PLISCHKE, ELMER—*American Government: Basic Documents and Materials*

SPROUT, HAROLD and MARGARET—*Foundations of National Power,* 2nd Ed.

LANCASTER, LANE W.—*Government in Rural America,* 2nd Ed.

GOVERNMENT IN RURAL AMERICA

BY

LANE W. LANCASTER

Department of Political Science
University of Nebraska

SECOND EDITION

D. VAN NOSTRAND COMPANY, INC.

TORONTO   NEW YORK   LONDON

NEW YORK
D. Van Nostrand Company, Inc., 250 Fourth Avenue, New York 3

TORONTO
D. Van Nostrand Company (Canada), Ltd., 228 Bloor Street, Toronto

LONDON
Macmillan & Company, Ltd., St. Martin's Street, London, W.C. 2

Preface

The second edition of this book maintains the purpose of the first edition, namely, to construct a picture of government in rural areas as a going concern and to describe the government and administration of the rural county, township and school district in the United States.

Developments of two sorts have made desirable a revision of the book. The first of these is the conscious evolution of a new pattern of relationships among the three levels of government in the United States. The most striking example of this is found in the arrangements set up for the administration of the social security program; but no local function has escaped the influence of state and federal programs, all of which have lost their provisional and tentative character and may now be regarded as aspects of a permanent *national* policy.

Organically connected with the development of a new pattern of intergovernmental relationships, it is reasonable to conclude, is the progressive urbanization, as it were, of modes of thought and of administrative procedure in the governance of the countryside. This sort of change cannot be demonstrated by statistics, and much of what is said about it is quite frankly speculation, based upon a considerable body of observed facts, but still speculation. It is hoped that, if such "philosophizing" as the author indulges in has actually a factual basis, it will at least prove suggestive.

In a sense, this book may be regarded as an attempt to summarize the findings of special studies. Although I am quite sure that I have not read everything that has been written on every aspect of the subject for the past fifteen years, I have made a conscientious effort to survey all the important literature available in a good library. No one can do the reading connected with such a task without forming certain conclusions—conclusions from which there is sure to be dissent. All one can do is to hope that such conclusions are not intruded too obviously into the description of institutions and processes, and that they are the sort which a reasonable person might reach.

There is, in both editions, one omission about which something should be said by way of extenuation. I have not discussed local units as political districts, although I am aware, of course, that many of them serve as legislative and other electoral areas and, as such, are vitally important in the democratic process. One cannot do everything, however, and my failure to "cover" this part of the subject may perhaps be excused by the fact that it is adequately treated in all the standard textbooks on political parties and state government.

The treatment of public education may seem unduly long. For this I make no apology. Those who write and those who read books on government are committed to the proposition that citizenship must *to some extent* be a rational matter, and I do not see any better formal device for helping to make it such than the public schools.

In the work of revision, I have pestered many people. Without knowing it, perhaps, my colleagues at the University of Nebraska have contributed to my thinking, although they are, of course, not responsible for what may have happened to their wisdom in its passage through my mind. I have learned much in conversation with A. C. Breckenridge, John P. Senning, and L. E. Aylsworth. Roger V. Shumate, whose knowledge of state and local organization in Nebraska is unrivaled and whose judgment is invariably shrewd, has patiently responded to my questioning on numerous points. I am indebted to many colleagues throughout the country, and to many public officials who have courteously answered my queries, though already burdened with pressing duties. It would be ungracious to bury my thanks in the sepulchre of a footnote. I have also laid under heavy contribution the labors of scores of investigators whose work appears in many research reports, and who, I hope, will endure an anonymity from which a textbook writer can do so little to rescue them. Miss Ruby Wilder, Chief of the Documents Room in the Love Memorial Library at the University of Nebraska, has been unfailingly cheerful in adding chores for me to the annoyances connected with her exacting responsibilities. I hope my wife, Margaret F. Lancaster, will understand my own realization of the inadequacy of formal thanks in a preface for her faithful labor in typing the manuscript, reading the proofs, and setting me right on many matters of literary style.

L. W. L.

University of Nebraska.

Contents

vii

Contents

Contents

CHAPTER 1

Rural Life and Rural Government

This is a book about the operation of government in rural areas. In these areas the principal units employed are towns, townships, counties, and school districts.[1] Government in such units involves essentially the same problems as those met with in managing the affairs of a populous state. The differences are principally of scale. The endless adjustments of interests go on in one place as well as in the other, and the devices by which public tasks are performed vary much less than is commonly supposed by those who think in terms of the responsibilities and the mechanisms of larger political organizations.

How we shall describe government depends in large measure upon our notions of what is actually most important in the process. If we hold the view that government is a mechanism for framing and enforcing rules, then we are likely to look upon it as the embodiment of force. There can be no doubt, of course, that in the last analysis government gets its work done because of its authority to command the property, the services, and even the lives of those who live under it. Modern thinking about government, however, tends to lay less emphasis upon commands and punishments and more upon the public services performed. If one takes this point of view, he will think of government much as he does of a large commercial or industrial establishment. He will incline to judge it in terms of the quality of its services and the price he must pay in taxes and will be scarcely conscious of coercion.

---

[1] In ordinary speech the word "town" refers vaguely to any relatively compact collection of people larger than a mere crossroads hamlet and smaller than a city. Here it is used to designate the unincorporated areas of general governmental powers in the New England states and New York state. A "town" in the popular sense, when incorporated, may be known as a village or a city, the designation being determined largely by state law. Generally speaking, the term "city" refers to the larger municipalities, although in some states a population of 1,000 suffices to take a community out of the category of villages. In a few states, as in Pennsylvania and New Jersey, some medium-sized incorporated places are called boroughs.

1

As between levels of government there are few important differences so far as procedures are concerned. When a county board lays out a highway, it is difficult to see any difference between their official action and that of the federal authorities when they decide upon a construction project. When a local school board employs a superintendent or makes ordinances for the conduct of the local schools, what it actually does differs very little, except in the extent of its operations, from similar decisions reached by state and federal authorities in the employment of personnel or in the making of rules for conducting the public business. When a county attorney takes action against a landowner for failure to remove a hedge obstructing traffic, what he does is very like what the attorney-general does when he takes action against the violator of certain state laws. In all of these actions much the same processes are involved. There are, to be sure, legal and constitutional differences but, so far as the ordinary citizen is concerned, all are acts of government.

Government everywhere involves the translation of public wishes into rules binding upon citizens, the purchase and use of materials, the employment and management of personnel, and the enforcement of rules of action and conduct upon all within the jurisdiction of the authorities. Under these heads will fall the doings of legislatures, courts, commissions, boards, and officials of every sort. Such matters are done somewhat differently and with varying degrees of efficiency by federal, state, and local officials, and it is worth something as a matter of information to know just how they are done; but aside from this it is a mistake to consider government as something which can be divided into compartments labeled "national," "state," "county," and so forth. If this point of view be kept in mind, it seems to the author that the subject of rural government will be studied in truer perspective.

THE RURAL POPULATION

Fewer movements in history have been more dramatic than that by which the Western world has been urbanized. The United States attained its political independence only a generation or two before the technological revolution began to have its characteristic effect of drawing people from the countryside and into industrial and trading centers. As Figure 1 indicates, between 1890 and 1950 the relative proportions of urban and rural population were almost exactly reversed. In the earlier year about two-thirds of our people were classed as rural; in the latter the same proportion was living in city or suburban areas.[2] Although the drift to the cities has been continuous for many decades, the *rate* of rural growth has tended steadily to fall behind that of the cities at every census since 1880. The figures for 1950 show that during the preceding ten years the population in urban areas increased by more than 18 per cent, while that in rural areas grew by only 7 per cent. Cities grew at a faster rate than the population generally, whereas the rate of rural increase was only half the national rate. The 1950 census shows, moreover, that there has been an even greater exodus than usual from the farms

RURAL AND URBAN POPULATION

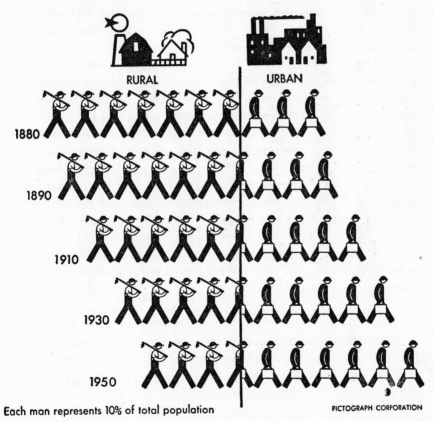

Each man represents 10% of total population   PICTOGRAPH CORPORATION

FIG. 1. Rural and urban population.

[2] It is true that the definitions of urban and rural were changed by the Bureau of the Census in the intervening years, but this change does not seriously affect the generalization in the text.

GAINFULLY EMPLOYED

AGRICULTURE
1940
1950

MANUFACTURING
1940
1950

TRANSPORTATION
and
COMMUNICATION
1940
1950

SERVICE TRADES
1940
1950

Base figure of one million workers

Fig. 2. Gainfully employed, 1940 and 1950.

since 1940. In the ten-year period there were losses of rural population in 17 states, and in 30 states more than half the total population is now classed as urban.[3]

The full extent of this transformation is not appreciated, however, until the rural figures are further analyzed. The Bureau of the Census now divides the rural population into two categories—rural-farm and rural non-farm. The rural-farm population consists of those persons actually living on farms; the rural non-farm includes those who live in villages and hamlets located in rural territory. When this distinction is taken into account, it is seen that the rural-farm population is only 15 per cent of the national total; the rural non-farm group makes up 20 per cent of that total. In other words, only one person out of seven in the nation lives on a farm, whereas one out of every five is in the country but not of it, in the sense of being engaged in farming. The people in this latter group are employed in village stores, filling stations, motels, or in such enterprises as small-scale lumbering, mining, or the processing of farm products.

The decrease in the rural-farm population is reflected in the

FARM LABOR PRODUCTIVITY

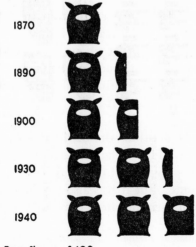

1870

1890

1900

1930

1940

Base figure of 100

Fig. 3. Farm labor productivity, 1870 to 1940.

[3] 1950 Census of Population, *Preliminary Reports, Series PC-7, No. 1*, Feb. 25, 1951; *Preliminary Counts, Series PC-3, No. 10*, Feb. 16, 1951.

sharp decline in the number of those gainfully employed in agriculture. This decline was particularly sharp between 1940 and 1950 and is shown graphically in Figure 2. In the former year 19 per cent of all workers were engaged in farming; in the latter, somewhat less than 13 per cent. This decline is, of course, a continuation of a long-time trend. In 1870 more than half the national working force was on farms and as late as 1900 more than a third were so employed. This shift in occupations is attributable to two facts. The first is the great expansion of other sectors of the national economy. The second is the constantly increasing productivity of farm labor because of the mechanization of agriculture and the development of superior grades of grain and livestock. Farm productivity, as shown in Figure 3, is three times what it was in 1870. This has released hundreds of thousands of workers for absorption into other callings, most of them in cities and villages.[4]

THE TRANSFORMATION OF RURAL SOCIETY

With fewer than 15 per cent of our people directly engaged in farming, with only a third living in rural territory, and with both categories apparently destined to decrease further in the future, it is fair to ask whether the old division between "urban" and "rural" is any longer a realistic one. There is undoubtedly some limit to "urbanization," but it is clear enough by now that a transformation is taking place which will produce a culture pattern far different from that which prevailed when the leading industry was farming. This transformation is being brought about by science and technology and these are characteristic products of urban and industrial society. What is happening is that farming and farmers are being made a part of a new pattern for which it is too early to suggest a descriptive term.

Under American conditions the distinctive thing about farming has been its isolation. This isolation has been spatial in the sense that our public land policy, west of the Alleghenies at least, created the isolated farm home. But it was also psychological, since around the prevailing type of farming there grew up a culture quite differ-

---

[4] 1950 Census of Population, *Preliminary Reports, Series PC-7, No. 2*, Apr. 11, 1951; H. Berger and H. H. Landsberg, *American Agriculture 1899-1939* (1942), p. 253. A leading agricultural expert says that if productivity follows the long-time trend it will be 140 per cent above the 1940 level in 1960. Louis H. Bean, "Agricultural Capacity," Ch. 24 of J. Frederic Dewhurst and associates, *America's Needs and Resources* (1947), pp. 619-20.

ent from that found in cities, a culture with a distinct set of ideas about personal conduct, legitimate social aims, and the proper province of government. Fifty years ago it was common and reasonable, even if unkind, to caricature the farmer as a "rube" and a "hayseed," for he was different in his appearance and in his conduct from city dwellers. No farmer now fits the old stereotype; he and his children tend to be indistinguishable from the general population, aside from the occasional "character" who, in any case, is found in all social groups. Although a residuum of well-defined rural traits, such as individualism, familism, contentiousness, and a belief in equalitarian democracy, may be long in disappearing completely, it seems clear that the farm and village population is ceasing to be distinctive even in these respects.

Perhaps no better summary statement of the effect of urban and technological influences on the farm population can be found than that of Turner in the 1940 *Yearbook of Agriculture,* which bears the significant title "Farmers in a Changing World." After speaking of the social and economic effects of urbanization, Turner continues:

"The intellectual effects, although less recognized, are not less important. First, the folklore and folk-techniques of the historic rural economy are being displaced by scientific knowledge and machine technology; and, second, through the improvement of communication, the traditional isolation of the rural community has almost completely disappeared. The mentality of its members, although not touched directly by the physical routines of urban life, is constantly played upon by stimuli originating in urban life. The mental organization of the farmer today is far more influenced by routines and impulses having origins in machines, science, the market, and the city, than was that of his antecedents who, in the face of physical danger and by hard manual labor, transformed the wilderness into tillable fields." [5]

It may not be amiss to illustrate this general and rather abstract statement. The first thing to be noted is that the physical isolation of the farmer and the villager is rapidly coming to an end. There still are, of course, remote settlements and farms that are inaccessible during some seasons, but these grow more and more exceptional.

[5] Ralph Turner, "The Cultural Setting of American Agricultural Problems," pp. 1019-20. Reference may here be made to other statements of these influences in Baker Brownell, *The Human Community* (1950); Granville Hicks, *Small Town* (1946); Walter Goldschmidt, *As You Sow* (1947); and W. Lloyd Warner, *Democracy in Jonesville* (1949).

The rapid extension of good roads has made the farmer as mobile as any other group. The 1945 Census of Agriculture reported that two out of three farms were directly served by all-weather roads and that 20 per cent more were within two miles of such a road. Good roads have increased the mileage of rural mail routes and, through these, the mail-order houses have reached the remote corners of the country. The variety of products now available to the rural population is almost as wide as that found in cities, so that the differences between the farmer and the city dweller in clothing, house furnishings,

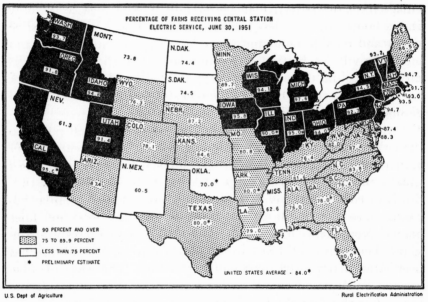

FIG. 4. Farms receiving central station electric service, June 1951.

and mechanical contrivances are no longer marked. Improved roads have also made possible graded and better-equipped consolidated schools and have provided easy access to the social, trade, and cultural advantages of villages and small cities.

A further result of technological advances is the mechanization of farming and the increase in the quantity and quality of agricultural production. It was reported in 1949 that the total investment in farm machinery was probably $8 billion and that cash expenditures alone in 1946 had totaled $1.5 billion. Between 1940 and 1948 the number of tractors on farms doubled, and there were increases of 20 per cent in the number of automobiles, 80 per cent in trucks, 150 per cent in grain combines, 100 per cent in mechanical corn pickers, and more than 150 per cent in milking machines.[6]

Much of this mechanization of farm labor has been made possible by the phenomenal progress of electrification in rural areas. In 1935 only 11 per cent of our 6 million farms had central station electric service. By 1950 nearly nine farms out of ten were electrified, and there were only nine states in which fewer than two-thirds of the farms enjoyed this service. The extent of this service for the country as a whole is shown in Figure 4. It would be difficult to overestimate the cultural effects of this development in making rural and village life more attractive and profitable. Electric service not only makes household tasks less burdensome, but it also makes possible steady and reliable radio and television reception, street lights and movies in villages, better lighting in schools, churches, and community centers, and the elimination of much of the drudgery of work on the farm itself. Rural electrification alone has gone far toward closing the gap between rural and urban mores.[7]

Accompanying the growing application of mechanical power to the tasks of the farm have been improvements in the techniques of agricultural production. For example, growers find that hybrid corn usually increases yields by 20 per cent, and the result is that two-thirds of corn acreage is now planted to hybrid seed. Similar advances have been made in the breeding of other food and fiber plants. New plants have been introduced and new uses are constantly being discovered for farm products. Livestock of all sorts has been steadily improved by scientific breeding. The effect of these various developments has been not only to increase output on the farms, but also to make it possible for farmers and villagers to enjoy in the country advantages not so long ago available only in large cities.

The technological revolution of our day has not been without its effects on rural government and administration. One obvious result has been the mechanization of such services as road construction and maintenance. In all but a few very backward areas the horse and the ox have given way to the motorized grader, bulldozer, and snow plow. But mechanization has invaded other areas with what may

---

[6] *Report of the Secretary of Agriculture, 1948*, pp. 83-4. Incidentally, this mechanization had caused a reduction of one-third in the number of draft animals on farms, thus releasing 15 million acres of cropland for the raising of human food.

[7] Rural Electrification Administration, *Report of the Administrator*, 1950, pp. 13-15.

well be almost revolutionary results. Local rural governments are no longer universally strangers to business machines, scientific assessment procedures, central purchasing, scientific accounting, budgeting, and reporting—all procedures developed in industrial society. Not all of these are feasible in all rural units, but few rural officials are completely ignorant of their existence and their advantages. There are doubtless still unreconstructed conservatives who plant in the dark or the light of the moon, attribute good fortune or disaster to the inscrutable will of the Almighty, and believe that what was good enough for Moses is still good enough, but the work of the weather bureau, the marketing association, the soil conservation technician, and the governmental research organization is rapidly thinning their ranks.

THE NEW PATTERN OF RURAL LIFE

This brief discussion has made it clear that urban and industrial forces are in process of working a complete transformation in traditional rural culture. Farming has been mechanized and has become a business instead of what has often been called "a way of life"; farm units are growing larger, and the large ones are in many sections of increasing social and economic importance; the acquisition of farms seems to be growing more difficult; and farmers have accepted such city folkways as installment buying and urban merchandising and standardizing methods. We have long been used to thinking in terms of the rural-urban contrast but, actually, this contrast has almost ceased to exist. "Restricting our thinking to distinct 'rural' and 'urban' types does not make possible a classification of all the cases which can be shown to exist. This being the case, we have begun to think in terms of 'continua' of relationship between the two types." [8] In short, we have already a new society for which we have no accurate descriptive term. We are certain that it is no longer rural, but the persistent rural heritage in our thinking makes us wonder how humanly satisfactory it will be.

Critics of the new pattern of life are both numerous and vocal. Most of what they have to say turns upon the alleged destruction of the traditional local community by industrialism and technology. It is assumed that life in the face-to-face groups found in rural and village society is more natural to men and women than membership

---

[8] Irving A. Spaulding, "Serendipity and the Rural-urban Continuum," **16** *Rural Sociology* 29-36 (Mar. 1951).

in the vast and impersonal occupational groups which in urban society have replaced the old geographical ties. The city is looked upon as parasitic on the country, drawing to itself not only vast portions of the wealth created by the latter, but being dependent upon rural migration for its growth, since its own rate of natural increase is far too low to maintain its population. The skills of the farmer are considered as involving the whole of man in contrast to the specialism of industrial society which calls into action only a part of his personality. It is alleged that industrial society, with its emphasis on expertness, efficiency, and centralization, makes power and domination human goals rather than neighborliness and cooperation. In short, urbanism and industrialism are said to have destroyed the natural community and put nothing in its place capable of satisfying humane aspirations.[9]

No informed or thoughtful person can deny the force of this criticism. There is plenty of evidence to indicate that the small group nearly everywhere is in eclipse. Both political and industrial organization grows more impersonal and centralized and what is purely personal and local seems to count for less. It is a fair question whether anyone can understand political or industrial units of the size and complexity now almost universal. Such "natural" units as the small open-country villages of fewer than 1,000 inhabitants have been steadily losing population in many sections and, in those which have managed to hold their own, observers report political apathy and social disunity. Functions long in the hands of towns, townships, and villages have been transferred to the county, the state, or the nation. It is not necessary to assume that life in the traditional local units was idyllic to agree with the remark of John Dewey that "the local is the ultimate universal and as near an absolute as exists," and that something like a restoration of its significance is urgent.

On the other hand, the changes wrought by technology are here to stay and even the critics of the new culture pattern do not go to the length of demanding their abolition. If the sense of community is restored it will have to be done in a world of the movie and the airplane, the industrial monopoly and the powerful national state, a

---

[9] See Baker Brownell, *The Human Community* (1950); Arthur E. Morgan, *The Small Community* (1942); A. Whitney Griswold, *Farming and Democracy* (1948). The substance of the last-named book, so far as American conditions are concerned, appeared as "The Agrarian Democracy of Thomas Jefferson," XL *American Political Science Review* 657-681 (Aug. 1946).

world characterized by fretful discontent and an apparent need for artificial stimulation. Man's integrity as a citizen will have to be established in the world as it is, not in a fanciful one created as an escape from one we may happen not to like.

There is some reason to believe that men generally, and not only the social theorists, are seeking relationships more satisfying than those characteristic of modern urban and industrial society. For a generation there has been a growing awareness of the values which are inherent in the small unit—the village, the small town, or the rural hamlet—as an understandable basis of common citizenship. There is evidence of this not only in the community surveys of professional sociologists, but also in the work of self-appraisal done by community councils and similar local groups. Inventories of community resources have enlisted popular support in many cases for better government, more efficient schools, and forward-looking policies with respect to recreation for the young, libraries, public health facilities, and other community interests.

Even "centralization" has paradoxically aided in the restoration of community influence. State- and federally-aided programs have given in many instances new life to local governments simply by supplying them with money enough to engage in significant work. Examples are to be found in the cooperative arrangements for the administration of the social security, the secondary road, soil conservation, and hospital construction programs. Even comprehensive planning of the physical and social resources of the community has made converts in spite of the doubts of traditionalists. Whether these developments can, in some degree, convert the Great Society created by scientific advances into something like a Great Community may still be in doubt, but "if the technological age can provide mankind with a firm and general basis of material security, it will be absorbed in a humane age." [10]

AGRICULTURE IN AN INDUSTRIAL SOCIETY

The problems of rural political and administrative organization and the solutions suggested for them arise alike out of the transformation of farming from a way of life to business conducted for a profit, and hence tending to become an integral part of an industrialized national economy. For a generation after 1880, at which date the urbanization and industrialization of the nation began to be in-

[10] John Dewey, *The Public and Its Problems* (1926), p. 217.

tense, problems of governmental organization in rural areas were neither serious nor pressing. Over most of the country, the county, the town, and the township continued to be in fact what they had always been in law, agents of the state in assessing property, collecting taxes, preserving order, and recording land titles. The more complicated functions resulting from technological advances or demanded by a population acquainted with higher standards of public service had not yet been added to local responsibilities.

The automobile had not yet appeared to revolutionize highway construction; administration of the "poor laws" was uninfluenced by notions of scientific case work; cost accounting, scientific assessment of property, mechanical bookkeeping, and so on were still to be created by the exigencies of a competitive business system and passed on to government. On the whole, the customary machinery of local government, dating in many cases from the seventeenth century, continued to serve reasonably well the needs of a population which was, in general, prosperous and able to pay for the few and relatively simple services required. The farmer could be forgiven for feeling some complacency about his place in society and his instruments of self-rule.

Shortly after the turn of the century, however, "the farmer was no longer master of his own destiny. He plowed his acres, harvested his crops, and fattened his stock, but no longer for himself alone. He fed distant New York and Philadelphia as well as Manchester, Trieste, and Prague overseas. He had become a producer of foodstuffs, of wheat, of cotton, or pork, or cattle, just as his fellow Americans had become producers of hats, or of cotton cloth, or of cheap tin pans. He had become, in short, a man of business, selling what he made and buying what he, his womenfolk and his children needed." [11]

The extent of this agricultural revolution may be appreciated by reading what Emerson had written about farming in his youth: "When men now alive were born, the farm yielded everything that was consumed on it. The farm yielded no money, and the farmer got on without. If he fell sick, his neighbors came to his aid; each gave a day's work, or a half a day, or lent his yoke of oxen or his horse, and kept his work even; hoed his potatoes, mowed his hay, reaped his rye, well knowing that no man could afford to hire labor

---

[11] Louis M. Hacker and Benjamin B. Kendrick, *The United States since 1865* (1932), pp. 164-5. A very good brief treatment of this transition is Harry J. Carman and Carl T. Schmidt, "The American Farmer in a Changing World," XXXIX *South Atlantic Quarterly* 413-426 (Oct. 1940).

without selling his land. In autumn the farmer could sell an ox or a hog and get a little money to pay taxes withal."

The implications of this change are so vast that it would require volumes to explore them. The integration of agriculture into an economy shaped by urban and industrial forces presented the farm population with complex problems in production, distribution, and marketing, as well as in social and political organization. Adjustment to the new order was made difficult because farm people had for centuries lived in a barter, and not a money, economy. In the strange new world the farmer found himself both the beneficiary of industrialism and its victim. Technology enabled him to produce more with less land and labor; yet he normally received a smaller share of the national income than the industrial population. Between 1899 and 1939 agricultural production increased 50 per cent while industrial production increased fourfold. During the same period, the farmer's share of the total income fell from 21 per cent to 12 per cent, while industry's share rose from 19 per cent to 30 per cent. The new and disadvantageous position of the farmer arises from the fact that prices for his products are normally more sensitive to changes in the industrial economy than are those of the things he must buy. He can control neither the amount of his production nor the price he receives for it to anywhere near the degree open to other producers, while conversion of the farm "plant" to new and different uses is a difficult and painful process indeed.

This long-term imbalance between agriculture and industry has been accompanied, as we have seen, by a steady decline in rural population. This decline has coincided with a tendency to socialize services. Such services as schools, libraries, hospitals, roads, and public health facilities are not only growing in number but in their expensiveness as well. As population decreases, more and more rural communities have found it extremely difficult, if not impossible, to support these functions from their own resources. In many areas the general property tax grows steadily more burdensome and tends to approach the limits of its productivity. It is, however, the only tax well fitted for local rural administration, and hence the only one which is consistent with our theory of local self-government in which financial ability has always been an important element.

Every attempt to get at taxpaying ability more accurately or more equitably than through the property tax requires a much wider area than the traditional unit of local rural government. Better indices of ability are to be found in personal and corporate incomes, estates and inheritances, and excises, and taxes on all of these are ill-adapted to local administration. Even if it were politically feasible to revise the entire tax structure of the nation so as to reserve certain sources of income to each of the levels of government, such a change is sure to be some distance in the future. In the meantime the search for a wider area for the support of local functions proceeds by more indirect methods. The most frequent suggestions for finding such an area are the consolidation of small local areas, the transfer of functions from small areas to larger ones, and the development of systems of financial aid from the federal to the state governments and from the latter to local authorities. Experiments with all of these are now under way. Whatever their outcome in detail, it is certain that the resulting system of government in rural areas will be significantly different from the traditional one.

In the long run the effectiveness of local rural government and the preservation of some measure of local control will depend upon the prosperity of farming. Whether anything like permanent "parity" between agriculture and industry can be attained is largely a matter of speculation. Twice since the first World War farmers have lived through severe depressions, marked by ruinously low prices, and accompanied by widespread tax delinquency, the growth of farm tenancy, mounting private and public indebtedness, and a sharp curtailment of public services. In 1952 agriculture is relatively prosperous. Prices are near or even above parity, tenancy has decreased from its high point in 1930, there appears to be no serious problem of tax delinquency, farm indebtedness is only half what it was during the 1930s, and there is for the moment no problem of farm surpluses.[12]

The relatively satisfactory position of agriculture may, however, be only temporary. The surpluses of farm products which were basic to the "farm problem" of the 1920s and 1930s have disappeared for the moment for two reasons. The first of these is that per capita and total demand for food products increased because of an unexpected growth in population. The second is that foreign purchases of American food products have been encouraged by the national

[12] For facts and figures on farm finances see *Agricultural Finance Review*, vol. 13, Nov. 1950, and the supplement to the same volume, May 1951, published by the Bureau of Agricultural Economics, Department of Agriculture.

policy of loans and grants around the world. Since the census of 1950 the rate of population growth has equalled that of the preceding decade and the urban population has enjoyed a high level of prosperity. If public and industrial policies are such as to maintain full employment, the farmer may possibly enjoy a long period of prosperity. The foreign trade policy seems less reliable as an element in the problem. Most serious students are of the opinion that unless we are willing to buy from foreign countries we cannot expect indefinitely to sell to them. "Continued onesidedness in our world trade will inevitably inflict further damage on our agricultural exports; and we must not forget that the damage exists, even if we cover it up with loans and grants to foreign countries. Foreign nations are still buying more from us than they are selling to us for one reason alone—we provide the money. Nevertheless they are running out of money fast. Onesidedness in trade cannot continue indefinitely in any event . . . Ultimately, unless we buy more from foreign countries, we shall not be able to do business with them at all." [13]

If our foreign trade policy is one which disposes of our agricultural exports only by public subsidies, our domestic policy towards farming is equally "artificial." There is a sense in which agriculture is a managed industry, the managers being the multitude of agencies within the federal Department of Agriculture. The domestic subsidies adopted to preserve parity are simply less well concealed than the loans and grants by which foreign trade is maintained. Neither policy is "natural." There is, moreover, a glaring inconsistency between a domestic policy directed at greater production and a trade policy aimed at disposing of surpluses. Responsible farm leaders probably disapprove of all subsidies on principle and accept them only as ways of keeping agriculture a going concern until more consistent policies can be formulated. Such policies would presumably seek to produce full agricultural and industrial production, full industrial employment, and freer international trade. Whether such policies will be supported by political and industrial leaders is at least doubtful, but unless they are, agriculture as a basic industry will feel justified in demanding the same sort of support, however artificial, which other groups have succeeded in obtaining.

---

[13] *Report of the Secretary of Agriculture, 1949*, pp. 3, 6-7; see also Marguerite C. Burk, "Changes in the Demand for Food from 1941 to 1950," **XXXIII** *Journal of Farm Economics* 281-296 (Aug. 1951) and Lawrence Witt, "Our Agricultural and Trade Policies," *Ibid.*, **XXXII:** 159-175 (May 1950).

AGRICULTURAL POLICY AND LOCAL GOVERNMENT

Although our policy toward agriculture is a national one, it has had in practice important decentralizing effects of significance to local communities. These effects are observable not only in the machinery used in administering various programs, but also in the programs themselves. The principal agency of securing what the farmer regards as economic justice is the Production and Marketing Administration. This authority, although a division of the Department of Agriculture, rests ultimately on locally elected marketing associations, thus providing local participation in the national plan. Moreover, throughout the farm program there is an extensive degree of interlocking of agricultural administration with organized farm pressure groups, the latter being federations of local associations. Thus, the Soil Conservation Service is connected with the National Association of Soil Conservation Districts, the Rural Electrification Administration with the National Association of Rural Electric Cooperatives, and the Extension Services of the state colleges of agriculture with the various local branches of the American Farm Bureau Federation. These interconnections involve the participation of very large numbers of individuals and farmers' organizations and give some assurance that the "grass roots" point of view will not be ignored by national and state administrators.[14]

Certain substantive programs of the Department of Agriculture are of prime importance to local government not only because of their use of local personnel but also because of their probable long-term effect on farm productivity and rural stability. Chief among these are the soil conservation program and the promotion of land use legislation by state and local governments.

Until very recent years public policy toward the use of land aimed at getting under the plow, or at any rate in private hands, as much of the public domain as possible as rapidly as this could be accomplished. The general theory of our land laws was that the public good would be best served by building up a class of small owners. This policy was in line, of course, with prevalent individualistic economic theories. Some of its results, however, have been unfortunate. As a leading authority puts it, Americans in practice have not learned to love the land but have, for the most part, regarded it

---

[14] See Charles M. Hardin, "The Politics of Agriculture in the United States," **XXXII** *Journal of Farm Economics* 571-583 (Nov. 1950).

as something to exploit and as a source of immediate financial return. Even if this harsh judgment does not apply to all farmers, it is true that few without external stimulus have been willing or able to apply measures to prevent the depletion of the land by natural forces.[15]

Erosion of land by wind and water, often aggravated by unwise management of crop land and by overgrazing, is estimated to cause an annual monetary loss of $400 million and to have been responsible already for total damage of $10 billion. Soil scientists tell us that nature requires from three hundred to a thousand years to build one inch of topsoil, which by the millions of tons is annually washed or blown from American farm and grazing land. Methods by which this loss can be prevented are well known to conservationists. Although progressive farmers here and there were applying these methods many years ago, there was no national policy of soil conservation until the mid-thirties of the present century.[16]

The soil conservation program of the federal government constitutes an interesting and significant chapter in the evolution of local rural government. This program operates through local soil conservation districts organized under state laws which meet with the approval of the Soil Conservation Service of the Department of Agriculture. The local districts are organized by a state soil conservation committee upon the petition of the owners of contiguous land. Once set up the district is administered by an elective local committee. The services of the technicians of the Soil Conservation Service are available to the members of the local district in planning and putting into effect the proper conservation practices. Compliance with the approved plan entitles the farmer member to government payments.

Of the nearly two billion acres of land in the United States slightly less than one billion are classed as land in farms. Roughly two-thirds of this latter figure is considered as having the best crop potentialities, although only about 340 million acres are described as "really" good, and only 62 million acres are completely safe from

---

[15] Consult H. H. Bennett, *Soil Conservation* (1939) ; Leonard A. Salter, Jr., "Do We Need a New Land Policy?" **XXII** *Journal of Land and Public Utility Economics* 309-320 (Nov. 1946). The name of this journal was changed to *Land Economics* in 1948.

[16] On the general subject of soil conservation the following will be found useful: Ward Shepard, *Food or Famine: The Challenge of Erosion* (1945), Edward H. Faulkner, *Plowman's Folly* (1943), Bernard Frank and Anthony Netboy, *Water, Land and People* (1950), and Russell Lord, *To Hold This Land*, Department of Agriculture, Miscellaneous Publication No. 321 (1938).

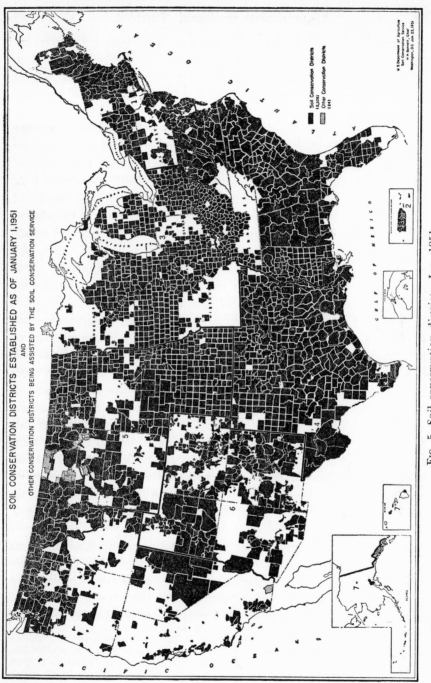

SOIL CONSERVATION DISTRICTS ESTABLISHED AS OF JANUARY 1, 1951
AND
OTHER CONSERVATION DISTRICTS BEING ASSISTED BY THE SOIL CONSERVATION SERVICE

Soil Conservation Districts
(2,225)
Other Conservation Districts
(24)

U S Department of Agriculture
Soil Conservation Service
H H Bennett, Chief
Washington, D C Jan 23, 1951

FIG. 5. Soil conservation districts, Jan. 1951.

19

erosion. During 1938, the first year when payments were made for the adoption of approved erosion control practices, 69 soil conservation districts covering 36 million acres, were organized. By 1951 more than 2,300 districts covering a billion and a quarter acres had been set up. The distribution of these districts is shown in Figure 5. At the same date the chief of the Soil Conservation Service reported that his field staffs were working with 18,000 neighborhood groups including more than 133,000 farmers. Farms within soil conservation districts totaled over four million and contained crop land of about 850 million acres. Farmers by now are convinced for the most part of the value of conservation measures, and the principal obstacle to more rapid progress is the serious shortage of technicians.[17]

It may be going too far to say, as does Griswold, that the soil conservation districts are the "elementary republics" of which Jefferson wrote; but there can be little doubt that they do encourage local self-government with respect to a fundamental concern of the farm population. The success of the system is, moreover, an interesting illustration of the fact that a centrally sponsored program may have the effect of strengthening local control and enlisting local interest.

LOCAL LAND USE REGULATION

Whereas much of the soil of the nation needs rebuilding, much is so unproductive as to make unrestricted private exploitation contrary to the public interest. In nearly every part of the country large areas which ought to be withdrawn from cultivation are still being farmed by a shifting and often shiftless population at a mere subsistence level. When the indiscriminate cutting of timber has gone on unchecked for generations, as has been the case in the Lake states, the Appalachian slopes, the Ozarks, and in parts of the Pacific Northwest, very grave problems are created for local governments. As marginal or submarginal farm land or cutover forest land ceases to be productive, the owner is unable to pay taxes on it. When a local government has within its jurisdiction a large area of tax delinquent land, the only course open to it, if it is to raise sufficient reve-

---

[17] *Report of the Chief of the Soil Conservation Service for 1950.* It should be added that some degree of erosion control is accomplished by the enforcement of conditions attached to loans made by private banks and public lending agencies. An excellent comprehensive article on the legal and administrative aspects of soil conservation is Edwin E. Ferguson, "Nation-wide Erosion Control: Soil Conservation Districts and the Power of Land-Use Regulation," **34** *Iowa Law Review* 166-186 (Jan. 1949).

nue, is to increase taxes on land still able to pay its way. These higher taxes tend to increase delinquency of land hitherto self-supporting and hence to aggravate the initial difficulty. The situation is not helped, of course, if the local government takes over the tax delinquent land which then ceases to make any contribution to the revenue.

There is literally no escape from situations of this sort, or at least none open to the local authorities. No matter how greatly property valuation decreases, so long as any population at all remains, local services have to be performed, and at a cost which tends to be stationary. In such areas state aid becomes necessary, with the result that in some communities in the Lake states and in upstate New York many people at various times have been reported as receiving all or a part of their living from public sources because of their employment in local services heavily subsidized by the state. Subsistence farming, so called, often means that people are living in what amount to rural slums. For the country as a whole the Soil Conservation Service estimates that 80 million acres of land should be withdrawn from agriculture. To do this would require the resettlement of about half a million families at a cost of $1,000 a family. The purely human problems involved in thus moving people about are clearly staggering.[18]

It is situations of this sort that have led to the adoption of rural zoning laws, often at the prompting of the federal government. The zoning of property in cities with respect to its use, the size of structures, setbacks, proportion of the lot occupied, and so on, has become almost universal. Although the situations met with in the country are unlike those encountered in cities, the idea of zoning is identical though novel in rural thinking. Land which is marginal or submarginal for agriculture should be zoned for use as public forests, game refuges, and recreation grounds, and its use for farming forbidden. Zoning in rural areas adjacent to incorporated places may go further and regulate structures and commercial and industrial uses not in harmony with the physical environs or inconsistent with the public health, safety, or welfare.

The most recent survey shows that 175 laws exist in 38 states authorizing zoning outside the limits of incorporated municipalities. "Of these 102 in 31 states empowered a total of 1,165 counties to

---

[18] See Robert W. Hartley, "Rural and Regional Development," Chapter 29 of J. Frederic Dewhurst and associates, *America's Needs and Resources* (1947).

zone; 50 in 12 states authorized towns or townships to adopt ordinances; and 23 pertained to other units of local government." [19] It is important to note that these figures refer only to enabling acts which the local governments are free to adopt or not as they see fit. At present 71 types of ordinances have been adopted by county governments over the country. Half of these are comprehensive in character creating residential, industrial, agricultural, forestry-recreational, and unrestricted use districts. Nineteen ordinances specifically permit the creation of forest and recreational districts. The enforcement of use restrictions in the open country is important as making it possible in time to retire unproductive land from agriculture and restrict it to uses in harmony with its character.

Rural zoning has obvious possibilities as a device for encouraging the rational use of land. Everything depends, however, upon the intelligence and vigor with which the zoning ordinance is enforced. On-the-spot surveys seem to indicate that the movement is still in its infancy. In many rural counties and townships zoning exists only on paper, for it has been difficult to interest rural people in its possibilities. Only a few local land-use committees have been active in enforcing land-use plans and ordinances. Perhaps the cautious conclusion of the latest study sums up the present situation adequately. "Rural zoning is a flexible tool that can be readily shaped to serve the needs of rural people. Realization of its full potentialities awaits the touch of adaptative imagination. . . . It is emphasized that the legal raw materials of zoning—the basic types of regulations —were urban created; that in the past these raw materials have been reshaped in an effort to serve the rural community. Today in our changing rural economy, new problems and goals call for new zoning techniques. It is probable that rural zoning will again prove to be a flexible community tool." [20]

In another generation it is quite probable that there will be no distinctive subject matter for a book on rural government. It is al-

---

[19] Erling D. Solberg, "Rural Zoning in Transition," *Agricultural Economics Research*, Vol. III, No. 4 (Oct. 1951), Bureau of Agricultural Economics.

[20] Erling D. Solberg, *op. cit.*, p. 140. Of the recent literature on rural zoning, the following may be referred to: Robert B. Goodman, "The Regulation and Control of Land Use in Non-Urban Areas," and W. A. Rowlands, "Zoning for Agriculture, Forestry, and Recreation in Wisconsin," 9 *Journal of Land and Public Utility Economics* 266-271, 272-282 (Aug. 1933); Johnson and Walker, "Centralization and Coordination of Police Power for Land-Control Measures," *Ibid.*, 17: 410 (Aug. 1941); G. S. Wehrwein, "Administration of Rural Zoning," *Ibid.*, 19: 264 (Aug. 1943); and Leonard A. Salter, "County Zoning and Post-War Problems," 18 *State Government* 187 (Oct. 1945).

together likely that the differences between rural and urban people, mores, and modes of economic and political organization and tactics will have been largely erased. The farmer now reads the same national newspapers and magazines, hears and sees the same radio and television programs, wears the same clothing, sends his children to the same schools and colleges, joins the same pressure groups and, in other ways, behaves himself as do people who live in the different physical surroundings of cities. And the ways in which he gets himself governed tend to differ less and less from those followed in cities. This transition is already far advanced and its effects on rural government and administration are evident in the discussion that follows.

CHAPTER 2

Area and Structure—The New England Town

The historic areas of local government in this country were the county in the South, and the town in New England. Both of these were "natural" areas in the sense that they were based upon methods of land owning and cultivation and the social groupings of the people. The machinery of government of each served a population which was to a rather high degree self-conscious and well-knit, and the areas originally blocked out incorporated with considerable accuracy a social group which possessed a good deal of real unity of needs and aims and purposes.

In the so-called middle colonies a mixed form of government was developed, in the structure and working of which are found elements of each of the others. Within the county, which existed for certain purposes, were the towns which preserved, or attempted to preserve, the town meeting and certain other features of the New England town, and which were represented as such on the governing body of the county. This mixed form was carried westward by the advancing emigrants and still exists in a group of states including Illinois, Michigan, Wisconsin, Nebraska, South Dakota, and Missouri, where it shares with the typical county organization brought from the southern seaboard states in the local government of the state.[1]

Whatever the details of this development may have been, it should be pointed out that for many years the county, town, and township were organs of *general* government. That is to say, the proper authorities in each area were charged with a considerable variety of functions such as the preservation of the peace, health, and safety of the people, the building and maintenance of highways and other public works, the assessment of property and the collection of

---

[1] It should be noted, however, that in some of these states, e.g., Nebraska, the adoption of township organization is optional with the people of the county. In 1933 twenty-one townships in a Minnesota county were abolished and their duties handed over to the county board.

taxes, and such other duties as might be imposed upon them by the state legislature.

THE CHAOS OF AREAS

Hence for a generation or more after the foundation of the Republic it is proper to look upon local rural government as being predominantly in the hands of the county, town and township officials. Comparatively few other areas were created until well along in our history, and local government organization was simplicity itself

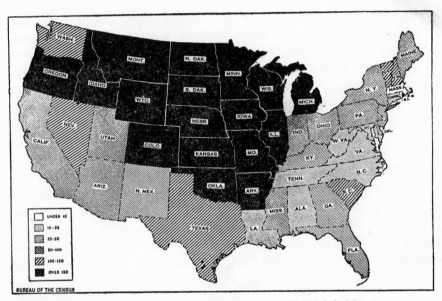

FIG. 6. Number of local governments per 10,000 inhabitants.

when compared with what we find today, when it is estimated that something like 165,000 local authorities are engaged in doing the work originally confided to a relatively few public bodies. Figure 6 gives some idea of the distribution of these areas of government.[2]

The intricate character of our present local government structure —composed as it is of counties, cities, villages, boroughs, towns, town-

---

[2] Anderson in 1945 reported over 165,000; see his *Units of Government in the United States* (Public Administration Service No. 83, 1945); with regard to school districts it should be pointed out that in many cases these coincide with other areas such as cities, counties, or townships. Anderson lists 3,050 counties, 16,262 incorporated places, 18,998 townships, 118,308 school districts, and 8,382 other units. For an excellent recent discussion of the whole subject see Part Six of *State-Local Relations*, a report of the committee on state-local relations of the Council of State Governments (Chicago, 1946).

ships, school districts, and a bewildering host of authorities organized for special purposes—is attributable to a number of forces.[3] In the first place, the growth of incorporated towns and cities created a large number of problems which the older organizations of the county, township and New England town were either legally incompetent to handle because of their restricted delegated powers, or for which the rural inhabitants of such areas were unwilling to pay. A solution for this difficulty was sought in the separate incorporation of cities, villages, towns, or boroughs. In most cases the authorities of these new areas were vested with powers commensurate with the special problems calling them into existence, though for some purposes they continued to form a part of the county, town, or township. Only rarely—as in the case of some twenty Virginia cities—were they set entirely aside from the county of which they were originally a part. The separate incorporation of cities and other urban centers proceeded at varying rates in different parts of the country. The New England towns were very loath to have their unity destroyed, and for many years the creation of cities and boroughs went on very slowly in that section.[4] In the West where the town and township were not indigenous institutions, there was not the same opposition to the establishment of new governmental units in urban portions of a township. Separate incorporation was in fact made very easy by requiring only a few hundred or a thousand inhabitants as a prerequisite for municipal status. This fact accounts for the comparatively large number of "cities" throughout the West and Middle West. Although such separate incorporation did not destroy the legal existence of the township, it has undoubtedly weakened it as an institution of self-government, not only by giving a ma-

---

[3] For the general subject of local areas consult the article by Phillips Bradley on "Administrative Areas" in the *Encyclopedia of the Social Sciences;* J. A. Fairlie and C. M. Kneier, *County Government and Administration*, pp. 476-508; F. H. Guild, "Special Municipal Corporations," **XVIII** *National Municipal Review* 319-323 (May 1929); Lane W. Lancaster, "Our Scrambled Local Government," **232** *North American Review* 438-445, 559-568 (Nov.-Dec. 1931). The most recent accurate count is that reported in the monograph by William Anderson referred to in the last note.

[4] See, for colonial incorporation, J. A. Fairlie, *Essays in Municipal Administration*, Ch. IV. It should be said, however, that even in New England numerous districts for special purposes, such as water, fire, lighting, sewer, and improvement districts were created within individual towns and given an organization more or less independent of the town authorities. Consult C. H. Clark, "Connecticut Boroughs," in *New Haven Colony Historical Society Papers* **IV;**120 f.; F. G. Bates, "Village Government in New England," **VI** *American Political Science Review* 367-376 (1912). In his enumeration of units of government in 1945 Anderson lists 890 special districts in the six New England states.

jority of its inhabitants a set of interests different from those of the rural fringe, but also by withdrawing from the township officials the bulk of the taxable property of the area and leaving them too few functions to hold the interest of citizens in township affairs. Separate incorporation also had unfortunate results in creating suspicion and enmities between the village or city and the population in the surrounding rural territory.[5]

A second force favoring the multiplication of areas of local government has to do with the spread of popular education. Ever since the acceptance of the dogma of universal education, the elementary schools of the United States have been considered the especial care of the local inhabitants. For by far the greater part of our history, over most of the country, the school district has been the typical area for local school administration. The school district may be defined as an area devoted to the support of a single elementary school.[6] It is likely to be quite small, serving what might be called a rural neighborhood, and in the vast majority of cases the school plant to this day consists of a single one-room, one-teacher building. Taking the country as a whole, the number of such districts greatly exceeds that of all other local areas. As late as 1947-48 it was estimated that there still remained, in spite of a strong movement for consolidation, more than 75,000 one-teacher elementary schools in the United States. These were located in something over 99,000 separate school districts. Something specific will be said later about the government and administration of local school districts, but it should be pointed out here that they are doubtless the most tenacious of all our local institutions. Local citizens have been jealous of their ancient prerogatives with regard to the education of the young, and in no field is popular interest greater or centralizing influences more sturdily resisted.

The historical areas of the county, town, and eastern township were to a large extent "natural" in the sense that they corresponded more or less accurately with the problems of interest to their inhabitants. Travel was difficult and infrequent, functions were few, sim-

---

[5] In the opinion of rural sociologists the antagonisms are in process of disappearing and villages are rather generally casting in their lot with the surrounding rural territory. See the chapter on "Rural Life" by Kolb and Brunner in *Recent Social Trends*.

[6] The legal definition is, of course, somewhat different. That given here is suggested as being more in line with the facts of rural organization. Other areas beside the school district as here described are used for the administration of local schools. These are discussed in the chapter on education.

ple, and almost entirely strictly local, and the existing agencies were competent to manage most of them satisfactorily. When commerce ceased to be local, when travel became less arduous and the mobility of the population increased, and when the advance of science created new problems for government to solve, the old agencies ceased to correspond with social realities.[7] A community occupying a portion of a county or township, or even of two adjoining counties or townships would find itself faced with a problem not felt by a majority of the inhabitants of the legal area. Such a problem might be the need for fire protection, the disposal of waste or sewage, a supply of water, facilities for irrigation or street lighting, the building of bridges, the provision of a library, or any of a score or more of other necessities or amenities. Since the matter was of no particular interest to the county or township as a whole, those immediately concerned might incorporate as a special fire, water, or other district. Thus would come into existence a new governmental unit, supplied with tax-levying and borrowing powers and with more or less machinery and equipment—including always a payroll! The functions performed by such districts might theoretically be accomplished by the creation of special assessment districts under the control of the county or other larger unit, but very often there were legal or constitutional obstacles to such procedure. It must also be confessed that often less respectable motives were controlling. Where constitutional or statutory debt limits were about to be reached, they might be indirectly evaded by the incorporation of a new district.[8] For the courts in many states have held that the general borrowing margin is available to the new corporation even though it may cover the same territory and involve the same people as one already operating under a different corporate name.[9] It may also be suggested that to the local

---

[7] "Indeed, the multiplication of local units has probably been largely due to the increase of public functions and the need of adjusting administration to actual conditions in the presence of traditional units that seemed too rigid for quick and serviceable adaptation." A. C. Millspaugh, *Public Welfare Organization* (1935), p. 181.

[8] The existence of "civil" and "school" townships throughout Indiana is an example of a wholesale effort to circumvent the stringent constitutional limitations on local indebtedness found in that state. The constitution of Indiana, as of other states, imposes these limitations on "municipal corporations." The courts have interpreted these words to include all types of local areas.

[9] The constitution of South Carolina, after setting a debt limit which municipal corporations may not exceed, proceeds to provide that, where several corporate bodies operate within the same territory, the total debt of all such units shall not exceed a certain somewhat larger percentage of the valuation of the whole area covered. This, however, is not a usual provision, and in some states it is possible, by the creation of special districts, to accumulate a debt as great as a fourth of the assessed valuation. Cf. Report No. 1 of the *Commission to Investigate County and Municipal Taxation and Expenditures* (N. J. 1931).

politicians the creation of a new legal entity is by no means an evil since, in one way or another, it will increase the spoils at their disposal.

These factors working together have produced a situation in which the local government of the United States is now managed by something like 165,000 different authorities.[10] Except in New England where the town has preserved much of its original vigor, there is scarcely a state which does not have many thousand such authorities, while in the neighborhood of such cities as New York and Chicago, problems which are to all intents and purposes common to the entire urban population are parceled out among literally hundreds of different bodies and officials. Most citizens everywhere live under and support at least three or four such authorities. Nearly everywhere the voter lives under a county government; in many parts of the country he supports in addition a township government; perhaps he lives in an incorporated city or village; he is invariably a resident of some sort of school district; and in many places he supports also the machinery of a sanitary, fire, water, irrigation, or other special district.[11]

The Weaknesses of Small Areas

Perhaps as good a way as any to understand some of the evils of such a system of local government is for the reader to study the situation in his own community. A map showing the boundaries of the various areas whose governmental machinery he supports will indicate almost immediately the way in which the potential unity of his community has been broken up. It will very likely be evident that the only area for which he feels a lively loyalty is the village which serves as his trading or cultural center, or the county (if he lives in the open country) at whose seat he pays his taxes, transacts his legal business, or markets his products. From the authorities of such

---

[10] A local government authority as the term is used here must meet the following conditions: It should have its own governing body; this body should be independent of other local governments and must not be a mere board acting for another local corporation; and it must possess an independent power to raise revenue.

[11] After defining Metropolitan Chicago as including the territory within 50 miles of State and Madison Streets, Merriam in 1929 listed 1,673 independent governments in that area—4 states, 16 counties, 203 cities, 166 townships, 59 park districts, 10 sanitary districts, 188 drainage districts, and 1,027 miscellaneous authorities. See *Chicago: A More Intimate View of Urban Politics* (1929). Since Merriam wrote there has been a reduction in this number, but as late as 1938 there were still 358 governments operating in the Cook County part of the metropolitan area. See Victor Jones, *Metropolitan Government* (1942), p. 16. In 1942 that portion of the Chicago metropolitan area lying in Illinois and Indiana contained 821 local units. See *State-Local Relations* (1946), p. 190.

areas will proceed most of the services in which he has a continuing interest. The others, dealing as they do with fragments of government and administration, will at best enlist his interest only spasmodically. This development may be regarded, of course, as symptomatic of the fact that the ancient community has ceased to exist. The creation of new legal entities is simply an attempt to meet a situation and not of itself a force creating a new and unsatisfactory one.[12]

An examination of the ballot in such a typical community will disclose other weaknesses of considerable importance to the smooth working of responsible government. The voter, after making his choice for state and perhaps national officers, must mark his ballot for a long list of county, city, or village officers, for township trustees, for members of school district boards, and perhaps also for directors or trustees of one or more special districts which have been carved out of the territory of the county. With such a ballot he is in no position to make a choice which will place in definite hands undivided responsibility for community administration.[13] The conduct of the public business is, on the contrary, divided among a score of petty officials and boards, no one of whom can easily be held accountable, and yet nearly all of whom have some power to levy taxes, incur indebtedness, and otherwise obligate taxpayers. In short, the multiplication of local areas has had the effect of creating a horde of jobholders far more numerous in most communities than the public business requires.

From still another point of view the large number of governmental and administrative areas detracts from efficient administration. With regard to many matters of general interest to a large area, the effect of the existence of a multiplicity of independent authorities is to prevent the pooling of the resources of the larger community, thus condemning many of the smaller areas to a pinch-penny policy fatal to efficiency. If, for example, a county is divided into

---

[12] This problem is not peculiarly American. In spite of some changes in the direction of greater simplification made in England fifty years ago, the administrative map of that country is still by no means simple. See W. A. Robson, *The Development of Local Government* (London, 1931) Part I. *The Municipal Year Book and Public Utilities Manual* (London, 1949), reports 14,313 units of local government in England and Wales. See J. H. Warren, "The Structure of Local Government" and R. J. Roddis, "Reorganization of Local Government in the Thinly Populated Areas," XXII *Public Administration* pp. 3-15 (London, Spring 1944).

[13] Moreover, under such a decentralized system, elections are so frequent as to be a burden to the voters. Thus, inhabitants of incorporated villages in New York state have four elections each year and five in presidential election years.

numerous townships or highway districts, each charged with the construction and care of roads, it is obvious that various unfortunate results will follow. In the first place, there will be no authority competent to deal with the area as a whole. Whether or not there is a highway system planned with reference to the general needs of the county will depend entirely upon the willingness of the many districts to cooperate in a unified plan—a willingness seldom met with because of the persistence of mutual jealousies and petty parochialism. Moreover, such districts are bound to vary in size and taxable wealth and, therefore, in the quality of the work done. One district will maintain excellent highways while its poorer neighbor will be the object of the righteous indignation of every traveler. Such a system further conduces to inefficiency by encouraging the excessive purchase of supplies and equipment,[14] a large part of which is used only a small portion of the year, and by multiplying the opportunities for jobbery in buying materials and awarding contracts. Much the same thing may be said concerning the maintenance of school and drainage districts and other areas within a county. Anyone who has observed the actual conduct of administration in any of these fields can readily call to mind cases in which a school district, supporting a school excellent from every point of view, will exist alongside one so poverty-stricken as to be unable to meet even the modest minimum standards set by the state without taxing itself unconscionably and perhaps receiving in addition substantial aid from the state. Moreover, situations of this sort occur in counties amply able to provide a well-conceived program of education or public works, if the multiplication of areas did not make impossible the pooling of the resources of the larger unit. In the opinion of some persons these inequities are the necessary price of local self-government. To others such an issue is not involved, or, if it is, the price paid is felt to be exorbitant. And there are still others who go further and say that the inadequacy of our small local units leads many in despair to call for greater centralization and thus the destruction of local self-government. Thus Robson, writing of English conditions, says: ". . . when reform is seen to be needed at a specific point, many people who dislike incompetence immediately jump to the conclu-

---

[14] When local highways in North Carolina were taken over by the state following legislation of 1931, an inventory of the equipment owned by the counties and road districts showed that buying had been done recklessly and extravagantly in many of them. See Paul W. Wager, "State Succeeds in Highway Business," **XXII** *National Municipal Review* 59-63 (Feb. 1933).

sion that centralized administration is the only alternative to local government. Parochialism . . . can easily become not merely a dangerous foe to the efficient development of public services on modern lines but also the unwitting means to an undesirable centralization of control." [15]

Nor should we forget that the larger the number of governmental areas, the larger the number of officeholders which the public must support. It is easy, of course, to lose one's sense of proportion when dealing with this subject and to wax fervent if not eloquent about the dangers of bureaucracy. Every modern government with numerous social responsibilities requires large numbers of public servants, and there is little hope of greatly reducing these numbers so long as the public insists upon new services. Nevertheless there is always present the tendency for governmental agencies to be overstaffed, and hence for the taxpayer to be compelled in one way or another, to support a personnel beyond the strict needs of the public service. The fact that many of these petty positions involve no salaries or only nominal ones is not of controlling importance in this connection. It must be recognized that most public jurisdictions in this country make their appointments on a political basis, no matter what the ballot form may be or the other legal and formal methods of choice. Many men can always be found to accept positions carrying no salary because of the "honor" involved, the opportunity for free advertisement, or the chance for indirect access to the means of private gain. In this way many of our powerful political machines are built up, and the private citizen is compelled in numerous ways to suffer from that "unending audacity of elected persons" of which the poet wrote.

REDUCING THE NUMBER OF AREAS

When we survey the actual machinery by which we now attempt to perform the work of local government there can be little doubt that a crying need is for such a reduction of the number of authorities as will simplify the voter's task, enforce official responsibility,

---

[15] W. A. Robson, *The Development of Local Government*, pp. 60-61. The latest American study concludes that the "states and the Federal government are unnecessarily burdened with financial and administrative responsibility forced upon them by the inability of local governments to perform tasks which are appropriate to local action. The possibilities of enlarging and strengthening local self-government are consequently reduced." See *State-Local Relations*, p. 197-8. Quoted with the permission of the Council of State Governments.

restore, if possible, the unity of government, and reduce the number of officeholders. To state these desirable objectives is comparatively easy; to suggest a plan for their realization is one of the most difficult problems in the whole field of local government. We deal in some detail elsewhere with specific suggestions for reconstructing our political and administrative map. This chapter will be devoted mainly to a discussion of the machinery of local government in the principal areas now employed.[16]

Ideally, perhaps the best solution from the standpoint of the theory of democracy would be to endow each "natural" area with complete machinery of government. That is to say, each community used by the inhabitants of an area as a trading and cultural center might be made the seat of a government equipped to deal with all the problems primarily of local interest arising in the district. The New England town was, in reality, a legal entity of such attributes and, in isolated cases, still serves acceptably as the governmental agency for satisfying general community needs. In some regions, as in the South, the county has succeeded in enlisting the loyalties of its inhabitants to such a degree as to be perhaps an acceptable unit for reflecting popular desires. Where this is the case there is little reason for disturbing matters. Usually, however, it is difficult to find so-called "natural" areas into which a county might be divided or which might feasibly be incorporated as municipal governments. Much labor has been expended by sociologists and rural economists in attempting to locate "communities" in various parts of the country. Whatever their researches may indicate as to the irrational division of our rural territory at present, they give us little help in redrawing the map of local government.[17]

In fact, if such a map were drawn in terms satisfactory to the sociologist, we should probably find ourselves equipped with far more machinery than at present, since legal recognition of the "commu-

---

[16] School areas are reserved for treatment in the chapter on education. For schemes of reform see the chapter on the Reconstruction of Local Government.

[17] For studies of rural community organization the following may be consulted: E. D. Sanderson, *The Farmer and His Community* (1922); E. D. Sanderson, *The Rural Community* (1932); T. B. Manny, *Rural Municipalities* (1930); J. F. Thaden, "Natural Community Areas" in *Michigan Local Government Series* (1933); B. L. Hummel, "Community Organization in Missouri," *Mo. Agr. Exp. Sta. Circular No. 209* (Sept. 1928); E. A. Taylor and F. R. Yoder, "Rural Social Organization in Whitman County," *Wash. Agr. Exp. Sta., Bulletins No. 203 and 215* (June 1926 and June 1927); Dwight Sanderson and W. S. Thompson, "The Social Areas of Otsego County," *Cornell Agr. Exp. Sta. Bulletin No. 422* (July 1923); but see the discussion of the community in A. C. Millspaugh's *Local Democracy and Crime Control*.

nity" would doubtless involve the incorporation of an even larger number of areas than we now have. Whatever sentimental advantages might be derived from such a procedure, we may as well recognize at once that it would run counter to every demand of an age in which the actual if not the self-conscious community is far wider than that which finds its center on a village green or the court house square. It is despair of finding any satisfactory basis for democratic government which has led some writers to abandon the attempt and to search in interest groups and associations for a new basis for such a community of interest as will keep alive the technique of democracy.[18]

The means of travel and the conditions of modern administration require larger rather than smaller areas of government. Although it may be more difficult to muster public opinion and maintain interest in local self-government over wide areas, the desire to do these things must yield to the demands made by the actual conditions under which the public business is now conducted. The people cannot forever continue to support a form of government at once inordinately complicated, expensive, irresponsible, and inefficient. The real problem is to find a unit sufficiently large to permit the use of modern methods of administration, and to make this area correspond as nearly as may be to that in which a real community spirit exists. The first of these objectives should probably be our immediate aim, for all experience shows that nothing which is not efficient can long endure, no matter under what form it may operate. But before this is attempted we should examine the structure of our existing units, leaving the discussion of reform for separate treatment later.

The New England Town

With the exception of a portion of northern Maine and a comparatively few incorporated cities where there are only vestiges of town government, the entire territory of the New England states is divided into towns. According to Professor Anderson's enumeration in 1945 there were 1,440 of these units. The New England town as

---

[18] On this point the reader will do well to consult A. D. Lindsay, *The Essentials of Democracy;* Mary P. Follett, *The New State;* John Dewey, *The Public and Its Problems,* Chs. V and VI. There is an excellent discussion of this issue in Chapter XIII, "The Unit and the Unity," of R. M. MacIver, *The Web of Government* (1947); see also the chapter by John D. Lewis entitled "Some New Forms of Democratic Participation in American Government" in Jasper B. Shannon (ed.), *The Study of Comparative Government* (1949).

an area of government differs from the township elsewhere in that it is considerably smaller and irregular in shape. It is also an unincorporated area, whereas in other states towns are incorporated municipalities, except in New York state where the term "town" is used in much the same manner as in New England. Originally, the New England town was more or less coextensive with the parish and might be looked upon as the political aspect of the early religious congregation. In the beginning the town consisted of a compact settlement which grew up around the town hall, the church, and a fort or stockade, plus the outlying fields of the inhabitants. As time went on and the need for protection grew less, the population extended beyond the village center into a number of more or less distinct communities which, in time, were set off as new towns. In some cases the people in these new towns were dissenters from the original church and moved out when their doctrinal differences were no longer to be tolerated by the majority in the parent town. Thus, for these and other reasons, the original three towns of Connecticut grew by division or migration until there are now 169.[19] In population these towns show great variations, the largest being one in Massachusetts with nearly 50,000 inhabitants, the smallest one in Maine with a population of nine. The median population varies from 677 in Maine to 4,400 in Rhode Island. In area the town is considerably smaller than the Middle Western township, most towns containing between 25 and 30 square miles as compared with an average of 44 in Michigan, 34 in Indiana, and 51 in Kansas. Again, whereas the Middle Western township is normally a square area, the New England town is irregular in shape, following the features of the landscape or conforming to what were originally "natural" community areas.

In the states of Massachusetts, Connecticut, and Rhode Island a great many of the towns are thickly populated and, although they do not have municipal charters, they are empowered by the statutes to perform the functions generally carried on by cities elsewhere. In northern New England, however, the town is primarily a rural area, although in nearly all cases there is a village center for whose inhabitants the town government performs services usually required by small urban communities. In such sections, however, the thing which gives the town its distinctive character is the fact that the village center is not separately incorporated, as is usually the case far-

---

[19] Anderson counted 480 towns in Maine, 312 in Massachusetts, 224 in New Hampshire, 238 in Vermont, and 32 in Rhode Island.

ther west, but continues as part of the town. The New England town, then, is an area containing both rural and urban territory,[20] and performing both rural and municipal functions.

The county has had only a slight development in New England. Thus, in Connecticut, substantially the only county functions are the enforcement of the weights and measures laws, the care of the county jail, the provision of quarters for the Superior Court, and the management of a home for dependent children.[21] In Rhode Island, each of the five counties has a sheriff, but he is chosen by the state legislature and his salary is a charge on the state budget. In 1941 it was reported that counties in Massachusetts spent only three per cent of all the money spent for government in that state. County budgets are approved by the state legislature and county government costs are paid by the cities and towns within each county. Massachusetts counties have some functions with respect to roads and bridges, maintain prisons and quarters for sessions of the state courts, are areas for probate work and the registration of deeds, and support agricultural schools.[22] As to the Maine county a competent observer has remarked that "there is good reason to believe that its activities could be carried on more effectively by either the state or the municipality."[23] In New Hampshire it was recently asserted that "the county's early functions in connection with highways have virtually disappeared, its welfare responsibilities are less than a fifth part of all relief . . . and its law enforcement functions have been greatly reduced since the state police were created."[24] The taxing and appropriating authority for the New Hampshire county

[20] Though villages are not separately incorporated, considerable use has been made of special districts to look after such needs as sewerage, water supply, fire protection and so on. Anderson found 132 of these in Connecticut, 106 in Massachusetts, 57 in Rhode Island, 48 in Vermont, 2 in Maine, and 8 in New Hampshire.

[21] See Henry J. Faeth, *The Connecticut County* (Institute of Public Service, University of Connecticut, Jan. 1949). In 1950, the Connecticut Commission on State Government Organization, in its report to the legislature, said: "We . . . recommend the abolition of the offices of sheriffs, and with them, of the counties as units of government. This represents a redistribution of functions, not an elimination of services. With strong state government and strong municipal government, the county is obsolete in Connecticut," p. 44. I am informed that legislation to carry out this recommendation failed to pass the 1951 legislature only because of technical differences in the bills adopted by the two houses.

[22] This information was supplied by the Hon. Henry F. Long, Commissioner of Corporations and Taxation, in a letter dated November 10, 1949.

[23] Lawrence L. Pelletier, *Financing Local Government*, published in 1948 by the Maine Municipal Association and quoted with the permission of the author and the Association.

[24] See the pamphlet by James M. Langley, *The End of an Era: County Government Is Obsolete* (1945).

is the legislative delegation for the county. Total county costs in 1947 were about $2,500,000. No new functions have been added to the county for nearly a century, and county lines are ignored in the administration of state functions.

The functions performed elsewhere by the county are in New England the responsibility of the town. This makes towns the most vital factor in the system of local government in that region. Not only is this true, but the town, being an historical unit with a stable population[25] and a long history, has entered far more deeply into the popular consciousness than is the case with the Western township. Moreover, the town is usually the product of an actual growth, not the result of the surveyor's calculations. While the town organization may exist very largely to perform services for the village center, the unity of the community is preserved by considering both village and country as parts of the same whole.

TRADITIONAL TOWN GOVERNMENT

The original government of the New England town approached that of a pure democracy. The ultimate and actual working sovereignty—under the law of the state—was vested in the body of adult male citizens qualified to vote in town meeting. Here the needs of the town were debated and voted on, the budget was adopted and taxes levied, and the administrative officers were elected and their work passed in review before the voters. The annual town meeting was a social as well as a political event. It was the occasion for "visiting" and making merry, as well as for debating and voting, and presented an opportunity for much shrewd comment by local "characters" who enlivened its sessions. A great deal of praise has been heaped upon the town meeting, and much of it has been deserved. It inculcated a feeling for public affairs in ten generations of citizens; it gave thousands of men a valuable training by affording them the opportunity to rule as well as to be ruled; and it nourished a sense of loyalty to the town which, though it might be regarded as merely parochial, was nevertheless a stabilizing force of great social value.[26]

---

[25] The census figures indicate that in the rural sections of New England the proportion of the population born in the town, the state, or in the region is larger than in any comparable area of the United States.

[26] Thus the Supreme Judicial Court of Massachusetts stated: "No small part of the capacity for honest and efficient local government manifested by the people of the commonwealth has been due to the training of citizens in the forum of the town meeting.

The functions of the town were the immediate responsibility of the selectmen, of whom there were usually three, and a long list of minor functionaries. These were chosen at the town meeting, and the tendency was to limit terms to a single year, although re-election was permitted and was, in fact, common. In practice town affairs were managed almost entirely by the selectmen and the town clerk. The selectmen constituted an administrative board in general charge of the town business, subject to the directions of the annual meeting, with power to appoint certain officials not chosen by popular election, and with general supervisory authority over such town functions as were not committed to other officials. They prepared and published the warrant which served as the agenda for the town meeting, prepared the budget of proposed expenditures, acted as agents of the town in incurring debt, admitted persons to the roll of voters, exercised general oversight over the care of highways and the relief of the poor, and generally managed the town in the intervals between meetings.

In many ways the clerk was the most important town official. He was also chosen annually, but was commonly re-elected year after year so that in many towns he became a sort of permanent undersecretary for all the town departments. He performed not only the routine secretarial duties in connection with the town meeting and the meetings of the board of selectmen, but was also the keeper of a bewildering variety of records. In his office land titles and mortgages were recorded, marriage and other licenses were issued; he kept and revised the list of voters, arranged for such matters as the town printing, the posting of legal notices, the custody of official bonds, the acknowledging of oaths, and the attesting of documents. He conducted the official correspondence of the town, represented it in its contacts with the state government, and acted as the official auctioneer in the disposal of property seized for non-payment of taxes. In short, from many points of view the town clerk overshadowed all other town functionaries, being more important in the eyes of the townsfolk than even the selectmen. This was because of the fact that he tended to be the only permanent official in the town. Even today there are numerous cases on record of clerks who have served twenty,

---

. . . The practical instruction of the citizen in affairs of government through the instrumentality of public meetings and face-to-face discussions may be regarded quite as important as their amusement, edification, or assumed temporal advancement in ways heretofore expressly authorized by statute and held constitutional." *Wheelock v. Lowell*, 196 Mass. 220, 81 N. E. 977 (1907).

thirty, or even forty years, and there are a few cases in which father and son between them have held the office for nearly a century. Having a command of the town business far more extensive than that of any other town official, he tended to become the living repository of the town's governmental tradition, the unofficial historian and genealogist of the community, father confessor to the general public, and keeper of the selectmen's conscience.

The organization of town government is indicated in Figure 7. A word of explanation is necessary with respect to this and other organization charts. There is almost literally no such thing as a "typical" town, township or county government. There is not only considerable variation among the states in the statutory requirements as to official agencies, but also significant differences in local practice. Charts, then, are only approximately descriptive of actual organization and may or may not correspond to what is in operation in the student's own local jurisdiction.

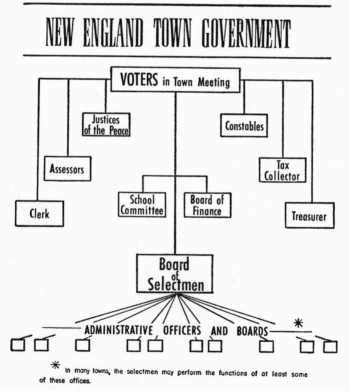

Fig. 7. Organization chart of New England town government.

A description of the governmental machinery of the New England town does very little to indicate its importance in our political history. The traditional apparatus of town government can today be seen in comparatively few out-of-the-way places; its spirit is basic to an understanding of many things in American government and politics. For the distinctive thing about the New England town was that it was a community. The towns were originally settlements of neighbors and co-religionists whose contacts were frequent and face to face. The town meeting which Jefferson praised so highly was but an adaptation to the civil concerns of such a community of a device long familiar in the conduct of church business. Much learning has been spent in trying to prove various ingenious hypotheses as to town origins. Some scholars have seen in the governmental arrangements of the original towns the logical working out of precedents established by the Teutonic tribes of medieval Germany; others have attributed the genius for local self-government to qualities somehow inherent in the "Aryan" branch of the race. A better judgment seems to be that of Channing to the effect that "the exact form that local institutions in the English colonies assumed was due far less to Teutonic and Aryan precedents than to local economic conditions, previous political experience and the form of church government and land systems that was found to be expedient." [27] The New England settlers, faced by hostile natives, an ungracious climate, and a stubborn soil, evolved a system of small and compact settlements. The soil would not support a large population, and personal safety demanded village life. Moreover, the form of church government, under which the individual congregation was largely independent of any authoritarian control imposed from above, was naturally adapted to the secular affairs of the community. Town government grew out of such a set of conditions.

Probably town government, in common with other forms, always had its seamy side. On the other hand, it would be difficult to overestimate the influence of the town on the form and especially on the spirit of American government. The idea that community affairs should be debated and settled in town meeting has had remarkable vigor. Though fitted most nicely to the economic and social conditions which gave rise to it, the notion that public questions may be settled by talk soon crossed the Hudson, scaled the Alle-

---

[27] Edward P. Channing, *Town and County Government in the English Colonies of North America*, p. 5, quoted in John F. Sly, *Town Government in Massachusetts*, p. 57.

ghenies, and took possession of the political thinking of men on the western frontier who lived under conditions which were in complete contrast to those existing in New England. Now it is precisely upon the feasibility of conference and debate as means of deciding public questions that political democracy must rest its case. As the functions of government in the future grow more and more to be based upon the findings of the exact sciences, the field of debatable questions may be progressively narrowed and matters to an ever-increasing extent may be referred to the decision of the so-called experts.[28]

The tradition of conference, as long as it persists, may be counted on to furnish a counterbalance to the tendencies toward officialism which appear in every industrial society, and to insist on making the real though subtle distinction between questions of policy and questions of technique. The New England contentiousness, institutionalized in the town meeting, will long remain a standing challenge to the pretensions of the expert to usurp the part assigned centuries ago by Plato to his philosopher-kings. This challenge is an indispensable function in every modern state.

Taking all things into account, the New England town government was an admirable device. We may well admit that it was inquisitive and gossipy, that it gave too liberal rein to the crank, the bore, the windbag, and the trouble-maker, that it put a premium on talk, and that it was tolerant of somnolent administration. But in spite of these defects it had the sovereign merit of bringing the rulers and the ruled together, it made easy the ventilation of grievances, it encouraged an intelligent and disinterested attitude toward public questions, and it fostered at its best a keen sense of the reality of the community. In an age when the community was self-conscious it institutionalized the neighborliness of the village.

Town Government Today

In the more rural parts of New England the old machinery of town government functions much as it always did. That is to say, where the town is still an actual community it gets on quite well with a type of government which assumes the existence of a stable and homogeneous population, and it does not encounter difficult

---

[28] The writer has seen no better treatment of the fundamental importance of debate and conference than that found in Chapter II of Sir Ernest Barker's *Reflections on Government* (1942).

problems of administration. Where these conditions do not occur modifications have been substantial. These have proceeded along three lines. The first of these involves changes in the town meeting itself. After a certain point has been passed in population growth and density—say, 5,000 persons in the relatively limited area of an average town—questions of administration come to grow more difficult and such questions do not lend themselves to solution by general discussion. Moreover, in such towns the homogeneity of the population has been destroyed by the influx of strangers to the native political and governmental tradition. Factions multiply, minority groups become insistent, and meetings come to be tumultuous, unrepresentative, and the sport of wire-pullers. In a number of the larger Massachusetts towns this situation has led to the adoption of the limited town meeting, in which a rather large body of elected representatives exercises all the powers previously possessed by the town meeting itself, under the guidance of the finance committee of the town.[29] "The town meeting, the last survival of direct democracy, found that a heterogeneous population and increased numbers limited, and in some cases destroyed, its effectiveness as a policy-making body. The board of selectmen discovered that it could not administer efficiently the many new and technical services demanded by a population nurtured in an industrial economy. The municipality, once a sociological as well as political unit, awoke to find that, with the increased mobility of its people, the community had disappeared. Finally, as the crowning insult, the state either increased its supervision of local government or assumed itself the functions formerly performed at the local level." [30]

In other parts of New England where the town meeting itself has not yet been modified, the growing incompetence of both the meeting and the selectmen in matters of finance has led to the creation of finance committees to furnish leadership and guidance to the town. The need for some such leadership is evident upon reading Professor Hormell's description of how financial matters are disposed of in the typical town meeting in his own state of Maine: "The voters in the

---

[29] John F. Sly, *Town Government in Massachusetts*, Chs. VII and VIII. In these towns any voter may speak but the voting is done by the elected representatives. There is a lively account of town life and town politics in Clarence M. Webster's *Town Meeting Country* (N. Y. 1945), Ch. 8.

[30] Lawrence L. Pelletier, *Financing Local Government* (Maine Municipal Association Handbook No. 6, Hallowell, Maine, 1948), p. 10. Quoted with the permission of the author and the Maine Municipal Association.

town meeting have, to guide them in voting appropriations, nothing except the unrelated and unclassified articles in the warrant, and financial items similar in character in the annual report. The chaff has not been sifted from the wheat. The needs of the town are not considered as a whole; nor are they considered in relation to the available revenue. The value of one activity is not weighed against that of another. Many of the articles calling for large expenditure are introduced by private individuals who have no comprehensive knowledge of the needs of the town. Often an unwise article championed by a fluent speaker is approved, while some necessary service is, perchance, entirely unprovided for. It is not uncommon for the articles near the top of the warrant to receive unquestioned approval, while equally important articles, accidentally coming near the end of the warrant, are summarily dismissed, after some 'watch-dog of the treasury,' with pencil and paper in hand, announces that the town has already appropriated more than the usual amount." [31] The finance committee is an unpaid board of citizens with the general duty of advising the town on all matters having to do with taxation and expenditures. It frames the budget and holds hearings upon it prior to the regular town meeting; it may approve or disapprove matters placed upon the warrant calling the meeting; it may formulate a long-time public works program; and advise both the selectmen and the meeting as to the creation and retirement of town debts. In some cases, if it has held public hearings upon the budget, its recommendations may not be exceeded by the meeting; and in any case it must be consulted in such matters.[32] Since New England communities quite generally contain a good many men and women with long experience in private business, in local and even state government, finance committees are often able groups, deserving and enjoying the respect of the public. Their influence seems to have been uniformly good.

When town functions were few and simple, the selectmen were able to discharge them successfully. In the more populous communities, however, the old system has broken down in recent years with the growing demand for new public services. In some places this has

---

[31] Orren C. Hormell, *Budget-Making for Maine Towns* (Bowdoin College Bulletin, New Series No. 64-1, 1916), p. 6. Quoted with the permission of the author.

[32] Finance committees exist in about three-fourths of the towns of Massachusetts and Connecticut and in about one-fourth of New Hampshire towns. While not required by law in Maine, many towns have them.

led to the adoption of the manager plan, although in many the idea of a manager was and still is repugnant to the population.[33] In the latter cases improvement in administration has been sought by conferring wide powers upon the town engineer or superintendent of highways, and by centralizing other functions, such as finance, under one responsible head. The manager plan itself, however, has spread rapidly within recent years and is now found in many quite small and largely rural towns. At the end of 1951 it was reported that there were 91 managers in Maine, 5 in New Hampshire, 15 in Vermont, 8 in Massachusetts, and 7 in Connecticut.

In most rural towns the chief modern changes have had to do with functions rather than with structure. Under present conditions the typical rural town is too small in area and population, and in many cases too poor in taxable resources, to render efficient and eco-

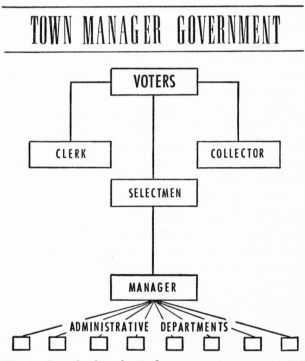

TOWN MANAGER GOVERNMENT

FIG. 8. Organization chart of town manager government.

[33] As Sly says: "It is not possible to reconstruct a local government without attention to those common feelings and traditions which have been the result of long-continued practices and it is asking much of a Massachusetts community to abandon a town meeting for a manager—a term that falls harshly after three hundred years of direct democracy." *Town Government in Massachusetts*, p. 25.

nomical service. The survey of state and local administration in
New Hampshire by the Brookings Institution pointed out that, of
224 towns, 148 had in 1930 fewer than 1,000 inhabitants, that 20 of
them had fewer than 200 people, and that in 85 of them there were
population decreases both in 1920 and 1930. In spite of these facts
and "though modern means of transportation and communication
have shortened distances and though public services have become
complicated and technical in character and state-wide or regional in
extent, the town has shown little if any capacity for territorial expansion." [34] Much the same situation exists in Vermont. A committee of the Vermont Country Life Commission some years ago
expressed the belief that "if the present town system could be rather
drastically modified or even entirely superseded, the state would be
benefited with regard to the special problems considered." This
same group pointed out that the town boundaries at present mean
very little in terms of the trading habits of the people, and that in
the school system a considerable amount of readjustment has already taken place, along lines followed by some of the churches in
widening parish limits. [35]

Towns generally in rural New England have not made extensive
internal changes to meet these inadequacies of area and financial
capacity. There is still the town meeting, the selectmen and a long
list of administrative officers, unpaid and serving in their "spare
time." [36] In personnel also much the same group takes the lead, "a
sort of untitled squirearchy recognized as the solid, permanent, and
benevolent element of the community, though now increasingly
composed in the larger places of energetic citizens from less distinguished ranks." [37] That the system continues to work as well as it
does is due very largely to the undoubted fact that "qualities of con-
servatism, thrift, stability, and intelligence are combined with comparatively widespread administrative capacity and no little ingenuity

---

[34] *Report on a Survey of the Organization and Administration of State, County and
Town Governments in New Hampshire* (1932), p. 79.

[35] Henry F. Perkins in *New England's Prospects* (1933), p. 208; for figures on the
financial and economic status of Vermont towns in recent years see Sheldon W. Williams, "Governmental Costs and Taxes in 150 Vermont Towns," and John J. Dalton and
Sheldon W. Williams, "An Economic Study of Local Government in Fifty Vermont
Towns," *Bulletins No. 546 and 532,* Vermont Agricultural Experiment Station, 1948
and 1946 respectively.

[36] The Brookings Institution Survey in New Hampshire reported a total of sixty
officers in the town of Wilton with a population of 1,724, while Greenville had fifty-
five, though its population was only 1,319.

[37] John F. Sly in *New England's Prospects*, p. 419.

in obtaining practical results." The persistent ability of the town to retain its identity, its vitality, its community consciousness, and the loyalty of its inhabitants, together with its peculiar institution, the town meeting, has had as a chief result a growing tendency to assign administrative functions to larger units, such as special districts, the county, and even the state, and to strengthen state supervision over town functions of more than strictly local interest.[38]

---

[38] There is an excellent study of politics in a New York town in Granville Hicks' *Small Town* (1949).

CHAPTER 3

Area and Structure—County and Township

THE COUNTY AS AN ADMINISTRATIVE UNIT

The one virtually universal unit of local government in the United States is the county. In the South and West it is generally a vigorous organ of administration; in New England it is dwarfed by the town; but almost everyone in the nation lives within the boundaries of some county. The latest count indicates that there are 3,050 counties, or 2,998 if we omit New England. The five counties of Rhode Island actually have no powers of local self-government. Other areas in which no county government exists are a number of South Dakota counties incompletely organized, the five counties of Greater New York, a number of areas such as Denver, Baltimore, San Francisco, St. Louis, and Philadelphia, in which city and county governments are substantially consolidated, and the 24 Virginia cities which exercise county powers.

An examination of the total figures enables us to separate the urban from the rural counties. The average county has a population of about 50,000. This figure, however, is very misleading because it conceals the vast differences between counties at the extremes of population. Thus the most populous county is Cook County, Illinois, with about 4 million inhabitants; at the other extreme we find Alpine County, California, and Loving County, Texas, each with about three hundred inhabitants. "Nearly a fourth of all counties have less than 10,000 inhabitants, nearly a third from 10,000 to 20,-000, and over a fourth range between 20,000 and 40,000. In other words, four-fifths of all counties have less than the average population. The median county has about 17,000 inhabitants and the largest single group of counties (543) ranges from 10,000 to 15,000." [1] Of more significance for our purposes is the fact that in four-fifths of

---

[1] William Anderson, *The Units of Government in the United States* (Public Administration Service No. 83, 1945), p. 19.

the 2,998 counties there is no municipality with as many as 10,000 inhabitants. It would be substantially correct to say, therefore, that 2,400 of our counties are distinctly rural areas. This method of calculation may result in counting some counties as rural that are in reality urban, because counties containing several municipalities under 10,000 population may actually be predominantly urban in character and others may contain relatively large unincorporated urban areas. The errors arising from this way of calculating, however, do not invalidate the general conclusion. Certainly more than three-fourths of all counties are rural, and the rural county is the typical county.

If we look at the counties from the point of view of their area, the contrasts are quite as striking as in the case of population. To take the extremes, the largest county is San Bernardino, California, with an area of 20,175 square miles. This county alone is larger than the states of Vermont, Massachusetts, Connecticut, New Hampshire, and Rhode Island taken together, or the states of New Jersey, Delaware, and Maryland. The smallest county is Arlington in Virginia with an area of 25 square miles. The average area of all the county units enumerated by Professor Anderson is 961 square miles. But, as in the case of the population average, this figure gives a false impression. About half of all the states have county areas of from 400 to 800 square miles. In the Western and Mountain states of sparse population the counties tend to be very large, the average county in Arizona containing over 8,000 square miles; while in the more thickly settled portions of the South and East the average size is much smaller, being 334 square miles in Kentucky and 368 square miles in Georgia.

If it is permissible to use such a word at all, one might say that the "typical" American county is an area of about 600 square miles, containing approximately 20,000 inhabitants, and having within its borders no incorporated municipality with as many as 10,000 people. These figures may seem to be useless information until we reflect that we must examine, as a part of a general investigation of the problems of rural government, the question of how effective our traditional areas are under modern conditions. In reaching a judgment on such a problem, we do not have very accurate or concrete tests, yet tests of a sort are being applied constantly, if unconsciously, in the routine administration of local affairs. Every time a local tax rate is set, or a budget prepared, or a highway projected, there is implicit in the planning some notion as to the sufficiency of the unit for which it is intended. Our task is to make the attempt at least to arrive at some general conclusions as to the effectiveness of the county as a area within which the typical governmental functions must be performed.

The county, in the contemplation of the law, is a more or less convenient area laid out under state authority for the local performance of functions regarded as largely or primarily of state concern. These functions are, for the most part, those which any government has to perform to secure its own existence, such as the collection of revenue, the enforcement of the criminal law, the peaceful adjustment of private disputes, the recording of land titles, the provision of highways, and the care of the poor. All of these the state itself would have to do if there were no local areas of government. The county was created to act for the state because such a decentralization of administration was thought convenient, wise, or expedient. Legally, it is but an agent of the state with little or no discretion as to the selection of the duties which it will discharge. Within recent years the statutes of a number of states have increased the optional powers of counties so that in a number of cases a county, by adopting such statutes, might almost reach the stature of a true municipal corporation, many of these newer functions having to do with the satisfaction of local needs rather than with the execution of state policy.[2] However, few rural counties seem to have availed themselves of these powers, the vast majority remaining simply agents of state policy.

THE COUNTY AS A UNIT OF SELF-GOVERNMENT

It would be a mistake, however, to draw the conclusion that the county is an abject instrument of the central state government. It is well established in law that such county functionaries as sheriffs and prosecutors are *state* officers. Between this legal notion and the actuality there is, none the less, a great gap, a gap created by the fact that such officers are chosen by local election. It is also important that an unreal distinction not be drawn between the idea of discretion in selecting the functions to be performed by local officials

---

[2] Charles M. Kneier, "The Development of Newer County Functions," **XXIV** *American Political Science Review* 134-40 (Feb. 1930); M. H. Satterfield, "The Growth of County Functions since 1930," III *Journal of Politics* 76-88 (Feb. 1941). Since many of these statutes are permissive, they may be adopted only by a few counties specially interested in gaining new powers. An article reviewing county government progress is scheduled to appear in the March 1952 issue of the *American Political Science Review*.

and a discretion in the choice of means to be employed in performing these functions. It will be convenient to discuss together these two points, namely, the influence of the local choice of officers upon the nature of the county, and the kind of discretion possessed by these officers.

Anyone who will take the trouble to consult the standard commentaries on the law of municipal corporations will find that courts rather generally tend to minimize, by implication at least, the importance of local election. In reality, this fact is the crucial one. For "our constitutional local self-government has consisted rather in the right of the people of the localities to choose the officers who are to execute the laws, both general and local, than in any right of the people of the localities to determine what branches of administrative activity they shall take up." [3] Those who argue from the legal premise that local officials are merely ministerial and that therefore local machinery should not endow them with a representative capacity quite forget that their local choice makes them something more than mere mouthpieces of a hypothetical central will.

Responsibility to the local electorate also signifies that a mere discretion as to *means* of action may, in practice, come very close to being the same thing as a discretion as to *what* shall be done. In view of the actual conditions of governing, far too much is made of the academic distinction between "politics," or the formation of policy, and "administration," or the implementing of that policy through a series of executive acts. Such distinctions are an aid to clear thinking, but it is possible to make them only by an effort of abstraction. In actual government what the books call "politics" shades by scarcely perceptible degrees into "administration." The tone, temper, and drift of a policy are set by the acts of those who administer it at first hand. The very substance of the "will of the state," declared with all the solemnity of statute law, may be altered in the hands of locally chosen officials, as their action is warped and twisted in response to the pressure of local interests. In a typical rural county, when provision is made for the poor, when property is assessed for taxation, or when highways are laid out and contracts let, it is futile to regard these acts as merely ministerial. In reality, they are the very stuff of village and rural politics.

Finally, it avails us little to say that officers with merely ministerial duties ought not to be chosen by a political process such as elec-

---

[3] F. J. Goodnow, *Principles of the Administrative Law of the United States*, p. 168.

tion. As a matter of practical politics there is every reason in the world for doing just that. This is true because of the fact that to nine citizens out of ten the satisfactoriness of government is determined almost solely in terms of the efficiency of administration with regard to their private concerns. It is idle to attempt to interest the generality of men in such a matter, for example, as the "scientific" assessment of property; what they are mainly interested in is that their own assessments shall be low, and the candidate who seems most likely to secure this desirable result will get their votes. For the majority of rural voters at least, the textbook distinction between "politics" and "administration" simply does not exist. Both categories are rolled into one—politics.[4]

These considerations have a direct bearing upon the question of the effectiveness of the county as an area of administration. Because of the fact that officials have continued to be elected locally the tradition has insensibly grown up that certain governmental functions are local in their nature, to be administered within local areas, with a minimum of supervision from above, and to be financed by the local revenues. There was a time when this theory was favored by actual conditions. Schools existed to teach the three "R's" to persons destined for the most part to remain in the community; roads were maintained by local labor, with local materials, and for purely local traffic; the poor were reasonably a charge upon the community since the causes of poverty were normally not connected with complex conditions beyond the local area; knowledge of disease was rudimentary and methods of dealing with it were less costly, less complicated, and less effective. Moreover, wealth was distributed fairly equally, and the methods of administration were not so expensive as to be beyond local resources. There was thus a strong case for regarding all such functions as local.

THE CHARACTER OF COUNTY FUNCTIONS

What is the situation today? About three-fourths of the cost of state and local government is incurred in the fields of education, highways, welfare, and public health. All of these are infinitely more

---

[4] "The people who participate in local self-government and show emotional attachment to it expect somewhat different things from it than do the statistician and the political scientist. They are concerned not so much with efficiency as with personal relationships. When friendliness permeates government, it wastes time and money, but it is quite possible that human foibles, such as sociability and charity, have a legitimate place in governmental organization." Arthur C. Millspaugh, *Local Democracy and Crime Control*, p. 55.

expensive than they were even a generation ago. Not only is this so
—it is now useless to deny that they are broader in their bearing than
the small units within which they happen to be administered. Thus
the Minnesota State Planning Board reached the conclusion that
law enforcement, education, health, relief and welfare, road building, and the assessment of property for taxation have all ceased to be
matters of purely local concern and that the state now has a prepon-
derant interest in the proper administration of these services. A recent study of county consolidation in Colorado lengthened this list:
"Certain functions such as supervision and maintenance of highways, policing, health work, the support of tuberculosis work, the
financing of old-age pensions, the care of the unemployed and certain
other welfare works are no longer confined to local areas but are of
state and national scope." [5] All of these matters are, in reality, state-
local functions, and the day cannot be forever postponed when we
shall recognize the state as the focal point in the formulation of policy and the development of accepted standards of administration.
That this is the direction in which we are moving seems clear when
we attempt an objective examination of the county as an administrative unit.

In seeking for a "yardstick" to be used in appraising the adequacy of existing units of government, Millspaugh discusses the
findings of numerous local investigations with reference to such
criteria as efficient and economical administration, possession of
sufficient financial resources, and convenience in rendering services
and maintaining contacts between government and citizens.[6] His
findings may be briefly summarized. Since the "essential purpose of
administrative districting is to provide public service with maximum effectiveness and at minimum cost," the district used should
be large enough to warrant an efficient staff and to keep it continuously occupied. The chief element determining the volume of
work is population. It is concluded that the minimum population of
a service unit should not be less than 25,000 in any part of the country. For some functions or in some sections of the country the figure

[5] *Report of the Committee on Administrative Units of the Minnesota State Planning Board* (Dec. 1934), pp. 4-5, 29; S. R. Heckart and G. S. Klemmedson, "County Consolidation in Colorado," *Colorado Agricultural College Bulletin No. 406* (Dec. 1933),
p. 54.

[6] *Local Democracy and Crime Control*, Ch. IV. This book is really concerned only
obliquely with the problems of crime control. It is, in fact, an admirable critical appraisal of various recent proposals for the reform and improvement of local administration and the reallocation of functions.

may be considerably higher. If population were the sole criterion, about seventy per cent of our counties could not qualify as acceptable service units.[7]

Those who wish to preserve local self-government are agreed that no substantial amount of it can be possessed except by units able to pay their own way. This means that each local unit should be able to pay for effective government out of its own resources. In the end this involves measuring the wealth of each community as represented by its general property, since the tax on general property is the principal source of local revenue. Although we know that our counties vary greatly in their assessed valuations, we know very little about the variations in real value among the counties, and very little about differences in taxpaying ability. However, we do know something about per capita wealth and local tax rates and we have the advantage of numerous local studies which make use of these criteria of local ability. The testimony of these investigations is unanimous to the effect that per capita expenditures are higher in the smaller units of government, and there is rather general agreement that somewhere about 20,000 population a point is reached below which the overhead cost of government becomes disproportionately high. On the basis of our present knowledge we seem justified in saying that, the country over, "a county with a population of 20,000 or more would be most likely to have taxable resources sufficient to support adequately a number of substantial functions."[8] Again seventy per cent of our counties are found wanting.

The third criterion examined by Millspaugh is that of convenience. It has always been assumed that the area of local government should be such that citizens might reach the seat of government without traveling an unreasonable distance. For this reason counties have generally been laid out with reference to prevailing modes of travel, and many of them are, of course, very small according to modern views of distance. If no account be taken of the fact that a large area will increase the total expenditures for certain services, such as highways, and if no attempt be made to make the county area correspond with the "natural" community, then it may be concluded that the maximum area of a county may vary from 900 to 6,400 square miles, the figure taken depending upon the location of the county seat, the distribution of the population to be served, and

---

[7] *Ibid.*, pp. 80-86.
[8] *Ibid.*, p. 96.

traffic and highway conditions. If we take the lower figure we find it only a little smaller than the average county and half again as large as the typical county. If the larger figure be taken, it is ten times as great and nearly seven times the size of the average county. In either case we may conclude that, under modern conditions of travel, counties generally could be much larger than they are.[9]

Such analyses lead to the tentative conclusion that the county under present conditions is too small in population and area and too weak financially to encourage or support an efficient administrative organization or competent personnel. So long as the functions discharged within its boundaries were local in their implications, there was no pressure upon traditional governmental forms. Since most of these functions are now seen to have wider bearings and to involve ever-mounting costs, proposals for reconstructing county areas, reforming county organization, and reallocating county functions are legion. These are reserved for later discussion, and we content ourselves here with examining the organization of county government as it exists in the rural sections of the country.

THE ORGANIZATION OF COUNTY GOVERNMENT

For the discharge of the various county functions there has been built up in all the states—except New England—a rather complex organization. Powers and duties are divided between a more or less extensive list of individual administrative officers and the general supervisory authority known as the county commissioners, the board of supervisors, or simply as the county board. The individual officers, such as the county clerk, the sheriff, the prosecutor, and the treasurer, usually find their duties rather minutely prescribed by statute and owe their responsibility to the law, as that mystical force may be set in motion by aggrieved persons or by such other officials as may have the right to call them to account. Their duties may best be discussed in connection with the various local functions. Here we shall be concerned primarily with the "county board."

County boards are constituted in accordance with two general plans. In a majority of the states the board is a small body of three or five members chosen at large from the county or from districts into which the county is divided for this purpose. In some states they are nominated by the district in which they live but elected by the

---

[9] *Ibid.,* pp. 97-101.

voters of the entire county; in others they are both nominated and elected by districts.[10]

In a group of states in which the example of the New England town has been strong, the townships into which the county is divided are the units for the choice of members of the board, which is known as the board of supervisors. This type of board is found in New York, Michigan, Wisconsin, in most of the counties of Illinois, and here and there in states farther west. Since even in counties small in area the

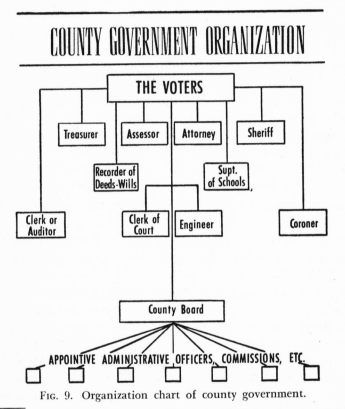

COUNTY GOVERNMENT ORGANIZATION

FIG. 9. Organization chart of county government.

---

[10] Of the 3,050 counties, the governing board consists of three members in 1,363 and of five in 872. In 87 counties the members are elected by districts, in 645 some are elected by districts and some at large, and in 1,189 counties all are elected at large, a district residence requirement being imposed in 629 of these. There is a complete summary of these requirements in Paul W. Wager (ed.), *County Government across the Nation* (1950), pp. 10-13. This book presents an analysis of county government in a "typical" county in each of the 48 states. The latest comprehensive study of county governing bodies in statistical form is *County Boards and Commissions* (Governmental Organization Report No. 2, Bureau of the Census, 1947). A more or less traditional county government organization is shown in Figure 9.

number of townships is likely to be large, county boards in these states vary in size from 16 members to 141 in Wayne County, Michigan, in which Detroit is located. The average board has about 25 members.

In some sections of the country there are variations from these two types. In Connecticut where the county is of slight importance, the board is chosen by the state legislature, in practice upon the nomination of the county's delegation in that body. In Georgia, the ordinary, or probate judge, is given many of the powers commonly vested in county boards, though in that state many duties are also vested in a board of roads and revenues. In Alabama, the county board is variously known as the Board of Commissioners or Board of Revenue, but the machinery of county government is provided largely by special legislation which frequently names the probate judge as chairman of the board. In a few other Southern states—Virginia, Kentucky, Tennessee, and Arkansas—the former English system of delegating administrative functions to the justice of the peace has been preserved. In these states board members are chosen from magisterial districts into which the county is divided, and the board numbers generally from six to nine members.

County board members are chosen for two or four years, and their terms are usually so arranged that the membership is only partially renewed at each biennial election. In a great majority of rural counties, the duties of the position require only a part of the incumbent's time and he is quite commonly paid a small sum per day plus necessary mileage when actually engaged in county business. To prevent abuses the laws of most states limit the number of meetings of the board or the total amount of salary and mileage which may be paid each year.

In the case of small boards, the organization for business is extremely simple, all matters being usually discussed by the whole board. It is a matter of common observation, however, that in many places informal agreements exist by virtue of which each member is responsible for a certain portion of the business. In states having large boards it is customary to create committees to make preliminary studies and submit recommendations to the full membership. This seems to be almost unavoidable because of the difficulty of assembling the whole board at frequent intervals. Where the membership of these committees is stable, they are very often reported as exercising a wholesome supervision over various portions of the county administration. On the other hand, frequent occasions are made for committee meetings and this has increased the overhead expenditures.[11]

What kind of men are elected to county boards? Observation leads one to believe that they are as satisfactory products of the electoral process as are found on other levels of government. Farmers, active or retired, small tradesmen, country bankers, insurance solicitors and real estate dealers, physicians and lawyers, professional politicians, and a nondescript class of men who make the salary or per diem eke out an otherwise precarious living—the list looks suspiciously like the one that might be made out for any other post. County boards reflect rather well the qualities, aspirations, and points of view of their constituents—which is all that representative government can be expected to do. If they are somewhat sleepy and easy-going, with a tendency to let things go at loose ends, an examination of the people whom they serve will usually reveal the same attributes. The record will very likely show that, according to their lights, many have served with great devotion—a fact which must be set over against the usual dismal indictments of investigators. Friendliness and accessibility rather than technical brilliance or administrative skill are the qualities sought for and appreciated by the rural population. It is probably within the mark to say that board members are normally honest and well-intentioned, but not very well informed or in close touch with developments in public administration.

The "Courthouse Gang"

County boards do not exist in a vacuum, and it will not do to treat them as if they did. A more realistic picture of such bodies is gained if we try to see them as a part of the unofficial "invisible" government which, on every level in the United States, really makes "the wheels go 'round." It is safe to say that, in nine-tenths of the counties in the United States, public affairs are in the hands of what the irreverent call the "courthouse gang." This "gang" may be described as a more or less permanent group of elective and appointive officeholders together with private individuals whose business normally brings them into contact with public officials. Among the latter will usually be found contractors interested in county road and

---

[11] A. W. Bromage and T. H. Reed, "Organization and Cost of County and Township Government in Michigan," *Michigan Local Government Series* (1933).

bridge construction, printers who want county contracts and favors in the passing out of jobs too small to require competitive bidding, purveyors of various supplies used in the county buildings and institutions, lawyers in criminal and probate work, ex-officials who have grown old in party service and who have become masters of the lower sorts of intrigue and so habituated to playing politics as to make residence at the county seat a psychological necessity, bankers likely to sustain close relations to the county treasurer in the not too vain hope that they may "take care of" public funds at a profit to themselves, and a ragged company of lesser fry attracted to the county town in the hope of eking out an uncertain income by jury duty, custodial positions, and other "pickings." Anyone who has lived in or even visited a county seat with his eyes and ears open will readily recognize many of the *dramatis personae*.

No one, however, can draw an adequate picture of politics as it is played in the typical county without taking into account many other more subtle relationships. It is necessary to remember that those in office have in their charge large amounts of public property and the disposal of large sums of public money. With the best of intentions and the greatest ingenuity the controlling state legislature could not enact laws which the local "ring" with more or less ease could not circumvent or turn to its own benefit. Moreover, officials must be given some discretion in performing their duties, and once this discretion is granted, the honest enforcement of law is left as a precarious hostage to those in office. Whatever the geographical location may be, the courthouse is certainly the political center of the county. To it and from it run the tangled threads of influence and power, favoritism and discipline, by which the somewhat furtive gentlemen in power keep the "organization" intact. The doings of the gang are perhaps not so dramatic as the gorgeous pillaging of a Tweed or a "Doc" Ames, and they have certainly not had so good a press, but no veteran need feel diffident in the presence of his urban brethren. The mere fact that the stakes are smaller in the average rural county does not mean that the game need not be played with acumen.[12]

To all these considerations must be added the fact that the county is not only an administrative area but also an electoral district. From

---

[12] "Indeed, probably little happens in the White House that has not been enacted before in every county court house in America. The difference between the average run in statesmanship and the average run in peanut politics is merely in the size of the counters, and not in the rules and the run of the game." William Allen White, *Masks in a Pageant* (1928), p. 161.

it are chosen members of one or both houses of the state legislatures who, since they are normally graduates of the school of courthouse politics, are likely as law-makers never to lose sight of the road up which they have traveled. All who suggest, therefore, that the state should "do something" about county affairs when they are unsatisfactory must take note of the fact that the state is something not very different from the aggregate of the districts composing it.

POWERS OF THE COUNTY BOARD

The statutes establishing the machinery of county government usually vest the county board with the "management of county affairs" or charge it with the "supervision of the affairs of the county." Language could not be more specific, and yet such phrases give a totally false picture of the powers actually exercised by the board. In reality the "business of the county" and "county affairs" have been committed to numerous officials in no way subject to control by the board. Almost all of these officers are popularly elected. They may be of a different political faith from that of a majority of the board and, in any event, there is no guarantee that they will be friendly to the board. Each looks to the statutes for his powers and to the ballot box for his vindication. The board cannot normally order these officials to do or refrain from doing anything, and although they may have a finger in business of first-rate importance, the board can do little beyond annoying them by withholding money for deputies and supplies. Annoyance is not supervision.

All this does not mean, however, that the county board is either useless or without power, for it still remains the center of the county governmental structure and has many duties to perform. It will be useful to comment on these.

1. Although the board is powerless to exercise any effective supervision over the elective county officers, it has full power over those whom it appoints. The number of these continues to grow, for the short ballot agitation has at least had the effect of preventing an increase in the number of elective officers. New functions have added to the list of county employees, and the statutes usually provide for their appointment and control by the board.

2. Although its range of freedom is being cut down by the expansion of state power, there still remain many questions of policy for the board to decide. It must, for example, still determine what undertakings shall be launched, what buildings and institutions shall

be built, what permissive statutes shall be adopted for the county, what and how much equipment shall be bought, and what roads and bridges shall be built.

3. A most important function involving the expenditure of much money is the awarding of contracts. The statutes of most states contain detailed provisions on the subject, but it is usually impossible to draw them in such a way as to do away with the possibility of incompetence or worse. Any discretion is likely to be abused if dishonest men are on the board, and too strict requirements may hamper honest men. In many cases, members of the board, although honest enough, are incompetent to pass upon the terms of a contract when the work to be done is complicated or involves processes outside the range of their usual experience. The history of rural county contracts is a record of ineptitude, slovenliness, and corruption, though there is perhaps less of the last than in the cities.

4. The board has a growing power to appoint minor officials and to make rules and regulations for various county institutions. Appointments are almost universally under the spoils system, and there is evidence that nepotism is widespread in spite of stringent provisions against it in the statutes.

5. Until the passage of the federal Social Security Act in 1935, the control of the county board over welfare functions of all sorts was substantially complete, except insofar as the state might influence local policy. The new federal policy, however, severely limits the powers of the county board with respect to the administration of old age assistance, aid to dependent children, aid to the blind, and aid to the totally and permanently disabled, all of which are financed in part by federal grants. There is thus left to the board a more or less complete control of general relief, except in those cases where the state government contributes financial aid, and to maintain a poor farm and to name the members of the board administering relief.

6. The board normally is responsible in large part for the purchase of supplies of various sorts for the county offices and institutions. There is evidence here of a good deal of waste and extravagance though it is not of a spectacular nature, and little or nothing has been done in the typical rural counties to improve matters. In only a few counties is there sufficient business to justify a purchasing agent, but in all of them something could doubtless be saved by making one individual responsible for the ordering and custody of supplies. There are also possibilities for improvement to

be found in a more extensive use of statutes placing the state's purchasing facilities at the disposal of the local units, but they are as yet largely unexplored.

7. The final responsibility for passing upon claims and allowing bills against the county belongs to the board. In the average county there are few places where the machinery is as disorganized as at this point. The result is that claims are frequently padded and, in many cases, the same goods or services are paid for more than once. In some counties the whole matter has been reduced to a system under which one person—usually the county clerk—receives and files all claims, investigates to see that goods and services have been received, and recommends payment or rejection to the board. There is urgent need that some such centralized control be made universal, since otherwise board action is bound to be careless and perfunctory.

8. As the policy-determining body of the county, the board is vested with a number of duties in connection with finances. Among these are the making and adoption of the budget, the fixing of the tax rate, and the equalization of assessments as between areas and individuals. The average county board is in no position to discharge these responsibilities efficiently. Many of the expenditures nominally under its control are made mandatory by state law. It has normally no power to investigate the conduct of the elective county offices, and therefore no basis upon which to criticize their requests for funds. Unless its personnel is of unusually high quality it is even unable to pass judgment upon the needs of services directly under its control. The assessor, auditor, and treasurer are not responsible to it, and it is therefore crippled at the outset so far as its financial duties are concerned.

9. Finally the county board approves official bonds, supervises the machinery of state and local elections, and performs a number of miscellaneous functions imposed upon it by the statutes. None of these is of sufficient importance to justify discussion here.

TOWNSHIP GOVERNMENT

The area known as the township exists in sixteen states to the number of nearly 18,000.[13] In New York, New Jersey, and Pennsyl-

---

[13] The township exists generally in Indiana, Iowa, Kansas, Michigan, Minnesota, New Jersey, New York, Ohio, Pennsylvania, and Wisconsin. It is found in parts of Illinois, Nebraska, Missouri, and the Dakotas. In a number of other states administrative districts called townships exist, but have no political organization of importance. In New York, the term "town" continues to be used.

vania it emerged almost as spontaneously as did the New England town, and during its early history it exhibited many of the same features of structure and operation. It was irregular in area and not much larger than the New England town and was to a considerable degree a natural community. In the states farther west the township was a ready-made area laid out by the federal surveyors while the land was still a part of the national domain. Although some attention was here and there paid to natural features of the landscape, these townships were for the most part square areas six miles in each direction, containing therefore thirty-six square miles.[14] It was the policy of the national Congress, seconded by the early state governments in the Northwest Territory, to supply the as yet sparse or non-existent population with the decentralized machinery of local self-government then so lauded in New England. In the words of Jefferson, these townships were to be "pure and elementary republics." Hence these squares on the map were endowed with governing powers and provided with a complement of officeholders.[15]

THE DECLINE OF THE TOWNSHIP

The township outside of New England has had, however, little vitality in spite of strenuous efforts to make it a vigorous exemplar of local democracy. It has been kept alive largely by artificial respiration in its early years and latterly by the stubborn inertia of vested interests. These influences have been so far successful that we cannot yet celebrate its demise. There are a number of reasons why its history has been so different from that of its New England original. The chief of these is that its boundaries did not correspond either to the social groupings of the people or to the methods of land cultivation. For this reason it seldom embodied a real community. Settlements of human beings are not likely to go up hill and down dale and across rivers to please the government surveyor. Large farms tended to create isolated farm homes and thus to minimize the importance of the village center as the focus of community life.[16]

---

[14] This was the so-called congressional township. Usually the civil township was identical with it in area, although in the more sparsely settled states several congressional townships were often combined to form a civil township.

[15] Thus the Michigan constitution provides that "each organized township shall be a body corporate, with such powers and immunities as shall be required by law," and goes on to require the annual election of a supervisor, a clerk, a commissioner of highways, a treasurer, no more than four constables, one overseer of highways for each highway district, and not more than four justices of the peace.

[16] In many New England towns compactness was enforced by by-laws forbidding the erection of buildings more than half a mile from the meeting house.

Moreover, the population which flowed into the West was not homogeneous in its origins or its political traditions. The town meeting, for example, had no special hold upon natives of Virginia or Maryland—to say nothing of Germans, Swedes, and Irish. Finally, it soon became the practice to set apart the compactly built portion of the township as a city or incorporated village, thus withdrawing its government from the township authorities who, therefore, with diminished functions and resources, busied themselves with the concerns of a scattered population of farmers. Some striking examples of this separate incorporation in Michigan are pointed out by an able student of local government in that state. The law of Michigan provides that villages of from 750 to 2,000 population may incorporate as fifth-class cities independent of the government of the township. The incorporation in 1928 of the village of Brighton as a city left the township of Brighton with 654 inhabitants. When the 1,207 inhabitants of the city of Watervliet received a charter, there remained but 948 people in the parent township.[17] The mere fact that the citizens of these villages sought a municipal charter is striking evidence of their possession of a community consciousness not possessed by the township as a whole. By contrast, it is clear that whatever may happen to the New England town either through changes in its structure or in its relations to the state government, its sense of unity is such that it stands in no danger of such violent disruption.

The township is significant both as a unit of representation and as an organ of local government in rural areas. Where it is used as a unit for constituting the county board—as is the case in New York, Michigan, Wisconsin, and most of the counties of Illinois—it results not only in large bodies but also in the perpetuation of a parochial point of view. Such figures as we have indicate that large county boards are considerably more expensive than small ones and, while it is a matter of opinion, there is no reason to believe that the larger ones are more efficient. On the contrary, their very size tends to throw the real decisions into the hands of committees, the board as a whole giving but a perfunctory approval to their recommendations.[18] If there is a value to local residents in preserving represen-

---

[17] Arthur W. Bromage, "County Government in Michigan," XVI *Papers of the Michigan Academy of Science, Arts, and Letters* 449-450.

[18] See M. Slade Kendrick, "A Comparison of the Cost of Maintenance of Large and Small County Boards in the United States," *Cornell Agricultural Experiment Station,* Bulletin No. 484 (1929). The figures cover the large-board states of Michigan, Illinois, and New York and the small-board states of Iowa, Montana, Kansas, Indiana, and Ohio.

tation of areas *as such,* it is of a character not easily measurable, and it is at any rate doubtful whether such values depend upon the retention of an area as small as the township. If the people insist upon this type of representation, it would seem possible to secure its values through the use of a larger district. Finally, the question should be raised whether it is desirable to choose bodies like county boards by a process which assumes that they have primarily representative functions. Even if we grant that, to some extent, their members reflect the views of the electorate, we must still admit that the bulk of their work is administrative and supervisory. A body with such duties certainly need not contain a score or more members.

TOWNSHIP OFFICERS AND FUNCTIONS

Our chief interest, however, is in the township as a governmental area. In some states township affairs are managed by one or more elected trustees or supervisors, with whom may be associated, as in New York towns, other elective officers such as the highway superintendent or the justice of the peace. In a few states the township meeting still has a shadowy existence but nowhere has it had a vigorous life. In Indiana, the territory of the township has two legal aspects. It is both a civil township and a school township. In the case of both, however, a single official, the trustee, is the responsible head of affairs. The principal responsibility of the civil township is the maintenance of the unimproved roads, either directly or through contract with the county. It no longer has any important functions with respect to the care of dependents. The school township covers exactly the same territory and is simply the area for the management and financing of rural elementary and secondary schools. The trustee is assisted by an elective advisory board which must be consulted before certain acts may be performed.[19]

Where the township lingers on in populous urban sections, as in parts of Pennsylvania and New Jersey, it is permitted to perform such an extensive list of functions as to make it in reality a true mu-

---

[19] The Dr. Jekyll and Mr. Hyde character of the Indiana township is due to the constitutional prohibition of a local debt in excess of two per cent of the assessed valuation. Since the civil and school townships have been held to be separate entities, this device simply doubles the borrowing capacity. See Clyde F. Snider, "Township Government in Indiana," II *Indiana Studies in Business,* No. 1; F. G. Bates, "The Indiana Township—An Anachronism," XXI *National Municipal Review* 502-504 (Aug. 1932). Figure 10 shows how township government is organized in Ohio.

nicipal corporation.[20] With these we are not concerned since they can scarcely be called typical. The rural township exists primarily today for maintaining country roads and, in a few cases, managing the schools. Although it has something to do in some places with the assessment of property and the enforcement of the election laws, the bulk of its expenditures are for roads and schools.

Over large parts of the country, practically the only thing that keeps the township alive is the fact that it is responsible for the care of minor roads. Where this is still a township function, it may be directly in charge of the township board or it may be divided among

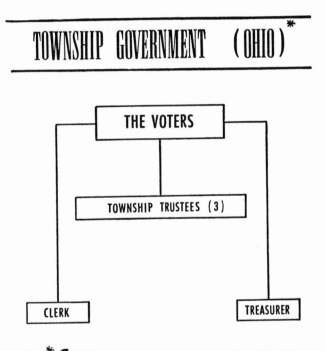

TOWNSHIP GOVERNMENT (OHIO)*

THE VOTERS

TOWNSHIP TRUSTEES (3)

CLERK   **TREASURER**

* *Source:* Paul W. Wager, COUNTY GOVERNMENT ACROSS THE NATION, Chapter 15. The voters may elect also not more than two justices of the peace.

Fig. 10. Organization chart of township government.

[20] The largest town in New York State has a population of over 259,000, while Pennsylvania has one with 56,883 inhabitants, and New Jersey one of over 39,000. The median population is 1,648 in New York, 1,805 in New Jersey, and 1,221 in Pennsylvania. West of Pennsylvania, the median population is nowhere as large as 1,500, and in Nebraska, Minnesota, Kansas, and the Dakotas it is less than 500. See William Anderson, *The Units of Government in the United States,* pp. 33-34. Among seventy-five townships in six Michigan counties, Bromage and Reed found eighteen supplying street lighting, eighteen fire protection, eleven libraries, four parks, and three water.

district supervisors each responsible for a few miles. Neither system is successful. The township is too small an area either to afford skilled superintendence or to use road equipment economically. Road repairs tend to be made in accordance with the pressures of neighborhood groups or even of individuals, and there is, of course, no opportunity to plan with reference to the county or state highway systems. The obvious inability of the township to care for modern traffic needs has led to widespread dissatisfaction in those states which still leave it any responsibility for the roads. Already township roads have been transferred to the county in Michigan, and to the state in Pennsylvania, and various types of control from above over planning and engineering are found elsewhere. It seems only a question of time until the township will cease to signify in this field of administration.

There are three states—Indiana, and North and South Dakota—in which the township exists very largely for school purposes. Where this is the case the township rather than the school district is the unit for financing and managing elementary schools.[21] While such an area may seem superior to the small district, educators generally do not encourage any extension of its use except where local conditions are unusual. The New England town is even yet a natural unit and as such may serve acceptably as a school district, and there may be real communities elsewhere with township boundaries suitable for organization about a consolidated school. These things, however, can seldom be claimed for the typical Middle Western township, and it seems a good deal more reasonable to favor the school consolidation movement or the county unit plan.

Very little indeed can be said for the township as a health or welfare unit. "The township as a health unit served its purpose when public health was limited to the use of quarantine to prevent the spread of communicable diseases and the control of environment by superficial inspections. Little was required beyond a hammer, a box of tacks, and red cards."[22] The whole scene has changed since this constituted the equipment of health officers. Few, if any, rural townships can afford the necessary trained workers or the expen-

---

[21] In Indiana, however, the township trustee has no authority over schools in incorporated cities or towns, unless the incorporated town has elected to abandon control of its own schools.

[22] A. W. Bromage, *American County Government*, p. 245; see also N. F. Sinai, "Organization and Administration of Public Health," *Michigan Local Government Series*, pp. 36-41.

sive equipment required to carry out a modern public health program. The retention of the township as a health unit at all simply means that money is spent to employ thousands of untrained part-time functionaries doing ineffective work. It would seem wise to recognize this obvious inadequacy and transfer this function to county or district units. This transfer is in fact already in rapid progress.

The relief of the poor has ceased to be a township function. Prior to the inauguration of the federal social security program, township welfare work consisted almost entirely of outdoor relief—and usually of the most rudimentary character. Cases coming to the notice of the supervisors were normally handled by the time-honored method of giving "grocery orders" until the local funds were exhausted. Until the depression of the 1930s, the typical rural township authorities were generally ignorant of modern methods of welfare work and, if not ignorant, at any rate suspicious. Years of deepening distress, however, exhausted local funds and forced reliance upon county, state, and even federal welfare organization. The designation of the township as a poor relief unit goes back to the days when the relief of poverty could reasonably be regarded as a local responsibility. The mixing of jurisdictions which has marked the effort to meet emergency conditions bears witness not only to a realization of the complex nature of the causes of poverty but also of the inadequacy of such a unit as the township. A county welfare department with the supervision and guidance of state and federal authorities can in the future manage outdoor relief far better than it was done by the average township.

THE FUTURE OF THE TOWNSHIP

If this is an accurate account of the township, it is not surprising that it has few defenders. The vast majority of townships are condemned on every count. They are too lacking in social unity, too small in area and population, and too weak in taxable resources to become vigorous units of government. There is not a function now performed by the township which could not be better performed by other units. And in fact it is being slowly starved to death. The county and state are stripping it of such functions as the care of roads, poor relief, and public health, while the incorporation of villages and small cities has depleted very seriously its taxable resources. The village, whether incorporated or unincorporated, has in fact become a much more important factor in rural government than is generally realized. In 1940, incorporated villages alone numbered 10,441 and had a population of 8,879,112; unincorporated villages numbered 8,918 with a total population of 4,901,478. The total population of those two types of villages was 13,780,590—24.1 per cent of the total rural population. Moreover, in the decade 1930-1940 the population of these villages increased faster than either the rural or urban population as a whole.[23] The steady encroachment of the county on the one hand and the growth of village populations on the other are very practical protests against the inadequacy of the township.

Formal abolition of the township is beset with a number of difficulties. In many states it would require a constitutional amendment. Still more to the point is the fact that the number of township officers is so large as to constitute a powerful vested interest. If, for example, all the township officers permitted by the constitution of Michigan were chosen in every township we should have an army of more than 16,000. These, together with their friends and families and hangers-on, might easily determine such an issue. In spite of a supposed American aversion to what is called bureaucracy, most rural and village people apparently seem to enjoy their turn in office, and the township form of government gives such opportunities to a very large share of the population. These offices are petty and part-time, but politically they are probably far more significant than the choicer "plums" at the state house. In any event they seem to be significant in the lives of many people. Defenders of the small government unit often rationalize this appetite for crumbs of power by saying that in this way the small unit trains people in the responsibilities of government. But, as Anderson says, while "education and experience in self-government are undoubtedly of value, it is doubtful whether all other considerations should be subordinated to this one." Moreover, as will be pointed out later, the values associated with local self-government do not require an excessive number of units.

Finally, it may be argued that the township represents the last remaining area in which the population can "run things" to suit themselves. It must be remembered, however, that twenty-five of

---

[23] The incorporated village is a center containing from 250 to 2,500 inhabitants. See T. Lynn Smith, "The Role of the Village in American Society," *Rural Sociology* (Mar. 1942), and E. de S. Brunner and T. Lynn Smith, "Village Growth and Decline," *Ibid.* (June 1944).

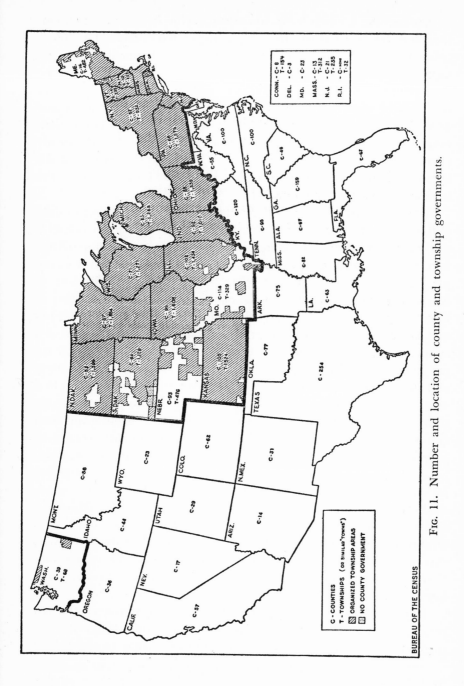

Fig. 11. Number and location of county and township governments.

69

our states never had townships and that eleven others never gave them any important powers. This is pretty good evidence that they are not indispensable units of government even in the states where they now exist. What we are doing is keeping alive mere shells of government, staffed by do-nothing officials whose titles are empty ones and whose salaries are gifts. If, as seems clear, the most hopeful way of attacking the problem of administrative inadequacy of local areas is through the reallocation of functions, the persistence of the township as a legal entity simply delays this attack or compels illogical subterfuges. The elimination of this area, either through its outright abolition or through the process of attrition, might be expected to reduce the overhead cost of local government, bring about greater uniformity in the quality of governmental services, and equalize the burden of taxation.[24]

---

[24] Figure 11 shows the present location and number of organized townships. Townships may be abolished by vote of the people of the county in Minnesota, Illinois, Missouri, and Nebraska. In Oklahoma the only townships still in existence are engaged solely in the liquidation of their debts. Current developments in township government may be followed in the *National Municipal Review*. There are some illuminating factual discussions in the chapters dealing with township states in Paul W. Wager's *County Government across the Nation*.

CHAPTER 4

Legal Aspects of Local Rural Government

THE LEGAL POSITION OF RURAL UNITS

In early England, shires and hundreds were in fact districts with large powers of local self-government. The strongly centralizing influences of the Norman and Plantagenet dynasties converted them into districts for the local administration of national law. Though never in practice reduced entirely to the level of mere administrative districts, local areas both here and in England have, since the sixteenth century, remained as distinctly subordinate units, and the legal presumption is that each is a creature of the state, no matter what the historical facts as to their origin may be. In the United States, however, the courts have usually attempted a division of these areas into two general classes: those which are created primarily with a view to the policy of the state, and those created primarily for local purposes. In some states, all these local units are called indiscriminately municipal corporations, but as a rule a distinction is made between municipal corporations proper and quasi-corporations. In the case of municipal corporations, the emphasis is placed upon their possession of *corporate* powers—that is, those powers useful and necessary for purposes of *local* government; in the case of such areas as counties and townships, the courts lay emphasis upon the fact that they are merely agents for the performance of *state* functions—that is, they are *political* and *governmental* rather than corporate and proprietary. When the latter areas are endowed with corporate powers, these powers may be used only to aid them in carrying out their more strictly political and governmental functions. Or it is sometimes said that counties, townships, and other quasi-corporations are created by the state without the solicitation or consent of the inhabitants, whereas such consent and request are assumed to have existed in the case of the municipal corporations proper. The net effect of this reasoning is to place the chief areas of rural government rather far down in the list of public corporate bodies. However, they are of higher rank than such purely administrative areas as park and drainage districts, since in practice they always afford some opportunity for self-government.

In any event, as a matter of law all public corporations and quasi-corporations of every sort derive such powers as they have from the state.[1] And all may be regarded as agents of the state, the main distinction being that the state does not use municipal corporations in quite the same way or to the same extent for its own peculiar governmental purposes.

Whereas the subordinate *legal* position of the county and other districts is clear enough, a mere reading of judicial decisions and textbooks on public law would not give one a correct idea of the actual position of our political subdivisions in the government of a state. The legal supremacy of the state is normally exercised by the legislative body, and its powers are in all states extensive, although it is well to point out that they are nowhere by any means unlimited. The chief limitations are those found in (1) the state constitution, (2) the political customs and the common sense of the legislature, and (3) the federal Constitution, statutes, and treaties.

LEGISLATIVE CONTROL OF LOCAL UNITS

With these three limitations in mind we are ready to examine the legal power possessed by the state over local units of government. The extent of this power may be stated briefly: subject to constitutional limitations the power of the state legislature over counties, cities, townships, and other local agencies is plenary. Such agencies are created solely at the will of the legislative body. Their powers and duties are prescribed by the legislature and may be widened or narrowed at its discretion. What the legislature gives it may take away and, unless the state constitution forbids, there is nothing to prevent the complete abolition of such authorities and the assumption of their duties by the state government.[2]

---

[1] *Atkin v. Kansas*, 191 U. S. 207 (1903). Even in the case of "home rule" cities, possessing charters locally drawn and adopted, the power to make such charters is derived from a constitutional grant emanating from the people of the *state*. *City of Fargo v. Sathre*, 36 N. W. (2d) 37, 50 (N. D. 1949); *Dodge County v. Kaiser*, 11 N. W. (2d) 348 (Wis. 1943).

[2] *State ex rel Linde v. Taylor*, 156 N. W. 561 (N. D. 1916); *County of Sacramento v. Chambers*, 164 Pac. 613 (Cal. 1917); *O'Neal v. Jennette*, 129 S. E. 184 (N. C. 1925); and consult J. F. Dillon, *Commentaries on the Law of Municipal Corporations*, 5th ed., Vol. 1; Eugene McQuillin, *Law of Municipal Corporations*, 2nd ed., Vol. 1.

The power of the state legislature—in the absence of federal or state constitutional provision—being absolute, it follows that it may be exercised for any purpose deemed wise by the legislature. Thus, the control of the legislature over county property has been subjected to few limitations by the courts. In the contemplation of the law a county exists entirely for the performance of state functions. It is simply a more or less convenient area for doing certain things of a governmental or political character which the state, if there were no counties, would have to do directly. Hence, it is doubtful if one can speak of the county as possessing any property. It is generally held that such corporate powers as a minor subdivision possesses are granted with strict reference to their utility or necessity in carrying out what are essentially state powers. In a sense, then, property held by the county is really state property and, therefore, at the disposal of the legislature. The only limitation upon this power which the courts will admit is that property held by a county may not be directed by the legislature to be applied to private purposes or used for the benefit of persons other than residents of the county. "The funds raised by taxation in the county are subject to the direction and control of the legislature for public use in that county, and the property of the county, acquired by funds raised through taxation, is property of which the state can direct the management and disposition, so long, at least, as it acts for the benefit of the public in the taxing district." [3] There is, moreover, judicial authority for the assumption by the legislature of the county board's appropriating authority. Thus, the supreme court of Indiana in 1932 ruled that "the General Assembly has the power to require a county to make specific appropriations without regard to the usual procedure, and in such cases the General Assembly in effect makes the appropriations and the act of the (county) council amounts merely to registering in the proper form the will of the General Assembly." [4] This discussion and the cases cited are perhaps sufficient to indicate that, as a matter of law, such governmental agencies as the county and the township are completely subject to the will of the state. "The will of the state" must, however, be declared by human agen-

---

[3] *State v. Board of Commissioners of Douglas County*, 189 N. W. 639 (Neb. 1922); in this case the court awarded *mandamus* to compel the commissioners to furnish quarters in the county courthouse for the Omaha municipal court; *Baker v. Hickman County*, 47 S. W. (2d) 1090 (Tenn. 1932); *State v. Lucas*, 85 N. E. (2d) 154 (Ohio, 1949).

[4] *State v. Steinwedel*, 180 N. E. 865 (Ind. 1932); on the authority of *State v. Melker*, 105 N. E. 906 (Ind. 1914).

cies and is found on examination to be nowhere as absolute as might
be assumed. In so far as it is declared by the state legislature its absolute character is limited in several ways. "The will of the state," of
which constitutional lawyers and certain judges speak with such unc-
tion, is delivered through (1) the constitution and (2) the statutes.
The first of these may be regarded as a statement of the "fixed" principles in accordance with which the government is normally to be
conducted. The latter are to be looked upon as a series of attempts
made from time to time by the legislative body to meet concrete
problems of government and administration-attempts which must,
of course, be subject to frequent revision. Moreover, both constitution and statutes—so great is the poverty of language and the ignorance of statesmen—must be more or less constantly interpreted by
the courts to bring their terms into some fruitful relation wih reality. Finally, tradition and political and social custom, and the
common sense of those in power, have a great deal to do with the
actualities of government.

Restrictions upon Legislative Control

In many ways the most important restrictions upon the power of
the state legislature are imposed by the state constitution itself.
Some constitutions contain very few such restrictions, others are
loaded with them. It will be useful to summarize those which may
be regarded as general, that is, those found in a considerable proportion of state constitutions.[5]

1. One of the most general limitations on the power of the legislature is the frequent prohibition against special legislation for local
units of government. This is frequently stated in the form of a requirement that local affairs shall be regulated by acts of general
application. Experience has shown that some such requirement is
necessary to prevent legislatures from using their power to favor,
for political reasons, certain local areas, or to punish political opponents by tampering with local governments and their powers. For
example, a survey of local government in Alabama in 1932 disclosed
a situation leading to the following comment: "The result of the vast
mass of legislation for individual counties of the state is a mass of
uncoordinated and uncodified legislation, carelessly drafted and as
carelessly passed. . . . The passage of local laws, many of them ob-

---

[5] For a good brief discussion see Charles M. Kneier, "The Legal Nature and Status
of the American County." 14 *Minnesota Law Review* 141-156 (1930).

scure and of doubtful constitutionality, creates administrative confusion in the counties affected . . . and brings unnecessary litigation into the courts. . . . To make matters worse, the comparative ease with which local bills may be passed has made them an effective means by which petty political and personal interests may be served." [6]

On the other hand, if such a prohibition were strictly applied it would have the effect of compelling the legislature to deal with vastly different local situations in the same manner. If, for example, the legislation dealt with the structure of the government, the requirement that it be general in form would have the effect of forcing all governments into the same rigid mold. The practical necessity of managing local affairs with some reference to real needs has led very generally to an interpretation of the constitution which will permit classification of local units. Substantially the only valid basis for such classification is population.[7] On this basis the counties or other subdivisions may be grouped into a small number of classes, each containing units of approximately the same population. Thereafter, legislation applying to all the units in a certain class will be held by the courts to be general within the constitutional meaning of that term. It is, of course, possible for the classification to be so made that each group will contain but one or two subdivisions. This has been done in some states and has been upheld by the courts, though it is not the usual thing.[8] It has the effect of nullifying the mandate of the constitution. On the whole, however, just principles seem to have been followed in most states where classification is permitted, and it may be said that the requirement of general legislation has protected local governments from the worst excesses

---

[6] *County Government in Alabama,* Vol. 5, pt. 4, of a survey of state and local government by the Brookings Institution, pp. 20-21 (1932). The situation is even worse in South Carolina; see Columbus Andrews, *Administrative County Government in South Carolina* (1933). A recent thorough study is Hallie Farmer, *The Legislative Process in Alabama* (Bureau of Public Administration, University of Alabama, 1944).

[7] "There can be no proper classification of cities or counties except by population. The moment we resort to geographical distinctions we enter the domain of special legislation, for the reason that such classification operates upon certain cities or counties to the perpetual exclusion of all others." *Commonwealth ex rel Fertig v. Patton et al.,* 88 Pa. St. 258 (1878). Cf. *Adams v. Beloit,* 81 N. W. 869 (Wis. 1900); *State v. Carmean,* 295 N. W. 801 (Neb. 1941).

[8] Thus in California, legislation in 1911 created a class for each of the fifty-eight counties and, under the decisions of the courts of that state, there seems to be no way to restrict the legislature in the matter of creating new classes. See *County Government in California* (Final Report of the California Commission on County Home Rule, 1931), pp. 28, 74; and cf. *Longan v. Solano,* 65 Cal. 122.

of partisan legislatures, while it has not prevented the latter from dealing with most individual cases on their merits. When, as in the case of very populous urban counties, there seems no way by which their affairs may be legally handled by either general or special acts, a grant of county home rule, at least as to matters of structure, may offer a way out of the difficulty.

2. There are certain rather more specific questions concerning local affairs which the legislature is frequently forbidden to touch. In this class of provisions are those having to do with the boundaries of local areas, mainly counties. Unrestricted legislative power to alter county lines, to divide, or to combine counties, would create temptations to gross abuse which legislatures would probably find impossible to resist. Prevention of these abuses is sought to be accomplished in various ways. In at least one state—Oklahoma—the counties were created by the constitution itself, and the supreme court of the state subsequently held that this fact prevented the legislature from creating new counties.[9] Since an absolute prohibition against altering county lines would prevent genuinely desirable changes, such alterations are frequently permitted if a certain procedure, intended to minimize opportunities for corruption, is followed. For example, an extraordinary majority of the legislature, such as a two-thirds vote, may be required. Or, alterations may be made if they do not reduce the area or population of the unit to be affected below a certain fixed figure. One interesting provision quite frequently found is that which forbids any alteration of the county limits which will cause any boundary line to be nearer than a certain number of miles from the county seat. In some states no new county may be created unless the proposed area has a certain assessed valuation or a certain minimum population. Further, it is often provided that no change in a boundary shall take place until it has been ratified by the local voters. Ratification is likely to be difficult to secure especially if, as in some states, there is a constitutional provision that the new county shall assume its just share of the debts of the county from which it is taken.

The whole question of dealing with the boundaries of local areas is complicated by the fact that the county, for example, regardless of its area or even its population, is often used as a representative district or part of one. Since it is quite frequently provided that in laying out such districts a county shall not be divided, any change of county boundaries is likely to result in difficulties.

---

[9] *Frantz v. Autry*, 91 Pac. 193, 311 (Okla. 1907).

3. In a majority of the states the legislature is now forbidden to move county seats. In most settled communities there is now apparently little danger of this power being exercised, but the inclusion of such a prohibition in the constitution is reminiscent of many a "county seat fight" of fifty years ago in the newer parts of the country. On the creation of a new county a certain village was normally designated as the county seat either by statute or by popular vote in the county. Here the county buildings were erected and here gathered all those elements of the population who found residence at the county seat convenient, lucrative, or merely pleasant. In short, a considerable number of vested interests grew up, all feeling themselves dependent upon keeping the seat of government in the community. But some quite accidental happening might destroy the hopes of the county town for commercial eminence and lead to the rapid growth of a rival town, a raw settlement with no past and small future prospects when the county was first carved out. However desirable it might be to change the county seat, there is plenty of evidence to show that, where legislatures were free to do it, there has been considerable politics of the usual shoddy and furtive sort. The detached student who reads the accounts of county seat "fights" of fifty years ago in the yellow pages of a newspaper file may be amused at the schoolboy tactics of rural villagers on these occasions; but to the hotel-keeper on courthouse square looking through his fly-specked "plate glass" window at the deserted and tumbled-down hitching-rail across the way, it was no joke! In a few states it is still possible for the legislature to initiate a measure looking toward a change of the county seat, but when this is the case, the proposal is subject to a vote of the people in the county concerned.

4. In a considerable number of cases the state legislature is forbidden by the constitution to abolish the popular election of local officials. Though it is perhaps true that legislatures would normally defer to the ancient tradition of local election, nevertheless this prohibition is not without significance. As the American notion of local self-government has actually developed, it consists very largely in the retention of this "right" by local residents. If the legislature were free to withdraw the privilege of voting for such officers, counties and townships might speedily be reduced to the level of mere administrative districts. It is clear from what has been said above that *what* is done in a local area is determined by the state legislature. Local residents of a county, for example, are only rarely permitted by law to adopt new functions. Local self-government con-

sists almost entirely in the privilege of choosing the officers by whom delegated functions are to be carried out. This, of course, is not to minimize the importance of local self-government. Any observant person can recall numerous cases in which the "will of the state" has been effectively nullified through the choice of officials unfriendly to the state's policy. As will be pointed out later, a number of procedural devices exist by which officials may be compelled to do their legal duty, but one may be pardoned for venturing the opinion that the majority who choose such lukewarm officers are not likely to be zealous in invoking *mandamus* against them. Those who are persuaded that administration would be improved by central appointment and supervision of local officials must realize that any wide resort to such a practice would spell the end of local self-government as we have hitherto known it.

Perhaps the greatest restriction on legislative bodies, however, is that imposed by the fact that their members are themselves the products of local politics and are devoted to traditional conceptions of local self-government. The typical legislator is not likely to interfere with the working of a system of local government with which his own fortunes are so deeply involved. Moreover, he is prone to cherish the belief that the "folks back home" know their needs better than officials at the capital. This may, of course, be doubtful, but it is none the less a powerful bulwark against legislative and administrative centralization.

New Functions of Rural Government

As has been pointed out above, counties and townships were originally created almost wholly with a view to state policy. As merely more or less convenient areas within which state functions might be performed, it followed logically that, in the contemplation of the law, they were creatures of delegated powers. When the possession of a power was in question, the doubt was resolved against them. Having comparatively few functions to perform, such areas possessed few of the corporate characteristics of a city. Proprietary powers were construed strictly with reference to the delegated functions conferred upon them.[10] This state of the law squared measurably well with the facts so long as a sharp difference existed between urban and rural life. In recent years, however, these differences in certain

---

[10] For example, the local area cannot hold property or spend money or lay taxes except in connection with some function expressly delegated to it by statute.

respects at least have tended to disappear. What some sociologists
have referred to as "rurbanization"—the obliteration of the ancient
differences and the creation of a new synthesis of urban and rural
mores—has proceeded to the point where the rural resident demands, within the necessary physical limitations, the same standard of living as the city-dweller. This has given rise to a whole set
of new problems and a demand for new powers to meet them. When
a county, for example, becomes conscious of the value of a recreational policy, a hospital and a public health problem, the need for
a library, or the possibilities involved in regional planning, it must
be equipped with legal powers not differing very greatly from those
conferred upon municipal corporations proper.[11]

In a growing number of cases this changing character of the
county has been recognized by the state legislature through the conferring of general police powers; and rules and regulations made
under such grants of power have been upheld by the courts.[12]
Where the county has become highly urbanized so that it differs little from a municipal corporation, it has been found advisable to
increase its discretion in the matter of choosing governmental machinery by providing a number of optional county charters or even
permitting the county to frame or adopt its own charter. While
there has been in some quarters considerable interest in county
home rule, the device would seem to be of limited application. So
long as counties generally continue to be primarily local areas for
the administration of state functions, it would appear both necessary
and wise to confine home rule to the choice of the frame of government, rather than to interpret it to mean the right of the county to
choose freely the functions which it will perform.

JUDICIAL CONTROL OF LOCAL GOVERNMENT

Local administration in English-speaking countries having seldom been organized in the form of a hierarchy of officials, the responsibility of public functionaries is normally regarded as being a responsibility to the law. "Responsibility to the law" is a mouth-filling
phrase but it means little unless it is conceived of in terms of human

---

[11] See Charles M. Kneier, "The Development of Newer County Functions," **XXIV**
American Political Science Review 134-141 (Feb. 1930); M. H. Satterfield, "The Growth
of County Functions Since 1930," **III** *Journal of Politics* 76-86 (Feb. 1941); also, the annual summary entitled "County and Township Government" in the *American Political
Science Review* by Clyde F. Snider.

[12] *Ex parte Junqua*, 103 Pac. 159 (Cal. 1909); *Ex parte Stephen*, 114 Cal. 278 (1896).

agencies to secure its enforcement. So it comes about that the proper performance of public functions is largely dependent upon the alertness of citizens in watching the work of their rulers and setting in motion the legal machinery needed to enforce the statutes. In other words, it is up to the citizen to look out for his own interests when these interests seem to be threatened by official action.

It is a well-established theory of our law that no official shall be irresponsible in the exercise of the powers delegated to him by statute. For failure to act, for wrongful action, or for action contrary to the intent of the law he may be held responsible in precisely the same way as any private citizen. The classic statement of the position of officials under "the rule of law" was made by Mr. Justice Miller of the Supreme Court of the United States in *United States v. Lee:* "No man in this country is so high that he is above the law. No officer of the law may set that law at defiance with impunity. All the officers of the government from the highest to the lowest are the creatures of the law and are bound to obey it. It is the only supreme power in our system of government and every man who by accepting office participates in its functions is only the more strongly bound to submit to that supremacy and to observe the limitations which it imposes upon the exercise of the authority which it gives. Courts of justice are established, not only to decide upon the controverted rights of the citizens as against each other, but also upon rights in controversy between them and the government." [18] Nor does the American official have the advantage—if it be an advantage—of having his official conduct examined in a special tribunal such as the administrative courts found on the continent of Europe. In short, the enforcement of official responsibility may be secured by either civil or criminal action in the ordinary courts, the procedure in such cases being essentially the same as is invoked in those in which private parties are involved. Broadly speaking, no public officer may plead his official status in extenuation of any act which would be illegal if it were committed by a private citizen.

The courts may exercise their criminal jurisdiction so as to influence the conduct of officials in two different ways. In the first place, the violation of an official command may lead to a prosecution in which the court is required to pass upon the power of the official to issue the order which has been disobeyed. If the court finds that the official acted beyond his legal authority, the field of administration

---

[18] 106 U. S. 196 (1882).

is to that extent limited. The control of the criminal courts is strikingly demonstrated in those cases where a jury is used. If the law or order in question has to do with the enforcement of a policy unpopular in the neighborhood, it may be impossible to obtain a conviction. In such instances state policy remains a dead letter.[14]

The criminal jurisdiction of the courts may also be invoked against public officials, to restrain or to punish them, either by private persons or by the prosecuting officer of the state or local district. The extent to which this type of control is effective depends almost entirely upon the content of the criminal law, that is, the extent to which it permits this sort of control over administrative officers. Although this kind of prosecution may be initiated by either a private person or by the state through its law officers, the actual conduct of such actions is in practice left in the hands of the latter. And since the latter have wide discretion in prosecuting matters turned over to them, the efficacy of this method is largely dependent upon the zeal of the state's attorney. While he may be under a positive obligation to take vigorous action against alleged wrongdoers, he may also at the same time be an integral part of the local political machine and thus have every practical reason for neglecting his duty. In such cases he may have to be superseded by an official detailed from the attorney general's office.

Civil Liability of Rural Units

The responsibility of officials to the law may likewise be enforced by civil action in the courts.[15] Such action may, if the statutes permit it, be taken by bringing suits against the government, or by seeking damages from the official as an individual. The right of the government to maintain suits against natural or artificial persons is in general unquestioned, but the liability of government to suit by private individuals is by no means so clear. It is a common principle of the law that a state may not be sued in its own courts without its consent. Since the areas in which we are primarily interested are viewed by the courts simply as portions of the state created for the more convenient administration of state policy, a suit against any one of them would be in effect a suit against the state and hence

---

[14] Control by the criminal courts is briefly discussed in Frank J. Goodnow, *Principles of the Administrative Law of the United States* (1905), Book VI, Division II, Ch. III. The role of the grand jury in investigating and controlling local officials is discussed in Chapter 9.

[15] Consult Goodnow, *op. cit.*, Book VI, Division II, Ch. II.

prohibited under the principle given above. This immunity of the local government is based upon considerations of public policy which forbids "that the state shall be made a defendant in litigation without its consent, and as counties are regarded as parts of the government the exemption is in good reason also extended to them, unless a statute exists expressly allowing the maintenance of actions against them." [16]

A somewhat different line of reasoning is followed in the case of cities. Here the degree of liability is commonly greater. This is based upon the belief that cities perform two sorts of functions. On the one hand, they are agents of the state in the enforcement of governmental powers. On the other, they are agencies of local government endowed with powers and privileges deemed of peculiar value to the local residents.[17] They are assumed to have been established at the solicitation or with the consent of the inhabitants involved, and this request or consent is considered evidence that incorporation confers benefits of such a nature as to subject cities to liability for the wrongful use of their corporate powers. In the exercise of governmental powers, however, the city enjoys an immunity from suit by private persons in the same way as the county whose duties are regarded as wholly governmental.[18]

While it may be said that the law grants to such areas as counties an immunity from suit for wrongful acts of the public authorities, there has appeared in recent years some tendency to modify this rule. This has been particularly marked in cases where acts of a county in the use of its property or in the performance of its functions have caused property damage to landowners. In 1932 the supreme court of Oregon had before it a case in which a county, in building a highway, had appropriated private property without going through the usual procedure of condemnation. While the court held that a county was not liable to prosecution for tort, the plaintiff

---

[16] *Rapp v. Multnomah County,* 152 Pac. 243 (Ore. 1915); *Wold v. City of Portland,* 112 Pac. (2d) 469 (Ore. 1941). Cf. *Marion County v. Rives and McChord,* 118 S. W. 309 (Ky. 1909); *Commonwealth v. Boske,* 99 S. W. 316 (Ky. 1907).

[17] *Commissioners of Hamilton County v. Mighels,* 7 Oh. St. 109 (1857); *El Paso County v. Bish,* 33 Pac. 184 (Colo. 1893); *Jones v. New Haven,* 34 Conn. 1 (1867).

[18] Liability may in all cases, however, be imposed by statute and this has been done by some states. See C. W. Tooke, "Extension of Municipal Liability in Tort," **XIX** *Va. Law Review* 97-120 (1930); E. M. Borchard, "Government Liability in Tort," **XXXIV** *Yale Law Journal* 1-45, 129-43 (1924-5) and *Ibid.* **XXXVI,** 1-41, 757-807, 1039-1100 (1926-7); Edgar Fuller and A. James Cosner, "Municipal Tort Liability in Action," **54** *Harvard Law Review* 437 (1941). Cf. *Snyder v. Binghampton,* 245 N. Y. S. 497 (1930).

might waive his tort action and declare upon an implied contract. The court had held in a previous case that a county might be sued for trespass upon private property when such an invasion amounted to a taking of land without condemnation. "A careful consideration of the complaint in the case at bar leads us to the conclusion that it states facts disclosing an appropriation of property by defendant county. Such an appropriation implies an agreement to pay the damages attendant thereupon." [19] Likewise, the supreme court of Minnesota in 1920 held a county liable when sparks from an engine of the highway department kindled a fire which spread to land nearby and destroyed private property. The county was held liable on the ground that it might not cause "a trespass upon the lands of an adjacent proprietor. This is a breach of duty owing, not to the public at large, but to the private owner." [20] The logic of this has been criticized by some courts, and it is doubtful if the county can be held free of liability in the case of torts and held responsible in damages for similar acts which are distinguished, if at all, only by giving them different names.[21] Judicial attempts to draw such a distinction may best be explained, perhaps, on the theory that, when the courts are impressed by the evident justice of a plaintiff's claim, they are willing to resort to questionable logic to afford practical relief.

The limited immunity against suits for breach of contract which the states enjoy does not ordinarily extend to their subdivisions. As a general rule counties, townships, school districts, and other local authorities may be compelled at the suit of private parties to perform contracts made in the course of their functions.[22]

THE EXTRAORDINARY REMEDIES

We have seen that the administration of public affairs may be controlled to some extent by the courts in the exercise of their ordinary civil and criminal jurisdiction. In many, if not most cases, the ordinary judicial process is sufficient guarantee that those in authority will not so act as to injure private individuals, or as to perpetuate

[19] *Kerns v. Couch et al.,* 12 Pac. (2d) 1011 (Ore. 1932).

[20] *Newman v. St. Louis County,* 176 N. W. 191 (Minn. 1920); *Clark v. City of Brainerd,* 298 N. W. 365 (Minn. 1941).

[21] *Dempster v. Grafton County,* 184 Atl. 866 (N. H. 1936).

[22] There are some exceptions, however. See *Buck v. Indiana Construction Co.,* 138 N. E. 356 (Ind. 1923) and *Duncan v. Willits,* 57 Atl. 369 (Del. 1903), cited in C. M. Kneier, "Legal Nature and Status of the American County," 14 *Minn. Law Rev.* 156 (1930).

a course of action likely to establish an unwise public policy. In a considerable variety of circumstances, however, the forms of action available in the ordinary jurisdiction of the courts do not in reality afford the sort of remedy which meets the needs of private parties or advances the cause of orderly administration. It may, for example, be of vital importance that an act be done which the law says shall be done. It would often amount to a denial of justice to require a person threatened with injury by official neglect, to wait until he had suffered the injury and then attempt to redress it by appropriate civil action, or even by criminal prosecution. It is not damages which are desired; nor would conviction of an offending officer meet the situation. Likewise, substantial justice may frequently be satisfied only by the prevention of an official action which is *prima facie* likely to work irremediable injury. All this is but another way of saying that what is needed in such cases is some way of reaching and controlling official *action* rather than the *persons* involved.

To meet such conditions there have been evolved a number of actions known generally as the extraordinary remedies. These are called extraordinary because they may not ordinarily be invoked if any other remedy is available.[23] At common law these remedies were regarded as prerogative in their nature, since they were developed out of the reserved judicial power of the British Crown which was held not to have been exhausted by the creation of the ordinary forms of action. The word "prerogative" in this connection is usually interpreted to mean that the allowance of these remedies is within the discretion of the court to which application is made. However, some of them are so important for the maintenance of individual rights that they early became *writs of right,* that is, issued as a matter of course on probable cause shown. In any event all of these remedies have in some respect been regulated by statute, and few or no general principles may be stated with regard to their use.[24]

The most important of these remedies are the writs of injunction, *mandamus, certiorari, habeas corpus,* and *quo warranto.* The writ of *mandamus* may be defined as an order of a court command-

---

[23] See Goodnow, *op. cit.,* Book VI, Division II, Ch. IV; J. A. Fairlie and C. M. Kneier, *County Government and Administration,* pp. 80-89. The classic text is James L. High, *A Treatise on Extraordinary Legal Remedies* (1896).

[24] The student will find very serviceable articles on these various writs in the *Encyclopedia of the Social Sciences,* and illustrative cases in James Hart's *An Introduction to Administrative Law* (1940). The extraordinary remedy known as *prohibition,* not being of importance in the control of administrative officials, is not discussed here.

ing a public official to do an act which he is obliged by law to do, but has refused to perform.[25] *Certiorari* is a writ used to review the procedure of a subordinate authority exercising powers which are judicial in their nature, for the purpose of amending or annulling an order or decision made by that authority.[26] The writ of *habeas corpus* is an order addressed to an official holding a person in custody to present such person before the court so that inquiry may be made as to the legality of his detention. *Quo warranto,* for which in most states a form known as "information in the nature of *quo warranto*" has been substituted, is the proper method for trying title to a public office where, for example, two persons may lay claim to the same post.[27] Although private persons in some jurisdictions may set in motion the machinery of the courts for such a purpose, action is generally brought in the name of the state by the attorney-general or other law officer. This is because of the fact that in theory a public office is a franchise derived from the sovereign state, and therefore only the state is interested in protecting its bounty from usurpation.

Of the legal remedies, the most important for the purpose of controlling public administration is the *mandamus*. *Mandamus* will not be granted if any other remedy is available to the complainant —such, for instance, as civil suit—unless such remedy, if available, is obviously not adequate in the circumstances. The adequacy of other remedies is, of course, a question for the court. The writ of *mandamus* has been issued by the courts to compel officials to publish a statement of audited claims, to repair a highway, to levy a tax, to pay judgments secured against the county or other unit, to call local elections, to set up various funds required by the statutes, to lay out commissioner and supervisor districts, and to perform a host of other acts, important from the point of view of individuals likely to be injured by inaction, or from the point of view of orderly administration.

---

[25] *Basset v. Atwater*, 32 Atl. 937. (1895); *People v. Fowler,* 127 N. E. 793 (1920); *State v. Essex County,* 23 N. J. L. 214 (1851). The writ may in proper cases be directed to private parties.

[26] "A *certiorari* at common law was an original writ, issuing out of Chancery, or the King's Bench, directed in the King's name, to the judges or officers of inferior courts, commanding them to return the record of a cause depending before them, to the end the party may have the more sure and speedy justice before him, or such other justice as he shall assign to determine the cause." Bacon's *Abridgement;* see *Beasley v. Beckley,* 28 W. Va. 81; *Miller v. Sacramento County,* 25 Cal. 94 (1864). The subordinate authority need not be a court, properly so-called. It is sufficient if its action on the matter before it requires the exercise of a quasi-judicial authority.

[27] *Ames v. Kansas,* 111 U. S. 449 (1884); *State v. Sullivan,* 47 N. W. 802 (1891).

In proceedings for *mandamus,* and to some extent in others of the extraordinary legal remedies, the courts are limited by the rule that questions of fact or expediency will not be inquired into. "This principle," says Goodnow, "is applicable whatever be the rank or character of the officer to be controlled. Be he never so humble, if he has discretion he is to exercise it free from any control; be he never so influential he must act in accordance with the law." [28] This rule as to the freedom from control of discretionary acts is subject, however, to one exception. The courts in some states will review the action of administrative officers when their findings are unsupported by the evidence or there is reason to suspect fraud or bad faith.[29]

In practice, the *injunction* is more frequently resorted to than *mandamus.* The courts will issue it only when the applicant can bring his case under one of the usual classes of equitable jurisdiction, such as those in which is involved breach of trust, possibility of irreparable injury, or the likelihood of a multiplicity of suits. When issued, the writ of injunction takes the form of an order directed to the official complained against, commanding him to refrain from performing a certain act. Failure to obey the order subjects the offending official to summary punishment for contempt of court. The initial order remains in force for a limited period during which a hearing is held, at the conclusion of which it is either made permanent or is vacated. In most states the right to demand an injunction is extended, either by common law or by statute, to all citizens or taxpayers on the theory that each has a sufficient interest in the expenditure of public funds or the performance of public functions to give him a standing in court.[30] As a matter of fact, most applications for the writ are made with the intention of protecting the public against the assumed injury to the treasury through the performance of *ultra vires* acts, the misapplication of funds, or the expenditure of moneys for purposes not clearly public, and are commonly known as "taxpayers' suits." Thus the writ will issue to prevent the collection of an illegal tax on property, to restrain the illegal creation of a

---

[28] F. J. Goodnow, *Principles of the Administrative Law of the United States,* p. 433.

[29] "The courts will not control the discretionary acts of county commissioners done within their statutory powers where fraud or abuse of discretion is not clearly shown." *Bowden v. Richter,* 69 So. 694 (Fla. 1915). For example, *mandamus* will not be issued to compel officials to enforce a statute or an ordinance prohibiting the sale of liquor or regulating the parking of automobiles. *State ex rel Wear v. Francis,* 8 S. W. 1 (Mo. 1888); *State ex rel Beardslee v. Landes,* 271 Pac. 829 (Wash. 1928).

[30] See *Crampton v. Zabriskie,* 101 U. S. 601 (1880); *Place v. Providence,* 12 R. I., 1 (1877); *Williams v. Gallatin,* 128 N. E. 121 (1920).

debt, to prevent the awarding of a contract in an illegal manner, or the holding of a bond election where there has been imperfect compliance with statutory proceedings, to prevent the laying out of roads over private property, and to prohibit the paying out of sums of money for goods and services unauthorized by law.[31]

Since an act of interpretation by some administrative official is in reality involved in the enforcement of every law,[32] it has been found necessary to establish a final and authoritative agency of interpretation. In the American system this final authority is the courts. Nearly every circumstance of their creation points to a desire to render them at least relatively independent of the forces which operate upon an elective or, at any rate, politically controlled administration; hence the longer terms of judges, their security against removal, the requirement of a minimum professional fitness and, in some cases, their choice on a non-partisan ballot.

Whatever else we may think of a system of government under which the competence of public authorities is ultimately determined by the courts, certain things at least must be conceded. In the first place, the courts, in relying upon adjudicated cases as authority for decisions on matters before them, establish within the law a security which, when clearly examined, is of the highest importance to men in their dealings one with another. Those who rail against the so-called usurpation of the judges do not calculate carefully enough the possibilities under any conceivable alternative scheme. It is entirely possible that a scheme of deciding each case "upon its merits" would import into the law an intolerable uncertainty, in the end productive of more evil than would appear possible on a superficial view. In the second place, with special reference to the direct and indirect control of local officials by the courts, it cannot be doubted that the courts, in this country at least, are more competent bodies than the typical legislature to protect the public against the mistakes, the imbecilities, and the downright extortions of audacious

---

[31] See, for examples, *Dyer v. Erwin,* 33 S. E. 63 (Ga. 1892); *Jones v. O'Connell,* 107 N. E. 731 (1914); *Denver v. Pitcher,* 129 Pac. 1015 (Colo. 1913); *Lewis v. Turner,* 76 S. E. 999 (Ga. 1912); *Cruse v. Police Jury,* 92 So. 679 (La. 1922); *Rogers v. Common Council,* 25 N. E. 274 (N. Y. 1890); *New London v. Brainard,* 22 Conn. 552 (1853).

[32] "There is hardly a proposition of any moment to be settled by county authorities but that they are called upon to act on data from which diverse conclusions may be reached. Not infrequently the citizens of the county differ as to the course to be pursued. It is impossible in our complex civilization to prescribe the exact manner in which every official act must be performed. Hence the manner of doing an act within the power of the governing officials of a county must be left largely to their discretion." *Dunn v. Beck,* 86 S. E. 385 (Ga. 1915).

elected persons. Indeed it is impossible to conceive of a legislative body doing more than creating the relationship of trustee, leaving the myriad specific incidents of such a relationship to be developed by the judges.

It is necessary constantly to call ourselves back to the simple and obvious, yet fundamental, truth that government consists essentially —at least as it works from day to day—of certain persons called officials exercising authority over other persons. The exercise of authority involves placing in the hands of such persons certain powers —powers over public property, powers over private property (and hence over income), and powers over personal conduct. Men possessing such authority are, of course, under a more or less constant temptation to abuse it, for, even though they may not consciously desire to seize excessive power, it is easy for them to convince themselves that what they wish to do is in the public interest.

One practical approach to the solution of this ancient feud between liberty and authority lies in the direction of making difficult this equation of interests. A crude method of doing this is to shorten terms of office so that men may not form the habit of command; the "recall" is another, though it is to be noted that here we are using what is after all a questionable expedient to enforce a judgment as to the public good; the devices of direct legislation do a part of the official's work for him, although, as is well known, the judgments expressed by the electorate may in reality be those of active minorities. But even if all these devices are recognized, they cannot, in the nature of the case, cover more than a tiny section of the field of government and administration.

Finally, though we have no wish to minimize the importance of the courts as agents for controlling the administration, it is very probably true that they have seldom stood out long against the realization of a clearly expressed public desire. A locally chosen judiciary is, after all, only a little less sensitive to public opinion than are other officials, no matter how much we may allow ourselves to romance about the dignity and aloofness of the judicial office. The ocean of precedents which is the law can supply support for almost anything desired by a predominant public interest. The oracular utterances of black-robed judges are but feeble echoes of the forces which really matter in the governing of men. Judges are not automata; they do not do their work in a vacuum; they are not unmindful more than others of what is going on beyond the courthouse square. It is well not to have too many illusions about them. "The great tides and currents which engulf the rest of men, do not turn aside in their course and pass the judges by . . . The law, conceived of as a real existence, dwelling apart and alone, speaks through the voices of priests and ministers the words which they have no choice except to utter." [33]

One final word is in point. The retention of a system under which the acts of public officials are subject to review and control by the courts can doubtless be justified so long as the character of the local service remains what it is at present. Considering the equipment of the personnel drawn into that service, it is perhaps wise to put it under some sort of tutelage. It is hopeless to expect popular election to supply us with competent persons to man the various technical services, and so long as this remains our method of recruitment in rural areas, the ignorant blundering of such persons ought to be corrected when individual rights or public well-being are threatened. There is no greater need today than the creation of an able public service which, guaranteed security, adequate salary, and social esteem, may safely be entrusted with the management of the public business.

---

[33] Benjamin N. Cardozo, *The Nature of the Judicial Process,* p. 168.

CHAPTER 5

The Conditions of Rural Administration

On whatever level of government we find it, public administration may be briefly defined as the management of men and materials to carry out the policies decided upon by the political branch of the government.[1] In other words, it is the *business* side of government, and in theory there is no reason why it should involve principles different from those found effective in other types of business. Any analysis of the conduct of public administration would mean discussing the accepted principles governing (1) the recruitment and management of personnel; (2) the methods of solving concrete problems having to do with material and work procedure, such as purchasing, accounting, budgeting, and reporting; (3) the conditions, human and otherwise, which affect both of these.

PUBLIC ADMINISTRATION AND THE SOCIAL ENVIRONMENT

The principal objective of this chapter is to point out and illustrate the fact that the character of public administration is influenced deeply and in a controlling fashion by the environment, social and psychological, within which it is conducted. In this respect the usual textbook definitions of administration are defective. For it is not too much to say that administration is as truly a part of the culture and civilization of a country as its arts, its customs, its sports, and the manifestations of its religious life. One can scarcely doubt, for example, that the characteristics of the French bureaucracy answer to fundamental traits in the French national character; that the Prussian officialism was the expression of the passion for order

---

[1] For brief definitions see L. D. White, *Introduction to the Study of Public Administration* (3rd edition, 1948), p. 1: "Defined in broadest terms, public administration consists of all those operations having for their purpose the fulfillment or enforcement of public policy"; W. F. Willoughby, *Principles of Public Administration*, Ch. 1; F. J. Goodnow, *Principles of the Administrative Law of the United States*, p. 14. The reader will find very stimulating the essay entitled "The Study of Administration," by Woodrow Wilson, published in the *Political Science Quarterly* in 1889, vol. II, pp. 197-222.

and discipline bred into Germans by generations of authoritarian rule; or that the peculiar combination of business efficiency and *noblesse oblige* found in the British civil servant is a precipitate of a thousand years of struggle for self-rule under aristocratic leadership. The quality of administration is conditioned at every turn by the desires, opinions, and views of the people concerned, by the extent of their education, formal and informal, by their background as individuals and by the body of traditions possessed by them as a social group. "Administration has its roots deep in the history of a people. It is an expression of their collective life. It is nourished by their affections and aspirations. It is fashioned by the interplay of their interests. It is warped by the persistence of their prejudices. Its form, its character, and the direction in which it grows are influenced by fundamental conditions—racial, geographical, topographical, traditional, psychological, economic and social." [2] As great musicians are not produced by a population indifferent to music, and philosophers do not arise among a people not given to speculation, so sound administration does not flourish where people are indifferent to its aims and unacquainted with its processes. This is particularly true of a democratic society where it may be taken as almost axiomatic that the administrator attains only such standards as the people among whom he works are able to understand and appreciate. It is not true to the same extent in a monarchy where the civil service is insulated from the direct play of popular wishes by its independent and semimilitary status; but it is emphatically the case in a social democracy where there are few barriers between the civil servant and the electorate.

It is significant that the bulk of the administrative and business talent for which the United States is famous is found not in government but in business. The reasons for this are complex. In part it is due to the fact that the pecuniary rewards have always been greater in private enterprise than in the public service. In part it is traceable to a traditional suspicion of government generally, to the belief that, on the whole, government has been a great evil. And to some extent it may now be ascribed to conscious efforts to perpetuate this

---

[2] *Report on a Survey of the Organization and Administration of the State, County, and Town Governments of New Hampshire* (Brookings Institution, 1932), p. 63; see also Leonard D. White, *Introduction to the Study of Public Administration* (1948), Ch. II, "The Form and Spirit of Public Administration in the United States," John M. Gaus, *Reflections on Public Administration* (1947), Ch. 1, "The Ecology of Government."

attitude by certain leaders of opinion who have good reasons for holding it.[3] In spite of this belief every crisis in our affairs has demonstrated that we have a great supply of administrative talent. We have not lacked it; rather, conditions have not favored its use by the public. In business as traditionally conducted under the regime of private capitalism, there were few democratic elements; autocratic management was tolerated, if not welcomed, at least as long as dividends were forthcoming. On the other hand, the very idea of self-government implies that questions of administrative technique shall be involved in those of *opinion,* and that the notions of the governed shall be heeded by their rulers, however ill-founded they may, in fact, be. All of which is but another way of saying that, in a democracy, what the mass of the people believe will get itself translated in the end into governmental action.[4]

To use the words of an author quoted above, the question to ask ourselves is, does "the totality of the social, economic and political forces and historical traditions" in rural society differ from those found in cities to such an extent as to make rural administration in any way distinctive? Aside from the information which might be conveyed there is little to be gained by discussing rural administration as a separate entity unless there is something distinctive about it. And we shall find that what is distinctive is not so much the nature of the problems met with as the conditions which have to do with the feasibility of applying to them approved solutions. The sociologists give us some suggestive material on this subject, though perhaps their generalizations deserve more scrutiny than they usually get.

---

[3] Mr. Justice Frankfürter makes the suggestion that both our distrusting and burdening government betray "some unresolved inner conflict about the interaction of government and society," *The Public and Its Government* (1930), p. 170.

[4] There is a great deal of nonsense written about bureaucracy in government. It is generally talked about as if it were confined to government, whereas any observant person constantly meets with it in his contacts with large business organizations such as railway companies and department stores, to say nothing of some of our modern labor organizations. It seems, in fact, to be a function of size and complexity, whether these attributes be found in government or in other groupings of human beings. On the subject of this paragraph see: John Dickinson, "Administrative Law and the Fear of Bureaucracy," **XIV** *Journal of the American Bar Association* 513-516; 597-602 (1928); Charles and William Beard, "The Case for Bureaucracy," *Scribner's Magazine* 91: 209-214 (April 1933); Marshall E. Dimock, "Do Business Men Want Good Government?" **XX** *National Municipal Review* 31-35 (Jan. 1931); Herman Finer, "The Civil Service in the Modern State," **XIX** *American Political Science Review* 277-289 (1925); Josiah C. Stamp, "The Contrast between the Administration of Business and Public Affairs," **I** *Journal of Public Administration* 158-171 (1923); and Ch. I of Dwight Waldo's *The Administrative State* (1948).

Rural Attitudes and Administrative Standards[5]

It may be well to begin with a statement concerning the approved standards of public administration and then pass to a discussion of the extent to which rural traditions and habits of mind make possible the realization of these standards. The question of fundamental importance to all administration is that of personnel. If things are to be well done, those in charge must know what they are about. In all but the simplest operations some training is needed, and conditions within the administration must favor the retention in the service of persons having such training.

An eminent French writer on public administration has stated as the three requirements of an adequate civil service, permanence, professionalism, and hierarchy.[6] These three standards mean briefly: (1) that those employed in the public service should be retained for an indefinite period and removed only for reasons having to do with their efficiency; (2) that the service should be regarded as a career for which men and women prepare in the same way as for any other profession, and in which they serve with equal loyalty successive administrations regardless of their political bias; and (3) that the various ranks should be subordinated one to the other in such a way as to place without the possibility of doubt the responsibility where it belongs in each case. Of course, these standards are not completely realized on any level of government, but they may nevertheless be considered as desirable ideals toward which to aim.

Conditions in rural areas at present do not favor the building up of a corps of permanent civil servants. Most officers in the county and other typical rural districts continue to be chosen by popular election, as a rule upon a party ballot, and for relatively short terms of office. The only other feasible method of choice would be appointment under some sort of merit system, designed to test the fitness of applicants. But the fact must be faced that the merit system

[5] A considerable portion of the remainder of this chapter appeared as an article entitled "Approaches to the Study of Rural Government" in the *American Journal of Sociology* for November 1933. The author is grateful to the editor of that journal and to the University of Chicago Press for permission to use the substance of that article here.

[6] A. A. Lefas, *L'Etat et les Fonctionnaires* (Paris, 1931), p. 95. Cf. the article on Bureaucracy by H. J. Laski in the *Encyclopedia of the Social Sciences*, and the essay on bureaucracy by Max Weber in H. H. Gerth and C. Wright Mills' *From Max Weber* (1946).

has made little progress outside the urban sections of the country. Generally speaking, the agricultural population has shown little or no interest, if not active hostility, toward proposals to build up a permanent staff of administrators on *any* level of government. The states that took the lead in adopting the merit system for filling offices were all urban states. Even today almost the sole examples of the use of the merit system for the choice of local officers in rural states are found in those services which are aided by national grants of money. With respect to the inroads made upon the old spoils system by the federal requirements, it is clear to most observers that state acceptance of the merit system was reluctant.[7] "The appointment of officials has seemed to the rural voter one way of enabling a little oligarchy to appoint its favorites and then extend its power, as indeed has often happened."[8] In his own local area the farmer has felt more or less consciously that the retention of the long ballot has increased his control over his local officials. This has perhaps been true in many cases, although in practice it has meant lowered efficiency, by removing the barriers between the official and various crude popular notions about the conduct of the public business. Moreover, the long ballot has often had the effect of turning over the local government to a small group usually referred to as the "courthouse gang" and owing no responsibility anywhere. However, the introduction of the short ballot and the merit system would involve nothing short of a revolution in rural political *mores*. The average farmer or villager can see no adequate reason why offices should not be "passed around." County, township, and village offices strike him as rather "soft jobs" and, after their holders have occupied them for a term or two, the general feeling is likely to be that they have had them "long enough," and that someone else should "have a chance" at them.[9]

---

[7] There were in 1947 twenty-two states having the merit system, but in very few of these did the law apply to rural units. There were civil service commissioners in only twenty-seven counties, many of them distinctly urban. White says that "by and large the counties remain the chief stronghold of patronage and of discreditable political rings, which are endowed, however, with extraordinary vitality and capacity for self-protection." *Introduction to the Study of Public Administration*, p. 322.

[8] J. M. Williams, *Our Rural Heritage*, p. 191.

[9] Over against the stock arguments against the long ballot, however, may be set the fact that in districts with a small population voters are likely to be well acquainted with candidates and hence in a position to choose with some wisdom between rivals. A Massachusetts commentator says: "The saving grace in the scheme . . . is the fact that incumbents are able to hold on to their positions and that they are regularly returned. Among the voters, who surely don't understand these positions any too well, there must be some residual common sense which tells them that a court clerk or register of pro-

The fact that with us the public service is not looked upon as a career, for which men and women may deliberately prepare as for other professions, is to be explained largely by the circumstance that the opportunities for profitable employment and reasonably rapid promotion and other recognition are, or appear to be, far greater in private industry and the older professions. It is often alleged by critics that there is in the United States no "sense of the State," and that this lack explains the relatively poor quality of our officials. This is a dark saying in more ways than one. If it means that there is with us a less lively appreciation of social solidarity and hence less desire to serve the commonwealth, it seems to the writer to be nothing more than a stilted way of stating a fairly obvious truth, which need not be obscured by the use of mystical language. Considering the utterly different circumstances, it can scarcely be said that our point of view toward the state suffers in comparison with that of Europe. If the public service beyond the Atlantic is attractive to a relatively high order of talent, it is to be explained largely on the ground that alternate careers are, on the whole, less lucrative than they are with us. There is no reason to believe that the passion for service is any more highly developed among Europeans than here. Were the opportunities for personal gain in the traditional professions, in business, finance, and the exploitation of natural resources as great in England, France, and Germany as they are in America, the youth of those nations would probably turn a deaf ear to the call to public service, and leave that field to the same type of persons that fill its ranks here. Finally, in older and highly stratified societies, the civil service has historically been regarded as the private preserve of the "upper classes," and may be looked upon as an extension of the circle of court officials immediately surrounding the person of the monarch. Its members, therefore, enjoy an esteem both because of their status in a social aristocracy and because of their closeness to the throne. Even minor functionaries enjoy a reflected glory from their superiors. All in all, it may be said simply that in Europe government posts are *good* "jobs"; with us, they are *not*—as yet.

The public service suffers from still another disability. Just because it is the *public* service, the employees of which are citizens as

bate should be kept in office." *Local Government in Massachusetts* (Bureau of Public Administration, Massachusetts State College, 1941), p. 23. Moreover, sheer apathy often works to keep many elective officers in office for long periods of time. See Kirk H. Porter, "The Deserted Primary in Iowa," **XXXIX** *American Political Science Review* 732-740 (Aug. 1945).

well as officials, its personnel must be managed in an impersonal and mechanical way. Promotions, salary increases, and other marks of distinction go by seniority and are too seldom based upon qualitative accomplishments, partly, no doubt, because the use of tests other than seniority is bound to create problems of morale among those affected. Work must be planned with reference to the pace possible to those of rather mediocre ability, and there is little incentive for the rank and file at least to exceed this pace. The demands of the people for "practical" results discourage the development of that initiative and curiosity which might make the service attractive to our ablest scientific minds.[10] This situation goes far to explain the fact that, in spite of some notable exceptions, our best medical men, engineers, chemists, physicists, and other scientists are found as a rule, not in the public service, but in the universities and in the laboratories of the more enlightened industrial establishments.

Signs are not wanting, however, that the public service in the United States is becoming increasingly attractive to the able youth of the nation. The civil service of the more populous states and cities, and the newer establishments of the federal government offer to their staffs not only security, but a feeling of importance and a sense of real power, as decisions of policy are perforce shifted from over-worked representative bodies, and the control of vast enterprises presents challenges to men anxious to feel themselves part of the "ruling class." Desirable as this sort of development may be regarded in some positions, there is still point in John Stuart Mill's remark to the effect that "the absorption of all the principal ability of the country into the governing body is fatal sooner or later to the mental activity and progressiveness of the body itself. Banded together as they are, working a system which like all systems necessarily proceeds in a great measure by fixed rules, the official body are under the constant temptation of sinking into indolent routine, or if they now and again desert that mill-horse round, of rushing into some half-examined crudity which has struck the fancy of some leading member of the corps; and the sole check to those allied though

---

[10] Compare, for example, the freedom of a scientist on a university faculty or an endowed foundation with that of an employee of a government bureau. A great deal of the latter's time and effort is consumed in such matters as routine correspondence, the answering of queries, and the making of various analyses for citizens, who, as the ultimate employers, may not be denied. However, even private foundations do not always escape this pressure for "practical" results, especially when they are financed by so-called "practical business men." Sinclair Lewis' *Arrowsmith* is a long commentary on this type of pressure.

seemingly opposite tendencies . . . is liability to the watchful criticizing of equal ability outside the body." [11]

THE INFLUENCE OF SMALL AREAS

Although the difficulties referred to above are common to every level of the public service, it seems that there are special circumstances militating against the development of a true professionalism among the employees of rural areas of administration.[12] In the first place, the scale of operations is so small as to make unattractive to first-rate talent the work to be done. There are few engineering, health, or welfare problems encountered within the limits of the typical small rural area sufficiently large to constitute a challenge to those trained to get results in those fields. Here and there in the state and federal services and in the largest cities may be found administrators of the first order of ability, but such is seldom or never the case in smaller areas. Even if public servants were released from their present bondage to the "courthouse gang," the prospect before them would not be alluring. Hence, the division of the country into thousands of petty areas is a standing invitation to Lilliputian administration. And it leads directly, of course, to the further fact that the number of employees is so small as to afford little or no opportunity for fostering the *ésprit de corps* which is so vital in the maintenance of administrative standards, even though the development of such an *ésprit de corps* admittedly involves dangers to democratic control.

In the second place, administration in the typical rural area is carried on much closer to those affected, so that officials act under the direct impact of popular ideas and prejudices. In a democratic society officials can nowhere entirely escape this pressure. In cities they are made to feel it through the ward leader and the "boss" who act as conduits to transmit popular views to those responsible for action. In the country, however, the whole relationship is much more personal. Officials are likely to be personally known to a large

---

[11] *Essay on Liberty* (Everyman ed.), pp. 167-8.

[12] A. N. Holcombe thus summarizes the leading characteristics of the traditional system of administration in rural areas: (1) the independence of administrative officers of one another and the decentralization of administration; (2) a settled tradition of political interference with the administration of public business; (3) reliance upon the popular election of administrative officers and upon the judicial review of administrative acts to protect the public against the abuse of administrative power. See his *The New Party Politics* (1934), p. 130. The student would do well to read all of the first chapter of this book: The Passing of the Old Party Politics.

proportion of the citizenship, and the public business committed to them will probably be considered the business of each constituent, whose opinion is bound to be shown at least outward respect.[13] This may not be an unmixed evil for there is wisdom in the remark of Beard that "history affords innumerable examples of sound judgments springing from the opinions of the nameless and unknown . . . and resulting in action afterwards approved by the arbitrament of mankind. . . . Beyond the technical specialties there is unity —a unity which must be dealt with by a competence transcending that of particular experts." [14] On the other hand, the larger scale upon which administration is required to be conducted in a city of any size makes it necessary to organize the administrative machinery in a hierarchical fashion. The farther this proceeds, the more impersonal the process tends to become and the stronger the tendency of the official personnel to escape popular influence—or at least control.[15] The city may be the "hope of democracy," as one author once believed, but it is difficult to see how those of any considerable size can escape the control of a virtually irresponsible governing group. The great diversity of interests met with in cities and the weakness of the neighborhood tie have prevented until the present such an organization of the electorate as will make possible anything like the continuous pressure on administration found in rural districts. The "public" in the country is far less heterogeneous than in

---

[13] "If a candidate wins, he finds himself under constant pressure from the exaggerated importance of the personal relations in his electorate. In matters of official policy he must ever think in terms of personalities. Even a minor deputy at the courthouse was able to say: 'Every taxpayer treats you as if you were working for him personally, as if he paid your whole salary.'" A. C. Blumenthal, *Small Town Stuff*, p. 305. On this same point Sorokin and Zimmerman say that official position in rural communities "gives very moderate rights to the holder. For this reason it does not 'elevate' the rural official class much above the socio-political status of the mass of the agricultural population." *Principles of Urban-Rural Sociology*, pp. 82-83. On the importance of the face-to-face relationship in rural communities see, F. H. Allport, *Social Psychology*, p. 384.

[14] C. A. Beard, "Government by Technologists," **LXIII** *New Republic* 119 (June 18, 1930). Cf. A. N. Whitehead: "The discoveries of the 19th century were in the direction of professionalism so that we are left with no expansion of wisdom and with greater need for it. Wisdom is the fruit of a balanced development. It is this balanced growth of individuality which it should be the aim of education to secure." *Science and the Modern World*, p. 246.

[15] "It is the public service which is the repository of that sublimated sort of egoism which is the preservative of Power. Permanent officials bring to the maintenance and enlargement of their offices, which in their innermost hearts they regard always as a piece of property, and which they have often inherited, the diligence of a lifetime." Bertrand de Jouvenel, *On Power* (1948), p. 122.

cities. In the latter the administration is likely to have its different branches spasmodically under fire from various interest-groups specially affected by their activities. In the country the populace is much more homogeneous and is therefore a good deal more effective in bringing pressure to bear upon officials. The strict, impartial, and efficient enforcement of the law demands a certain impersonal attitude, and the expert administrator must be in a position to act as the conditions of his problem demand without having to defer overmuch to the prejudices and opinions of his ultimate employers. These conditions are seldom met with in rural communities.[16]

"COMMON SENSE" AND "SCIENTIFIC" ADMINISTRATION

Finally, the spirit and technique of modern scientific administration encounter in the rural regions the highest development of the amateur tradition and the most elaborate worship of the homespun virtue of "common sense." The conditions of life and labor in agricultural communities do not favor the growth of specialized skill nor respect for exact and painstaking technique. Farming is not so much a craft as a whole group of skills. The farmer is in some sense a biologist, an engineer, a carpenter, a machinist, a plumber, a mason, and a businessman. The mere listing of these skills is enough to raise the presumption that he is likely to act in each capacity by rule of thumb. Nothing in the farmer's or villager's life, at least until the dissemination of city-born ideas, has familiarized him with expert ways of doing things. A jack-of-all-trades himself, living, at least traditionally, a self-sufficient life, he sees little need for special training. If a broken bit of harness will serve well enough for a hinge on the henhouse door, why will not any "honest" or "practical" man do for public office? "Common sense" is a virtue highly prized; expertness, in some dimly felt way, connotes "uppishness" in its possessor.[17] Common sense, rule of thumb, has of course been

---

[16] Under modern conditions it seems to be true that as the area grows larger the influence of minority groups on policy increases in a way not possible where the population is smaller and more homogeneous. Certainly one of the real dangers in "centralization" consists in the possibility that minorities will push their advantage to extremes ruinous to the general welfare. Cf. The essay, "The Paradox of Representative Government," by Harold W. Stoke in John M. Mathews and James Hart (eds.), *Essays in Political Science* (1937), pp. 77-99, and the comments on pressure groups and the general welfare in V. O. Key's *Politics, Parties, and Pressure Groups* (2nd ed. 1947), pp. 196-204.

[17] "Farmers did not feel companionable with a well-informed man. They were uneasy in his presence and quick to suspect that his learning gave him a sense of superi-

responsible for many of our ills in a mechanical age. Thus, nearly all modern scientific inventions, such as flying, have been condemned by the generality as contrary to "common sense." In personal relations and in those manual arts where exact measurement is not of the essence, there is and always will be room for "guessing," "sizing up," and "calculating"; but where a basis of exact science exists the exclusive use of our time-hallowed "common sense" is often fatal. Filling out grocery orders at the rate of three dollars a week, leaving the "slack" to be taken up by charitable neighbors, is a crude application of common sense; the apparatus and technique of the welfare worker is the accepted modern answer to the problem of dependency and poverty.[18]

This is not to say that the cities are the only places where sound administration will be found or that the rural districts are a vast waste of incompetence and inefficiency. Observation shows that no such generalizations are justified by the facts. But it is clear that the city-dweller is much more receptive to the idea of administrative expertness. For the modern city is an exemplification on a huge scale of the principle of the division of labor, that is, of specialization. The jack-of-all-trades finds little opportunity for a display of his "bag of tricks" in an environment where the keenness of competition gives the palm to him who excels in a relatively narrow field. On the other hand, so long as every circumstance and tradition of country life tends to foster a belief in the adequacy of the home-made, and the validity of what comes close to mere superstition, we may expect rural affairs, at least on the administrative side, to be in the hands of incredible witch-doctors. Indeed the progressive urbanization of the nation seems the most promising way to rescue large

---

ority. . . . This attitude has survived in the rural population." J. M. Williams, *Our Rural Heritage*, p. 163. On the other hand, the many witticisms still current about "experts" are often enough justified. "Expert" is a word to conjure with and it is not surprising if its use has been overdone in many cases.

[18] Speaking of the pioneer democracy of Jackson, which set the tone for much of our thinking since, Croly says: "The average man, without any special bent or qualification, was, in the pioneer states, the useful man. In that country it was sheer waste to spend much energy upon tasks which demanded skill, prolonged experience, high technical standards, or exclusive devotion. The cheaply and easily made instrument was the efficient instrument, because it was adapted to a year or two of use and then for supersession by a better instrument; and for the service of such tools one man was likely to be as good as another." *The Promise of American Life*, pp. 63-64. For further material on the subject of this paragraph consult N. L. Sims, *Elements of Rural Sociology;* P. Sorokin and C. C. Zimmerman, *Principles of Rural-Urban Sociology;* J. M. Gillette, *Rural Sociology;* L. L. Bernard, "A Theory of Rural Attitudes," XXII *American Journal of Sociology* 630-649 (Mar. 1917).

sections of the population from the bondage of so-called "practical" men.[19]

RESPONSIBLE THEORY, IRRESPONSIBLE PRACTICE

The realization of the principle of hierarchy would require the organization of the public service to be arranged in such a manner as to place each important function in the hands of definite individuals, each of whom would have in charge a specific portion of the work for the performance of which he would be held responsible by his superiors. Such an arrangement involves in reality both the idea of permanence and that of professionalism, as well as a semi-independent status for the administrative branch of the government. In the municipal, state, and federal services this type of organization has made some progress. It scarcely need be said that it is seldom or never met with in rural government. The typical county, for example, is practically never organized in such a way as to show any recognition of a distinction between the political and administrative work which it has to do. A large number of officials performing routine tasks are still elected by popular vote. No single person in the entire organization is legally in a position to give orders to subordinates and enforce compliance with those orders. Such responsibility as these persons may bear is owed, not to administrative superiors, but to the electorate as a body. And in practice this too often means responsibility to a political party or even to a coterie of wire-pullers and spoilsmen. Nor does this end the story. With very rare exceptions the functions of rural government have not been departmentalized to such an extent as to place in definite hands the responsibility for their performance. The management of finances, highways and public works, charities and corrections, and education is parceled out among numerous authorities, all of whom must act together to get results and any one of whom may easily disclaim responsibility when things go wrong. When critics refer to our county organization as being "without head or tail," they are simply using a colloquial expression to point out the absence of what we have referred to as

---

[19] In this connection it is interesting to contrast the activity of farmers in supporting various "movements" for reform in state and national politics with the quiescence of the same groups in the presence of abuses in their own local governments. Such reforms as have been instituted in county government, for example, seem usually to have been introduced by carpet-baggers either from an urban center within the county or even from more distant cities. Waldo makes the point that the ideal of the American writers on public administration has been predominantly an urban ideal. *The Administrative State* (1948), p. 7.

hierarchy. Since a hierarchical organization of administration depends in the end upon the achievement of permanence and professionalism in the personnel, our failure to attain it is to be explained largely by the same set of rural attitudes toward the public business.[20]

The Old Attitude and the New Order

While much depends upon a well-organized and well-trained personnel, this alone cannot insure good administration. Experience has shown that sound methods of transacting public business are almost as important. Among the phases of local administration where this fact is most clearly illustrated may be mentioned accounting and budgeting, the purchase of supplies and the awarding of contracts, the allowance of claims against the treasury, the custody of public funds, and the reporting of official actions. Though private enterprise is not free from scandals in all of these matters, being still shot through with fraud, chicanery, favoritism, and an unconscionable secretiveness, it must be admitted that its record is, on the side of efficiency at least, better than that of the public authorities. Good accounting methods, for example, are as vital to the administrator as the logarithmic tables are to the engineer; yet in this field our rural governments make but a poor showing. In an effort to get at actual costs and to enforce responsibility for expenditures, most of our states provide for the installation and maintenance of a system of uniform accounts by local governments, and often go further and provide for periodic audits by a central authority.[21] While such statutes are in a few states enforced with considerable effectiveness, this does not seem by any means to be the rule. The subject of accounting has little dramatic appeal and the outlay required to make such laws effective seems out of proportion to any discernible imme-

---

[20] This is not to be taken as an argument in favor of applying the principles of organization and management found successful in cities to the rural agencies of government. The feasibility of such changes is briefly discussed in the chapter on The Reconstruction of Local Government.

[21] "In 1941 forty states had statutes providing for central supervision of accounting for one or all classes of local government. . . . The accounting procedures of counties are supervised in thirty-seven states; of municipalities in twenty states; and of other governmental units in thirteen states. Seventeen states review local accounting for both counties and municipalities only. Thirteen states exercise the supervision over all local governments." *State-Local Relations*, p. 28. For local finances generally, see Wylie Kilpatrick, *State Supervision of Local Finance*, Publication No. 79, Public Administration Service, 1941.

diate benefit.[22] The result is that in not more than half a dozen states is the law enforced in such a way as to enlighten the taxpayer or confer any substantial benefit upon the local officials subject to it.[23]

There is, of course, no reason to doubt that a vigorous enforcement of such laws would be extremely worth while. On the other hand, it is not hard to understand why they are for the most part inoperative. The typical farmer is himself a poor businessman, keeping his accounts, if at all, "in his head," and judging the profit or loss of each year by the crudest methods imaginable. It is little wonder that we hear of authenticated cases where official "accounts" consist of penciled entries in pocket notebooks, or in which the "report" for a year's business is little more than an exercise in subtraction showing a balance or a deficit. Such methods, after all, accord with "the custom of the country," and should cause no special wonder. The absence of any adequate system of accounts makes impossible the existence of sound budget methods, with the result that plans for expenditures do little more than comply with the modest minimum requirements of the statute—requirements which in the last analysis can be enforced in fact only by cumbersome legal process.

Much the same story may be told with reference to the purchase of supplies and the awarding of contracts. Although these items account for a large proportion of all local expenditures, the officials in charge seem in many cases to be guided by no very respectable principles. In buying supplies one of the principal objectives often seems to be to see to it that the public business is distributed as widely as possible among local merchants, or at least among such as are politically friendly to those in power. The letting of contracts,

---

[22] Williams suggests that the farmer had little use for ideas unless they were somehow connected with his practical activities. "He was apt not to care for a background of thought that would give him an insight into his problems, but rather for information that served his practical interest at the moment or satisfied his curiosity about familiar things. This lack of interest in the broader aspects of their problems tended to make farmers men of poor judgment." *Our Rural Heritage,* p. 165. The opinion may be hazarded that imagination as well as interest is lacking and that this may go far to explain the unwillingness of rural legislatures to lay down and support with appropriations a program the results of which do not promise to be immediate or "practical."

[23] It is only fair to add, however, that in many cases the form of public reports issued by state officials is such as to make it very difficult to secure a good picture of local affairs. These shortcomings may be attributed in some degree to the fact that state supervisory officials rarely have adequate funds.

when not tainted with downright fraud, is too often unintelligently done by men who think of construction in terms of equipment and processes long since laid aside by private contractors, and who are thus incapable, whatever their intentions, of making a sound judgment as to the reasonableness of bids received. Purchases and contracts are two fields of public administration peculiarly fitted for expert handling; yet the rural tradition and background support an easygoing inefficiency in both.

A visit to the various offices in a typical rural county will often afford a demonstration of the backwardness of these areas in adopting new methods of office practice, and the general parsimoniousness of the rural population in the conduct of public affairs. Rural officials find it easy to get on without various mechanical office aids, the use of which would probably save money in the end by reducing labor costs and stopping various leaks. Here we see at work perhaps the same jack-of-all-trades attitude that the conditions under which farmers conduct their private affairs have forced upon governmental agencies. In communities long insulated from contact with developments in the larger world of affairs, the traditional way of doing things yields but slowly to persuasion. The immediate cost of modernization is a telling argument against it, no matter what the possible future economies may appear to be. These latter seem to be so largely a question of opinion; under the traditional regime, affairs have been administered without positive disaster and this fact reinforces the argument as to the wisdom of letting well enough alone. Besides, vested interests often grow up around antiquated procedures. Long-hand recording and copying and district-school methods of calculation supply with "jobs" many who would be displaced by the newfangled equipment.[24] Nepotism is probably widespread in many rural areas, and in any event the neighborliness of the countryside, celebrated in song and story, is tolerant of ways which "take care" of a perhaps excessive number of public servants.

The Question of Cost

The penny-pinching notions of economy so widely held in rural areas, though they are the despair of those who would move ahead faster than the democratic mass, are not difficult to explain. Rural governments rely almost entirely for their local revenue upon taxes

---

[24] It must be added, however, that there are hundreds of units in the country where there actually is too little business to justify the mechanizing of local offices.

on tangible property. The burden is immediate and inescapable. The first duty of officials is to keep down the levy, and the temptation is to do this by what in reality may be shortsighted methods. Ownership of real property is more general than in the cities, and the "irresponsible proletariat" hardly exists. The pressure for economy is more direct, universal, and unremitting than in any other part of the community.[25] In the second place, administration according to modern standards is extremely expensive. A program of social services combining all the demands of zealous reformers would lay a crushing burden upon the typical rural community with its present narrow tax base and the scanty resources of its citizens. Business in many rural areas is still conducted on a basis not very far removed from barter. At least the average small farmer is not accustomed to handling large sums in cash. The item of salaries alone involved in a modern program of social welfare and public works, though it seems reasonable to those used to thinking in terms of approved standards, strikes the farmer as grotesquely high—and actually is, in view of the meager resources of many rural units. Here, as in other areas, but to an exaggerated degree, a good deal of our mediocre service is traceable to an unwillingness or an inability to pay for adequate performance.

What is saved by the time-honored methods of work is, of course, often lost in driblets, not only through inefficient office practice and excessive payrolls, but through petty graft in the letting of contracts and the purchase of supplies, through careless allowance of statutory fees for unneeded or at best perfunctory discharge of nominal functions, and so forth. None of these losses is large enough to create a scandal, many of them are honestly, though mistakenly, regarded as proper perquisites of office, and nearly all of them involve directly or indirectly dozens of persons in the community. It is perhaps for these reasons that reform moves with leaden feet.

THE OUTLOOK FOR GOOD ADMINISTRATION

A good deal of popular suspicion of vigorous and efficient administration arises from the belief that government is an evil and that its agents should, for the good of the people, be kept within the narrowest bounds. The evidence we have seems to indicate that this suspicion is more marked in the country than in the cities. The

---

[25] Still more fundamental perhaps is the fact that a hazardous occupation such as farming makes frugality a virtue. And it may be but a step from frugality to parsimony.

habit of self-help is strongly developed in a population where success or failure depends upon one's own efforts or at any rate upon
natural forces which have from time immemorial seemed largely
beyond human control. Primitive conditions surrounding the crises
and misfortunes of life—birth, death, illness, accident, and calamity
—put such a premium upon informal community or neighborhood
action, that there are to this day many rural communities in which
much of what is done by appointive officeholders in cities is performed by such organizations as the grange, the churches, or other
voluntary groupings of the people. Such matters as library service
and the annual "clean up day" in rural villages will readily occur to
the observer.

Furthermore, functions in the open country have normally been
simple enough to be managed by the improvisations of amateurs.
The greater complexity and urgency of problems confronting a city
government quite naturally result in their being handed over to a
class of specialized officeholders. Even today it remains true that,
over great stretches of the country, the necessary functions seem few
and simple enough to cause the inhabitants to be indifferent to plans
for greater efficiency brought forward by reformers and humanitarians. The old suspicion of government seems to have the facts of
rural life on its side. It remains to be seen whether and how rapidly
immemorial rural habits and attitudes are altered by such developments as more reliable control of insect pests and plant and animal
diseases, to say nothing of the artificial production of rain.

The concept of simplicity in rural government is a delusive one.
The contact of the rural population with the money economy has
led to the appearance of social instability and insecurity even in the
country. The exhaustion of the soil by unwise cropping has made
clear the need for land-use planning and has, in many cases, so weakened the resources of local units as to make necessary the development of new and complicated financial relationships involving every
level of government; the shrinkage of markets abroad, the fluctua-
tion of urban purchasing power, and the unpredictable changes in
consumers' tastes make inevitable the development of a public program for agriculture; while population shifts on a vast scale, improved communication agencies, the growth of farm tenancy, and
the existence of what amounts to a rural proletariat, the changing
content of public education, and newer knowledge of the cause of
disease and social maladjustment, foreshadow the expansion of gov-

ernment even in rural areas. The one fact which is common to all of these problems is that they can be met, if at all, only through "varied and extensive political arrangements, and that these arrangements are largely administrative in nature." [26] Can a population long habituated to weak and diffuse government conducted by untrained citizens in their spare time accustom itself to a new organization of political power, one of the most important ingredients of which is certain to be administrative discretion?

In the end the issues presented by the growth of political power will have to be met by country and city alike. Bureaucracy has been aptly called the "core" of modern government and its acceptance is inevitable, even though opposition to it has been the burden of countless defenses of free government. However eloquent such defenses may sound, it is clear that we have reached a point where free government itself can be preserved only by strengthening its administrative arm. Thus we are involved in what appears to be a paradox: the only way by which, in a complex and interdependent society, we can preserve even a tithe of our primeval "liberty" is by increasing the authority of those agencies whose possession of power is an apparent invasion of liberty. The record of predemocratic governments was, on the whole, such as to justify the traditional American preference for weak government. Does a reconstructed modern democracy promise anything better? The indecision and fumbling of orthodox democracies here and abroad have brought the democratic dogma everywhere into eclipse. Men affect to see in the democratic state simply another engine of exploitation, distinguished from older tyrannies, if at all, only by the elaborate machinery of elections and so forth which, they say, serves only to heighten an illusion which remains nevertheless an illusion.[27]

The best the defenders of democracy anywhere can say today is that it is better than any feasible alternative, not that it is actually the best form of government. The fervent eloquence of its earlier romantic prophets falls strangely upon modern ears attuned to the cynical charges of its detractors. Is there any way by which the servants of the modern state can be prevented from falling into the age-old habit of converting themselves into its masters? Is the paradox involved in preserving liberty by strengthening government a real

---

[26] John M. Gaus, "American Society and Public Administration," in J. M. Gaus, L. D. White and M. E. Dimock, *The Frontiers of Public Administration* (1936), p. 93.

[27] This is a large part of the burden of the thoughtful book, *On Power*, by Bertrand de Jouvenel (1949).

or apparent one? Those who believe that free government is still both possible and desirable may feel some confidence in the hope that our great wealth may be so used as to give to all of us that security without which men nowhere value freedom. The democratization of higher education holds out some hope that those who administer our common affairs may be in some organic relation to those whom they serve. The American facility for organization may guarantee that over against the possessors of governmental power will always stand groups interested in preserving their own rights and equipped to collaborate fruitfully with their "rulers." Even the faith which once led to the gallant defense of free institutions may not be beyond recapture. As city and rural problems become identical in their essential nature, country and city alike may learn to construct the machinery to meet them.

CHAPTER 6

Financial Administration

Broadly speaking, everything that government does costs money, for all that it does requires the services of individuals and the use of materials. While considerable service is rendered free, the bulk of mankind require compensation for their labor, and dealers in necessary commodities are invariably interested not only in the return of their investment but also in a profit. There is a persistent notion in the minds of many that government somehow differs from private individuals in its power to command the services and commodities which it needs. While this is perhaps a tribute to the prestige of government, it is bad public finance. For there is no alchemy about government; its officials wave no magic wand; it has no mysterious source of revenue not possessed by ordinary citizens. In the end its income depends upon the income of its citizens, for the taxes, fees and other forms of governmental revenue must be paid from the surplus which private persons and corporations have in hand after paying the necessary costs of maintaining life and conducting business operations. Therefore, the complicated business of levying and collecting taxes and deciding upon the size of various fees resolves itself into a series of decisions intended to discover indices of income from which taxes may be paid. The only important way in which public finance differs from private finance—aside, of course, from its greater complexity—is found in the fact that government possesses the sovereign power to compel the payment by the individual of a portion of his income to defray the expenses of the public business. It is easy, however, to make too much of this distinction. After all, our privately owned "public utilities," since they furnish what have come to be essential services, possess what amounts to the power to tax. Even the public power to tax has definite limits in practice, since no responsible official interested in retaining office will ignore entirely the taxpaying ability or inclinations of his constituents.

The administrative machinery of every revenue system may be regarded, therefore, as a set of arrangements for uncovering and tapping taxpaying ability. And every object of taxation may be looked upon very largely as a more or less rough measure of such ability. During our history up to the present time the possession of property has been taken as a fair test of taxpaying ability, and by far the greater part of *tax* revenue for local purposes has been derived from a levy on property. This proportion in the case of some units exceeds ninety per cent. This so-called general property tax may be defined as a tax upon the value of all property, real and personal, tangible and intangible, within the jurisdiction of the public authority laying the tax. Legally and theoretically, the term "general" means exactly what it says, and a general property tax administered as the law directs would involve setting a value upon every form of property and collecting a certain proportion of this ascertained value in the form of a tax. In other words, houses and lots, books, pianos, jewelry, cattle, horses, automobiles, stocks, bonds, mortgages, promissory notes, and all the other scores of types of property would have to be taxed if the tax is to be a "general" one, since all of these things presumably have some value.[1]

THE GENERAL PROPERTY TAX

There is no tax in our system which has been more widely condemned than that on general property. Criticism has come not only from those upon whom it falls with what seems to be disproportionate weight, but also from a host of investigators who may be considered disinterested. Impatient persons go so far as to say that, if it is good at all, it is so because "an old tax is a good tax." This aphorism contains this kernel of truth: a tax so old has long since been capitalized, so that, although the ownership of property may not be the sole test of ability to pay, it is certainly an important one. More careful students concede that the tax is a productive one and that it constitutes a stable element in the total revenue system. Even if its real defects are admitted, anything like its abolition would involve a complete overhauling of the entire system. It is not surpris-

---

[1] It should be pointed out that a very large proportion of property is for one reason or another exempted from taxation. It has been estimated that in 1942 real estate to the value of more than $26 billion or 18.2 per cent of the total in the United States was exempt. More than 25 per cent of this was located in New York State. See K. P. Sanow, "Property Tax Exemption," **19** *State Government* 108-114 (Apr. 1946).

ing that practical politicians and administrators shrink from the unpredictable difficulties of such an enterprise.

In an agricultural society, where ownership of property was fairly widespread and where it consisted almost entirely of tangible goods, the general property tax had a good deal to be said for it. In such a society the possession of tangible property was a relatively fair measure of ability. However, with the appearance of new forms of intangible property following the invention of the corporate form of business enterprise, and the growth of public and private debt, tangible property ceased to be a fair measure of taxpaying ability. For a generation or more its inequity has been denounced by public and private investigators in unmeasured terms, and its serious modification, even its abolition, has been demanded by a growing body of opinion. That little has been done in either direction is explained by a number of reasons. In the first place, what is familiar is preferred to what is new. In the second place, those who pay the bulk of the real property tax, farmers and small home-owners, are not organized in the same way as other groups, and hence are unable to make their influence felt decisively with legislative bodies. Finally, there is a feeling that new taxes designed as a matter of theory to relieve the burden on real property may turn out in practice to be not substitute taxes but *additional* taxes, to be spent by more or less predatory officeholders.[2]

At all events, the tax on "general" property remains the principal source of tax revenue for local purposes in most of our states, and local authorities are compelled to do the best they can with a faulty system. The heart of the problem, of course, lies in finding a value for the object to which the tax is to apply. This amounts to saying that the officer finding the taxable value makes a judgment as to the income-producing ability of the particular piece of property, or its value in terms of human satisfactions, and hence decides in the first instance what its owner shall pay for the support of government. This process is known as assessment, and the official who applies it, the assessor. Unless his judgment in the first instance or upon immediate review is reasonably correct, every subsequent step in the process is vitiated by the initial blunder, since no system of review

---

[2] On the other hand, it is probably true that pressure from rural legislators is at least partly responsible for the recent precipitous decline in the state's use of the general property tax and the growing use of such levies as those on motor vehicles, gasoline, personal and corporate incomes, sales, and business licenses.

involving the application of mathematical formulae can intelligently correct his errors.

FINDING THE VALUE OF PROPERTY

In view of this fact the administrative machinery for reaching taxable values is of first-rate importance. In about one-half the states of the Union, assessing officials are chosen for towns or townships or equivalent local areas; in the other half the responsible officers are county officials. The general rule is to choose such officers by popular vote. It would probably be difficult to devise a worse method for filling these posts. This is not to say that assessing officials should not be responsible to those who pay the bills of government; the real questions are, to whom is such responsibility really owed, how may it best be enforced, and what system is best adapted to get the most competent officials. When the district is as small as a town or township, the candidate for office is likely to be influenced in his work by various personal considerations and by the unseen but active pressure of important local potentates.[3] The oftener he stands for office, the more careful he must be to avoid antagonizing taxpayers. If he is honest, there is a good chance he may be defeated. If he becomes an adept at wire-pulling and tight-rope-walking, he destroys his ability, if he ever had any, to administer his office efficiently. Even when the county is the unit for the choice of the assessor, much the same criticism may be made, though it is possibly true that he will be somewhat less beholden to local interests in view of the larger electorate involved.[4]

No matter which area is used, however, choice by popular vote will seldom give the best results. This is true because under modern conditions the work of making a correct assessment of the scores of types of property is highly technical and requires a trained official.

---

[3] Powerful corporate interests such as utility companies have been known to be active in opposing the abolition of locally chosen assessors, since large properties, being outside the everyday experience of the assessor, are likely to be undervalued. See the *Third Report of the (N. Y.) Commission for the Revision of the Tax Laws* (Leg. Doc. No. 77, 1932), p. 49 of Memorandum No. 3. The committee on state-local relations of the Council of State Governments reported in 1946 that there were more than 26,000 primary assessment districts in the United States.

[4] It was reported in 1944 that there were 1,785 assessing districts in Michigan. In 1,266 of these the assessing was done by the township supervisors. Only 91 of all assessors were appointed. The Rural Property Inventory Project in 1939 found that more than ten per cent of the 1,500,000 descriptions on the township tax rolls were erroneous. See Milton B. Dickerson, *State Supervision of Local Taxation and Finance in Michigan,* Mich. Agr. Exp. Sta. Special Bulletin No. 327 (Apr. 1944), p. 19.

The elective process seldom if ever secures such officials. In the opinion of experts little improvement in the conduct of the assessing function can be expected until two reforms have been carried out. In the first place, an area at least as large as a county should be adopted for assessment purposes. Such an area would be large enough to demand the services of a full-time and well-paid official and, in most cases, wealthy enough to support a proper office organization to insure that the work would be done in accordance with approved principles of "scientific" assessment. In the second place, the assessor should be made appointive. This is not suggested as a means of taking the office "out of politics" as that expression seems generally to be understood. One of our cherished delusions is that we may accomplish this result by a mere change in our machinery. As a matter of fact, there is no mechanical means in a democracy by which any office can be taken "out of politics." [5] The whole question, like most others, is a relative one. Under what sort of system is pressure of an undesirable sort *more* likely to be reduced? On the balance it would seem reasonable to suppose that an appointive assessor would be *somewhat better* shielded from the direct play of the *least desirable* sort of pressures, and that the appointing authority would act under a *more* vivid sense of public responsibility than do the voters at the polls.

It must be admitted, however, that neither of these suggested reforms has as yet made much progress. The people generally have been loath to give up the privilege of voting for the assessors, and the smaller units of government have so far successfully resisted most attempts to deprive them of the control of their assessing machinery.[6] Here and there improvement is taking place slowly through the influence of tactful state officials in educating local officers in better methods, and through the pressure of the better-financed and staffed bureaus of research and taxpayers' leagues.

[5] "It is surprising to note how frequently arguments are advanced that this or that subject should be 'taken out of politics.' Looked at rigorously, it is a somewhat pathetic admission that democratic or parliamentary government is not wholly fitted for its entire task." Alexander Gray, *The Socialist Tradition* (1946), p. 144.

[6] "The prestige value of public office, the addition of the slender *per diem* to the slender income from other sources, and loyalty to the party to whom they owe these honors and emoluments combine to make the 2,700 elected assessors throughout the rural areas of the state convinced campaigners in support of the *status quo*. . . . Successful candidates (for the Legislature) when confronted by bills designed to abolish or alter the jobs of these mudsills in the political organization . . . will think twice before they jeopardize their chances for renomination." *Third Report of the (N. Y.) Commission for the Revision of the Tax Laws* (Leg. Doc. No. 77, 1932), p. 49 of Memorandum No. 3.

But it may be argued that fundamental reforms depend not so much upon changes in machinery as upon a comprehensive overhauling of the entire tax system. Taking the country as a whole, real estate, especially small residential and farm properties, bears a disproportionate share of the tax burden.[7] This has been true for many years, and the disproportion tends to grow greater with the increasing industrialization of the nation and the appearance of new forms of property. There is a slowly growing conviction among small property owners that the possession of real property is no fair test of income-producing ability. This belief has been responsible within recent years for such proposals as limitations upon tax rates and schemes for exempting rural homesteads and city homes from the property tax. Tax limitation laws have not generally proved effective in reducing the real tax burden since the necessary costs of government are too often simply defrayed from the proceeds of loans. The exemption of homesteads could scarcely have any other effect than to compel the adoption of some other tax. If either of these proposals should be successful in "relieving" small properties, it is essential to realize that such a result would render virtually nonproductive the only tax which local governments are able to administer. Any substitute tax would almost certainly be in the hands of the state government. In this case the control over local revenues and hence over local functions would be shifted from local residents. Local groups seeking to relieve property through the adoption of such schemes do not seem sufficiently to have considered this possibility.[8]

---

[7] The evidence for this is voluminous. The reader is referred to: Clarence Heer, "The Rural Tax Problem," 8 *Social Forces* 114 (Sept. 1929); *The Fiscal Problem in New York State* (National Industrial Conference Board, 1931); *Report of the Commission for the Revision of the Tax Laws*, referred to above; the papers by Eric Englund and Richard T. Ely in the *Proceedings of the National Conference on Land Utilization* (1931); and numerous bulletins dealing with the tax burden and assessing methods published by the Agricultural Experiment Stations of such rural states as Minnesota, Texas, Wisconsin, and Oregon. In their *Elements of Land Economics* (1924), R. T. Ely and E. W. Morehouse state: "An examination of the statistics of state and local taxation . . . warrants the . . . statement that, unless present taxation policies are changed, we shall approach the time when the government will confiscate through taxation the entire value of farm land, since it will take practically all the annual net income from land in taxes." (Pp. 317-318). Most of the standard textbooks on public finance make the same point. See Alfred G. Buehler, *Public Finance* (2nd ed., 1940), pp. 439-441.

[8] For information upon the effect of tax limitation laws see the discussion in *State-Local Relations*, pp. 103-112, and F. Leroy Spangler, *Operation of Debt and Tax Rate Limits in the State of New York* (Special Report No. 5, N. Y. State Tax Commission, 1932).

ASSESSING METHODS

Under present conditions how does the assessor find the value of the things to be taxed? With the best of intentions and the most modern equipment the task is a difficult one. It may be assumed that most assessors have good intentions, albeit a bit easygoing in their attitude toward the work and somewhat amenable to "influence" if carefully exercised.[9] But they are likely to be poorly supplied with equipment. In the larger cities, assessors are usually furnished with maps and record books for preserving essential information about real property, and various more or less "scientific" rules have been worked out for getting at value. But in rural districts this is almost nowhere the case. The assessor is likely to continue to list property "the same as last year" or to call upon his own knowledge of local transfers, land productivity, and so on, as guides in reaching his conclusions.[10] In general there seems to be too little connection between the office of the register of deeds and that of assessor, and hence too little attention to sale prices. The office equipment, if there is an office,[11] is likely to be meager and antiquated and will continue to be so as long as the assessing district is a village or a township. One of the improvements which a larger district with a larger tax base would permit would be a better-equipped central office and a closer attention to record-keeping.

---

[9] "The larger property owners in some districts have always fixed their own assessments. Some of them are now serving notice on the assessors that they intend to reduce their assessments. In some cases the reduction demanded is as much as ninety per cent of the previous assessment. The assessors have never had a proper technique for valuing large properties and they have always been obliged to accept such valuations as the owners have been willing to turn in." *The System of Taxation in Maine* (Report of the Recess Commission on Taxation, Dec. 1934), p. 84.

[10] A certain amount of local knowledge is, of course, indispensable, and the most highly centralized system, if it is to endure, would find it desirable to avail itself of the store of information possessed by those in constant touch with the local market. As to assessing methods, the New York Commission on the Revision of the Tax Laws said in 1932: ". . . it is doubtful whether thirty towns (out of 932) could be found . . . where the assessment methods have changed in any particular since the state adopted its first constitution (1777)." Sampling indicated that many towns were working "without maps, without building records, and without any plan of comparative valuation." (*Third Report*, Memorandum No. 3, pp. 27-29.) In 1946 the committee on state-local relations of the Council of State Governments reported that the new assessing techniques "despite the fact that their effectiveness has been proved, have yet to be applied by a large sector of local government."

[11] Rural assessors are likely to transact their business from their homes or literally "carry their offices in their hats."

THE REVIEW OF ASSESSMENTS

The work of the assessor who makes the original assessment is nowhere final. His work is subject to review and revision by a higher authority, known variously as the board of review or the board of equalization. This board in most states acts for the county and is either elective or *ex officio,* in many instances being the board of commissioners or supervisors with the addition, perhaps, of one or two other county officers.[12] The board of review usually has power to equalize values as between the various taxing units in the county, so that the incidence of a county-wide tax will everywhere be approximately the same; and it may, on complaint of taxpayers, raise or lower (and thus "equalize") assessments placed against individual pieces of property.[13] The work of such boards seems nowhere to be satisfactory. They can almost never have any accurate first-hand acquaintance with the property involved and are likely in their blundering way to increase the inequities of a bad original assessment—unless indeed they rely, as they often do, upon the advice of the assessor in which case their "review" is useless. As a rule, boards of review do not seem to be very active bodies. Their work of "equalizing" as between taxing districts is usually done in a perfunctory fashion. Appeals by individual taxpayers are not frequent, the average citizen regarding the whole process as a bother and very likely a useless one at that.

MISCELLANEOUS SOURCES OF LOCAL REVENUE

While the general property tax is the chief source of local revenue it is not the only one. The figures compiled by the Federal Bureau of the Census show that about two-thirds of all local revenues are derived from property taxes. In the case of counties, property taxes constitute 96 per cent of total *tax* revenues. More than 90 per cent of township and town *tax* revenues come from the property tax, and in school and special districts the *entire tax* revenue is from that source. The principal remaining sources of income are licenses and

---

[12] For details consult *State and Local Taxation of Property* (National Industrial Conference Board, 1930), pp. 61-62.

[13] If the state levies a tax on property, there is a State Board of Equalization with the function of equalizing as between counties. Such state boards also often assess certain properties such as railroads and other utilities which are statewide in extent. For state tax purposes the values so found are distributed among the various counties according to various rules laid down in the law or worked out by the state board. Decisions of boards of review may be appealed to the courts.

fees for various services and privileges, subventions and grants from the state and federal governments, fines and forfeits of various kinds, sales of property, and the earnings of those business enterprises upon which the local government may have embarked. Fees and licenses differ from taxes proper in that they are not paid unless the service or privilege is desired, and they are roughly proportioned to the value of the benefit conferred, while a tax is a compulsory payment exacted without reference to any special benefit received by the taxpayer. A subvention is a sum of money paid by one government to another. This item on the credit side of the local budget tends to grow larger. This is because the state has been found to be a better unit for the administration of certain kinds of taxes than the local unit. Such taxes as those on gasoline, incomes, and inheritances are best managed by the larger unit. However, since the residents of local areas contribute to them, it has been thought desirable that a portion of the sums collected be redistributed to counties and other subdivisions. In some cases, the state simply acts as the collecting agency and distributes the entire proceeds of the tax to local districts in accordance with some principle assumed to be equitable. The proceeds of certain other taxes, however, are handed back to the local areas only under definite conditions as to the use of them. These sums are usually referred to as grants-in-aid and are at present used in connection with the performance of such functions as highway construction and maintenance, public education, and public health. The most recent estimates indicate that about one quarter of the total local revenue is made up of payments from the state government.[14] No special local problems are presented by such sources of revenue as fees and licenses except perhaps when some of them are earmarked for certain purposes or are required to be kept in special funds. Subventions and grants-in-aid, on the other hand, raise significant questions as to the relations between the state and its local units. These questions are discussed in the next chapter.

THE BUDGET SYSTEM

The next process in financial administration is fixing the rate of taxation, and this cannot be done until needs are determined. This

---

[14] See Ruth G. Hutchinson, *State-Administered Locally-Shared Taxes* (1931) where the growth of this system is very adequately dealt with. As is pointed out in the next chapter, the distinction between shared taxes and grants-in-aid is largely arbitrary.

involves the preparation of a budget. At the present time the laws of thirty-seven states require counties to prepare annual budgets, but these laws do not seem to have produced any particular improvement in local government finance in most of the rural areas of the country.[15] A number of reasons may be assigned for this failure. The laws in many instances content themselves with making the requirement of a budget without setting up any standards of budget-making for local officials to follow. In most cases no machinery is supplied for seeing that the law is carried out, and so long as the local authorities go through the motions of presenting and publishing figures purporting to be a budget, the statute is generally regarded as having been complied with.[16] In a few states, central authorities are charged with the duty of supervising local budget-making; in others, county authorities are set up to enforce local compliance with the law. Neither system has been conspicuously successful. A state authority is usually too distant to be conversant with local conditions and is able usually to do little more than exercise a perfunctory supervision over the *form* of the local budget. County supervisory authorities are often *ex officio* boards, as in Ohio, and seem disposed to regard this part of their work as a "side line."

Finally, it must be admitted that the idea of a budget is still somewhat of a novelty in the United States. No administrative device is easier to define and no concept of the public business is more "taking" when it is talked about on the stump or recommended by those interested in putting "more business in government." Under actual conditions, however, both popular and official interest is likely to wane when confronted with masses of comparative figures and— to most people—the dull intricacies of accounting. The idea is simplicity itself, as it is usually presented; its operation involves careful thought and constant attention to details, hence men shrink from the implications of its thoroughgoing practice.

[15] "Forty-one states require the preparation of budgets by all or some of their local governments. Thirty-seven states require budgets for counties, and twenty-eight states for municipalities. Other local governments (not counting school districts) must prepare budgets in twenty-two states. Originally, budgeting was required with respect to current operations only; gradually, however, budget demands have become more inclusive, and now also cover both capital outlays and debt transactions in many states." *State-Local Relations,* p. 30. A table showing these requirements in detail accompanies the discussion. See also Wylie Kilpatrick's "State Administrative Supervision of Local Financial Processes," in *Municipal Yearbook* (1936).

[16] Passage of such laws and then failure to do what is necessary to make them effective is, of course, a common political trick. No local official is discommoded by the law on the books; yet the legislator may virtuously claim to the reformers that forward-looking legislation has been passed.

A real budget is a complete financial plan covering governmental needs and resources for a determinate period of time, usually a year. It is based upon estimates made by those in charge of governmental functions, but it is *not* simply a series of guesses. No budget can be accurate or adequate which is not based upon accounting data embodying actual previous experiences as recorded in completed transactions, and upon constant current study of costs and price trends. Moreover, the authority responsible for collecting data and preparing the budget should be in a position to oversee the conduct of the administrative functions of the area which he serves. Unless this condition is fulfilled no budget plan can be sure of presenting an accurate picture of future needs and resources.

If this ideal is conceived of in terms of the bulky and elaborate budgets of large units of government, it is, of course, not likely to be realized in small rural areas. In such jurisdictions, however, an intelligible budget need not be an elaborate one. It can be quite comprehensible without being so. It is not ordinarily beyond the powers of the officials of small areas to prepare an expenditure plan which can be understood by citizens willing to give attention to it. The truth of the matter seems to be that officials are often unreasonably handicapped by old-fashioned accounting methods which make local finance unreasonably complex. Local talent and industry, assisted perhaps by sympathetic advice from state officials, would even now be adequate if these antiquated procedures were abolished.

In general, however, progress depends upon the creation of certain conditions of local administration which at present do not exist. In the first place, there must be changes in the structure of local government which will place real responsibility for financial planning upon a definite person. This authority should preferably be one engaged solely in administration or, at any rate, not connected with the appropriating authority. The usual organization of county government, for example, where a board has general supervision of county affairs, violates an essential requirement of sound budget practice in that those who do the spending also very largely determine their own needs. There is, under these circumstances, no internal check since the appropriating and spending authorities are one and the same. The laws of some states, without attempting fundamental changes in the structure of county government, have realized this weakness at least to the extent of placing the formal responsibility for preparing the budget upon some official other than the county board, such as the county clerk, the auditor, or account-ant.[17] In general, however, it would seem that these requirements lead to nothing beyond a system in which the official designated col-lects estimates from the spending agencies and presents them to the county board or other appropriating authority. It is difficult to see how it could be otherwise. Unless the official charged with pre-paring the budget is allowed to exercise some control over the de-partments asking for funds, his function is bound to be restricted to collecting figures the accuracy of which he is in no position to ques-tion. For unless such an official has power to maintain constant con-tact with the various services, by way of investigation or oversight, he is, of course, unable to know whether the estimates submitted to him represent real needs or are justified by the past performances of the departments. In short, it appears essential to make those struc-tural changes in local governments which would provide each with a head responsible for financial planning and empowered to get the data for his task.[18]

What has just been written may be regarded as a statement of the ideal in public financial planning. The essential features of such a system may be summarized as follows:[19]

1. The budget should consist of estimates embodying a care-fully thought-out program of work, prepared preferably by the ad-ministrative officer who will be responsible for carrying out the program. This program should be prepared in the light of the expe-rience of previous years and should, if possible, be based upon accu-rate information as to costs, kept by those in immediate charge of each function of government.

2. These estimates should be carefully correlated with available and expected revenue. This part of the budget plan should indicate

---

[17] Questionnaires received by the Governments Division of the Bureau of the Cen-sus in 1945 revealed, in 25 of the 41 states reporting, some official designated by the gov-erning body "to act on its behalf in performing duties or in supervising finances and functions." See Edward W. Weidner, "A Review of the Controversy over County Ex-ecutives," **VIII** *Public Administration Review* 22-23 (Winter 1948); L. H. Adolfson, "County Clerk as Manager," **34** *National Municipal Review* 125-128 (Mar. 1945); W. L. Bradshaw, "County Managerial Tendencies in Missouri," **XXV** *American Political Sci-ence Review* 1008-13 (Nov. 1931).

[18] Whether or not such an internal reorganization as is here suggested is feasible is discussed in the chapter "The Reconstruction of Local Government."

[19] The reader should consult the standard works by A. E. Buck, *Public Budgeting* and the *Budget in Government of Today* (1934); L. D. Upson, *The Practice of Munici-pal Administration*, Ch. IV; J. A. Fairlie and C. M. Kneier, *County Government and Administration*, Chs. XVIII and XIX.

clearly the nature of each proposed expenditure—whether for current upkeep or maintenance, additions to plant or equipment, or payments on principal or interest on the public debt; and the revenue sources from which such payments are to be made, whether from general taxation, license fees, special assessments, or from borrowing.

3. The estimates ought to be so stated as to be readily intelligible to the body—usually laymen, of course—who are to do the appropriating. For example, ideally, requests for funds should be supported by a record, in terms of units of work done, of what was accomplished with the funds granted for the last year, and proposals in the same terms for using the money requested for the following year.[20]

4. In the interest of clarity and efficiency, the ordinance or resolution appropriating money should be a single document so worded as to permit a maximum of control with a minimum of interference with administrative officials in carrying out the work program.

5. Machinery should be set up in the local unit for seeing, *as the money is spent, not only that it is spent legally, but that the government is securing value received.* An external audit at the end of the budget period can determine finally the *legality* of expenditures; only a system of current internal administrative control can give assurance as to their *efficiency* and *legality* before they are made. It should be pointed out that much less progress has been made in this part of the budget procedure than in any other.[21]

The typical local budget, of course, does not fulfill these requirements, and local financial planning is generally a rule-of-thumb affair. Estimates are based upon a more or less casual judgment of needs as they may be guessed from the previous year's experience and are the result of various compromises among the different services requesting funds. The desire for economy and a low tax rate is

---

[20] Unit cost accounting is a recent development in public departments. Brief discussions will be found in Chs. VIII and XV of W. B. Munro's *Municipal Administration* (1934) and in the works by Upson and Buck referred to above. See also *Public Reporting*, Publication No. 19 of the Municipal Administration Service (1931), and the pioneer study, *Governmental Reporting in Chicago* by Herman C. Beyle (Chicago, 1928).

[21] Consult the article "Accounts, Public" by A. E. Buck in the *Encyclopedia of the Social Sciences*, for the changing concept of the audit. See also Ch. V on Accounts by William Watson in A. E. Buck (ed.), *Municipal Finance*. "Local audits by state staffs or state-supervised private auditors are mandatory for counties in thirty-six states, for cities in sixteen states, and for other local governments in twelve states." *State-Local Relations*, p. 29.

a marked characteristic of rural administration everywhere, and the appearance of frugality may be secured by the postponement of expenditures which arrive later in disconcertingly large amounts. Where the law requires the publication of the budget figures, as is true in most cases, the figures which reach the public are seldom wholly trustworthy and almost never give an adequate picture of what has been done or what is planned for the future. Where audits are required to be made and published, they seldom afford the taxpayer much real enlightenment, unless he is willing to spend hours interpreting to himself the dreary pages of figures which ought rather to be interpreted in terms of work done. For this latter task, however, there is on most levels of government too little imagination. The upshot of all this would seem to be that local authorities, taking the country as a whole, are for the most part guessing their way along and achieving a result which is tolerable only because our wealth has been such as to enable us to bear with comparative ease a burden which would crush the rate-payers of less favored nations. On the other hand, one would be naive to think that a so-called "model" budget system is feasible in the case of the typical rural area. Considering the small sums involved and the untrained personnel normally found in these communities, it would be merely comical to suggest the adoption of such counsels of perfection. Far-reaching reforms in area and structure will have to precede the introduction of a system of this sort.

THE COLLECTION OF REVENUES

While the most important single reform suggested by critics of local government has been the adoption of scientific budgeting, there are other administrative problems of a financial nature which are of sufficient importance to deserve separate mention. Although the duty of collecting revenues is a merely ministerial one, involving no discretion, a good system of collection is of considerably more importance than it would appear to be on a superficial view. "Standards of collection in a majority of localities have generally been low, and the improvement of collection procedures is one of the most urgent and difficult problems in the field of local finance." [22] A poor system will be costly to operate and will thus violate one of the established canons of a good tax system in taking from the taxpayer more than is strictly needed to meet the claims of government.

---

[22] *State-Local Relations*, p. 93.

Two problems present themselves as a result of any survey of present methods of local tax collection—the area used and the method of paying the collecting officer. The town or township is the unit most frequently used in New England and in New York, Pennsylvania, New Jersey, Michigan, and Wisconsin. In three others, Illinois, Missouri, and South Dakota, a combination of the county and the township is used; while in the remaining thirty-four states the county is the unit. In addition, school and other special districts in some parts of the country have their own collectors independent of the town or township in which they are situated. Under modern conditions there is no good reason why such a multitude of officials should be engaged in the work of collecting taxes. The plan by which a single county official, usually the treasurer, collects the sums due to every unit within the county should be made universal. Recent studies show that where this plan is followed the cost of collection is less than half what it is in New York where each town, village, and school district has its own collector.[23]

Centralizing the collection of revenues in some such area as the county would be an important reform. Not only would it reduce the administrative overhead involved in the maintenance of hundreds of petty officials; it would make possible the abolition of the fee system of compensation, the use of modern equipment, and the employment of more competent officials. Payment by fees is still a widespread practice for which little or nothing can be said.[24] The whole fee system originated in a day when government had little to do and when doing that little was a part-time job. The fee, in this case a percentage of the sum collected, was long looked upon as a fair equivalent for the service rendered. Under simpler conditions the fee system was inexpensive and adequate. Under present conditions, however, the system as applied to tax collections reveals on examination "another hidden story of inefficiency that has hitherto been given no consideration whatever. We will search the reports of state tax commissions in vain for data showing the cost of tax col-

[23] M. Slade Kendrick, "Collection of General Property Taxes on Farm Property in the United States with Emphasis on New York," *Cornell University Agricultural Experiment Station Bulletin No. 469* (June 1928), pp. 4-5, 43-4; *State and Local Taxation of Property* (National Industrial Conference Board, 1930), pp. 71-2; Alvin Hansen and Harvey Perloff, *State and Local Finance in the National Economy* (1944), pp. 74-5.
[24] The collector is paid by fees in fourteen states, by a salary in twenty-four states, and by a combination of the two systems in the others. See Kendrick, *op. cit.*, pp. 4-5. There is a good discussion of the fee system in the *Third Report of the (N. Y.) Commission for the Revision of the Tax Laws* (Leg. Doc. No. 56, 1933), pp. 67 ff.

lections, current or delinquent. We rarely find any note of the amounts uncollected and finally uncollectible due to indifference, cowardice, or political bargaining, resulting in additional burdens upon the punctilious and conscientious taxpayers." [25]

An examination of the political realities, however, makes clear the difficulties in the way of abolishing the fee system. There were at one time in the state of New York alone, outside the counties in the metropolitan area, more than 11,000 collectors. In the country as a whole, there must still be several times that number. The fees realized by each of these individuals are, of course, petty, but there are doubtless hundreds of cases in which they constitute "easy money" by which minor officials eke out a precarious living. It may also be assumed that each collector is a person of some political consequence in his community, likely to have some influence in the choice of legislators who alone can bring about changes.

PUBLIC PURCHASING

In the performance of its activities, every government is required, as is every private business, to use large quantities of perishable and durable commodities. Even small units purchase scores and hundreds of items—soap, chalk, concrete, fabricated steel, ink, business machines, medicines, food, oil, gasoline, motor vehicles, and so forth. Perhaps in local governments generally, from 20 to 30 per cent of all current expenditures are for supplies. If the operating costs of local rural units amount to more than three billion dollars per year, and if 20 per cent of this sum is accounted for by supplies, even modest savings at this point would run into millions of dollars.

Traditionally, the operating departments of local units have bought supplies when and where it pleased their desires. If the highway superintendent needed spades or shovels or rubber boots, he bought each as he required them, in such quantities as he thought would "do," and from the most convenient or friendly retail dealer. Although other departments might need the same articles, combined buying was, and still is, seldom resorted to. It is not hard to see the inefficiency of such methods. Even if the operating head of a department and the retailer are both completely honest, the government could not get as good value as if one person were made responsible for all buying of this sort. The advantages of centralized

---

[25] *Third Report of (N. Y.) Commission for the Revision of the Tax Laws,* pp. 67-8.

purchasing are thus summarized in the *Book of the States:* "While it is difficult to determine the savings made through centralized purchasing, there is evidence that they are about 20 per cent. Such savings result in many ways. Better over-all administration is supplied, coordinating the buying and use of supplies by the departments. Specially trained staff replaces the larger number of employees who were buying for the various departments. More competitive bidding and lower prices result from bid-offerings being sent out from a single office for larger quantities. Unnecessarily large varieties of different types of commodities purchased are reduced through standardization programs. Specifications are developed for the particular quality of the material needed. A testing and inspection program assures actual delivery of amount and quality of commodity purchased." [26]

The movement for centralized purchasing has made considerable progress in our state governments, forty-two of which now provide for some degree of central buying.[27]

About three hundred of our largest cities are also committed to the system, a few having quite elaborate organizations for buying, testing, standardizing, and storing commodities used in large quantities. The movement has made relatively little progress in areas of rural government. Most of the counties which buy through a central agency are in urban or suburban areas, and even in these, numerous exceptions are made, such as school and highway supplies, which continue to be purchased independently. A number of states authorize their political subdivisions to buy through the state purchasing agency, about one-fifth of them permitting local school systems to buy on state contracts. Some of the state leagues of municipalities offer a buying service to their members. It is almost impossible to discover the extent to which local units avail themselves of such services, but the impression one gets from the literature of local government surveys is that they are not much used.

Although there are no doubt very considerable obstacles in the way of anything like a general adoption of central purchasing in rural units of government, the principal reasons why they have not gone further are tradition, inertia, and private greed. A fully equipped purchasing office, managed by an expert buyer, and sup-

[26] Edition of 1950-51, p. 179. This caution may be added: it is possible to make a purchasing program so rigid as to deprive operating heads of a desirable discretion. This discretion may be abused, of course, but it is necessary to take that chance.

[27] Details may be found in the *Book of the States,* 1950-51, pp. 182-187.

plied with all the paraphernalia needed to do a scientific job would, of course, be quite beyond the resources of the typical rural county or school district; but there would seem to be no very respectable reasons why a good many products could not be bought by a state agency on standard specifications and distributed to the various units or by local units on state contracts with vendors. Take, for example, such things as the printed forms used by assessors, clerks, treasurers, and other local officers. The number of these things is generally known well in advance of their use and could be bought in such quantities as are needed through a central agency. This suggestion is usually met, however, with various persuasive, if specious, arguments emanating from local job printers and country editors, who now make a good thing of requirements of this sort and can always claim that they should not be compelled to compete against "outsiders" who quite possibly would underbid them. Moreover, obstacles to change are found in a certain somnolence of administration in the open country, and a suspicion of new ideas, explained perhaps by the somewhat slower spread of ideas in rural sections. An efficient scheme of central purchasing would require considerable planning and a good deal of attention to market movements and technological changes, and rural governments have not ordinarily shown themselves inventive along these lines. Genuine improvement in this field awaits a series of fundamental changes in governmental organization which are probably in the distant future.

PUBLIC EMPLOYEES

The effectiveness and, to a considerable degree, the popularity of any government, depends upon the character and ability of the subordinate personnel. The typical citizen, after all, judges his government by what it gives him in the way of concrete services. He wants the roads to be passable, the schools to be responsive to his views, the water supply adequate, and the fire department efficient. We cannot reasonably find fault with this pragmatic attitude, nor condemn him if he fails to get excited over judicial review, or the delegation of legislative power, or any of the other questions which professors of political science are disposed to regard as "fundamental." In the long run, these latter issues *are* perhaps vital, but in the short run, the citizen is interested in keeping out of the ditch on his country road. And, while administrative ability is doubtless rare, and important in proportion to its rarity, the real work of mending roads and delivering the mail and catching criminals is done by those persons whose names do not appear on official letterheads or on the cornerstones of public buildings. In a very real sense, those who "run" the government are the men and women engaged in the humdrum and laborious work of recording deeds, issuing drivers' licenses, patrolling lonely roads, pouring concrete, making blueprints, and "taking dictation." Let his elective officials be never so brilliant, the citizen will be right in judging his government in terms of the job done by comparatively humble persons far down on the roll of officeholders—people who endure anonymity, whether or not they have a passion for it. If this be true, a problem of first importance in the administration of a government is that concerned with the recruitment and management of the subordinate civil service. Modern practice in financial administration emphasizes the close connection between this problem and the more inclusive one of budget-making, and for that reason, we discuss it here.

The latest official figures indicate that the public service in the United States—federal, state, and local—consists of 6,677,000 persons. Just about half of these, 3,250,000, are employed by local units, 1,440,000 by school districts and 1,800,000 by other local authorities. This means that, for the nation as a whole, about one person in twenty-five works for some governmental agency. On the local level, the figures above would be considerably larger at certain seasons when construction work is extensive and, in some departments, at rush times. Some indication of the cost of maintaining this army of civil servants is supplied by the fact that the total state and local payroll in April, 1951 was just under a billion dollars.[28] Contrary to the popular belief, by no means all of this outlay is for "clerks." Counties, for example, nearly everywhere maintain courts, the work of which, from every point of view, ought to be in competent hands; the same thing may be said of engineering staffs, and of health, welfare, and law enforcement agencies. The waste, extravagance, and inefficiency, to say nothing of the human tragedy, involved in the partisan political management of such services, are beyond computation. The county jail and the poor farm not only exemplify man's inhumanity to man—they are the result of certain attitudes toward public administration which militate against any sensible or scientific handling of the problems of government which are involved.

---

[28] Figures are taken from the Bureau of the Census publication, *Public Employment in April 1951*, issued in July of that year.

The traditional way of filling administrative posts in this country has been to use them as rewards for party services.[29] A society which has gone to great lengths to prevent the existence of a standing military force does not object to, but good-naturedly tolerates, a system of civil administration which involves nothing short of quartering upon the public a standing army of occupation. While this inconsistency has caused reformers and believers in good government considerable pain, it is to be explained, we venture to think, on grounds other than human perversity. The technological revolution which altered all the conditions of public administration is a comparatively recent thing, the implications of which have yet to be grasped in many fields where they are full of significance for the future. Over vast stretches of the country, where leisurely administration produces no perceptible harm, and where social conditions do not favor the pretensions of an expert class, it has been largely useless to argue against a persistent neighborliness which tolerates an easygoing favoritism in such matters as the choice and management of a civil service. In many rural sections, nothing seems more natural and less open to criticism than the use of minor public posts as a means of taking care of the community's unfortunates. The idea of an expert and permanent public service contains a number of sophisticated notions not easily developed under the conditions of relative simplicity found in most rural regions even today. Moreover, the scale of administration in the typical rural area is so small that the problem of a trained personnel has scarcely emerged, and where it is recognized, its solution is quite beyond the competence of rural local government as now organized. The result of these factors is that in the vast majority of rural areas, county, township, and village services continue to be recruited by the spoils system of appointment. It is estimated by the Civil Service Assembly of the United States and Canada that no more than 15 per cent of all county employees are under merit systems. Teachers, of course, are chosen by something like a merit system, in so far as they must be certified by a state agency; but, aside from this group, the only employees who are relatively free from partisan control are those engaged in the

[29] Leonard D. White estimated that in 1937 there were about 250,000 potential patronage positions in the counties and rural subdivisions of the country, although he cautioned that "by no means all of these positions outside the merit system are actually used for party purposes." *Introduction to the Study of Public Administration* (3rd ed., 1948), p. 323.

local administration of programs financed in part by federal grants.

So far as the state governments are concerned, nineteen were listed in 1949 as having merit systems applicable to the entire state service, but most of the others used the merit principle only with reference to employees in the grants-in-aid programs and a few other special services such as the state library, the state patrol, or state hospitals. In about half a dozen states, all or some local units are required by statute to choose their employees under the merit system, but Massachusetts and New York seem to be the only states in which such statutes are enforced with any efficiency. Even where local units voluntarily adopt a merit personnel program, they obtain comparatively little help from the state. "The laws of only ten states provide for some measure of general supervision or aid for local personnel programs. In most instances, states provide services on an optional basis, and relatively few localities have exercised their right to take advantage of these facilities. . . . California, Minnesota, Rhode Island, Tennessee, and Wisconsin, perform civil service activities for all local jurisdictions on a fee basis at local option. In Maryland and New Jersey, local governments by majority vote may bring their personnel under provisions of the state civil service act; available data show that no local units in Maryland have taken advantage of this provision, while a number of New Jersey localities have voluntarily accepted merit systems. In New Jersey, state services are supplied without fee. The Ohio Civil Service Agency has some jurisdiction over the personnel matters of local units and in certain circumstances may recommend the removal of a delinquent commissioner. The state's power to regulate county personnel affairs is more stringent, but the state agency has suffered from lack of funds and has not acted energetically." [30]

In short, little progress can be reported with regard to personnel management in local services in rural areas. The idea of a bureaucracy is not congenial to rural modes of thought, and the merit system may be said to work best only in the urban portions of the country. This will probably continue to be a fair statement of the situation until such a reallocation of functions between the state and its local areas has taken place as will enlarge, at least constructively, the area within which public policies are determined and executed. Whatever virtues our present small areas may have from

---

[30] *State-Local Relations,* p. 39.

the point of view of decentralizing power, they will long continue to be serious obstacles to the introduction of approved methods of organizing the public service.

THE INCREASE IN THE COST OF GOVERNMENT

No matter how we view it, the last generation has witnessed a phenomenal increase in the cost of local government. After allowance has been made for such factors as the change in the purchasing power of money, increase in population, and so forth, it remains true that public expenditures are increasing faster than either the national wealth or the population. In this fact there has been found, of course, material for many a sermon on economy and hundreds of scorching denunciations of the "wicked" politicians. The explanation of the more extreme manifestations of this critical attitude is twofold. There is in the United States a deep-seated suspicion of governmental activity, which extends to doubting the wisdom of allowing public officials to spend money for any but the obviously necessary functions of government. People who hold this belief in its most extreme form seldom attempt to set forth precisely what putting it into practice would involve; and they would, of course, meet serious difficulties if they did so. When they give expression to these opinions, what they doubtless mean is that they prefer to choose for themselves the things for which they shall spend their money. This view is entitled to respect, even though those who insist upon this type of liberty may get, in the opinion of others, less for their money than government might obtain if it were to make the decision for them by the use of the taxing power. For liberty in these matters consists precisely in freedom to choose the objects of expenditure, unless there are strong reasons for thinking that the general good might be threatened by that very liberty.

There is, in the second place, the widespread notion that money spent by private persons is productively spent, while public outlays are in some way unproductive. It would, of course, be very hard to maintain this distinction successfully. Although the burden of taxation may not be equitably laid, it is altogether likely that we get a good deal more for our taxes than officious economizers are willing to concede. Every year millions of our citizens, exercising their "sovereign prerogative of choice," spend millions of dollars for worthless stocks, fake remedies, adulterated food, harmful cosmetics, and "courses" designed to make them beautiful, slender, charming, eloquent, or "successful." It would be a rash person who would claim that public spending is as wasteful as this. While one may hold that freedom may mean freedom to be bilked, one may at the same time hold that this freedom, as is true of many others, may have to be restricted if it threatens the general well-being. It may well be that, in ways not yet clearly understood, "the very processes of industrialization with its influences on our work, our leisure, our society, and our politics have let loose such powerful forces that self-preservation itself depends upon common action for their control. May it not be that this phenomenon is rapidly bringing us face to face with the necessity of reappraising our social, economic, and political institutions, of comprehending more adequately the direction in which our activities are moving, and of facing the prospect of gradual but radical transformation in the structure and operation of our tax system and our governments as well?" [31] If the point of view expressed in this quotation is sound, the problem of meeting our public expenditures is one which involves making a decision as to what we think worth doing by cooperative effort, as well as bringing about the changes in governmental machinery required to give effect to such a decision. Thus the control of expenditures is bound up with the far more portentous questions of social and political reform.

Until one stops to think about it, it would seem reasonable to expect general agreement as to the advisability of keeping down public costs. In reality, as a matter of practical politics, reduction of expense is not only a most difficult thing to accomplish—it is, nine times out of ten, actually an unpopular thing to advocate. For it is necessary to emphasize the fact that the government of any area represents at any given time not simply a set of arrangements for transacting the public business, but to an even greater degree, a certain adjustment and balance of various private and group interests.[32] And these interests normally depend for their existence upon public spending. Thus, very commonly, some more or less powerful interest in the "general public" will be found to have

---

[31] Benjamin P. Whitaker, "Some Implications of Increasing Public Expenditures," **XVIII** *Bulletins of the National Tax Association* 163 (Mar. 1933).

[32] "Competition is the law of life in government as much as in economics. All government programs are in varying degrees competing for allocations from a limited budget. Their share in the budget is determined by group and public support—support that cannot be assured by merely doing a good job except in the most clearly necessary functions." Norton E. Long, "Popular Support of Economic Programs," **XLII** *American Political Science Review* 334-5 (Apr. 1948).

charged itself with watching over the administration of a certain department or service which it wishes to see strengthened at all costs. In a country which has a tradition of being ruled by a competent and public-spirited ruling class, decisions as to the apportionment of expenditures are by tacit assent habitually left to be made by those presumed to know the various needs, by reason of constant contact with the public services. Where no such class and no such tradition exist, budget allotments are normally made as a result of the pushes and pressures (ultimately reducible to votes, of course) exerted by various groups outside official ranks.[33]

Each service under these circumstances comes to be, in the eyes of its supporters, almost an end in itself. All attempts to reduce its appropriations are met by the contention that, whatever may be the case with other services, this particular one cannot possibly get along with less money without endangering the very foundations of society.[34] There exists scarcely anywhere in our various governments any person or authority recognized as competent to speak for the people generally and endowed with power to compel each branch of the service to see its work in relation to the whole task of government. Nor is such an authority likely to emerge in the present confused state of our politics.[35] It is a curious fact that the growth of democracy, far from increasing the power of the "people," has had the effect of increasing that of minorities in the body politic. The multiplication of pressure groups creates for democratic government a baffling dilemma: the body erected to represent all of us against the demands of partial societies is increasingly the product of these

---

[33] Even where such ruling classes have existed, it remains to be demonstrated that they spent any more wisely than democratic governments have done. The possible stake of the bureaucracy in large public expenditures is treated penetratingly by Bertrand de Jouvenel, *On Power* (1949), p. 115.

[34] "This is a time when the public, as well as individuals, does not purchase or demand a large amount of what it really gets. The high-powered salesmen, promoters, and so-called boosting clubs, in fact, make the sales. If it were left to the public at large many of the so-called improvements which are in the nature of luxuries that are now sold to it would not be seriously considered." Clarence Smith, State Tax Commissioner of Kansas, "Control of Public Expenditures," in *Tax Digest* 9:259 (Aug. 1931). It is worth pointing out also that those clamoring for more funds are not always, or even very often, the "interests"; they are far more likely to be found among the lily-white reform organizations interested in an earthly New Jerusalem.

[35] "There is no surer road to political death than opposition to public expense. . . . The spending powers are the popular ones and are received with acclaim. . . . Political power rests largely upon the spending of the public's money. Those who prevent tax reduction or who are responsible for an increased expenditure are those who spend or get the tax money." Seabury C. Mastick, "Reduction of Local Budgets as a Measure of Tax Reform," *U. S. Daily* (Dec. 9, 1931).

same interests. Its obligation to occupy itself with what is common
to all of us, rather than with what is peculiar to each of us, is one
which it finds increasingly hard to discharge. Leaders occasionally
appear under circumstances which permit governmental emphasis
on the general good, but the simultaneous arrival of such leadership
and such circumstances is not a dependable feature of our politics.[36]

If the "general public" is really interested in the reduction of
public expenditures or, what is the same thing, the more efficient
spending of public money, the chief suggestions which may be
made follow.

1. Voters need to become far more critical of office-seekers than
they have been in the past. They must learn to recognize as a shyster
the candidate who promises in one sentence to lower taxes and, in
the next, to give the "grand old town of Millersville, the finest, the
most modern, etc. school plant in the state." A widespread ability
to make adequate judgments upon such pronouncements would retire to the cracker-barrel many a windy patriot who now disfigures
the political landscape. This is perhaps a counsel of perfection as
long as the population is so easily taken in by other forms of quackery, but in the end there are no substitutes for vigilance, and no
"system" or "organization" of government can take the place of intelligent and honest officeholders.

2. If there is any validity at all in the notion that the people can
control their government, it is weakened seriously by the unconscionable complexity of our governmental structure. We are involved in a vast web of small units born of conditions vastly different from those of today. Even experts find it difficult to make the
relationships between its various parts intelligible; to expect ordinary people, busy with getting a living and amusing themselves, to
deal effectively with such complexities, is to look for a degree of

---

[36] See the able essay by Harold W. Stoke, "The Paradox of Representative Government," in J. M. Mathews and James Hart (Eds.), *Essays in Political Science in
Honor of W. W. Willoughby* (1937), pp. 77-99. An even larger issue is raised by Alexander Gray: "We are living in an age when all manner of commodities and all manner
of services are being made more widely available, by a policy of subsidies, aids, subventions and what-nots. Free education leads quite logically to free textbooks and
free meals. Free medical attention quite logically to free medicines, and, without much
ingenuity, one might argue, to free bread and free milk. We have subsidized our agriculture and we have subsidized our coal. We live in a subsidized age. Whether a
universally subsidized and subsidizing society is also a communistic society is perhaps
a problem to be discussed by undergraduates and fallen angels." *The Socialist Tradition* (1946), p. 366.

political virtue and acumen beyond anything we have a right to expect. A system which requires every voter to be a political scientist and a man of leisure is absurd.

3. The whole question of allocating functions to various units needs thorough study. Where local units are incapable because of poverty or lack of technically trained personnel to manage functions traditionally assigned to them, there is no reason why any sentimental regard for "home rule" should stand in the way of a new functional alignment.

4. There is urgent need for improvement in the reporting of the public business. At present, official reports are not only issued too late to be of any value, but are usually so badly put together as to be unintelligible. It is significant that the public is normally informed, when at all adequately, through the work of private research associations rather than through the reports of its hired servants.

5. No reform can compare in importance with the creation of an able civil service. A staff of administrators, carefully chosen and guaranteed reasonable security of tenure, while not free from faults, would come closer than any other device of which the world has experience to affording the kind of disinterested and intelligent leadership which is now so sorely needed on every level of government.

6. Fundamental to all these considerations, however, is the necessity of our giving a clear answer to the ancient question, What is the proper sphere of government? What ought the State, in the words of Burke, to take upon itself to direct by public wisdom, and what ought it to leave, with as little interference as possible, to individual freedom? The bewildering working at cross purposes, the sordid scramble for preferment in every budget, and the general apathy of the bystander at the political struggles of the day, are symptomatic of our failure clearly to envisage the role of government in individual and group welfare. Until we have reached a consensus on the main question, public finance, like politics generally, will continue to be a confused business without definite objectives and hence without predictable direction.

CHAPTER 7

The New Pattern of Fiscal Relations

It would be completely unrealistic to speak of local finance as if it were a matter of concern only to the citizens of local areas. To use the term in this way would be correct only if the services rendered by local governments were paid for strictly out of local revenues. In the long run, this could be the case only if wealth were distributed in accordance with local needs, if none of this wealth had connections of any sort outside the local area, and if the functions of local government were of interest solely to local people. All of this could be true only in a society so thoroughly decentralized as to make each political subdivision completely self-contained. To a considerable degree this situation existed in early American society. When the economic and social contacts of the people were confined normally within the boundaries of the town, township, or county, it was "natural" that political arrangements—which always follow those set up for the more fundamental human relationships —should be associated with the territorial areas within which the primary concerns of life were organized. Self-government continued to be local as long as life was local; it had substance as long as the functions which it performed were solely of local interest; it had effective reality as long as it was paid for locally.

No argument is needed to show that these conditions no longer exist. It is difficult to name any function of substantial importance which is not of interest to an area far wider—to the state or even to the nation—than that of our familiar local subdivisions. Highways cannot be left to the independent administration of townships, even though only a little of the traffic over them may be destined for points outside. The state as a whole has an interest in the kind of schooling offered in every local district, since the products of the local system enrich or impoverish the citizenship of the state. The list can be extended to cover almost the whole field of government—

135

health, welfare, relief, tax assessment, public borrowing, public personnel, policing, judicial administration; all of these are of far more than local significance, and the most zealous advocate of home rule would not urge a return to our primitive decentralization. The logical area of administration for all such functions tends ever to be a larger one. So it is also with regard to financial support. As wealth flows in a larger proportion from industrial and commercial processes and from interstate transactions than directly from the mere possession of land, the local jurisdiction grows less and less able to tax it, and thus less and less able to finance its own services. Since counties, towns, and townships cannot, in the nature of things, levy taxes upon wealth which is non-local in its character, they find themselves restricted to the least elastic of all tax bases, general property. Thus the area of financial support also tends to be the larger unit, for it is only such a unit that can tap these new sources. Because of these developments the connection between state and local tax systems has grown steadily more intimate, and the line between what is state and what is local comes to be blurred.

THE TRADITIONAL REVENUE SYSTEM

Before the opening of the present century, both the state and the local governments depended almost entirely upon the general property tax to finance their activities. The prevailing system was to have property assessed and taxes collected by locally chosen officials who then remitted to the state treasury the proceeds of the state rate. Very often as many as five or six jurisdictions shared the same source, each imposing a rate sufficient to produce the required revenue. So far as the state government was concerned, little attempt was made to supervise the local assessing and collecting officials. The system worked quite well as long as the combined levies were relatively light. About the year 1900, however, the increase in the number and costliness of public functions showed the inadequacy of the traditional system. The use of the corporation instead of individual ownership created types of property which could not be assessed by local officials—franchises, stocks and bonds, and complicated varieties of physical property such as power plants, pipe lines, and railway terminals. On the other hand, the burden on such familiar sorts of property as land and farm buildings, equipment, and livestock grew heavier, either because the new forms of general property tended to escape taxation altogether, or because local assessors were more accurate judges of familiar kinds of property.

What happened in this new situation was that the state governments everywhere pre-empted the new and, as it turned out, vastly productive sources of revenue and left the tax on general property to the local units. The result of this has been striking. In 1902 the state governments were receiving 52 per cent of their total tax revenue from the general property tax. By 1950 the Bureau of the Census reported that property taxes of all sorts produced for state purposes only 3.4 per cent of *total* revenue. In the same year, the tax on motor vehicle fuel alone produced for states more than five times as much revenue, and corporate and individual income taxes together more than four times as much.[1] Twenty of the states had in 1948 abandoned the general property tax as a source of revenue for state purposes, and of those retaining it only seven received more than 10 per cent of their total tax revenue from this source.

LOCAL SELF-GOVERNMENT AND LOCAL POVERTY

In spite of the fact that the state governments had exploited these new and lucrative sources of revenue, experience gave no certain answer as to whether the state or the local unit should administer the various functions of government. If it is logical to transfer to the state the control of those sources of revenue which it can best administer, it is equally logical to transfer to it the control of those functions which are of more than purely local interest. But, of course, the matter was not settled on logical principles. The believers in the traditional dogma of local self-government did not discriminate as nicely as did the scholars between state functions and local functions. Indeed the matter is not yet settled. By and large, what happened was that local units retained substantial control over the usual functions in spite of the fact that their financial resources were severely restricted. At the same time the cost of these functions increased, and entirely new ones were steadily being added. If devotion to local self-government would not permit the transfer of these functions to the state in spite of the inability of the

---

[1] Indeed in 1950 motor vehicle and operators' licenses and motor fuel taxes accounted for more than one-fifth of all state general revenue. See *Compendium of State Government Finances in 1950*, Bureau of the Census, 1951. A great mass of figures on motor vehicle taxation may be found in the publication *Automobile Facts and Figures*, issued by the Automobile Manufacturers' Association. A current source is the *Tax Economics Bulletin*, issued monthly by the American Petroleum Institute.

local unit to pay the bills, then some way had to be found to increase local revenues.

There are a number of ways by which this might be done. One way would be to remove the limitations imposed by state constitutions and statutes upon the taxing and debt-incurring powers of local governments. In so far as the state draws its revenue from sources distinct from those used by local units, there could be no theoretical objections to such a course, and indeed prior to about 1930 such tax and debt limitations were relaxed in many states. But there are strong practical objections to this as a general policy. Although tax limitations may be evaded and have often led in fact simply to the creation of debts, they were widely believed to offer protection to real estate owners, and during the depression of the 1930's, there was a definite tendency to restore them and to make them more difficult to evade. To the extent that such limitations are actually effective, they increase the rigidity of the local revenue system and seriously cripple the local unit in rendering the services offered by it.[2]

In a few states the plan was followed for a time of separating the sources of revenue completely, assigning to the state the proceeds of the newer taxes and leaving the general property tax entirely to the localities. While this scheme did free the state from its former dependence on the locally assessed property tax, it has not afforded in practice any great relief to local units from the pressure for more revenue caused by the taking on of new functions or the greater costliness of established ones. As a matter of fact, separation of sources of revenue is based upon an unstated assumption that functions may be divided into those belonging to the state and those proper for local administration. In practice no such distinction can be made, and separation is a failure if it means that the state is prohibited from sharing its revenue with its subdivisions. Finally, although it is true that many taxes, such as those on corporations, are more efficiently administered by the state, it does not follow that the state alone should dispose of the proceeds. The local district has a strong claim to a share in such revenues not merely because it needs the money, but also because the locality supplies services of value to the corpora-

---

[2] A convenient review of the experience with property tax limitation laws may be found in *State-Local Relations*, pp. 103-112. This summary is based in large part upon William O. Suiter, "State Limits on Local Property Taxes," *Municipal Year Book*, 1936, and on Glen Leet and Robert M. Paige (eds.), *Property Tax Limitation Laws* (Public Administration Service, 1936).

tion taxed. As a means of relieving local needs, then, separation has not been successful, though it is still followed to some extent in a few states.[3]

Neither the relaxing of tax and debt limits nor the separation of sources of revenue has contributed very much to providing local units with revenue sufficient for their needs. Of far more significance are two fiscal devices developed within the last generation—the sharing of state-administered taxes with the local units, and the grant-in-aid. Although of comparatively recent origin, these devices are thoroughly established as parts of what may most accurately be called our *state-local* system of finance.[4]

State-administered, Locally Shared Revenues

Many of the newer taxes levied by the state to supplement its share of the property tax, or to make up for its relinquishment, are in their nature unfitted for local administration. It would be difficult if not impossible, for example, for local units except possibly our large municipalities, to administer an income, a sales, a motor vehicle, or a corporation tax. The county, city, or township may well argue that receipts from such taxes should be kept in the district where the transaction took place and be used as a means of relieving the burden of the property tax. To some extent this argument is met by the state-administered, locally shared tax. These taxes have been defined by a leading student as "those which are collected by the state and the proceeds of which are then distributed, at least in part, to the local divisions without losing their identity as the yield of specific taxes, and also those taxes which are locally collected but over which the state has such close control that either the state checks the actual tax bills sent out, perhaps sending them out, or checks the individual receipts, even receiving the money and making the distribution to the local districts in some instances."[5] Two

---

[3] "The difficulty with the separation of sources in the case of state and local governments is that of obtaining adequate revenues for local governments from the few taxes that can be administered by so narrow a jurisdiction. Even with the larger state jurisdiction this is becoming a problem. Nothing short of national administration will bring equitable taxation of many important resources. In fact the tax on real estate would seem to be the only important tax that can be really successfully administered by a narrower jurisdiction than the Federal Government." Mabel Newcomer. "The Coordination of Federal, State, and Local Tax Systems," **183** *Annals* 40 (Jan. 1936).

[4] Both the sharing of state-collected taxes and the granting of money to local units date far back in our history, but comparatively little use of them was made before about 1915.

[5] Ruth G. Hutchinson, *State-administered Locally-shared Taxes* (1931), p. 34.

things are necessary, then, to bring a tax within this category— (1) state collection or sufficient state supervision to insure that the tax is properly collected, and (2) actual local spending of the proceeds.

The growth in the number and significance of taxes of this sort has been striking. Miss Hutchinson found that before 1900 only seventeen tax laws provided for sharing receipts with localities. By 1930 there were 142, and a count made as of 1947 showed that 44 states shared 151 separate levies. In 1941, the latest year for which complete figures are now available, a total of $288,237,000 was distributed to the local units. The principal taxes thus distributed were those derived from motor vehicle licenses, personal and corporate incomes, and motor fuel. This sum amounts to about six per cent of all *tax* revenues of the state governments.[6]

If the proceeds of such taxes are to be distributed to the local units, the question immediately arises as to what basis shall be used. In the view of the advocates of extreme home rule, the state acts simply as the collector of these taxes because administrative efficiency requires such an arrangement, and the proceeds of the tax should be returned in full to the locality. This demand is based on the assumed "right" of the locality to collect the tax in the first place, a "right" given up only for reasons of administrative expediency. There are, however, a number of reasons why this view will not stand inspection. In the first place, it is impossible to localize the origin of some taxes and thus impossible to return them to the place of collection. The gasoline tax, for example, is collected from a limited number of distributors, but it is actually paid by thousands of motorists at hundreds of retail stations. In the second place, the return to the locality is likely to lead to reckless spending and thus fail to relieve the property taxpayer. Again, this mode of distribution ignores the actual needs of local units and probably gives wealthy units more than they ought to have, for the reason that collections are almost certain to be heaviest in those units where the purchasing power is greatest.

These arguments against the distribution of the total proceeds to the localities are sound if it is believed that these state-collected taxes should be used to relieve the local property tax or to assist the

---

[6] Figures for the period up to 1936 may be found in Hutchinson, *op. cit.,* pp. 38-9, 126-7, and in the article "State-administered Locally-shared Taxes" by Raymond Uhl and Anthony Vincent Shea in the *Municipal Year Book* (1936), pp. 367-389. The most recent treatment is found in *State-Local Relations*, Part III. In New York State alone, for the budget year 1945-46, shared taxes amounted to $114,100,000.

locality in performing some particular function. If we accept the opinion that the state is only a collector of these taxes, then there would be an inconsistency in allowing it to dictate the objects for which the shared taxes are to be expended.[7] In this case, the sums returned to the communities would go into the general treasury to be spent at the discretion of the local officials. But experience has shown that this way of handling the matter does not work. In the first place, local politicians too often have not used the shared taxes to reduce the general property tax, but have regarded them simply as additional funds to spend. Again, the functions to be aided by such taxes are in most cases of more than local interest, and the state is under strong obligation to see, if possible, that none of its subdivisions falls so far below a minimum level of performance as to affect the welfare of the state at large.

For these reasons it has been impossible for most states to confine themselves to collecting these taxes and distributing them to local units. They have accepted to some degree the responsibility for protecting local budgets and for seeing that essential functions of general interest are not neglected. To accomplish these ends, it has become customary to designate the use to be made of the shares distributed and to devise various formulae for determining the amount to be given to each community.[8] What formula is used to determine this amount depends, of course, upon the nature of the tax involved, and it is impossible to generalize. In the case of the gasoline tax, which is generally designated for highway purposes, various bases are used in the several states. Thus, such criteria are employed as the amount of the tax collected in the county, the area of the county, population, highway mileage, motor vehicle registration, and assessed valuation. With reference to this tax it is to be noticed that some states do not distribute it at all, but use the entire

---

[7] "The desire for local autonomy is based upon the belief that financial support and control must go together. As the amount of state aid, administrative control and supervision increase, and as functions are gradually transferred to larger units, the traditional doctrine is asserted in the belief that local property tax contributions still form such a large part of financial support that the situs of control should remain local." Russell J. Hinckley, *State Grants-in-Aid*, Special Report No. 9, New York State Tax Commission (1935), p. 172.

[8] This is usually called reapportioning, by which is meant returning taxes to local units on some basis other than their origin in such units; thus, gas tax funds may be paid to counties in the proportion which the road mileage, or the area, or the population of a county bears to the total mileage, area, or population of the state. State control of the use of such reapportioned funds is not necessarily involved in the idea of reapportionment, though the use of these bases is presumably an attempt to measure local need and thus affect local policy.

proceeds for state highway or related purposes, such as the state police. Specifically, figures for 1948 show that of $1,350,000,000 collected as motor fuel tax, $850 million was for state highway purposes, including the state police, and a little over $300 million was used for local roads and city streets.[9]

The fact that some states, at least, are now sharing these taxes in accordance with formulae intended to show local need is of great importance. It must be remembered that the theory of the shared tax is that the state is supplementing local revenues because the local tax base is no longer adequate to bear the costs of local government. But in spite of this theory, the states have an interest in most of the functions thus aided, and a certain degree of interference with local discretion is implied when the state reapportions according to its view of local needs. As the number of these taxes and the percentage which they bear to local receipts increase, we cannot avoid a situation in which the state will be controlling a larger and larger share of total local expenditures. Moreover, while the number of these taxes is increasing, the state governments are showing, if anything, a growing reluctance to share them with the localities. In many of the states they are not all shared even now, and, in the states which do share them, the proportion of the total proceeds returned to the localities tends to grow smaller. Actually we are in a transitional stage preceding state supervision of the functions aided by such taxes, for if the states cease to share them, the inadequacy of the local units will be made clear immediately, and there will be no way out except state assumption of the administrative as well as the financial responsibility for a large portion of local functions.

While the shared taxes are an important source of funds for local purposes, it is the opinion of close students of local finance that the device of sharing has a number of defects. In the first place, present methods of distributing these taxes take no account of local needs or existing tax resources. Secondly, from the long-range point of view, the amount of such taxes normally would fluctuate so widely with the business cycle that they can scarcely be regarded as a stabilizing element in the local revenue system. When local need for additional revenue is greatest, in times of recession, this is precisely the time when the proceeds of such levies as those on sales and incomes drop most precipitously. For this reason, local budget-makers cannot rely

---

[9] *Table G-3, Disposition of State Motor-Fuel Tax Receipts, 1948,* Bureau of Public Roads (Aug. 1949).

on these sources. Finally, although theoretically state payments of this sort may foster local freedom because they are expendable as the locality sees fit, they have not been allocated in practice without conditions, the majority of shared taxes being designated for specific purposes. They therefore have come closely to resemble grants-in-aid with implications of centralized direction and control.[10]

STATE GRANTS-IN-AID

A still more significant way in which the local need for revenue is being met is the grant-in-aid. A grant-in-aid may be defined as a sum of money paid by one unit of government, usually the "higher," to another to aid the latter in performing a function. Such grants may be made a single time or they may be made annually or biennially. Considered abstractly, the grant-in-aid differs from the state-administered, locally shared tax in a number of ways. It is usually made from the state treasury without reference to its origin as the proceeds of a particular tax. In the second place, it is made for the purpose of enabling the various local districts to supply services of substantially the same amount or quality. That is, the desire of the state to improve the quantity or quality of the services offered by local government is openly avowed. Again, since it is made for the purpose of aiding the locality, the state normally insists that certain standards of performance are adhered to by the local administrators or that other conditions are met.[11] Finally, the grant-in-aid is based upon the theory that the responsibility for supporting such functions as health, welfare, education, highways, and so forth cannot be arbitrarily divided between the state and local authorities, whereas the opposite theory is implied in the system of state-administered, locally shared taxes.

The grant-in-aid has been for many years an important source

---

[10] See *State-Local Relations,* pp. 131-2; *Report of Commission on Municipal Revenue and Reduction of Real Estate Taxes* (Albany, 1945); Henry S. Bitterman, *State and Federal Grants-in-Aid* (1938), pp. 45-46: "In New York shared taxes in 1929 amounted to $74,698,000 and dropped to $28,821,000 in 1934 despite the addition of new state-collected and shared taxes. The difference resulted in increased property taxes and curtailment of local expenditures—especially for highways. In Massachusetts shared taxes decreased from $31,786,000 in 1930 to $17,692,000 in 1932, and local property levies increased from $191,268,000 to $210,808,000."

[11] The state, as we have seen, often attaches conditions to the use of funds which it collects but shares with the localities. When such conditions are imposed, the shared tax becomes in effect a grant-in-aid, but the fact that the amount of money to be received by the local government is determined by the tax yield and not by specific legislative appropriation means that local officials will have a direct practical interest in it, since the basis for sharing will determine the amount to be received by the local unit.

of local revenue. As long ago as 1902 it amounted to 10 per cent of all local tax revenues; by 1950 it had been greatly increased in amount and had been extended to cover a variety of functions. In the latter year the Bureau of the Census reported that "aid to local governments—comprising both grants and shares allocated to local governments of taxes imposed and collected by the States— amounted to $4,011 million, or 30.4 per cent of all state general expenditure in fiscal 1950. This is 13.2 per cent higher than the 1949 aid amount. Nearly half of the 1950 sum, $1,982 million, was for school purposes; $773 million was for public welfare; and $576 million was for local streets and highways." These facts are shown graphically in Figure 12.[12]

The Council of State Governments estimated that, in 1946, school districts received 36 per cent of their revenue in the form of grants, counties 34 per cent, towns and townships 20 per cent, and special districts 3 per cent. Although the grant-in-aid is now a well-established part of the state-local fiscal system, its development has been very uneven over the country. In 1941, for example, state aid constituted less than 8 per cent of local revenues in five states, while, at the other extreme, it came to 37 per cent in Colorado, 40

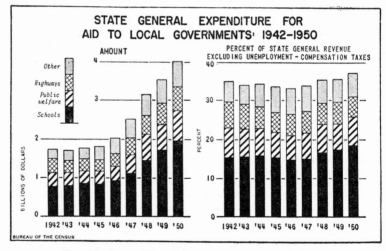

FIG. 12. State aid to local governments, 1942-1950.

---

[12] *Compendium of State Government Finances in 1950*, pp. 3, 28. The fact that these figures do not distinguish shared taxes and grants-in-aid is not important for our present purpose which is to indicate the new pattern developing in state-local fiscal relations.

per cent in Alabama and New Mexico, and 48 per cent in Delaware.[13] The proportion which grants-in-aid bear to total state revenues is very significant in showing the extent to which locally managed functions are involved in general state finances. It may be argued, of course, that the growth of the system of grant-in-aid will render more difficult local citizen control over governmental processes and finances, but such arguments have not been persuasive in practice with those responsible for fiscal policy on either the state or the local level.[14]

Taken together, state-administered, locally shared taxes and grants-in-aid probably account for at least a third of all local tax revenue and are, therefore, important elements in the state-local fiscal system. Although based upon somewhat different theories as to state-local relationships, it is evident that their effect on local government tends to be similar. Thus, it has been pointed out that, almost from the beginning, the states sharing taxes with the localities have imposed restrictions as to their use. Even though the source of these revenues—be it gasoline, motor vehicle, or corporation taxes —may remain distinct in a way not found in the case of the grants-in-aid, the fact is of little real importance, if the locality does not have a free hand in disposing of these funds. Hence, the state-administered, locally shared tax grows more and more to resemble the grant-in-aid, and there is a probability that as restrictions multiply even the theoretical differences will disappear and the system of shared taxes will be swallowed up in an enlarged system of grants-in-aid.

As a matter of fact, a system which largely ignores the former distinction between shared taxes and grants-in-aid has been in effect in New York State since 1946. The New York plan, because it very possibly supplies a pattern for other states, is worth describing. Essentially it abolishes the former complicated scheme of shared taxes and replaces it by providing for simple per capita grants at the rate of $6.75 per capita for cities, $3.55 for towns, and $3.00 for villages. In addition to these fixed grants which, it is to be noted, are made without reference to the source of the funds made available, the state assumes 80 per cent of the costs of public relief. State aid

---

[13] *State-Local Relations,* p. 68.
[14] For arguments on both sides see the publication *State Grants-in-Aid,* issued by the Council of State Governments in 1944, and Harold L. Henderson, "State Aids as a Possible Revenue Sources for Cities," 32 *Bulletins of the National Tax Association* 43-8 (Nov. 1946).

for education, highways, and public health is continued on the former basis. The total increase in state aid over 1944 is more than $50 million and the new program required more than $274 million in its first year of operation. Most significant of all, perhaps, is the fact that separate state budgets are set up for state purposes and for local assistance, thus emphasizing the continuing responsibility of the state for local functions, instead of treating the latter as addenda to the state's fiscal program. For the very considerable number of states in which at least a third of the budget consists of local aids, this feature may well become a model.

The Council of State Governments, after describing the New York plan as "a notable development in the history of state-local fiscal relations," comments as follows: "The per capita grants greatly stabilize local revenues. Simultaneously, the assumption by the state of a major portion of local relief costs effectively takes up a large share of increased costs during depression and thus has the effect of stabilizing local expenditures. In addition to this important two-way stabilizing effect, the New York plan achieves an admirable balance between maintaining standards (through the education and welfare grants) and leaving a large share of initiative to localities (through the per capita grants which are not specified as to use). Finally, the separate budgeting of local aid increases legislative control over the system." If, as the Council points out, the fixed grants may not take into account the variable needs of localities and may even keep some uneconomic ones in existence, the only pertinent comment would seem to be that these possible results are probably unavoidable in any plan which regards the preservation of local self-government as desirable.[15]

THE MEASUREMENT OF LOCAL NEED

The payment of sums of money by the states to their local units, no matter what the sources of these funds may be, raises many difficult questions of both policy and administration. If, as was originally urged in the case of state-administered, locally shared taxes,

---

[15] See *State-Local Relations*, pp. 136-37. The New York plan is described in the two *Reports of the Commission on Municipal Revenues and Reduction of Real Estate Taxes*, 1945, 1946. There is an excellent article by Robert F. Steadman, "Recent Developments in State-Local Fiscal Relations in New York State," in **32** *Bulletins of the National Tax Association* 198 (Apr. 1947).

money is returned to the community where it was collected, it is possible to obtain uniformity and efficient administration to a degree not likely if collection were made by each local authority. This method might be followed with no great disadvantage as long as the sums involved are not large. As soon, however, as significant amounts are returned, it is discovered that the actual needs of the various units do not vary with the yield of the tax. Indeed, rich communities are quite likely to contribute heavily to such taxes, and if the latter are returned to the place of origin, we find help being given to districts which do not need it, while others barely able to provide the essentials receive very little help. It is this situation which has caused most states to adopt the policy of distributing both grants and shared taxes on the basis of need, or of using some formula which will encourage more efficient local performance of the functions aided.

The measurement of local need inevitably involves difficult administrative problems. What are the most adequate measures of this need? And what is the standard of performance to which this need is necessarily related? A school district would obviously need less aid in order to offer instruction through eight grades than if it maintained a high school in addition; while the size of classes and the density of population would have a direct bearing upon the standard to be set. Hence, somehow it must be decided that a certain minimum quality and quantity of service is reasonable before it is possible to determine the ability of the local unit to supply this service unassisted. The units by which this quantity and quality are to be measured will vary, of course, with the function being considered. In general, however, it seems agreed that the state should use its resources to equalize the ability of both rich and poor districts by helping the latter to offer what the unit with average economic resources is able to supply. In the field of education, the development of formulae to measure local need more adequately and equitably has been the almost constant preoccupation of state school authorities.[16] The elements of the problem are so many and complicated, and conditions in different states vary so widely, that scarcely any two states have adopted the same means of determining the needs of local units. About all that can be said now is that methods

[16] See Council of State Governments, *The Forty-Eight State School Systems* (1949).

of measurement are far more refined than such earlier ones as assessed valuation and pupil and teacher censuses.[17]

Once the local need is determined, the knotty problem is faced of measuring the ability of each unit to furnish the service agreed upon. The problem here involves a judgment as to local resources, a judgment very difficult to make in general terms applying to all units. It would probably not be far wrong to say that most systems of aid require the local unit to demonstrate its willingness to supply the aided service by levying a tax at a rate determined by statute. A number of examples may be given to illustrate how local ability may be shown. In New York State, the measure of local ability to meet the minimum educational program which the state will support is the actual valuation of real property (as equalized by the state) behind each pupil in average daily attendance. High valuation districts are those having $40,000 valuation per pupil, middle valuation districts have $10,000 per pupil, and low valuation districts, $4,000 per pupil. The equalization quota is distributed in inverse proportion to local tax-paying ability, poorer districts receiving more than wealthy ones. In Connecticut, present statutes require each district to expend at least $140 per pupil in average daily membership during the preceding year, and the state grant is subject to reduction if the town fails to make such an expenditure. Under this scheme, while the town probably raises its revenue from a tax on property, its methods of assessment are not involved. School aid in Pennsylvania is predicated upon a local tax levied upon real property, reserving to the State Council of Education the authority to equalize values as found locally for county tax purposes. A somewhat similar system of school aid is in force in Illinois. So long as each local unit does its own assessing of property, there are certain to be some inequalities, but no state centralization of this function is likely to occur, and these schemes seem best adapted to compel a reasonable local effort of any that have been suggested.[18]

---

[17] See P. R. Mort and W. C. Reusser, *Public School Finance,* 2nd ed. (1951), Book III; *The Forty-Eight State School Systems,* Ch. VII; Francis G. Cornell, "Grants-in-Aid Apportionment Formulas," 42 *Journal of the American Statistical Association,* No. 237, pp. 92-104 (Mar. 1947); Morton Grodzins, "State-Municipal Fiscal Relations: A Critical Commentary," III *National Tax Journal* 1-17 (Mar. 1950).

[18] These formulae have been furnished the author by the state educational authorities. They refer principally to equalization grants, although it should be pointed out that special provisions are made for such services as school transportation, adult education, improvement of school plant and equipment, and the teaching of handicapped children.

State Aid and Uneconomic Units of Local Government

Distribution of shared taxes on the basis of their origin tends to ignore local needs. This is one horn of the dilemma. The other is this: if state assistance is used to equalize the amount and quality of local services, grave risk is run of creating a situation in which large numbers of local units will receive the bulk of their revenue from the state and, though ineffective as agencies of government, will thus be perpetuated. The number of these uneconomic units is large and they occur in almost every state.[19] In theory, there are two ways by which such a situation might be avoided. One would be to transfer to the state the administration as well as the financing of all of those functions of interest to the state as a whole. The other would be to create local units large enough to be able to support the functions now shared with the state. Neither solution, however, seems feasible at any time in the near future.[20] Aside from the serious technical obstacles in the way of such drastic changes, it must be remembered that they could be made only by legislatures which are deeply influenced, if not actually dominated, by representatives of those pauperized areas living off the bounty of the state. Whatever may be the strength of the sentiment of local self-government, these districts as a matter of fact do not seem at all to resent their dependent position, and their deputies seem quite willing to allow things to remain as they are.

All of this does not mean, however, that only a policy of drift can be followed. It is possible within limits to use the device of state aid in such a way as to discourage the performance of functions by ineffective local units. If state aid is used in such a way as to delay desirable structural changes, "the total tax burden remains unnecessarily high, local units which would disappear if it were not for state aid continue to exist, these artificially supported units impede the rationalization of local structures as a whole, and the final desirable

---

[19] "Aid for minimum standards, without careful planning, may be contradictory to the end of maintaining local freedom. Conversely, aid of all kinds may perpetuate archaic and inefficient units of government. This is an important dilemma facing state and local officials. State aid is a technique clearly superior to other immediate alternatives . . . available for the solution of local fiscal problems. In the long run, however, the enlargement of the area of individual local governments holds forth great promise as a fundamental solution to a large part of local fiscal difficulties. The danger is that state aid will postpone needed structural reorganization and thus act as a deterrent to the best solution of local fiscal problems." *State-Local Relations*, p. 136.

[20] These two "solutions" are discussed, though from a different point of view, in the chapter on the reconstruction of local government.

end of local units supporting the main portion of local activities is indefinitely postponed." Some states now realize the possibilities inherent in the grant system for avoiding these undesirable results. Thus the Pennsylvania system of school aids is based upon a teaching unit large enough to discourage, in all but exceptional cases, the perpetuation of excessively small districts—final determination of the validity of such exceptions to be made by the State Council of Education.[21] The New York law is drawn with the same end in view and may be assumed to have been responsible in part for a notable reduction in the number of very small districts operating schools. In Illinois, "except by special permission of both county and state superintendents, districts of small attendance may not receive state aid to continue operation. Unless the permit is granted, the pupil requirements are raised so that by 1953 the small high school must average fifteen attendance pupils per grade offered in the high school course, and by 1953 the elementary school must have at least fifteen pupils in order to receive state aid." [22]

State Grants and Local Self-government

The states, of course, do not share taxes or make grants to local governments without attaching conditions as prerequisite to receiving such grants. Even shared taxes are now very rarely returned without the attaching of conditions, even though this procedure may be inconsistent with the original theory; in the case of grants-in-aid, there is no pretense that the locality is free to spend them as it will.[23] Thus there arises another dilemma created by the financial inadequacy of the local unit. That dilemma may be stated thus: money given to local units without conditions governing its use has always led to extravagant spending, has not relieved the burden of the property tax, and has not contributed to a desirable equalization in the quality and quantity of services among the various parts of the state. On the other hand, the attachment of conditions to be met by the local units means inevitably the cutting down of local discretion and the growth of state supervision of the function

---

[21] *State-Local Relations,* p. 136; the Pennsylvania legislation is found in Act No. 515, 1947, and Act No. 536, 1949.

[22] *State Aid for Common Schools in Illinois* (Research Department, Illinois Education Association, Springfield, 1949), p. 4.

[23] The proportion of unspecified aid is shrinking. In 1925, "20 per cent of total state aid was unspecified. In contrast, unspecified aid for the selected years 1932, 1937, 1939, 1941, and 1944 varied between 10 per cent and 15 per cent of total aid." *State-Local Relations,* p. 69.

aided. This leads directly to what we call centralization. The larger the grants, the more pronounced this tendency will be, for, as the sums grow, the state will control a larger and larger share of the revenue at the disposal of the local authorities. The direct control may extend at present to only a relatively small portion of the local budget; the indirect control may cover a much larger part of it, since to these grants must be added such mandatory expenditures as the cost of the courts, the statutory salaries of local officers, and election expenses over which the local government has no power.

The simplest condition which the state may attach to its grant of funds is to earmark them for a special purpose, leaving the actual manner of expenditure to be decided by local officials. Beyond this there may be found a great variety of requirements imposed by different states, extending all the way from merely nominal ones to quite drastic controls. There would seem to be no limit to the purposes that may be accomplished by the use of state aid except the lack of ingenuity of legislators and administrators. In the case of highways, while many states do little more than earmark shared taxes and grants, there is a growing tendency to use both as a means of extending central supervision. In many states the approval of the state highway department is required before local plans may be carried out. It is significant that almost all recent investigations have led to recommendations for a greater degree of state control over local construction and maintenance. Grants for health work are not as yet greatly developed and those now existing do not fall into any well-defined pattern. Centralizing trends appear, however, in the practice of requiring localities to match the state grant, in state approval of local programs, and in the state's control over the appointment, quality, and training of local personnel. Matching may, as a matter of fact, imply a good deal of central influence, since the state grant may stimulate the locality to a point which it would not reach if state aid were not available, and since such aid is usually not forthcoming at all unless certain conditions are met locally with respect to the spending of all the fund, whether state or local as to its source.

STATE GRANTS AND STATE FISCAL CONTROL

With the steady growth in state assistance to localities either through shared taxes or through grants, it has become necessary to consider the desirability of possible controls to prevent local extravagance and to insure the proper expenditure of state funds. If the state is in any sense the guardian of the general interest, it must be noted that whatever controls are set up cannot be confined simply to that share of the local budget derived from the state treasury. This is true because grants from the state have had, in part at least, as their object the relief of local property taxpayers. As one able student puts it: "Only through fiscal controls correlating state assistance with property tax relief may actual tax reductions be effected. Obviously the greatest local tax relief will accrue from controls exercised over expenditures, indebtedness, and local budgetary practice and, insofar as the political considerations surrounding local autonomy will permit, from reorganization of local government and the reallocation of functions between local units and between local units and the state." [24]

Suggestions of the sort embodied in this quotation are examined elsewhere. At this point, it is only necessary to say that they probably indicate very adequately the pattern into which state-local relationships will tend to fall in the future. Indeed all of them have been experimented with somewhere, and most of them are being discussed wherever local government and administration are seriously investigated. Whether any reform embodying state controls, internal reorganization, larger areas, and functional reallocation can ever be very generally introduced would seem extremely doubtful. The variables in the problem are so numerous and so resistant to exact analysis and estimate as to make any sort of prophecy very dangerous. What is most needed, of course, is a greater degree of flexibility in the relationships among the various small local units on the one hand, and between these and the state on the other, as a necessary basis for experiments in widening administrative areas and in distributing state aids. Almost everything, furthermore, depends upon the actual strength of popular belief in "local autonomy." Very frequently this is simply a symbol used to lend apparent justification to the desires of vested interests, but whatever its nature the phenomena associated with it can be depended upon to be serious obstacles to the rational treatment of the problems of local-state relations.

---

[24] R. J. Hinckley, *State Grants-in-Aid,* p. 59. The problem, however, involves more than state-local relations for, as is pointed out in the report, *State-Local Relations,* previously cited, "a complete solution to the problem [i.e. the disparity of wealth between states] can not be found within the framework of state-local relationships; rather it must be sought in new and expanded financial programs stemming from the Federal government." P. 86.

STATE-LOCAL FINANCE IN A TRANSITION PERIOD

The set of rather complicated relationships growing out of the use of locally shared taxes and grants-in-aid is a perfectly normal development in a political system such as ours, in which we are still groping for an answer to the question of what is the proper administrative area. Logically, this question should be answered by the transfer to the state of both the support and the administration of those functions of more than strictly local interest. But government is not a matter of logic, and, because of this, few if any political systems have the degree of flexibility which such a transfer of power implies. The most illogical element in the problem is the persistence of the desire for home rule, which has a powerful emotional appeal. This feeling for the locality is a most important part of the psychology of Jeffersonian democracy. This philosophy was constructed to fit a society of small landed proprietors, each in charge of an almost self-sufficient family undertaking. In a society of this kind, the prevailing political subdivisions may be regarded simply as the isolated farm enterprise writ large, the rural neighborhood institutionalized. To put it another way, the decentralized system of government with its wide distribution of powers and its emphasis upon checks and balances reflected more adequately than any other the universal belief in the virtues of individualism and self-help. Against this background of theory and practice, it is clear that such devices as the sharing of state-administered taxes and the grant-in-aid are only blundering efforts on the part of locally chosen legislators to effect a compromise between the demands of local groups for the preservation of an individualistic society, and the insistent requirements of modern administration for larger areas, greater uniformity, and central control.

From still another point of view, the state-local system of finance illustrates the politics of the second best. For many years now, there has been an almost unanimous agreement among students that our whole tax system needs thoroughgoing revision. There is ample evidence of this in the widespread discussion of so-called "model" systems of taxation and in the growing consciousness of the existence of conflicts in taxation and of multiple taxation. Even if there were no vested interests to contend with, the technical difficulties involved in revamping a tax system are formidable. We need not wonder that legislators have refused to tackle such an enterprise but have preferred to go at it piecemeal. Hence the resort to tax-sharing and to grants-in-aid may be regarded as a half-conscious recognition by legislatures of the complexities in which the transition from a rural to an industrial and urban economy has involved us. They indicate also the unwillingness or inability of lawmakers to face the implications of this transition for the traditional tax system. Thus rural legislators, who, it is to be remembered, dominate even now in most of our states, although in theory opposed to central control and to new taxes, will nevertheless vote to increase such taxes as those on incomes, inheritances, and corporations, even when these taxes strengthen the central government, if the districts they represent are guaranteed a "cut" of the proceeds. Far from being ashamed of representing "pauper" areas, such men, when on the stump, frequently justify their votes by quoting figures showing how much more their constituencies received for roads and schools than they actually contributed to the state treasury. The excess appears to be drawn, as indeed it is, from the urban motorist, the holders of intangible property, and the city "slickers" generally.[25] Again, these types of financial aid are seen to be normal developments in a system such as ours, since they represent a workable answer to a problem to which a "logical" solution is not yet possible.

Even though an "ideal" fiscal system would undoubtedly involve federal as well as state and local taxing and budget procedures, any such "solution" will be, for the foreseeable future, beyond the limits of the politically feasible. Until and unless such a Utopian day dawns, adjustments will have to be made within the individual states. In this connection, one of our wisest and most experienced state financial administrators recently made this prediction: "It would seem obvious that the present system of grants and aids, even though in existence for many years, is still embryonic in the solution of the problem of state assistance to communities in need. The day is soon to dawn when every single state will realize that it has a need to watch out for the dollars of its citizens, regardless of the channels through which they flow, and that expenditures should be made with consideration for all of the citizens whether the state expends, the political subdivisions spend, or the state and the political subdivi-

---

[25] It is only fair to add, of course, that city-dwellers find numerous causes for resentment against the farmer. Consider the antagonism of New York City toward upstate legislators, urban flouting of prohibition as a tyranny born in the backwoods, and the opposition of the industrial centers to the processing taxes under the Agricultural Adjustment Act of 1933.

sions working jointly spend, so that while the revenues will be taken from all the citizens there will be an assurance that the distribution through expenditures will be to the benefit of all within the confines of the state." [26]

There is one further consideration. The types of control which are coming to accompany state aid are of the flexible administrative kind, rather than the more rigid legislative supervision embodied in statutes. It may perhaps be expected that such controls will be more sturdily resisted by the rural population than is likely to be the case with city-dwellers. After all there is a clearness about the statute, a certain appearance of finality, a kind of assurance of certainty, and a guarantee that the *status quo* will not be disturbed without adequate notice; while the ruling of an administrative officer has some of the attributes of a ukase from an inaccessible and irresponsible authority. Again, as pointed out by Holcombe, one of the leading characteristics of the "rustic administrative system" has been "a settled tradition of political interference with the administration of public business." [27] This interference is not necessarily to be interpreted in terms of partisan politics; it is, in fact, a good deal less political in that sense than it is in cities where party organization is much more rigid. It consists rather in emphasis upon neighborliness and friendship to the neglect of efficiency in the conduct of government. If John Smith has lost a leg, it is a decent thing to do to elect him county auditor, although he is a bit weak in his bookkeeping; it is a human thing to take care of the widows and other survivors of one's neighbors by appointments in the county service, even if their qualifications are not quite up to the standard prescribed by the state department. Countless investigations of local government business practices have shown that the spirit if not the letter of the statutes is violated, not in order that officials may profit personally, but so that someone who needs help may be favored by a "generous" interpretation of the law. In an environment where such attitudes are normal, it is difficult to make popular the sort of standards likely to be worked out by state administrators, who after all too often deal with the concrete public at a distance. Again, it must be remembered that village and rural society is self-conscious, homogeneous, and well knit, and likes to think of itself at any rate

---

[26] Henry F. Long (Commissioner of Taxation and Corporations, Massachusetts), "The State and Its Political Subdivisions," **18** *State Government* 62 (Apr. 1945).

[27] Arthur N. Holcombe, *The New Party Politics,* p. 130.

as self-sufficient. State agents sent to it to supervise the work of locally chosen administrative officers will probably be regarded with the suspicion reserved for all strangers. The very fact that they are sent with instructions to watch local officeholders carries the implication that the home talent is unequal in skill, an implication certain to be resented with an almost personal animus. The fact that the central representative shows himself expert in his knowledge of the statutes, far from helping him to become popular, is likely to count against him. The well-informed and competent man may be looked upon in a rural community as dangerous. Under conditions as they exist in rural America, "honest" men, "trustworthy" men, and men of "common sense" are usually preferred to the expert, whose very competence makes him incomprehensible to the average man and therefore brings him under suspicion. Every system of central control must be worked out with these considerations in mind.

It is fair to conclude, then, that the fiscal devices considered here are normal in a transitional period characterized by a high degree of tentativeness. Whether these decisions will, when the next period of relative equilibrium is reached, be swallowed up in a more coherent system depends upon the settlement of those larger issues involved in the change from the rustic to the urban politics of the future. The traditional system of taxation and administration in the United States was given its form when our society was overwhelmingly agrarian. It persists in an age when the creative forces in our national life are urban and industrial. It would not seem rash to predict that in the end these new forces will find political and administrative forms more consistent with their nature. For a considerable time to come the rural point of view will be too strong to be entirely ignored. It will have on its side constitutional and legal safeguards such as those securing it a disproportionate representation in state legislatures. A recalcitrant individualism will long persist as a powerful obstacle to the collectivist drift in policy. But this point of view has had its day and made its contribution, and the system of local government which grew out of it will give way to one more in harmony with the new age.

The Evolution of a New Pattern

The development of a state-local system of fiscal relationships has been the result of two factors. In the first place, the localities have traditionally performed the more costly functions of government—highway construction, schooling, welfare, and protection of persons and property—but have in most states operated under more or less restrictive tax and debt limits. In the second place, the states, though responsible for a limited number of less expensive functions, have a very much greater capacity for raising revenue. Out of this situation arose a demand for tax-sharing and grants-in-aid, with the result that nearly all of the functions once in the hands of local units are now jointly financed and jointly administered. This situation may be regarded as permanent, and the demands occasionally heard that these functions be returned to the localities may be dismissed as uninformed and completely unrealistic. The importance of state funds in the pattern of local expenditures was firmly established during the depression of the 1930's. Following this period local expenditures rose more rapidly than locally controlled revenues, and the dependence of the localities on the states has increased rather than decreased. The present situation is thus described by the Council of State Governments: "The business of state and local governments is a joint business. Virtually every major function these governments perform is a shared function. Localities are dependent upon states for enabling legislation, the provision of certain funds, the establishment of standards, and many other services. States are dependent upon localities for the efficient operation of a multitude of functions. The two levels of government have a complete mutuality of interests in serving the same population. . . .

"It is clear, nevertheless, that primary responsibility for a well-ordered system of state-local relations rests with the state governments. This responsibility springs principally from two facts: first, except for constitutional guarantees, the states are legal masters of local government; second, the states are superior to the localities in their ability to raise revenues." [28]

It is clear, then, on any showing, that the capacity of the states to support state-local functions is much greater than that of their local units. Although this is true of states *generally,* it does not follow that *all* states are able to assist their localities to the same degree. This results from the fact that the states vary greatly among themselves in wealth and, hence, in tax-raising ability, so that the poorest

---

[28] *State-Local Relations,* p. 8. In 1942 the localities collected about one-half of all state-local revenues, but disbursed approximately two-thirds of all state-local expenditures. The difference was made up by state aid. State debts are only about one-sixth those of local units and are being retired twice as fast. Between 1926 and 1942 the states increased their tax yields thirteen times as rapidly as the localities. *Ibid.,* p. 56.

states cannot support either the quantity or the quality of public services generally regarded as desirable. From this point of view, fiscal capacity is best measured by the per capita income of the inhabitants. Using this basis we find that in 1945 the per capita income of Mississippi was $556 and in New York $1,595. With the best will in the world, then, Mississippi cannot assist its local units to anywhere near the extent possible in New York. In other words, the greater fiscal capacity of the states is only a relative matter and, for that reason, a solution to the problem of equalizing the amount and quality of functions cannot be found within the framework of state-local relationships alone.

The evolving pattern of fiscal relationships has federal as well as state and local elements. Some idea as to the extent in which all three levels of government are involved in state and local finances is gained by examining figures as to the transfer of funds—a major method nowadays of balancing state and local budgets. In 1948, 14 per cent of the general revenue of the forty-eight states consisted of grants from the federal government. In the same year 30.5 per cent of general state expenditures was in the form of aids paid to local governments. This latter sum made up at least a quarter of all local revenues. Stated in dollars, federal aid to states amounted to $1,960,-114,000 in 1950, while state aid to localities came to $4,011,471,000. It is evident from these figures that state-aid to local units does not represent merely a transfer of funds given by the federal government to the states. The facts are not nearly so simple. Federal aid to the states exceeds state aid to the local units only with respect to public welfare and public health; in all the other areas state aid is greatly in excess of federal aid. But in the case of nearly all the federal grants a portion of the money, though passing through the state treasury, is expended by local officials with more or less supervision by the state departments involved.

A close examination of the administration of the functions aided would show an interfusing of state and federal influences at the local level. We have, in reality, a federal-state-local system of financing and administering most of the traditional local functions, and the relationships thus established are not likely to be dissolved. In fact, the states will not be able to realize their highest capacity in assisting localities unless, among other things, they become successful in acting as channels for distributing federal aid to the localities. For, just as the states are superior to the local units in their ability to raise revenue, so the revenue-raising ability of the federal government is greater than that of the states. This fact is of primary importance in connection with the business cycle. In periods of depression, the state and local governments, precisely because of their relatively smaller ability to raise revenue, are compelled to restrict functions —such as relief—at the very time when expansion is needed; whereas the federal government, with its enormously greater resources is in a position to assist the subordinate units in maintaining essential services. All of this amounts to saying that the economy is a national one and that fiscal arrangements are being adjusted to that fact. There are no longer state functions, local functions, and national functions, with appropriate sources of supporting revenues; there are simply *governmental* functions financed by levies upon the product of a national economy and administered cooperatively by all three levels of government.

It is much too early to assess the importance of these developments. Some things, however, seem already fairly clear. If it is now necessary to speak of *federal-state-local,* instead of local, functions, it does not follow that the new pattern of relations involves necessarily a weakening of local government. Paradoxically, quite the opposite seems to be true. The effect of state and federal aid in such fields as welfare and public health has been to put new life into units long considered moribund. Furthermore, while federal and state grants are not made without restrictions, controls have not been rigid, and ample opportunity has been preserved for the participation of local people. Finally, it is not too much to say that the more ample support made possible by grants-in-aid has brought to many local governments for the first time in their history an acquaintance with modern standards and methods of public administration which augurs well for the future of local self-government.

CHAPTER 8

Police and Justice

CRIME IN RURAL AREAS

Any discussion of present police services in rural areas becomes intelligible only if we understand the nature of the crime problem in the country. We are generally familiar with urban crime and the conditions which have made it a pressing problem. The concentration of population in metropolitan centers multiplies human contacts and gives rise to a certain amount of disorder under the best conditions; the existence of great wealth side by side with abject poverty increases the temptation to the less fortunate to assail the property of the more prudent or lucky; a mixture of races and religions imperfectly assimilated halts the formation of steadying traditions of orderly cooperation; while all those individual and social causes predisposing to a career of crime seem to operate with peculiar intensity in the urban environment.

In rural areas the "crime problem," such as it is, is not compounded of such elements, though some of them are present even there. Originally the disorder existing in other than urban areas consisted very largely of disputes over land boundaries, occasional tavern brawls, very rarely a highway or a postoffice robbery and, at long intervals, a murder.[1] Communities were well-knit, property

---

[1] Clarence Webster says, with reference to his portion of rural New England: "A few minor thefts and assorted misdemeanors of little importance are the extent of the town's crimes, except for acts of violence and sex. Every year or so an angry man strikes another a harder blow than he expected to strike, or some degenerate kills his wench, or a solitary farmer is beaten to death for the money he is supposed to be hiding. Such crimes of violence are not dealt with by the town; instead, a highly efficient state police steps in and sees that justice is done. Because of this and because any one town seldom has a murder more than once in half a century, we do not think of this crime as part of the real life of the community. Rather it is some strange phenomenon that visits us every so often." *Town Meeting Country* (1945), p. 218. Quoted with the permission of the publishers, Duell, Sloane and Pearce. Bruce Smith, however, states that there is some evidence that crimes against the person are now as frequent in the country as in the cities and that rural crime rates generally may be approaching those of urban areas. *Police Systems in the United States*, rev. ed. (1949), p. 34.

160

was fairly evenly distributed, want was almost unknown, and petty thievery was comparatively rare. And, of course, the more refined types of theft that are involved in various questionable devices of corporate finance were unknown until rather recently. The "gold brick artist" who once preyed upon the "hicks" was a transparently simple figure in contrast with the "investment" underwriter and financial prestidigitator of a gaudier era. As everyone who has read Dickens knows, life in cities a century ago had its vicious elements as it has today; this viciousness did not, however, spread to the country; and the present machinery in the country for the detection of criminals was evolved to meet the type of crime most prevalent; it has very largely stood still in spite of important changes in the equipment and operating methods of the criminal.

It is significant of the way in which the rural sections of the country are being swept into an urbanized world to note how the character of the rural crime problem has changed within recent years. The *professional* criminal is still a product of the city, but improved highways and the automobile have made it possible for him to transfer his operations to the open country and the small town, while making the large city his "hideout." "Every farmer's house and every crossroads general store and postoffice . . . is today only about one-eighth as far from the great city as it was twenty or twenty-five years ago." [2] Country store and bank robberies are eloquent testimony to the greater mobility of the criminal and, at the same time, evidence of the inadequacy of rural police protection.[3]

---

[2] Bruce Smith, *The State Police*, p. 9. ". . . a vast net work of improved highways and the well-nigh universal use of the motor car brought about an interchange of population which made its influence felt in all parts of the land. These new facilities virtually destroyed some of the spatial factors which hitherto had operated to distinguish rural from urban life. Coincident with such developments, there has come an expansion of manufacturing in rural areas so that 'at present some 4000 small centers of industry hold a population of approximately 4,000,000 persons who are in the country but not of it.'" Bruce Smith, *Rural Crime Control*, pp. 14-15. In preparing this chapter the author has drawn heavily upon this excellent study. This and the other quotations are used with permission of the author.

[3] In Ch. I of Smith's *Rural Crime Control* may be found an analysis of such data as exist bearing upon the growth of certain types of crime in rural communities. The figures given are, however, too fragmentary to warrant any safe conclusions as to the increasing prevalence of crime generally. There is a general discussion of crime in rural areas in P. Sorokin and C. C. Zimmerman, *Principles of Rural-Urban Sociology*, pp. 378-401. It is the conclusion of these writers that "rural or agricultural criminality, . . . is somewhat lower than that of the urban population as a whole, or those of the majority of the large occupational class with the exception of the professional and official groups." It is significant, perhaps, that such a comprehensive study as Kolb and Brunner, *A Study of Rural Society* (1946), contains only brief and incidental references to rural crime and delinquency.

In less obvious ways the city and the country have been brought closer together in the matter of crime. A recent report of the New York Crime Commission stated that while there was little professional crime in the rural counties of the state, little murder, and no alliance between officials and criminals, there nevertheless was a crime problem even in the country. The problem, said the commission, involved the "checking of tendencies towards delinquency. It is the problem of preventing that disintegration of character and of habits of respecting law and order that creates the soil in which criminal tendencies may grow." [4] This statement is supported by the data assembled by numerous surveys of social conditions in the rural portions of many of our states. There is, for example, an imposing body of evidence pointing to the decay of such traditional agencies of social control as the church, the family, and local community opinion. The decline of agriculture as an industry and the coming of good highways and the automobile have been forces making for the disintegration of those institutions which formerly performed a valuable service in supervising and controlling the conduct of members of a unified community.[5] On the other hand, positive agencies for counteracting such developments have scarcely shown themselves in the typical rural area. We are told very frequently that the curriculum of the rural school is ill-adapted to the needs of the children served, that recreational facilities are almost nonexistent, that social welfare programs are almost unknown, and that such institutions as the juvenile court are still in the future. In summary, the rural crime problem involves two situations: more or less frequent raids by the city-trained professional criminal upon the countryside; and the progressive disintegration of those agencies which have long stood as barriers against the forces making for delinquency. The second of these, if susceptible to treatment at all, may

---

[4] *Report of the (N. Y.) Crime Commission* (1930), pp. 198-199.

[5] "It is not too much to say that the suppression of rural crime has become a task of the first magnitude, which now challenges the attention of the rural sociologist, the justice official, and the student of public administration. The fundamentals of rural life are changing almost from day to day. A large and important part of our open countryside is undergoing a revolution in certain social, economic and political aspects. Extensive areas, without becoming cities in themselves, have acquired many of the characteristics of urban development. This process originated in improved transportation, the decline of agriculture, the rise of new industries in small towns and hamlets, and the flux of an heterogeneous population which has been drawn from the cities to the land and to its mills, its forests, and its mines. The commission of certain types of criminal acts appears to have been stimulated by such unsettling changes." Bruce Smith, *Rural Crime Control*, pp. vi, viii. It must be said, however, that the concrete evidence to support this general statement is as yet very sparse.

perhaps best be coped with by those preventive and therapeutic devices discussed under the heading of social welfare. The first demands repressive treatment by such devices of police and punitive justice as we have been able to develop. It is to these latter that we now turn.

* THE OFFICE OF SHERIFF

As soon as those acts which we now call crimes ceased to be regarded as merely private wrongs, and central government in early England ceased to rely upon informal community organization for the prosecution of wrongdoers, we discover the rudimentary beginnings of what we call a police system. Indeed, the germ of an officialism for the performance of police functions is met with in such devices as the tithingmen of Saxon days. However, the setting apart of certain men directly charged with the responsibility of keeping order and catching criminals did not take place until about the time of the development of the grand jury's present functions and the gradual decay of the old notion that the inhabitants of the county were as a body responsible for misdemeanors within its borders. The executive officer who became the representative of this changed point of view was the sheriff. The creation and success of this officer represent the final dominance of the centralized English monarchy over the feudal system of the early middle ages.

Prior to the Norman Conquest in 1066 the government of the English shire was to all intents and purposes under the control of the local lord or earl. This official was the military and civil chief in his county, dealing as an equal with the earls of neighboring shires and even with the early kings themselves. The existence of such a powerful local potentate was, of course, a standing threat to the universal supremacy which the Norman and Plantagenet kings set out to establish. The ties of allegiance by which local subjects were bound to the earls had to be broken, and an arrangement set up by which men everywhere should acknowledge the complete supremacy of the king. The instrument for accomplishing this change was the shire reeve or sheriff. Owing his appointment solely to the king and recognizing no local obligations, he entered the central administration as the open rival of the earls and succeeded eventually in destroying their power and influence in the shires. The sheriff came to be looked upon as the king's direct representative in the locality, discharging a great variety of functions pertaining to financial, judicial, and military affairs. Thus, he was active in the collection of taxes, in summoning and equipping troops, in serving various legal writs, in providing quarters for the royal court when it sat in the county, in summoning jurors, in executing the orders of the court, and in the maintenance of the jail and the care of the prisoners. With the passage of time the statutes conferred upon the holder of the office a formidable list of powers and duties, most of which, however, referred to one or another of those listed above. When the office was fully developed, its holder was an extremely important personage in his county, not only by virtue of the variety and importance of his duties, but even more so because he was the king's representative and a channel of communication between the central government and the local population.

Although by no means as important or as resplendent a personage in England now as he was in the sixteenth and seventeenth centuries, the office as we have known it here was introduced before its decline in the home country, and continues to this day with many of its historic functions—on paper, at least.[6] It exists as a county office in every state in the Union and is elective by the people everywhere, except in Rhode Island, for a term of two or four years.[7] In some states the sheriff is ineligible to succeed himself, a provision which has a good deal to do with his ineffectiveness as a police officer. In nearly every state the formal qualifications go no further than requirements as to age, local residence, citizenship, and possession of the privilege of voting. None of these, of course, has any value from the professional point of view. In practice the sheriff is a very commonplace character, the occupants of the office being drawn from the various occupations of the village or open country—farmers, storekeepers, butchers, carpenters, and so on. Surely the sheriff has come down in the social scale when we compare him with his medieval predecessor.[8]

---

[6] For the early history of the office in the American colonies see Cyrus H. Karraker, *The Seventeenth Century Sheriff* (1930).

[7] In Rhode Island election is by the general assembly. In thirty-eight states appointment is forbidden by the constitution. This is of obvious importance in its bearing upon the possibility of making the sheriff a professional police officer.

[8] "The average sheriff in Indiana is a married man, forty-eight years of age; he did not attend school beyond the eighth grade; his previous occupation was farming; he has been a sheriff not more than three years; he did not have any previous law enforcement experience. His annual salary is approximately $1,700 a year and he is certain that he will lose his job if the political party in power is defeated." *Report of the Indiana State Committee on Governmental Economy* (1935), p. 390; see also the *Missouri Crime Survey*, p. 65, for a list of sheriffs' occupations in that state, and Bruce Smith, *Police Systems in the United States*, rev. ed. (1949), pp. 81-89.

It is desirable to set down in summary form the powers and functions of the office before attempting to deal with the sheriff's work
as a law enforcement officer. "His important duties are usually the
service of writs and processes for the courts, executing court decrees
and maintaining the peace within the county. He may also attend
court as a bailiff, keep the jail, assist at elections, and collect taxes.
In no one county will he be discovered performing all these functions, but they are all a part of the duties of some sheriff somewhere." [9] It is obvious that most of these duties are of a civil nature
and not at all related to the business of preventing crime or appre-
hending criminals. And it is easy to infer from this fact that the
office ought perhaps to be abolished or at any rate seriously re-
formed. This would no doubt be a sound inference if government
were a matter of rational choices. Those who would either abolish
or reform, however, forget to consider that, politically speaking, the
sheriff normally occupies an almost impregnable position. There
is usually a fair salary attached to the office and this is supplemented
by various perquisites and fees which make it quite a "good thing"
for its holder. If the sheriff is the keeper of the county jail, as is normally the case, he has the appointment of a turnkey or two and a
matron.[10] These posts are frequently given to relatives of the sheriff and instances are not unknown in which they are held by members
of his immediate family. Moreover, if the sheriff can feed the prisoners in his care for less than the daily amount allowed by the
statutes—a feat which he does not find it hard to manage—the difference, in the language of the craft, is "velvet." In addition to these
"pickings," the statutes usually provide fees for the service of writs
and processes, and make liberal allowance for mileage for all official
travel within or outside the county.[11] In view of these facts, it is

---

[9] *National Commission on Law Observance and Law Enforcement* (Wickersham
Commission), No. 14 (Report on Police), pp. 128-129.

[10] In addition to these, the variety of his duties requires the sheriff in some cases
to employ deputies who are often paid by the sheriff out of his own pocket, which
means that he is compelled to get cheap help who thus become the victims of our
attempt to run the office on what amounts to a commercial basis.

[11] In many counties the post of sheriff is easily the most lucrative in the county,
when account is taken of the perquisites of office. "Cashing in" on these extras must
often require the possession of an India-rubber conscience. "In one county a reliable
investigation indicated that the cost of feeding a prisoner was eight cents a day while
the sheriff received forty-five. In many counties the sheriff is permitted, either directly
or through concessionaires, to sell special articles of food, tobacco, or other luxuries to
prisoners. He is thus permitted to starve them to the point where they or their friends
purchase food to supplement the daily ration. He thus enjoys the extraordinary privilege of reaping a profit not only from starvation but from the relief of starvation."
Raymond Moley, "The Sheriff and the Constable," *Annals*, vol. CXLVI, No. 235, p. 31.

well within the truth to say that the office is normally one which becomes "the aim and ambition of the rising politician rather than the
opportunity for service of the man genuinely interested in the administration of the law." [12]

The purely civil functions of the sheriff leave him very little time
to perform the police duties which are attached to his office, while
the fee system is admirably designed to turn his attention away from
the work of law enforcement. However, he is still recognized as the
only police functionary in the vast majority of rural counties. As
such he has the usual powers of a police officer and is assisted by
deputies whom he appoints. In addition he retains the ancient authority to raise "the power of the county" by calling on citizens to
join in the search for wrongdoers. The slightest observation, however, is enough to convince anyone that the office is poorly organized
for police work. In reality we have retained a medieval functionary
with almost unchanged status and powers to cope with a criminal
class which has completely mechanized itself and taken full advantage of every improvement in transportation and communication.[13]
The sheriff has remained elective while every other important police
officer in the world is now appointed. His direct and intimate connection with local politics discourages any idea he might have to be
more active in police work, while his relatively short term and his
frequent ineligibility to succeed himself prevent the acquisition of
enough skill to convert the office into an effective one for law enforcement work. And there is little hope of turning his force of deputies
into a real constabulary. Appointment of deputies is liable to be
made for political reasons and, in any event, such a group is likely to
be too small to warrant special training. In short, any force under an

---

[12] Raymond Moley in the *Missouri Crime Survey*, pp. 73-76. In speaking of the
commercial nature of the office Kilpatrick remarks that "the prisoner is victimized by
being made the object of profit-making by the entire sheriff's office; the sheriff is victimized by being compelled to enter the restaurant business to earn a salary for his
position. The public is victimized by a disguised salary method that puts a premium
upon the sheriff's ability as a farmer and cook to the neglect of preserving the peace."
Wylie Kilpatrick, *Problems in Contemporary County Government*, p. 488.

[13] The discrepancy between the equipment of the criminal and that of local peace
officers is strikingly put by the Montana State Crime Commission in its report issued
in 1930: "There are at times veritable reigns of terror along our main automobile
highways due to the influx of desperate and experienced criminals who commit many
crimes of violence and are beyond detention and detection before the forces of the
law can get into operation. Our inexperienced and untrained county sheriffs and deputies are ill-prepared to combat such situations."

elective head tends to be a makeshift affair.[14] In counties which are thickly populated it is possible to create and maintain a county force, but in the vast majority of rural counties any serious attempt to meet the crime problem will probably ignore the sheriff.[15]

Although the preceding paragraphs are not, it is believed, an unfair description of the office of sheriff and its potentialities, it is only fair to point out that there are exceptions to the general rule. The sheriffs themselves, in many cases, acknowledge the shortcomings of the office and in recent years have been active in suggesting improvements. Since 1940 they have been organized in The National Sheriffs' Association which, in 1950, had a total membership of 7,000 sheriffs and deputy sheriffs, including more than half of the nation's sheriffs. In line with the tendency observable in late years in other callings, the sheriffs are attempting through their association to professionalize the office. This has involved an admission on their part of the existence of the evils set forth in this discussion. The national association lists among its objectives the abolition of the fee system of compensation and the establishment of adequate salaries for the sheriff and his deputies; the ending of per diem feeding of prisoners; the elimination of the county jail as a place of detention for juveniles, alcoholics, and mental defectives; the adoption of traffic safety and crime prevention programs; the further extension of police communication systems; and the improvement in the condition and administration of county jails. The Association also is on record as favoring the removal of constitutional provisions against sheriffs succeeding themselves in office.

On the credit side it must also be pointed out that many sheriffs'

---

[14] Bruce Smith, in *Illinois Crime Survey*, pp. 341-342. "Regardless of the extent of the territory to be patrolled the numerical strength of such forces is rarely imposing or in any sense adequate to the task, largely because they are superimposed upon the village and township police systems which are in themselves hopelessly inadequate." Smith, *Rural Crime Control*, p. 72. See also R. E. Heiges, "Good-bye to the Sheriff," **XI** *Social Science* 137 (Apr. 1936).

[15] ". . . it may confidently be stated that the sheriff's office has lost touch with all but the most elementary requirements for dealing with rural crime." Smith, *Rural Crime Control*, p. 339. In Missouri, the governor expressed the opinion in his biennial message of 1923 that the sheriffs were abject failures, since, being generally untrained in their work and locally elected, they share the common desire of mankind to offend none of their constituents. In Connecticut, while the statutes vest a good deal of potential police authority in the sheriff, "in practice these powers are not exercised and the sheriff has largely been superseded by the officers of the state police in the execution of state laws. . . . In recent times the social and official prestige of the office has declined enormously." Henry J. Faeth, *The Connecticut County* (1949), pp. 21-22.

offices do not suffer by comparison with other law-enforcing agencies. Many are well equipped with the most modern crime-detection devices, some operate their own radio stations, and many have patrol cars supplied with two-way communication sets. Efforts are also being made, sometimes in conjunction with state universities and state police agencies, to afford training to sheriffs and their deputies. In connection with such improvements and aspirations, it is not amiss to suggest that a competent and well-intentioned sheriff may often be frustrated by a tight-fisted county board which is, therefore, the villain in the piece. On the other hand, the Association is apparently committed to the election of sheriffs on the ground that such a method of choice insures home rule, although it may be doubted if the elective system is appropriate. Finally, in view of the poverty of the great majority of our rural counties, professionalization of the office may be long in coming.

The State Police

As a matter of fact, many sheriffs, when asked about their law-enforcing duties, have admitted their lack of interest in this portion of their work and their preoccupation with their civil duties. In many cases, they are willing to see their police work turned over to some sort of state organization, and this seems to be the direction in which things are moving. At present all the states have police forces of some sort. Most of these began as traffic enforcement agencies, but today only twelve are so restricted, the others having general authority to enforce state laws.[16] In those states having true police forces, the types of administrative organization vary somewhat, but the intent in all cases is to create a professional force free from direct political influence, organized on a military basis, and so distributed as to afford protection to all parts of the state. Although political influences have not been completely eliminated in managing these forces, they have not been serious, and, on the whole, the state police have had a good record in affording protection to rural areas.[17]

---

[16] It is Smith's opinion that of the state forces possessing some degree of general police authority, only about a dozen are reasonably adequate to the task. *op. cit.*, pp. 173-82. Older books still of some value are August E. Vollmer and A. E. Parker, *Crime and the State Police* (1935) and David G. Monroe, *State and Provincial Police* (1941). A recent discussion of police administration and functions is O. W. Wilson, *Police Administration* (1950).

[17] It is necessary to point out, however, that the overwhelming proportion of highways is not in the state systems, and that country roads must be patrolled, if at all, by local sheriffs.

Some opposition from local officials has been encountered from time to time, but, generally speaking, relations seem now to be harmonious, state and local forces working together cooperatively. The state police are almost universally prohibited from enforcing local ordinances, except when invited to do so, and are usually forbidden to serve civil processes.[18]

THE CONSTABLE

If the sheriff is to be condemned as a police officer, still less can be said for the constable.[19] This official has been the object of quips and jokes at least since Shakespeare's day, and to say that he still deserves them is to put it mildly. Nearly everywhere he is elected by the voters of the town or township. In spite of the relative insignificance of the office the constable has constitutional status in twenty-one states. He is not salaried but receives fees for the service of process from the court of justice of the peace to which he is attached. In many sections it is difficult to get those elected to take the qualifying oath, and nowhere can any considerable proportion of those serving be said to make a serious effort to perform police duties. On the other hand, there are numerous cases on record where alliances exist between the justice of the peace and "his" constable to waylay passing motorists and divide the resulting fines and fees. Thus, in the *Fifteenth Annual Report of the Judicial Council of Michigan,* figures are reproduced from questionnaires from 63 counties showing that of 35,800 traffic cases reported for the period 1931-36, there were only 914 dismissals. In the words of the report, "this represents 97.5 per cent of convictions. These figures would seem to suggest that most traffic cases were handled by justices who

---

[18] In Connecticut, Massachusetts, Rhode Island, New Jersey, and Delaware, sheriffs do little criminal work, either the state or contiguous local departments assuming this responsibility. One observer writes that in Connecticut the state police department has so clearly demonstrated its superiority to town constables and deputy sheriffs that more and more of the rural towns call upon it for assistance, with the result that "one may predict that the time is not distant when the state police department will have assumed . . . the major role in police work in the state." Victor A. Rapport, "The Growth and Changing Functions of the Connecticut Department of State Police," **30** *Journal of Criminal Law and Criminology* 359-369 (May-June 1939).

[19] The careful student would do well to preface a discussion of both the constable and the justice of the peace with the following remark by Bruce Smith: "Though scholars have delved for their historical roots, and have traced their development through state constitutions and statutes, though systematic knowledge of their powers and duties has been compiled with a certain amount of care, the actual work and operation of these functionaries promise to continue for a time in the dim light of uncertainty which now surrounds them." *Rural Crime Control,* p. 30.

were quite sympathetic with the enforcing officers." In short, the office under modern conditions is little short of a nuisance, and there is no valid reason why its holder should not be relieved of his police functions and reduced to the status of a factotum to the justice of the peace. With the progressive decay of the justice system and the substitution of more competent courts, this result may possibly be accomplished. The Missouri Constitution of 1945 permitted the abolition of elective constables, and statutes carrying out this provision were immediately passed for all counties except those in which St. Louis and Kansas City are located. In Virginia the office was abolished in 1942, and its duties conferred upon the sheriff.[20]

THE CORONER

Of great potential importance in the detection of criminal acts and the apprehension of criminals is the office of coroner. Though the coroner today is in many places somewhat of a joke, the office was originally one of great dignity. The king's "Crowner" had it in his charge within his county to keep records of all matters of criminal justice, to collect for the king all goods and chattels of criminals, treasure troves, shipwrecks, and royal fish.[21] He also heard appeals of felony and the confessions and abjurations of those condemned to flee the realm, and kept the records of inquests. All of these functions save the last-named have long since disappeared, but under modern conditions this one may be of great importance. The law now generally provides that the coroner shall inquire into the cause of deaths produced by accident, or where there is reason to suspect foul play, or where the deceased had not had medical attention prior to his death. The coroner, if he suspects foul play, must summon a jury, examine witnesses, seize evidence, and aid in the apprehension of the guilty party.

It is clear from this brief statement that the office is best served when its occupant has both medical and legal knowledge. A coroner

---

[20] Striking evidence of the breakdown of rural agencies is found in the development of what amount to local vigilantes in those sections of the West and Mid-West which have been the scenes of numerous bank robberies. Some of these associations, composed in part of veterans, are quasi-public bodies since their members, though armed by bankers' associations, are deputized by the sheriff. In some places these units are so effective as to have secured from the underwriters a reduction in premiums on burglary and robbery insurance.

[21] There is an amusing chapter on the coroner in Sir A. P. Herbert's *Uncommon Law.*

incompetent in the first field would be incapable of making a sensible judgment as to the cause of death, especially since murder may have been accomplished through agencies leaving no trace observable to the layman. Examinations may be required by an expert pathologist or toxicologist, yet the records are filled with verdicts made by coroners who, to put it mildly, were mere ignoramuses. The legal duties of the office, such as the examination of witnesses and the weighing of evidence, are such that only a person with some legal training can perform them efficiently. In short, a good coroner should be in some degree a medico-legal expert.

It goes without saying that few of those holding the office can lay claim to skill or training in either field.[22] In fact, the office nearly everywhere is held in something approaching contempt and, because of this public attitude, the honor of holding it is small indeed. In many counties it goes by default; in many others it ranks simply as a wizened and wormy fruit from the political plum tree, being held by a dreary succession of down-at-the-heel party water-boys. The coroner is frequently paid by fees, and his tendency to do unnecessary work to swell his compensation has led to various limitations being placed upon his total income. If the coroner is wide-awake, however, he may add to his income by discreet connections with local funeral directors. Indeed it is a lugubrious fact that in a good many counties the office is held by an undertaker who thus is in a strategic position to add to his business!

Perhaps no better summary of the shortcomings of the office can be found than that which appears in the testimony of a committee of the American Medical Association in 1945: "The practice of selecting official medical investigators by direct vote of the electorate or by some form of political patronage has led to the systematic scrapping of invaluable experience, has placed persons in office who are not only inexperienced but not infrequently incompetent as well, has predisposed to partiality in the conduct of public business, and has discouraged from entering public service the very kind of physician that should be engaged in this important type of work." [23]

---

[22] In Connecticut, where the coroner is appointed by the Superior Court, he is required to be a lawyer and is further required to leave the medical duties of the office to an appointive medical examiner. This system has given general satisfaction.

[23] See the editorial comment entitled "Coroners Are Obsolete" in **XXXVIII** *National Municipal Review* 162 (Apr. 1949). For popular accounts of the office, see James Finan and Frederic Sondern, Jr., "The Scandal of Our Blundering Coroners," *Liberty* (Nov. 1949) and P. Martin, "How Murderers Beat the Law," 222 *Saturday Evening Post* 32 (Dec. 10, 1949).

If we intend to be in earnest about meeting the problem of catching criminals, the abolition of the office of coroner would be one of our first objectives. As things stand now, physicians of the better sort do not seek the office and hold it, if drafted, only from a sense of public duty. Considering the fact that tenure of the office involves more or less close contact with the lower order of political hacks, it is not strange that there is too little of this sense of public duty to cover the three thousand counties in the Union. Since the services performed by the coroner are not often needed, except when there is suspicion of foul play, it would seem logical to abolish the office and confer its functions upon the prosecuting officer, at the same time giving him power, when necessary, to retain competent medical assistance. There has been in recent years a strong tendency to deal with the matter in this way. In New York City, Massachusetts, Maryland, Virginia, and a number of other states, the prosecutor exercises the coroner's powers and is given authority to obtain expert medical advice. In some of the up-state counties of New York, the district attorney has been made the coroner by special legislative act, and one such official wrote in 1949 that he had "taken the whole coroner function in his stride without any added cost to the county." In the state of Washington, twenty-six counties of fewer than 40,000 inhabitants combine the offices of prosecutor and coroner. Rhode Island in 1949 enacted a statute, supported by both the state medical society and the state bar association, providing for the appointment by the attorney-general of a chief medical examiner with responsibility for all autopsies and with authority to name twelve medical examiners. Changes of this sort are calculated to give some dignity to this phase of law enforcement and to attract to the public service able and self-respecting medical men.

When the public is ready to cease regarding the office of coroner as the small change of the spoils system, its duties are likely to be dealt with along such lines. However, until urbanizing influences have spread farther, little change in the office may be looked for in purely rural regions. For in these districts, though the office of coroner will doubtless continue to add its peculiar hue to the somber picture of "practical" politics, in practice it is not likely to produce the scandals associated with the comparable office in our larger cities. Its relative obscurity will long preserve it, though if there should be a universal development of state police systems, the coroner's functions might well be transferred to this body acting in conjunction with the prosecutor.[24]

THE NATURE OF PUBLIC ORDER

The fundamental and inescapable duty of all government is the preservation of order, and it requires no acumen to see that if this duty is not performed the group which government represents cannot survive. The preservation of order has been frequently discussed with an almost exclusive emphasis on the detection of malefactors and their punishment. It is perhaps natural that this is so, for the wrongdoer in a society inclined to exalt the masculine "virtues" of boldness and "nerve" is to many a romantic and glamorous figure. But in a more fundamental sense, order consists less in the doings of policemen, prosecutors, criminal juries, and jailers than we are wont to believe. It involves rather the maintenance of the machinery needed to regulate the normal business and personal contacts between men in such a way as to provide grounds for the conviction that the State, to use the language of Burke, "is not a partnership in things subservient only to the gross animal existence of a temporary and perishable nature" but "a partnership in all science, a partnership in all art, a partnership in every virtue and in all perfection." A well-ordered community is one in which men generally have this conviction and hence go about their ordinary tasks with the assurance that others will not reap where they have sown, and that what is promised will be performed. The long record of quarrels about property, stopping short of violence, is evidence of the fact that civil justice is almost as much to be desired as security against the craft and stealth and force of the criminal. When we speak of justice, then, we refer not only to the problem of law enforcement in its usual narrow sense, but to a wider notion connoting such a state of orderly social relations as we have referred to above.

As soon as the social group became self-conscious, private retaliation for injuries, civil and criminal, created an intolerable situation in which the preservation of social peace was impossible. The dis-

---

[24] Consult the article on the coroner in the *Encyclopedia of the Social Sciences* and the articles cited there. Of special value, although no longer up-to-date, are: O. T. Schultz and E. M. Morgan, "The Coroner and the Medical Examiner," *National Research Council Bulletin No. 64* (1928); Raymond Moley in the *Missouri Crime Survey*, pp. 77-110; W. F. Willoughby, *Principles of Judicial Administration*, Ch. XIII; *Reports of the (N. Y.) Crime Commission* (1927 and 1930); Bruce Smith, *Rural Crime Control*, Ch. VI.

tinction was quite early made between those offenses which were direct or potential assaults upon the general welfare—crimes in the modern sense—and those differences constantly arising between private individuals, in the peaceful adjustment of which society as a whole had a direct or indirect stake. The assertion on the part of the state of an interest in both kinds of cases laid upon it the practical obligation of providing some regular machinery to safeguard the public good and to secure whatever adjustments would commend themselves to both parties to a private quarrel. It is obviously out of place here to attempt an historical review of the development of civil and criminal jurisprudence, but a review of this sort would show that such considerations, borne in upon the consciousness of men, led to the evolution of our present legal and judicial machinery. In the field of criminal law, the state not only furnishes at public expense the facilities for trying cases, but also takes upon itself the function of prosecuting offenders against its laws. In civil cases, involving disputes between private individuals, the parties themselves present their own arguments, and the state, in return for certain fees, confines itself to providing a presumably impartial process for reaching a conclusion binding upon both parties.

In the American federal system of government, the great bulk of both civil and criminal business is handled by the courts of the states. This remains true in spite of the fact that the growth of interstate business and the steady expansion of central power have added very greatly to the work of the federal courts. The efficiency of both civil and criminal justice in this country, then, depends very largely upon the character of the machinery provided by the individual states. In theory the state's judicial system is a unit, every court and all prosecutors and other attachés being engaged in the enforcement of *state* law. In practice such unity is realized to only a slight degree.

Of the great nations of the world, the United States is the only one in which the court system is not organized on a national basis. In most foreign countries, even the lowest courts are integral parts of a national system, heading up in fact as well as in law in the national capital. In the United States not only do we have forty-nine systems of courts, but there is within each of the states a degree of decentralization which foreigners find amazing. For, in reality, it is not the state but a smaller area, generally the county, which is the actual unit for the administration of justice. This comes about because of another peculiarly American device—the local election of judges and prosecuting officers. The use of small areas was doubtless forced upon early communities by conditions of transportation and communication which made essential the decentralization of judicial as well as other types of administration. Election of judicial officers was one of the first fruits of the Jacksonian "revolution" of a century ago and reflected the democracy's suspicion of the expert as a person not likely to agree with popular dogmas about equality.

⸱ THE COURT SYSTEM: THE JUSTICE OF THE PEACE

Throughout the rural regions of most of the United States, the court in which most petty cases are disposed of is that of the Justice of the Peace. This office is of very ancient origin, having been established during the fourteenth century, although it is now possible to trace it as far back as two centuries earlier. It was originally endowed mainly with executive police functions and took over many of the duties which had previously belonged to the constable, when that office was one of great dignity. At first the justice of the peace had few judicial duties, but as time went on the powers of this sort, formerly exercised by various ancient local courts of the hundred, the manor, and the sheriff, were transferred to him and he finally came to represent, in judicial matters, the power of the centralized monarchy. From time to time, administrative duties such as the maintenance of highways, the care of the insane, the licensing of taverns, and scores of others were imposed upon the justices within each shire until, in the eighteenth and early nineteenth centuries, it may be said that they were virtually the rulers of the English shire and altogether a most influential group in the local administration. Their strictly judicial duties were always largely in the field of criminal law, their civil jurisdiction being very narrowly limited. The office was developing rapidly during the seventeenth century when it was transplanted to America by the British colonists.[25]

In colonial America the justice seems everywhere to have been an official of considerable power and a person of social eminence in

---

[25] A comprehensive act relating to justices of the peace was passed by Parliament Dec. 16, 1949. Under it the justices retain certain licensing functions in non-county boroughs. The whole system was subjected to somewhat more rigorous supervision by the central government, but the justices remain laymen though supplied with the services of justices' clerks who are required to be barristers of at least five years' standing. An interesting provision of the act is (Sec. 17) that "it shall be the duty of every magistrate's courts committee, in accordance with arrangements approved by the Lord Chancellor, to make and administer schemes providing for courses of instruction for justices of the area." The Act is Ch. 101, 12, 13 and 14 George VI.

his community. His chief duty was to preserve the peace, and this he was expected to do through the exercise of his criminal jurisdiction. Except in certain Southern states where the influence of the migrating English gentry was strongest, his purely administrative duties fell into disuse in the new environment, but that the office was viewed as one of considerable prestige is evidenced by the fact that it is provided for in all but two of the state constitutions. And, under the conditions of the pre-industrial age, the office had much to recommend it. The law was not yet developed into that morass of refinements inseparable from a varied and complex economic order, and plain men were competent to manage tribunals devoted to settling the controversies of their neighbors. Distances were vast and travel difficult; hence visits of trained judges were infrequent. Isolation bred a distrust of central authority and a suspicion of gowned experts. What was wanted was quick justice in accordance with rough and ready principles comprehended by the mass of the people. The role was adequately filled by the court of the justice of the peace. The justice himself was likely to be a man of character and vigor, known and respected by his fellow-citizens in a sparsely settled community, and expected to dispose of the cases before him quickly and fearlessly so that he and the community might get back to their proper work of earning a livelihood. Thus, Andrew Jackson was a typical frontier judge, unlearned in the law, at least in comparison with the judges on the Eastern seaboard, but possessed of a vigorous character and a willingness to enforce his decisions, if necessary, by violent measures.

At present, the justice of the peace is everywhere an elective officer chosen in and for the town, township, or similar small area, and normally for a short term. The statutes quite frequently provide for two, three, or four justices for each township, but surveys indicate that many of those elected never qualify, and that of those who do a small minority handle the great bulk of the cases. Thus a survey of twenty rural townships in Michigan in 1941-42 disclosed that 362 cases were tried in one year or about one and a half cases in each township per month. During the same period two part-time (trained) city justices in Ann Arbor disposed of 4,711 cases. Assuming this to be a full load, each of the rural townships produced judicial business averaging about 1/260 of a one-judge load. In Indiana, although it is legally possible to have as many as 3,000 justices of the peace, actually only about 450 were serving; and in 378 definitely rural townships, there were in 1939 only eighteen justices, four of whom reported no business.

The author of the Michigan survey, Professor Edson R. Sunderland, concludes that "the supposed popular demand for a justice of the peace court in every township for the convenience of the community does not exist," and that "if the county, instead of the township, were to be made the unit for these courts of limited jurisdiction, and such courts were to be located in one or more of the principal centers of rural population, the result would correspond almost exactly with the actual practice as it is now carried out in Michigan." [26] Although the law requires him to be a voter and a resident, it almost nowhere imposes any qualifications as to his learning or legal experience. The result is that many justices are ignorant men, unfit to occupy even a minor judicial post. No salary is paid, the emoluments consisting of fees assessed largely against the losing party—hence the quip that the letters J. P. stand for "justice for the plaintiff."

Although in theory the justice is a part of the judicial machinery of the state, there is almost no supervision over his doings either by the higher courts or by other local officials. Indeed justices are generally lax, to say the least, in the keeping of the reports frequently required by the statutes. Thus a survey recently conducted by the New York State Commission on the Administration of Justice revealed that fewer than twenty per cent of the 3,670 justices made any such reports. The evidence from other states makes it clear that record-keeping by the typical justice is a joke.[27]

It requires no argument to demonstrate that under urban conditions the office is an anachronism. Civil suits and criminal causes in large cities are often certain to present problems beyond the abilities of untrained laymen, for the law has not stood still though the justice of the peace system has. This situation has been met in large cities

---

[26] See *Fourth Report of Judicial Council of Michigan* (1934), p. 170; a complete study of the system made by Professor Sunderland may be found in Part II of the 15th annual report of the Council (1945). There is an excellent study of the office in Indiana, entitled *Justice of the Peace Courts in Indiana,* by Gail M. Morris, published in 1942 by the University's Bureau of Government Research. I am much indebted to Dr. Edwin B. McPheron, Director of the Bureau, for letting me see a copy of this study from the Bureau files.

[27] *Report of the (New York) Commission on the Administration of Justice,* p. 14; Paul F. Douglass, *The Justice of the Peace Courts of Hamilton County, Ohio,* pp. 61, 66; Wylie Kilpatrick, *Problems of Contemporary County Government,* p. 128; Paul W. Wager, *County Government in North Carolina,* p. 227. Very thorough audits of the accounts of trial justices are made in both Virginia and Maryland.

by the creation of municipal courts, presided over by trained lawyers and subject to the administrative control of the local council. In rural sections of the country, however, the old system exists much as it always has, and, as it actually works, it discloses many defects. In early rural America, the administration of petty justice was concerned mainly with such civil suits as arose over neighborhood squabbles, and with criminal cases likely to arise in a self-willed and brawling population. Much of the grist which comes to the mill of the justice is still of this sort, and it may well be that in more remote sections he still serves adequately. It must not be forgotten, however, "that we live in a complex commercial and industrial age which has developed a highly technical and specialized body of legal principles and enactments peculiar to a period of maturity of law. . . . It follows that the justice of the peace of today is a judicial officer having jurisdiction over a great variety of crimes and civil causes who, to exercise such a jurisdiction properly and fairly, must be able to apply judicially a great multitude of laws." [28] Many of these considerations apply with some force even to rural justices, who, wherever they have been investigated, have shown up rather badly.[29] On the civil side, all but the most simple cases are quite beyond the typical rural justice, who makes an equally sorry showing on criminal matters. Payment by fees has favored in many sections the development of what amounts to systematic extortion. Scores of motorists can testify ruefully to the thriving business done by the rural justices and their constables in arresting and fining the unwary traveler. In civil matters the lower ranks of the lawyers usually work hand in glove with the justice of the peace in the bringing of petty actions, presumably to the advantage of both "court" and counsel! In short, under all but very exceptional conditions the office comes close to being a nuisance.[30]

---

[28] Chester H. Smith, "The Justice of the Peace System in the United States," **XV** *California Law Review* 119 (1931).

[29] "No subject concerning the administration of rural justice in Virginia elicited such uniformly unfavorable comment from county officials as that of the justice of the peace. If the system, as now operated, has any supporters the survey failed to disclose them." *County Government in Virginia* (Report of the Governor's Committee on Consolidation and Simplification in Government, 1924), p. 49.

[30] On the other hand the following sensible comment of Bruce Smith should be kept in mind: "Our own association with them convinces us that stupidity and corruption are no more common among them than among their fellows in the community, that their faults and virtues are common faults and virtues, and that they possess neither in any considerable degree. They are simply what they were perhaps intended to be; lay and inexpert arms of the law, who were to function in a primitive society

Reformers, of course, have not been slow to suggest improvements in the machinery for administering petty justice. In cities magistrates are universally required to be lawyers. The fee system has been abolished and adequate staffs for the court have been provided. In the country, all of these changes, for one reason or another, are harder to accomplish. While the wider areas perhaps make necessary a larger number of courts for small causes, the expense of securing adequately trained lawyers has prevented any general remedying of the present unsatisfactory situation. However, numerous investigations indicate that under modern conditions fewer justices would do the work just as well, and in most cases relatively few of those in office are readily accessible, so that the bulk of the business, in any event, is handled by a very small proportion of those serving. In some cases, it has been proposed to abolish the office of justice of the peace and substitute for it a district court serving an area larger than the township, such court to be subject to the supervision of the judge of the general trial court in the county, or perhaps to the board of county commissioners. In 1929 the Constitution of New York was amended so as to permit county boards to create one or more districts within the county in each of which a trained lawyer would act as judge with the powers formerly possessed by the justice of the peace.[31] Under the Virginia Trial Justice Act of 1942, a trial justice is named for each of the ninety-seven counties (although in a few cases a single justice serves two counties), is required to be a lawyer, and is paid an adequate salary. In nearly half the counties the justice sits exclusively at the county seat, while in others he sits in two or more places in the county where judicial business requires. The Virginia statute did not disturb the justice of the peace system, but it did provide that no justice of the peace may exercise any jurisdiction conferred by the act upon the trial justice, and required further that all attachments, warrants, and subpoenas issued by justices

that was too busy subduing a continent to pay much heed to problems of local administration and the requirements of local justice. If the squire now appears somewhat miscast for his role, it is because the whole environment in which he functions has undergone great changes." *Rural Crime Control*, pp. 260-261.

[31] *Report of the (New York) Crime Commission* (1930), p. 85. See also H. N. Fuller, *Criminal Justice in Virginia*, pp. 173-183; *Report of the Commission on County Government to the General Assembly of Virginia* (Dec. 1931); *Report of the Commission Appointed to Consider the Question of Criminal Costs in Virginia* (1932). I am informed by the executive secretary of the Association of Towns of the State of New York and by Mr. Leonard S. Saxe, Executive Secretary of the Judicial Council, in letters dated Jan. 30 and Feb. 24, 1950, that no county has as yet adopted this plan, except Nassau which operates under a special charter.

of the peace shall be returnable before the trial justice. The new system has given general satisfaction.[32]

In most states it would be difficult to alter the office of the justice of the peace very seriously without amending the state constitution.[33] This is never an easy thing to do, and in some states the justices occupy key positions in the local party organization and are thus able largely to control the action of the local representatives in the legislature. The Missouri Constitution of 1944, however, did abolish the office, and legislation of 1945 implementing its provisions transferred their work to trained magistrates.[34] In the light of our experience, it would seem best to transfer civil work as far as possible to fewer trained magistrates and make some provision by which they might act quickly on criminal matters as well. It should certainly be reasonable to suggest, in these days of improved highways, that there is no need for six, four, or even two justices in every township.[35] "We can but say that the supposed popular demand for a justice of the peace court in every township for the convenience of the community does not exist. If the county were to be made the unit for these courts of limited jurisdiction and the courts were located in the principal centers of population, the result would correspond in many ways to the actual distribution of the justice of the peace courts at the present. This would eliminate a few isolated rural justices, but no amount of investigation has been able to prove that the social loss would be more than negligible." [36]

---

[32] *Virginia Code of 1942, Sec. 4987.* A somewhat similar system exists in Maryland, each county being served by from one to fourteen trial justices.

[33] California and Missouri are the only states in which the office of J. P. is not protected by the Constitution. In a few others the constitution specifically permits the abolition of the office.

[34] *Missouri Constitution, Art. V, Secs. 18-25* and *Schedule, Sec. 4; Missouri Laws, 1945,* p. 765. Judge Laurance M. Hyde of the Supreme Court of Missouri writes that the new magistrates' courts "are really significant courts, which will give many people who have no contact with any other courts a better impression of our judicial system." "The Missouri Plan for the Selection and Tenure of Judges," 39 *Journal of Criminal Law and Criminology* 272-287 (1948).

[35] On the history of the office of justice of the peace, consult Charles A. Beard, *The Office of Justice of the Peace in England in Its Origin and Development* (1904), and the article in the *Encyclopedia of the Social Sciences;* on the system as found in England today see Pendleton Howard, *Criminal Justice in England* (1931), Ch. V. For the situation in the United States the following may be used: W. F. Willoughby, *Principles of Judicial Administration,* Ch. XXII; Chester H. Smith, "The Justice of the Peace System in the United States," XV *California Law Review* 118-141 (1931); A. B. Butts, "The Justice of the Peace—Recent Tendencies," XXII *American Political Science Review* 946 (1928); "The Passing of the Justice of the Peace," 12 *Virginia Law Register* 110 (1926); J. W. Manning, "Kentucky Justices of the Peace," XXVII *American Political Science Review* 92 (1933).

[36] Gail M. Morris, *Justice of the Peace Courts in Indiana,* p. 26.

General Trial Courts

In most American states the district served by the court competent to try the more important civil and criminal cases is the county
or a combination of contiguous counties.[37] The judge who presides
is elected—in many cases on a partisan ballot—by the voters of the
county.[38] Although regarded as a state official, perhaps even paid
directly by the state, he is seldom under any direct supervision by
the higher judicial authorities and is, in reality, a part of the state
system only because his decisions are subject to reversal on appeal
to the state supreme court. Such judges are, therefore, in the difficult position of owing a technical responsibility to the state, the laws
of which they administer, and their offices to the local electorate.
Under ordinary conditions they are far more likely to be punished
for failure to please the voters than for failing to discharge their obligations as state officers.

Under American conditions the fault here lies by no means in
the fact that judges are elected. In the opinion of those in a position
to know, there is no evidence that appointment secures measurably
better judges than election.[39] Here as elsewhere in the field of government, the cause of our ills lies deeper than the machinery in use.
There may be a certain advantage in centering the responsibility for
judicial and other appointments in the hands of a conspicuous official
such as the governor, but it is easy to overestimate the value of such
a change. Most of our governors are politicians who suffer from a
species of agoraphobia, the most marked symptom of which is a
chronic fear of exclusion from the good things of office. If such an
official is charged with making appointments to local judicial posts,
he is likely to consult the local party panjandrums, and the net result

[37] Where the state is divided into "circuits," each comprising a number of counties,
justice is brought to the locality by having the circuit judge sit in turn at the courthouse
of each county in the circuit.

[38] Election is not universal. For example, all Massachusetts judges are appointed for
good behavior and Connecticut trial judges are chosen by the state legislature for terms
of eight years. In the latter state re-election is the rule. There is an excellent study
entitled "Selection of Judges" issued as Publication 87 by the Illinois Legislative Council
in April 1948.

[39] Thus Raymond Moley says: "Considering what the sovereign democracy compels
its judges to suffer, it is served better than it deserves. American state trial judges are,
in spite of unfortunate exceptions, a hopeful group of public servants. The observer,
as he goes from state to state, comes to recognize that, in character and common sense,
judges are the best of those in public life." *Our Criminal Courts*, pp. 256-7. As to
the relative merits of appointment and election consult the article on Judiciary by H. J.
Laski in the *Encyclopedia of the Social Sciences*.

of this plotting differs little from what it would have been had the choice been with the electorate. This is almost certain to be the case unless powerful influences operate in the opposite direction. If the bar has high standards and is well organized for expressing its point of view, a good deal may be accomplished in the way of compelling the choice of competent judges.[40] But a well-trained bar is usually the product of high community standards able in any case to influence the personnel of government. Under either system, then, our local judges are likely to be rather accurately representative of what the individual communities are able to stand for in the way of public officials, and to mirror rather faithfully the point of view of the people of their districts.[41]

[40] On this point, however, Mr. Moley has the following to say: "Those who call upon the bar to reform the administration of justice are thinking of the profession in terms of a compact little guild. The bar in America has outgrown such a conception. The vast market for legal knowledge, the interrelations of the bar and business, the ease with which legal knowledge may be acquired in many of the less rigorous law schools, and the lax conditions of admission to the bar in many states have resulted in a vast bar membership very difficult to organize as an effective unit. The ever-present conflict between the personal-injury lawyers and their opponents is a basis of disunion altogether too difficult effectively to overcome, particularly when the selection of judges is concerned." *Our Criminal Courts*, p. 254.

[41] In Missouri, trial and appellate court judges (with a few exceptions) are appointed by the governor from a list of three nominees presented by Circuit and Appellate Judicial Commissions, composed of lawyers and laymen. At the expiration of a judge's term he "runs" not against another candidate but on his own record, the electorate voting on the question: "Shall Judge ———— of the ———— Court be retained in office?" In the opinion of lawyers the Missouri plan has given general satisfaction. See William W. Crowdus, "Improvements in the Missouri Judicial System," an address before the Ohio State Bar Association, May 15, 1947. A similar plan has been in effect in California since 1934. See Charles Aikin, "A New Method of Selecting Judges in California," XXIX *American Political Science Review* 472-4 (June 1935). An interesting popular article is Mitchell Dawson, "Judging the Judges," CLXIX *Harper's Magazine* 437-448 (Sept. 1934).

CHAPTER 9

Police and Justice (continued)

THE PROSECUTOR

The judge, of course, is only a part of the judicial machinery and often, indeed, only a small part. Popular suspicion of the expert has operated in many jurisdictions to reduce him to playing the role of umpire in the intricate game played by opposing counsel, and to enlightening the jury on points of law arising in the course of a trial. Because of the general lack of public interest in private disputes between individuals, and the rather more technical nature of such proceedings, the judge has perhaps a freer hand in the conduct of civil cases. But in the trial of criminal charges he is likely to be dwarfed in the public view by the prosecutor and counsel for the defense.

The lowest court of record in every state has attached to it a prosecuting official known variously as district attorney, state's attorney, prosecuting attorney, or simply prosecutor. In the great majority of states he is elected by the people.[1] It is his duty to bring charges against all those who are suspected of offenses against the criminal law and to proceed against them at their trial as representative of the public. Where he is elected in and for a county, he usually acts also as its adviser in civil matters and handles such routine affairs as the drafting of legal papers of various sorts. These latter duties, however, are much less significant than those which he discharges in the field of criminal justice.

It is not too much to say that the prosecutor is easily the most important part of the whole machinery of law enforcement. The mere statement of his legal powers and prerogatives is sufficient to

---

[1] The office is appointive in Connecticut, Delaware, Florida, New Jersey, and Rhode Island. In 26 states the prosecutor is paid locally, in 11 wholly from state funds, and in the others partly by the state and partly by local areas of various kinds. Details may be found in John A. Fairlie and Donald F. Simpson, "Law Departments and Law Offices in the States," 14 *State Government* 237 (Oct. 1941).

demonstrate this fact. In the first place, whether or not a suspected offender shall be proceeded against is entirely within his discretion. This is true because the number of violations of law is so great in most jurisdictions that to prosecute all cases would lead to terrific congestion. Hence, someone must have discretion to decide in which instances the public interest will be served by prosecuting. To a large degree, this discretionary power is a reality even in those states where indictment is still brought by the grand jury, since laxness of the prosecutor in gathering evidence and his refusal to cooperate with that body would very seriously hamper its work. Moreover, the grand jury almost invariably accepts the recommendations of the prosecutor as to the sufficiency of evidence and the general desirability of prosecuting. After prosecution has commenced, the entire conduct of the case is in the hands of the prosecutor. By his handling of cases he may delay the process as much as he wishes, may compromise with defendants on such terms as he thinks would meet with public approval, or he may even dismiss prosecution before it is completed. Finally, he is frequently consulted by the court in assessing the penalty after conviction and later by the appropriate authorities in connection with probation, parole, or pardon.

The occupant of such a position is bound to be a person of genuine importance to society. It is not too much to say that he holds the key to the problem of law enforcement. In rural sections it is not without significance that, as one writer puts it, "he is looked upon as the protector of the public in all things having to do with the enforcement of the law. In districts where there is no real police protection it is the instinct of the citizen when he has a serious matter to report to some public authority to go to the state's attorney. The office becomes a sort of clearing house for all sorts of information about real and imagined infractions of the law and irregular practices of all sorts, and its holder a sort of keeper of the public conscience, exceeding even the judge in prestige and influence." [2] The means by which he is selected and controlled are, therefore, of more than ordinary significance.

Almost everywhere the prosecutor is elected by the district in which he acts—a county or a small group of counties. In Florida,

---

[2] W. D. Knight in *Illinois Crime Survey* pp. 250-251. See H. M. Bates, "The Story of a County Prosecutor," **XLI** *Michigan Law Review* 915-919 (Apr. 1943).

Georgia, and New Mexico he is appointed by the governor; in Connecticut, by the judges of the Superior Court. In the last-named state it is almost traditional to fill vacancies on the Superior Court by promoting state's attorneys. Although in a special sense a sworn officer of the court, he is seldom in a position to conduct his office solely for the public welfare as it is defined in the statutes. For a large part of his time he is busily engaged in making for himself a "record" on the basis of which to seek further political preferment. Hence his discretion in prosecuting cases is certain to be deeply influenced by his calculations as to the result of his action when expressed in votes. That the office is one of great strategic importance in politics is evidenced by the large number of important American politicians who found the district attorneyship the first rung on the ladder to eminence.[3]

In practice the system of prosecution reveals certain factors which by no means aid in the efficient administration of justice. Where the county is the unit, the salary, outside of a few populous counties, is likely to be too small to attract the best legal talent in the neighborhood. One result of this has been the rise of the custom of electing as prosecutor some fledgling attorney who thus secures free office space from which to conduct his private practice, if any, and a small addition to his income from other sources.[4] In other words, he learns law at the expense of the county. This training is, of course, an asset to him in his campaign for more lucrative or important public office. If he has no political ambitions, his training in office is likely sooner or later to be useful to the more or less predatory private interests in his state who are willing to pay him well for what he has learned about the mysteries of the criminal law as a paid official of the public. Moreover, the internal organization of the

---

[3] "A study of 767 lawyer governors and members of Congress showed that forty-two per cent had been prosecuting attorneys and that seventy-five per cent of these had held that office as the first in their political career." J. A. Fairlie and C. M. Kneier, *County Government and Administration,* p. 252, note 37. The names of such potent politicians as the elder LaFollette and his son, Philip, Hiram Johnson, Thomas E. Dewey, and Earl Warren will readily occur to the reader.

[4] The Michigan Crime Commission in 1930 reported that one-third of the prosecutors of that state were under thirty-five years of age and two-thirds were under forty-five. In only ten of the eighty-three counties did the annual salary equal or exceed $4,000; in seven it was less than $1,000; and in more than half it was less than $2,000. The Commission concluded that "an impartial view would seem to indicate plainly that the several counties in the state have in most cases been receiving more than they have been paying for." *Report of the Michigan Crime Commission,* p. 30.

office in a typical rural county leaves much to be desired from the standpoint of sound administration. It is seldom that the prosecutor is equipped with sufficient assistance in securing evidence against lawbreakers or with proper help in keeping the records essential to the efficient conduct of the office. The county board is usually not much interested in such matters since the expense of the prosecutor's office is a mandatory one which they are anxious to keep as low as possible. An active and honest prosecutor in a sizable county would be required to spend all his time at his official duties if he would make up for deficiencies of this sort. Unfortunately the salary offered is so small as to make it unreasonable to expect him to devote more than a moderate portion of his efforts to his purely official obligations.[5]

It is without doubt true that the great weakness of the office of prosecutor in the United States is its political character. The duty of the prosecutor is to the state; his interest lies in cultivating those who have votes. However we may gloss it over, it must be admitted that the connections between organized vice and crime and political corruption are everywhere obvious. Most American counties—and not all of them in urban areas—are under the more or less benevolent dictatorship of the local courthouse gang. Investigations without number have shown conclusively that the prosecutor is the keystone of such organizations. It lies in his discretion to set in motion the machinery of criminal justice or to ignore infractions of the law. Plausible reasons can usually be found for either course of action and he will always be able to win to his side respectable, not to say pious, pillars of the community, no matter how reprehensible his conduct may seem to the moralist. So long as the office is filled by political means, its holder is likely to discharge his functions with reference to the political forces in the community rather than to theoretical considerations as to his abstract duty to the state. The state for him is the local voters. He is the embodiment of local nul-

---

[5] It is obvious that the accurate keeping of the records of the prosecutor's office is of the utmost importance in estimating the actual prevalence of crime and the efficiency of our arrangements for handling the problem. Yet a study of Nebraska county attorneys made in 1931 by Dr. Cyril Coombs revealed that the "official" and private records of some county attorneys were kept in the same files which were all moved out together when the incumbent left the public service! The same study turned up cases in which the county board brought pressure on the attorney to frame his informations against suspects so as to avoid the penalty of a jail sentence. Such action would lower expenses and thus make possible the lowering of taxes! From an unpublished M.A. thesis in the Library of the University of Nebraska.

lification of state policy.[6] It is difficult to see any solution to this situation.

Some improvement might be expected if the area of administration were widened and if the local prosecutor were brought under some sort of effective supervision by a state official. But, on the whole, it seems that little can reasonably be expected from either change. Those active gentlemen, the party politicians, have shown considerable ingenuity in evading other attempts to prevent the prostitution of public office and will very probably continue to do so in the future. It is, after all, the purpose of local self-government in a democracy to provide the people of a locality with what they want, and those who hold office, however exalted, by popular election, are likely to find ways of circumventing any attempt to compel the active enforcement of unpopular laws. State supervising authorities are, in most cases, men who have had their training in practical politics in local areas, and they are not very prone to forget these local connections, since the vigorous performance of a sworn duty is liable to cost them political support. Hence, though the statutes of many states provide for the removal of local law officers, the powers conferred seem to be only charily used in practice.[7]

Here, as in a great number of other problems concerned with the smooth functioning of government, genuine remedies for bad conditions require more than any mere changes in machinery. It is a quite common demand on the part of certain elements that this, that, or the other function be "taken out of politics." By this slogan it is doubtless meant that the officials charged with a public responsibility should be so chosen and supervised as to make them independent of the pressure of politics in the partisan sense of that term. But there is, in reality, no mechanical way of doing this. It is useless to rail at politicians. Their art consists in the shrewd calcu-

---

[6] The dual nature of the prosecuting function is recognized by the courts. Thus the Supreme Court of Kansas: "While public prosecutions are instituted and conducted in the name of the state, the interest of the state is the general public interest. The actual burden of law enforcement in a county . . . rests chiefly on the county. Aside from the public interest in the suppression and punishment of crime, the local financial interest in sustaining a meritorious judgment of conviction is a matter of substantial concern and the board of county commissioners has authority to deal with the matter in a business way." *Heinz v. Commissioners of Shawnee County*, 12 Pac. (2nd) 816 (1932).

[7] See M. H. Satterfield, "State Appointment and Removal of Local Law Enforcement Officers," **XII** *Southwestern Social Science Quarterly* 277 (Mar. 1932); C. M. Kneier, "Some Legal Aspects of the Governor's Power to Remove Local Officers," **17** *Virginia Law Review* 355 (Feb. 1931). In only ten states are regular reports (to the state) required of prosecuting officers.

lation of the balance of political forces in a community. At a given moment they may be regarded as acting in a genuinely representative character. What they produce may not be pleasing to reformers and may be even shocking to people of extraordinarily tender sensibilities, but it is going too far to say that it is so looked upon by voters in general. After all, politics, properly understood, may be thought of as that complex of forces by which the community makes known its wishes to the maligned politicians, who are quick to realize popular wishes and extremely agile in carrying them into action. "Politics" in the "bad" sense may be defined as the use of public office for private or non-public ends. In this sense, no one can doubt that the craft is practiced by many people, because government has the power to confer or withhold benefits and to establish an artificial equality among men. Manipulation of the forces of government, whether it be through the office of prosecutor or judge or senator, has for its object the perversion of the right reason of which law is regarded as the embodiment, in order that the natural inequality may be the effective order. Public officials stand at the center of warring forces—the ideal of justice on the one hand and the belief in the rule of the strongest on the other. Good legal authority can usually be found for any proposition no matter how scandalous, and "philosophers" will always be found to defend any course of action, however immoral it may seem. This is true because men have, for the most part, little ability to think with detachment and find it natural to rationalize their own desires into rules of general application. So long as the roots of privilege are as tangled and as extensive as they are, any attempt to enforce law fearlessly and without favor is sure to be only partially successful. Officials are quite as often the victims of these common human frailties as they are the villains in the piece. It is precisely because we expect more of those vested with the power of the state that we refused to pardon them for conduct which, in business and professional men, we are often inclined to applaud.

As long as the county continues to be used as the unit of prosecution, the chances of improving matters do not appear very encouraging. Since it is too small to be able to justify full-time well-paid officials, there is little reason to look forward to the professionalization of the office. Though it has been suggested that there is as good reason for a county department of law enforcement as for a highway department, there is little to be said for this suggestion, at least as it might apply to the vast majority of rural counties. The analogy seems to be a false one, for even a poor county has far more road work to manage than it has legal work. The growth in the number of state police systems and in the scope of their functions suggests to us that most local law enforcement work may be in a transitional stage between local autonomy and state direction. Indeed, the same thing may be said with regard to most traditional local functions. And it is for this reason that it has been asserted that in rural regions a "county 'department of justice' uniting policing and prosecution appears to have little to justify it." [8] The conclusion therefore would seem to be warranted that, unless the prosecuting function can be reorganized on a district basis under the supervision of the attorney-general of the state, matters will drift on much as they have in the past. Such a reform may be forced upon us by the demonstrated weakness of present arrangements in the face of the growing efficiency of organized crime, but there is as yet little evidence that events are moving in that direction.

THE GRAND JURY

Prosecution for crimes in the United States may be initiated either by action of the grand jury or by the process known as information. Provision for the use of the grand jury in bringing indictments is found in the constitutions or laws of all of the states, though it is nowadays in most of them an alternative method to the filing of an information by the prosecuting officer.[9] It may be said generally that where it has fallen into disuse as the usual way of presenting criminals for trial, it is still retained as an instrument for the investigation of official wrongdoing or of a situation in which disorder is so widespread as to make it unwise or impracticable to rely upon the efforts of the prosecuting officer.

The grand jury is such a familiar institution, at least to the extent that we read much about its doings in the newspapers, that we are likely not to consider its real character and the part that it has

---

[8] A. C. Millspaugh, *Local Democracy and Crime Control*, p. 242. The suggestion of a county department of law enforcement is found in an article by Alfred Bettmann in the *Journal of the American Bar Association* for July 1921.

[9] In twelve states—Arizona, California, Idaho, Louisiana, Missouri, Montana, Nevada, New Mexico, Oklahoma, South Dakota, Utah, and Washington—the constitutions permit either method of accusation; and in ten—Alabama, Colorado, Illinois, Indiana, Iowa, Mississippi, Nebraska, North Dakota, South Dakota, and Wyoming—the legislature is empowered to modify or abolish the grand jury. See Herbert F. Goodrich, "Does the Bill of Rights Need Revision?" *The Annals*, Sept. 1935.

played in the development of our criminal law. Originally, the commission of what we call a crime was a matter to be dealt with by the two or more persons immediately affected by it. The laws of the Saxons in England make it very clear that wrongs which we should now call crimes were a thousand years ago considered simply as personal injuries. It was left to the injured party to obtain satisfaction from the wrongdoer. There was no feeling that what we call the "public" had any special interest in the mode of redress, probably because there was no consciousness of anything like a "public." While it is believed by some scholars that there was something very like the grand jury developing in Saxon times, its real progress dates from the reign of Henry II (1154-1189). Probably because of the disorder produced in a growing population by the private settlement of grievances, or possibly because of Henry's desire to increase the business, and thereby the revenue, of the central courts, it was provided that each county in which the judges from Westminster held court should present evildoers before the Royal Justices at their periodical visitations. This was equivalent to placing upon the body of the inhabitants, presumably in a position to know what was going on in the county, the responsibility of maintaining order by bringing suspected persons to trial before the Royal Justices. It was therefore a direct assertion of the "public" interest in a whole series of acts hitherto regarded as of significance to the principals only. It may be considered as the birth of the modern notion of a "crime." [10] Later the original idea was modified by providing that criminals should be presented for trial by a body known as the grand jury. This consisted at common law of from twelve to twenty-three persons who on their oaths accused those whom they believed guilty of crime. In other words, they acted in a representative capacity for the whole body of the inhabitants of the county and, incidentally, provided a needed protection against arbitrary prosecutions by royal officials. In all its essentials, the grand jury has come down to us as it was early developed.[11] For the greater part of its existence, it may be looked upon as a group of neighbors specially sworn as pub-

---

[10] Assize of Clarendon, 1166; this may be found in Adams and Stephens' *Select Documents in English Constitutional History*. See Mrs. J. R. Green's *Henry II;* consult article on Grand Jury in the *Encyclopedia of the Social Sciences.*

[11] Statutes, however, have reduced the number of grand jurors in some states. Thus in Montana, Oregon, and Utah only seven are required of whom five are necessary to bring an indictment. In New York the grand jury may have twenty-three members but twelve may bring in a "true bill." For details, see W. L. Morse, "A Survey of the Grand Jury System," X *Oregon Law Review* 232.

lic officials to speak before the representatives of state power as the authentic voice of the community. Or they may be regarded as a lay element in the process of maintaining order, in contrast to the expert element found in the judge and prosecutor, who, it is suspected, are likely to take a somewhat different and less charitable view of local miscreants. Whether or not the grand jury is a success in filling these roles under modern conditions is a question which will be discussed later.

THE PROCESS OF INDICTMENT

Before we can reach a judgment as to the present-day effectiveness of the grand jury, it is perhaps worth while to ask ourselves what happens when it is used as the regular means of presenting suspected persons for trial. The first step taken in the handling of a criminal case comes with the arrest. This may be made either by an officer upon his own detection of a crime or at the suit of an individual willing to accuse the wrongdoer. Following arrest the suspect has the constitutional right everywhere to be taken immediately or within a very short time before an examining magistrate to have the cause of his detention inquired into. Here the testimony heard is usually that of the officer making the arrest. If the magistrate feels that a *prima facie* case has been made out, he may hold the accused for action of the grand jury. If the accused is charged with a less serious infraction of the law, he may be released on bail pending the meeting of the grand jury. The grand jury meeting takes place only upon the call of the judge holding court in the district and may be some weeks or months in the future. When the grand jury meets and has been instructed by the judge, the case against the accused is presented by the prosecuting officer in a secret session in which testimony on behalf of the accused is not heard. The prosecutor advises the grand jury on questions of law and prevents the introduction of incompetent evidence. If the evidence presented is such that, uncontradicted, a trial jury would have to find a verdict of guilty, the grand jury is required upon its oath to find a "true bill." The evidence presented before the grand jury may be given by witnesses or by the prosecutor or his agents and detectives. If a true bill is found, the case is set down for trial at the next session of the court.

It will be seen from this brief description that the accused, even if there were no grand jury, would receive at least two examinations—one before the committing magistrate and one before the trial jury. Ordinarily, then, there would seem to be no reason to regard the grand jury as performing any useful function in protecting the accused against arbitrary action on the part of the government.[12] If prosecution by information were permitted, certain definite advantages might be looked for. In the first place, the prosecutor would alone bear the responsibility for bringing charges, and in most cases this responsibility would be sufficient to deter him from bringing baseless accusations. In the second place, the grand jury may meet usually only upon the call of the judge. This may mean but rare meetings and, in the meantime, the suspected person may be under an unjust suspicion. Moreover, the cost of holding a term of the grand jury is by no means negligible, and the delays consequent upon calling it are likely to make conviction more difficult when the accused person is actually guilty. Again, in most urban districts and in a good many thickly populated country districts, the grand jury can no longer be regarded as a group of neighbors familiar with what has happened outside their immediate neighborhood. The grand jury is the typical product of an agricultural society and a sparse population where each man could with some reason be considered responsible for public order in his community. The modern development of police and detective services places at the disposal of the prosecutor the means for getting far more information about suspected crimes than any ordinary grand jury, made up by lot, is likely to be able to supply. As a matter of fact, the prosecutor under present conditions gives the grand jury almost all the information it has, so that for the most part it acts as a mere recording machine for registering decisions already arrived at by the prosecutor. This is recognized by the practice which has grown up of having the formal indictment prepared in the office of the prosecutor, ready for the signature of the grand jury.[13]

ACCUSATION BY INFORMATION

For the reasons that have been enumerated, it is the general belief of those who have investigated the process of indictment that

---

[12] The study by Morse covering more than 7,000 cases before the courts in 1929 and 1930 indicated that "there is little difference between the opinions of prosecutors and grand juries as to what should be done with the cases" and that "innocent persons would be as well protected under the information method as under the indictment method." X *Oregon Law Review* 154 (1931).

[13] It is also true that the grand jury is often not aware of its own powers for securing evidence and is hence more than likely to depend upon the prosecutor.

the grand jury under present conditions serves no useful purpose and ought to be abolished as the regular method of bringing accusation against suspected persons. The alternative method of information, now permitted in about half the states, is recommended as a substitute. The criminal information was defined by Blackstone as "an accusation or complaint exhibited against a person for some criminal offense. It differs principally from an indictment in this, that an indictment is found upon the oath of twelve men and an information is only the allegation of the officer who exhibits it." Where the information is used, it is brought by the prosecuting attorney upon his official oath. The basis of his accusation consists in the testimony of private persons willing to make accusation under oath, and of such other evidence as the prosecutor may be able to collect through his subordinates, police officers, or detectives. When filed in the proper court it sets in motion the machinery of trial.[14] Among the states where the use of the information is permitted, there is considerable variation in the circumstances under which it may be used. It is generally provided that for felonies or, at any rate, for capital offenses the grand jury alone is competent to indict. With this exception it may be used for any grade of crime in most states, although it should be noted that everywhere the grand jury remains as an alternative mode of accusation, being set in motion in a variety of ways, usually upon the motion of a judge or by popular petition.

There can be very little doubt that the procedure by information is destined to supersede the grand jury as a routine method of accusation. Professional legal opinion is almost unanimous in preferring it, informed laymen are generally convinced of its superiority, and every investigation of the "crime problem" in recent years has called for the abolition of this function of the grand jury.[15] The weight of this opinion is bound to count in the end. On the other hand, there are strong reasons for retaining something like the pres-

---

[14] The validity of the process was upheld by the Supreme Court of the United States, against the contention that it violated "due process of law," in *Hurtado v. California,* 110 U. S. 516 (1884).

[15] The evidence on this is voluminous. See the article by Morse referred to above which collects the opinions of 162 prosecuting officers and several hundred trial judges: X *Oregon Law Review,* 101-160; 217-257; 295-365 (1931); also the discussions in the *Missouri and Illinois Crime Surveys,* the article "The Grand Jury" in the *Encyclopedia of the Social Sciences,* and Raymond Moley, "The Initiation of Criminal Prosecutions by Indictment or Information," XXIX *Michigan Law Review* 403-31 (1931); "Grand Jury Encumbers Justice in Many States," XXIII *Journal of American Judicature Society* 25-27 (June 1939).

ent grand jury for certain eventualities. While it may be of little
value as representative body in speaking the mind of the community
in regard to the typical crime, it is not difficult to conceive of circumstances under which it would be an ideal spokesman for the general
public interest. As has been said above, the district attorney very
often, if not usually, occupies the key position in that complex organization of "politics" by which official power is placed at the disposal of private interests. It is easy to imagine a situation—indeed
they are constantly arising—in which an entire community may be
the victim of such an alliance. In a situation like this, the public's
legal protector himself is the head and front of a species of treason.
Unless some means exists to marshal the public's sense of justice,
there is no way of breaking the power of such a corrupt ring. For
emergencies of this sort, much may be said for a body constituted as
is the grand jury. The same thing may be asserted with regard to a
situation in which any local official is suspected of misfeasance or
malfeasance in office, and his political connections with the prosecutor are such as to make the latter loath to begin action against
him.[16]

Largely for these reasons, the grand jury still has a shadowy
existence in all states, including many in which its indicting function in ordinary crimes has disappeared in favor of the information.
In the latter states, the grand jury may usually be called by the judge
on his own motion or must be called by him upon presentation of
a petition signed by a certain number of local residents. Until some
other and more impartial guardian of the public interest is supplied
us, the arguments for the retention of the grand jury for such cases
seem cogent. "It is the age of organized official corruption and
crime, of rackets, of clever criminals with unlimited resources and
shrewd advisers, of schemes primarily designed to fleece large masses
of the public." When no crime has actually been committed, however, the prosecutor is powerless to act, though all may feel sure that
crime is in the making. Under these circumstances it is correct to
say that "the grand jury is the only powerful investigating body
known to our law today which wields the authority which he (the
state's attorney) requires but does not possess." [17]

---

[16] See G. H. Dession and I. H. Cohen, "The Inquisitorial Function of Grand Juries,"
XLI *Yale Law Journal* 687-712 (Mar. 1932).

[17] M. Nahum and L. M. Schatz, "The Grand Jury in Connecticut." **5** *Connecticut
Bar Journal* 121 (1931). As to the grand jury's independent power to investigate, the
courts have said: "To the grand jury and to it alone, is given the power of investiga-

The Trial Jury

One of the ancient Anglo-Saxon institutions which has entered deeply into our tradition of free government is trial by jury. Though this device originated apparently in the fiscal needs of monarchs, circumstances converted it into a piece of machinery which served well enough to speak the mind of the community on the crucial issue of guilt or innocence in the case of one of its members. Whatever its original purpose may have been, popular government appropriated it to its own special uses and set it up as a counterweight to officialism and expertness as represented by judge and prosecutor. In short, the jury as a sample of the community was there to declare the law as the community felt the *law ought to be*.

The essential notion in trial by jury is that a section of the community in which the controversy arose or the alleged crime took place should act in a representative capacity with the judge in deciding cases. It is quite commonly believed, of course, that the judge is judge of the law and the jury is judge of the facts. In a very real sense, however, the jury is in all states judge of both the law and the facts. Indeed, it is hard to see how it could be otherwise in a society which has once admitted the people to a share in the administration of justice. In a popular government, the people are by definition the strongest force in the community and this force will make itself felt no matter what the strict letter of the law may be.

It must be conceded that in times past the trial jury made a great contribution to constitutional liberty, and that the burden of proof is clearly upon those who would disturb or abolish an institution which has survived many vicissitudes of modern history. The mere fact, however, that it marked a great advance over such previous methods of reaching verdicts as compurgation or trial by battle can have little or no bearing upon the question of its fitness under modern conditions. In the controversy that has gone on concerning the jury system for the past generation, both of these considerations have been lost sight of in the zeal of the disputants. By one group,

---

tion without a specific charge." *Ward Baking Co. v. Western Union Telegraph Co.*, 200 N. Y. S. 865 (1923). "The court cannot limit the scope of the investigation of the grand jury." *U. S. v. Thompson*, 251 U. S. 407. The Kefauver Committee said in its *Third Interim Report* (1951): "The grand jury is the traditional organ of law enforcement charged with the responsibility of uncovering corruption in government and misfeasance and nonfeasance in office of public officials. . . . In order for grand jury inquiries to be effective, they must be freed from such hampering restrictions as are found in . . . laws which limit the terms of grand juries."

interested in "efficiency" and a bit supercilious perhaps toward the vagaries of "the twelve men of average ignorance," the jury has been condemned as a "relic of barbarism," the "arch obstructor of justice," and the "hope of the guilty." On the other hand, its friends have pleaded for its retention as a "bulwark of our liberties," and an exponent of the "common sense of the neighborhood," against the obscurantism of a permanent officeholding class.[18]

Recent Changes in the Jury System

If we close our ears to the din and commotion occasioned by the debaters and examine the facts, we discover that the argument is largely beside the point. In one way or another the use of the jury, once universal in both criminal and civil cases, has been whittled away until it may now fairly be regarded as a disappearing institution. This result has been brought about in a variety of ways. In the first place, the old rule of unanimous decision has in many states been seriously modified in criminal actions as well as civil controversies. Since unanimity was long an essential characteristic of the system, such a modification of the law amounts to a fundamental change in our system of administering justice. It is based on the growing belief that the attempt to find twelve men upon whom the evidence in a case will make the same impression and lead to the same verdict is doomed to failure and likely to lead to numerous situations in which the verdict will be dictated by one or more individuals able, by sheer obstinacy, to bring a despairing majority around to their own point of view.[19]

A still more serious inroad on the system is being made in those states where the statutes provide that a jury trial may be waived in civil cases and in some or even all criminal cases. In an increasing number of states the jury in civil cases is becoming the exception, and this has no doubt made it easier to relax the custom calling for such trial. With regard to civil cases the states have dealt with the jury in one of two ways. In some states, trial is before a judge only, unless one of the parties demands a jury. In others the party demanding a jury must pay into the court a fee covering in part at least the cost of impaneling a jury. In the state of Connecticut ap-

---

[18] There is a good summary of the arguments for and against use of the trial jury in W. F. Willoughby, *Principles of Judicial Administration*, pp. 500 ff.

[19] There is a good deal of variety in the rules of the states permitting verdicts by less than a unanimous vote. See G. R. Winters, "Majority Verdicts in the United States," **XXVI** *Journal of the American Judicature Society* 87-92 (Oct. 1942).

plication for a jury must be made in writing within a specified time. In practice, waiver of jury trial has proved popular with judges, lawyers of the better sort, with litigants, and with the general public. Such figures as we have indicate that the vast majority of litigants prefer the prompt procedure before a judge to the long drawn-out process involved in drawing a jury and instructing it with regard to an intricate mass of evidence, for example, as to technical business and industrial processes. Defendants without a real defense may be disposed to "take a chance" on a "hung" jury, but the new procedure has commended itself to most of those who are compelled to resort frequently to the law.[20]

It is difficult to mourn the passing of the civil jury. In a rude society where the neighborhood was closely knit, where transactions were relatively simple, and where a man might with reason be regarded as able to reach sound conclusions, there was a good deal to be said for the institution. There was always, however, something illogical in using a jury in civil controversies. From time immemorial, courts of equity have sat without juries and, in disposing of cases, have always ruled upon matters as important as those which arise in common law. Yet there has been little or no demand for the use of juries in equity except in connection with the granting of injunctions and the punishment of contempt.[21] Whatever the reasons for this difference in procedure—and they are largely historical —equity confines the difficult task of reviewing and weighing evidence to the hands of a person whose professional training has been directed toward enabling him to penetrate to the essentials of a case as it is presented in a mass of conflicting evidence, and to reach a decision uninfluenced by the appeals of attorneys with only an oblique interest in doing justice. Under modern conditions in which the bulk of civil cases involves rather complicated business transactions, a satisfactory jury, taking into account all the circumstances surrounding its drawing, is more than likely an accident. A single judge will probably do the work better and more promptly and, so

---

[20] The civil jury has been weakened also by the growing use of conciliation and arbitration in business disputes of various sorts. One commentator writes: "There is so much evidence of a growing tendency to dispense with jury trials in civil cases that a prophet could, without being outlandish, predict its ultimate abandonment." H. F. Goodrich, "Does the Bill of Rights Need Revision?" *Annals* (Sept. 1935).

[21] In the interests of accuracy, however, it ought to be pointed out that at the time when the jury was generally looked upon as the bulwark of popular liberties there was a rather widespread demand for its extension to equity cases. In recent years organized labor has pretty generally demanded the use of the jury in injunction cases.

long as a reasonable right of appeal is preserved, every legitimate private and public interest is served.[22]

Much of what has been said above applies with peculiar point to the civil jury. The use of the jury in criminal cases stands on somewhat different ground. It is not difficult to see that a chance aggregation of twelve jurors might be a very unsatisfactory body to sift the evidence and reach a verdict in a complicated civil case. In criminal cases, however, somewhat different matters are at issue. It is only rarely that a civil dispute will attract wide public attention or arouse public sentiment for or against plaintiff or defendant. Recurrent hysteria about so-called "crime waves," however, affords evidence that official zeal may overreach itself in behalf of what some are pleased to call "law and order." Law and order are necessary, but we are prone to forget that law may be declared in part by the people themselves, and that order is not necessarily the situation which finds favor with the robed figure on the dais. The history of the development of human liberty is one which reveals the jury as playing an important, not to say vital, role. It was and is the jury's duty to speak the mind of the community in a process in which officials may conceivably ignore the community and conceive law in terms of logical syllogisms or even of class interests. In an imperfect world we need to be reminded that the law is not made for the austere, but that it tends rather to be whatever "twelve men in a box" declare it to be—twelve ordinary men, not twelve archangels or bureaucrats or frock-coated "leading citizens."[23]

Perhaps even more can be said for the system of trial by jury in rural districts. Here even now there persist to a considerable degree

---

[22] Judge Clarence G. Galston of the Federal District Court for the Eastern District of New York suggests that intelligence tests be used in the choice of civil juries, remarking that "there is no rational or experiential ground which justifies the belief that a jury is natively endowed with qualifications requisite to efficient performance of its duties . . . jurors are no more heaven-sent than are the other groups participating in the trial of a law suit." "Civil Jury Trials and Tribulations," **29** *Journal of American Bar Association* 195-198 (Apr. 1943). The same suggestion is made by Judge Julius H. Miner (Chicago) in "The Jury Problem," **37** *Journal of Criminal Law and Criminology* 1-15 (1946).

[23] Thus Judge John J. Parker of the United States Court of Appeals: "My experience . . . convinces me that no better method of trying ordinary issues of fact, particularly in criminal cases, has ever been devised. But this is not all; no stronger bulwark, in my judgment, can be devised for protecting the innocent from oppression at the hands of the powerful. . . . The important matter of judging the guilt or innocence of a fellow-citizen whose life or liberty is at stake they [the people] have delegated to no one but have reserved for themselves, the jury not being elected or appointed, but chosen by lot from the body of the citizenship." "Improving the Administration of Justice," **27** *Journal of the American Bar Association* 71-76 (Feb. 1941).

many of the conditions favoring the satisfactory working of the ancient system. In civil cases, the issues are likely to be subjects of neighborhood gossip or transactions of a sort well known to a majority of the adult citizens. In criminal prosecutions the case is, if anything, stronger. There is more likely to be a genuine community point of view and there is certainly far less difficulty in securing juries than there is in the cities. Much of the agitation for changes in the system is based upon the fact that it does not work well under urban conditions. While this may be granted, it still remains true that about forty million people live under the simpler surroundings of the open country, and here the arguments against trial by jury are perhaps not so cogent. Nevertheless even the criminal jury has undergone great transformations within recent years. Trial by jury may be waived even in felony cases in fourteen of our states, while waiver may be had in misdemeanor cases in more than thirty. In such jurisdictions, trial is before the judge and seems to be widely resorted to with generally satisfactory results. It is to be assumed that even in rural districts modifications of this sort have been accepted.[24]

› Local Prisons

The custody and treatment of those convicted of crimes and misdemeanors present some of the most baffling problems in the whole field of law enforcement. Earlier theories were based very largely upon the idea that prisoners should be "punished." "Punishment" was to be inflicted not so much in order to deter the convicted from a repetition of their offenses, or to warn others, as to enable an outraged community to wreak its vengeance upon wrongdoers. Modern penology lays more emphasis upon preparing the convicted for reabsorption into society or even, if more advanced theories are followed, of treating him as if he were physically or mentally ill. In any case, modern methods tend to be less barbarous, more "scientific," and also more expensive. Against the old idea of "punishment" is set the new idea expressed by a former federal Director of Prisons: "The task of the modern prison includes an effort to prepare all of its

---

[24] The states permitting waiver of jury trial in criminal cases, with the dates of the adoption of the plan, are: Connecticut (1921), Indiana (1905), Maryland (1852), New Jersey (1898), Oklahoma (1911), Washington (1922), Wisconsin (1925), California (1928), Illinois (1930), Massachusetts (1929), Michigan (1927), Ohio (1929), Rhode Island (1929), and Virginia (1928). A complete discussion of the movement may be found in J. A. C. Grant, "Felony Trials without a Jury," **XXV** *American Political Science Review* 980-995 (1931).

prisoners against the day of their release. This is the reason for the demand that men in prison be kept busy at some productive task, that they be taught the rudiments of American citizenship, that their bodies be cleansed of disease and their minds cleared of delusions, that the physical, mental, and moral handicaps and maladjustments be removed." [25]

While the modern view is rather widely accepted in the abstract, the more ancient attitude has by no means been eradicated. For this reason, the administration of even modern prisons is necessarily a series of compromises. "On the one hand, prisons are expected to punish; on the other, they are supposed to reform. They are expected to discipline vigorously at the same time that they teach self-reliance. They are built to be operated like vast impersonal machines, yet they are expected to fit men to live normal community lives. They operate in accordance with a fixed autocratic routine, yet they are expected to develop individual initiative. All too frequently restrictive laws force prisoners into idleness despite the fact that one of their primary objectives is to teach men how to earn an honest living. They refuse the prisoner a voice in self-government, but they expect him to become a thinking citizen in a democratic society. To some, prisons are nothing but 'country clubs' catering to the whims and fancies of the inmates. To others, the prison atmosphere seems charged only with bitterness, rancor and an all-pervading sense of defeat. And so the whole paradoxical scheme continues, because our ideas and views regarding the function of correctional institutions in our society are confused, fuzzy, and nebulous." [26]

So intent is the community upon enforcing compliance with its mores, even savagely and without nice discrimination, that it is not to be wondered at that "scientific" penology has waged an unequal battle with reactions that are almost, if not quite, instinctive. The presence of two such contradictory views as punishment and rehabilitation accounts for the tragic dilemmas set forth in the paragraph above.

In rural areas, however, a number of factors operate which make difficult the adoption of a modern program. The typical local correctional institution is the county or town jail. This is used prin-

---

[25] Sanford Bates, Address before the Attorney-General's Conference on Crime, Dec. 12, 1934.

[26] *Federal Prisons, 1948* (Annual Report of James V. Bennett, Director, Bureau of Prisons, Dept. of Justice, 1949), p. 3.

cipally to confine prisoners awaiting trial for crimes, and offenders serving short sentences. In the vast majority of rural counties it cannot be satisfactory. The number of inmates is seldom or never large enough to justify any employment program or any but the most obvious curative procedures, or, indeed, the implementation of any of the accepted standards worked out by experts in penology.[27] A survey conducted in New Jersey in 1934 brought out the fact that there was a complete turnover of the population of the county jails every sixteen days. Even in the workhouses, containing short-term offenders, there was a turnover every sixty days. Under such conditions it is impossible to have a program aiming at reformation through the productive labor and education of the inmates. In rural states the average daily jail population is so small—usually under ten—as to make such a plan even less feasible. Moreover, the typical system of jail administration affords little opportunity for constructive penology. The county jail is usually under the control of the sheriff, and many sheriffs are not only without expert knowledge, but also probably share the traditional community attitude toward criminals. If, as is often the case, the sheriff is paid by fees, the management of the jail is a business proposition—and a sordid one at that. The jail becomes a boarding-house, and the temptation to treat its inmates inadequately in order to profit by it is often too strong to resist. The net result is that the jail becomes a squalid school of crime for its idle and exploited inmates.

That this picture is not presented too darkly is demonstrated by the findings of the Federal Bureau of Prisons which since 1930 has inspected local prisons to determine their fitness for boarding held-for-trial and short-sentence federal prisoners. During this period, of more than three thousand jails inspected, the Bureau has granted full approval to only 435 and approval for emergency use only to an additional 365. "And by no means are all the fully approved jails what we wish they were; many are merely the best we can find in localities where, from time to time, we need detention facilities." The Bureau has found that of 3,220 local jails inspected, not one rated as high as 90 on a scale of 100, and less than one per cent rated 70 or above. Eighty-three per cent rated under 50. The standards used by the Bureau are perhaps higher than average public opinion would insist on, but they do represent the judgment of those who

---

[27] A comprehensive statement of these standards may be found in the *Manual of Jail Management* published in 1948 by the federal Bureau of Prisons.

have given most attention to the problem. The conclusion of the Bureau as to the present conditions—a conclusion corroborated by dozens of local studies—is that "most jails even today contaminate and degrade those confined in them. This is inevitable since most of them are squalid and filthy; they are steeped in primitive retributive traditions; they lack adequate facilities to segregate offenders of various types, ages, and degrees of criminality; they permit most inmates, sentenced as well as unsentenced, to remain completely idle a greater part of the time; and they are usually operated by persons who are without qualifications for their tasks." [28]

There is perhaps something to be said for a local institution for the detention of persons awaiting trial for serious offenses, even though it may not be possible to make extensive arrangements for their employment, education, and recreation. But the county jail or similar institution, as actually used, has little to commend it. Persons being held for trial are not normally numerous, nor is their stay long; therefore there is nothing to be gained by herding them in with convicted criminals. As to the latter, it is clear that persons serving thirty, sixty, or ninety days are simply being "punished" in the average jail. While under sentence their earning power is stopped and their families run the risk of becoming public charges. A far more sensible arrangement would be to make greater use of probation in the case of minor offenses, permit the payment of fines in installments, and commit long-term offenders to institutions better able to offer a modern program looking toward reformation. As matters stand most local jails are monuments to society's desire to make the transgressor smart. A reasonable suggestion would be to allow counties to join in maintaining larger institutions and to strengthen state supervision over such prisons. Jails would then have a population large enough to justify the employment of trained supervisors, the adoption of an employment, educational, and recreational program, and the proper classification of prisoners. A smaller number of such institutions would also permit better central supervision. [29]

---

[28] *Federal Prisons, 1948,* pp. 48-9. See also *Report on a Survey of Probation in New Jersey* (1934); *Report of the Commission on Penal Institutions in Pennsylvania* (1931); J. F. Fishman, "The American Jail," **130** *Atlantic Monthly* 792-805 (1922) ; Henry J. Faeth, *The Connecticut County* (Institute of Public Service, University of Connecticut, 1949), p. 34.

[29] A Connecticut Legislative Commission to Investigate and Report on the Need for a State Jail Farm which functioned from 1931-39, after presenting the familiar depressing picture of conditions in the county jails of that state, concluded that "for the cost

While the local jail can probably never be an ideal correctional institution, certain improvements may be noted. Wider and more intelligent use is now being made of probation for adult offenders; children are no longer confined with seasoned criminals; and long-term offenders are commonly committed to larger institutions. The general public has grown aware of the shortcomings of the local jail, and jail officials themselves are showing a greater interest in improved standards of administration. Even the sheriffs, through the National Sheriffs' Association, have made the abolition of the fee system and of the per-diem food allowance a part of their program for making the office both more efficient and more dignified. Jails are almost universally under completely local control, but at least two states, Virginia and North Carolina, have recently established some measure of central control and inspection. These developments may eventually remove the inmates of the county jail from the ranks of society's "forgotten men." [30]

THE REFORM OF LAW ENFORCEMENT

The general inadequacy of our traditional machinery for the detection, prosecution, and punishment of criminal acts has been given within recent years unusual and dramatic publicity. The investigations of the Kefauver Committee of the United States Senate, and of a number of state and local crime commissions, have made clear what was long suspected, namely, that crime has become such a lucrative business that, as in many legitimate enterprises, it has been organized in what amount to syndicates and "trusts" operating without reference to political boundaries. It is now evident that our decentralized machinery of law enforcement faces an integrated organization of clever and ruthless men, possessed of ample funds, assisted by competent legal counsel, and able in many cases to secure the "protection" of police and prosecuting officers. It is true, of course, that the operations of the crime "syndicates" have been con-

---

of one modern, adequate, sanitary county jail of the old high-security type, a central state institution of the jail farm type could be built, which would serve all eight counties of the state adequately and at a tremendous saving over the ten present institutions." See Henry J. Faeth, *The Connecticut County* (Institute of Public Service, University of Connecticut, 1949), p. 34.

[30] The constitution of the National Sheriffs' Association lists among its purposes: "to advocate the elimination of per diem payments to sheriffs for feeding inmates of county jails; to advocate the elimination of the county jail as a facility for detention of juveniles, alcoholics, and mental defectives." This constitution is printed in the July-August 1949 issue of the *Sheriff's News Letter*.

fined largely to large cities; nevertheless, no part of the country is beyond their reach, and, in any event, the problem of dealing with crime is one requiring the concerted efforts of authorities at every level.[31]

The Kefauver Committee, while stating that "the enforcement of the criminal law is primarily a state and local responsibility," was extremely critical of our existing local arrangements. Its suggestions for improving local agencies give added point to the present discussion. "State and local law enforcement agencies," said the Committee," must consider such problems as:

> "1. The combination of small independent local police forces into larger regional units which will be adequately staffed and equipped to make criminal investigations and to deal with organized crime.
> 2. The elimination of the law enforcement responsibilities of the sheriff's office.
> 3. The more adequate policing of rural areas by state police units.
> 4. The closer integration of local police forces and local police activities with the work and efforts of state police units.
> 5. The provision of better methods of recruiting and training local and state police officials.
> 6. The provision of higher standards of pay for persons engaged in local law enforcement work.
> 7. The elimination of the traditional coroner's office and substitution of adequately staffed and equipped medical examiners' offices.
> 8. A clearer definition of the function and responsibilities of the local prosecutor in connection with the investigation of criminal cases.
> 9. The steps necessary to secure greater stability of tenure and greater professionalization of the local prosecutor's office.
> 10. The provision of a greater degree of centralized control of the work of local prosecutors, either through the Attorney General or the Governor's office.

---

[31] The final report of the Kefauver Committee (Special Senate Committee to Investigate Organized Crime in Interstate Commerce, established by Senate Resolution 202, 81st Congress) was made Aug. 31, 1951. At the same time a Commission on Organized Crime of the American Bar Association made its report. These two reports are the source for most of the brief discussion here.

11. The tightening of legal provisions concerning the removal of lax and faithless law enforcement officials.
12. More law enforcement officials should be brought under civil service regulations; in some cases these regulations should be revised in order to facilitate . . . separation from the service." [32]

Most of these recommendations, it is clear, involve much stricter state control than has yet been contemplated in most of our states. The American Bar Association Commission is even more insistent on state assumption of responsibility. Its report is worth quoting at some length:

"Local control of law enforcement agencies is characteristic of American political organization. It is based upon a well-founded and deep-seated fear of the dangers to liberty involved in the centralization of police power. However, *complete local control without any responsibility in local authorities to account to the State government for their administration of State law, is one of the principal causes of weakness in our system of administering criminal justice and in our defenses against organized crime.*

"State statutes should be prepared to make possible greater State supervision over local law enforcement agencies, the adoption of uniform law enforcement policies, and an improvement in the functioning of local law enforcement agencies. . . . Adequate State and local law enforcement is the key to the control of organized crime. However, we cannot obtain such law enforcement by traditionally organized agencies or through personnel selected by traditional methods. The one fact that stands out from the reports on police, prosecutors, and cooperation in law enforcement is that *the State must reassert its primary responsibility for the functioning of law enforcement agencies. . .* The provision of centralized State supervision over local law enforcement agencies is one of the most vital steps that can be taken to control organized crime and to improve the administration of the criminal law . . . The Commission recommends that model State statutes should be prepared which will have the following objectives:

"1. A greater measure of State supervision over criminal prosecution.

[32] Kefauver Committee, *Third Interim Report* (May 1, 1951), pp. 27-28.

"2. A greater measure of State supervision over the operation and functions of local police departments and the recruiting and training of policemen.
"3. Specialized State services in connection with crime detection, criminal identification, and criminal statistics.
"4. State inspection and audit services to local law enforcement agencies." [33]

It is not to be expected that the states will immediately or universally adopt all of these suggestions. They are, however, undoubtedly consistent with the long-time centralizing trend in state administration and many of them are likely to be realized in the future. Following or accompanying the Kefauver investigation, about a third of the states created crime control study commissions of one sort or another. In addition to such action, a number of them have not only adopted or strengthened legislation with respect to crime, but have also taken steps to strengthen state supervision of local officials. Other states have acted to strengthen the powers of the grand jury as a device for combating crime and official connivance at its perpetration. Recent state action has also given additional support to interstate crime control programs developed during the 1930's through uniform state statutes and interstate compacts.

---

[33] *Report of the Commission on Organized Crime* (1951), pp. 32, 61-62.

CHAPTER 10

Public Highways

THE LOCAL HIGHWAY SYSTEM

There are in the United States slightly more than three million miles of rural roads.[1] In discussing the rural highway system it seems best to use as a basis the governmental areas charged with highway administration. Using this basis we find that 572,000 miles are in road under the control of state highway departments. The remaining 2,361,000 miles are generally under the supervision of county, township, or other local officials. Local government units employ in highway work about 97,000 persons, of whom 67,000 are permanent employees and 30,000 seasonal.

Although our attention will be centered principally on those highways which are supervised by local authorities, it is important to note the part played by the federal government in road work, because of the influence which federal standards may be expected to have upon even secondary highways. Of the 358,000 miles of primary state highways, 232,000 constitute the primary federal-aid highway system as designated by the Federal Highway Act of 1921. The federal government and the states act cooperatively in constructing and maintaining these roads, although it is reported that a large amount of work is done by the states without federal assistance. These roads marked with the shield-shaped route markers are parts of the United States Highway System, although these markers do not mean that the federal government "owns" or even

---

[1] In revising this chapter the author has found most useful *Highway Practice in the United States of America* (1949) and *The Local Rural Road Problem* (1950), both published by the Bureau of Public Roads in the Department of Commerce. The *Annual Reports* of the Bureau and its annual publication *Highway Statistics* are indispensable. The Bureau also issued in 1951 *Highways in the United States*, an excellent popularization of data on highway maintenance and construction. Brief but informative articles on progress within the individual states appear in the issues of *Better Roads*, published monthly at 173 West Madison Street, Chicago.

controls them. Such roads are designed primarily for interstate and inter-regional traffic.

Federal aid, however, is no longer limited to the construction and maintenance of such highways. Under the Federal Aid Highway Act of 1944 a special portion of federal-aid money, amounting to 30 per cent of the total made available by Congress, is set aside for secondary or farm-to-market roads. In selecting the roads to be included in this system attention is paid to the value of the road in securing access to markets and in serving the needs of school bus transportation. This system now includes about 400,000 miles. The federal-aid primary and secondary systems now amount to about 750,000 miles, which means that federal aid is now available for about one-fourth of all rural highways, over which about 90 per cent of all travel passes.

We may say, then, that about 75 per cent of the total rural road mileage of the country, or nearly 2,250,000 miles, is under the control of local officials, most of them serving rural constituencies. Motorists generally are most familiar with the splendid highways upon which whole states are crossed in a single day, but it is well to remember that these roads are only a fraction of the whole. Thousands of miles of other highways must cross swamps, thread canyons, and get over hills to reach district schools, isolated mining and lumber camps, and remote hamlets of whose very existence the speeding tourist is ignorant. County and township commissioners and supervisors, road district overseers, highway superintendents and engineers by the hundreds, and laborers by the thousands are constantly engaged in keeping their neighbors out of the mud in rural sections far from the concrete strip over which rumble the transcontinental buses. In a very real sense the important highway problem is right here, not at the state engineer's office nor in the Bureau of Public Roads in Washington.

Viewed solely from the point of view of financial outlay, road building and maintenance is today a major governmental industry in the United States. Official figures show that state, federal, and local highway expenditures in 1950 amounted to more than four billion dollars. For county and local roads alone, excluding streets in incorporated areas, slightly over one billion dollars was spent. In the same year the state governments collected in highway-user revenues the sum of $2,300,000,000. Of this total $520 million was allocated for county and local road construction, maintenance, and debt service. Local road building and maintenance is then a billion dollar business and involves not only the comfort and convenience of those who use the highways, but also the prosperity of hosts of suppliers of materials, and contractors, and many thousands of highway workers.

The explanation of these huge expenditures is to be found in part, of course, in the more costly type of construction now demanded by the traveling public. It has been estimated that in 1906, roughly the beginning of the era of the automobile, total road expenditures amounted to $75 million. At that time there were not more than five miles of concrete rural highway in the entire country, not more than 1,500 miles of brick highway, and negligible mileages of bituminous or asphalt surface. The mileage of gravel road surpassed by far all other types of surfaced roads. By the end of 1949 the Bureau of Public Roads reported about 200,000 miles of high-type surface on local roads. Modern roads of the highest type are obviously far more costly than those of fifty years ago. Additional factors increasing costs were improvements in highway design which came with the passing of the horse-drawn vehicle, the development of heavier vehicles, especially trucks, and the invention and use of expensive earth-moving and construction equipment to replace earlier crude adaptations of farm wagons.[2]

Considered simply as an agency of communication, the modern road is of first-rate social importance. For by far the greater portion of human history, men have lived their lives in a physical isolation quite incomprehensible to the fast-moving present generation. The automobile brought good roads and good roads have been the foremost agency in destroying this isolation and in making possible that multiplication of human contacts upon which uniformity of culture depends. The farmer is no longer isolated. As is made clear by Figure 13 and by statistics gathered by the Bureau of Public Roads, eight farmers out of ten are closer, in point of time, to their amusements, their markets, and their seat of government than were city-dwellers fifty years ago.

"The nearest neighbor may be still as far away in miles, but not

---

[2] Even today "about half the total road mileage in the United States is unsurfaced. Many of these roads, because of their minor importance, will never be improved with more than low-type surfaces of sand-clay mixture or gravel or crushed stone. Such surfaces, if well built, are quite adequate for low volumes of traffic." *Highway Practice,* p. 148. Complete figures on types of surface are given in *The Local Rural Road Problem,* pp. 6-11.

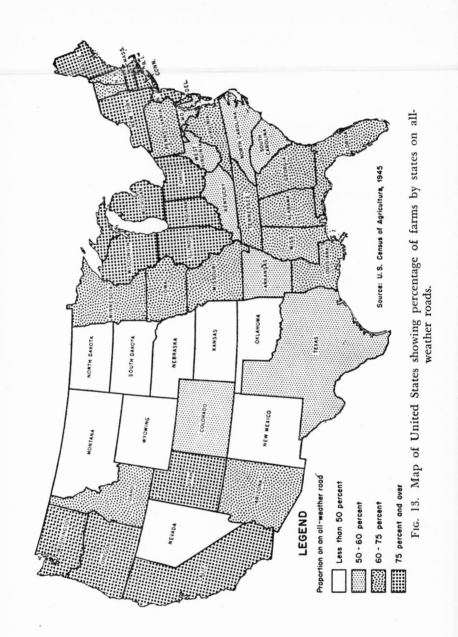

LEGEND

Proportion on an all-weather road

Less than 50 percent

50 - 60 percent

60 - 75 percent

75 percent and over

Source: U. S. Census of Agriculture, 1945

Fig. 13. Map of United States showing percentage of farms by states on all-weather roads.

in minutes. The 15-mile trip to town and back takes an hour instead of all day. The mail-order catalogue is no longer essential. Two out of every three farms are on an all-weather road, and 20 per cent more are within two miles of one. Crops can be hauled away and supplies brought in by truck without worrying about the mud. On the 6 million farms in the United States there are now five and a half million automobiles, two and a half million trucks, and nearly three and a half million tractors. And many another farm machine is powered or towed by gasoline engine.

"One of the most important changes brought about by the highways is through the use of school buses. The little red schoolhouse is rapidly being replaced by consolidated elementary and high schools, which are far more efficient in their use of funds and can give our children a better education, too. In the past 20 years the number of one-teacher schools has been cut in half, and the number of pupils riding school buses has multiplied five times. Nearly 6 million children now ride daily in 100,000 school buses to 46,000 schools. This is almost one-fourth of all the school children in the United States.

"Rural free mail delivery was slow and difficult when the mailman drove his buggy through the mud and dust. Now, there are 30,000 carriers traveling one and a half million miles of rural roads every day by car or truck. Their service is as regular as that of the mailman working a few blocks from the city post office." [3]

HIGHWAY UNITS

Whatever may be the standardizing effect of an expanding system of good roads, there can be no doubt of its influence on administrative agencies. Historically the construction and care of roads constituted a local function. In the North generally it was the responsibility of the towns or townships; in the South it devolved upon the county as the ultimate unit of local government. Methods of construction and maintenance were extremely simple, and the costs were largely for labor. Roads were periodically dragged with crude scraping devices and some slight attempt was made to secure drainage. Labor was furnished by neighboring farmers who quite often "worked out" their road tax by donating their own labor and the use of their teams of horses, oxen, or mules for an agreed number of days each year. Few scientific advances have had greater central-

---

[3] See *Highways in the United States*, p. 11.

izing influences than the successive improvements in the art of road building. This art stood substantially still from the time of McAdam (who died in 1836) until the perfecting of the automobile. The demands of motorists spurred to activity the chemists, physicists, and engineers to whom is due the network of all-weather roads now largely taken for granted. From the point of view of public administration, the effect of the automobile has been to render the township and the road district and, to some extent, even the county, obsolete. Yet no account of modern highway administration would be realistic which failed to mention the smaller units still engaged in highway work.

So far as the primary road systems of the country are concerned, these were quite generally brought under centralized control before 1920. This development was a striking one. Before 1900 only seven states had even a rudimentary system of highway administration. By 1917 all had some sort of highway authority and, during the ten years following, responsibility for the primary road system was everywhere definitely under state control. These changes in state administration are directly attributable to the entrance of the federal government into the field of highway construction with the Federal Aid Highway Act of 1916. Under this act no state could share in the federal funds which it made available until it had designated to the Bureau of Public Roads a system of state highways controlled by a single state agency. In most cases the process of centralization within the state followed very rapidly after acceptance of the provisions of the federal act.

These developments, however, did not directly affect county, town, and township highways, since the federal grants were at first made available only for primary roads. Local roads continued to be under the supervision of local authorities who yielded their prerogatives grudgingly and who, in fact, are still far too important to be ignored. Hence, what we really have is a national highway system responsibility for which is divided on one level between the central state authority and the federal Bureau of Public Roads, and on the state-local level between the state highway department and a large number of local highway authorities.

As nearly as can be determined more than 18,000 local governmental units have jurisdiction over local rural roads—about 3,000 counties, some 15,000 towns and townships, and several hundred special road and bridge districts. These vary in area from about a square mile to the more than 20,000 square miles in San Bernardino County, California. Road authorities may look after fewer than five miles to more than 5,000, and spend from less than $500 to more than $10,000,000 annually. The smallest district may have a single part-time employee, while the largest may employ five hundred workers.

There are a number of patterns of local highway administration. In New England the unit remains the town. In Pennsylvania it is for the most part the township. In the South and West local roads are usually under the jurisdiction of the county. In the remainder of the country, control is divided between the county and the township, except in Indiana, Iowa, and Michigan where, within recent years, the townships have lost their highway functions to the counties. Here and there in the township states, highway control is being transferred voluntarily by the townships to the county governments. In Kansas, for example, during the last 30 years this has happened in about half the counties. Finally, there are four states, Delaware, North Carolina, West Virginia, and all of Virginia except three counties, where all roads are under the state highway departments.

From the point of view of those interested in planning an integrated system, the large number of small units is a nuisance. The least defensible of these local authorities is the township which is seldom adequate to the job. There are two principal reasons why the township has been able to retain some of its highway authority in the motor age. The first is that it has always been possible to defend it on the ground that it preserves home rule. Before the coming of the county unit plan in Michigan it was argued that the services performed by the township are the only governmental activities over which the people have any direct control. "If we lose the township," it was said, "we will no longer have a voice in government." [4] Although this sort of argument conveniently overlooks the fact that self-government managed to survive in more than half the states that never had townships, it was long persuasive in some quarters.

The second reason for the persistence of the township is rather less respectable. The principal thing that has kept the township alive at all for many years has been road work. On this function 40

---

[4] A. W. Bromage and T. H. Reed, *Organization and Cost of County and Township Government* (Michigan Local Government Series, 1933), p. 85.

per cent of township budgets have been expended. Take it away and it would be difficult to justify, even to home rule advocates, the other 17 per cent which is spent for the salaries and expenses of township officers. It seems reasonable to believe that the most active defenders of the township have for many years been the officeholders. "It is the multiplication of these part-time, poorly paid, but relatively unproductive officials that makes township government so expensive and its perpetuation questionable." [5]

It is becoming clear to the general public, however, that the township as a highway unit is outmoded in the age of the automobile, and all signs point to its rather early liquidation. The chief reason why the township is losing out as a highway administrative unit is that modern road building, unlike some other governmental functions, demands machinery and management which the township unit usually cannot supply. There is simply not enough work in most townships to make possible the economical use of such machinery or to attract managerial talent. "Development in highway equipment, especially the motor grader, has greatly increased the range of an efficient maintenance crew, but the advantage of the newer equipment cannot be fully realized in operations of the smaller governmental units. The average township and small political subdivision must either use its own obsolete equipment or contract for maintenance service at rates far in excess of those experienced by governmental units of sufficient size to permit the effective use of a better equipment plant." [6]

As to management practices, it is not surprising to find that small units, such as the townships, have almost always in recent years made a poor showing. A survey conducted by the Board of County Engineer Consultants of the federal Bureau of Public Roads revealed that fewer than half of all local highway units were under the supervision of engineers. "Elected county governing body officials or surveyors manage county road affairs in about 1,050 counties of a total of more than 2,800. In approximately 640 counties road management is in the hands of a road superintendent or supervisor appointed by the governing body. Appointed or elected engineers are in charge of road work in about 850 counties. It should be noted, however, that more than 80 per cent of the engineers are employed

[5] Paul Wager, *County Government across the Nation*, p. 37.

[6] *The Local Rural Road Problem*, pp. 43-4. A great mass of data to the same effect was turned up in surveys of state and local administration made through the 1930's in New Hampshire, Iowa, Mississippi, Kentucky, North Carolina and other states.

in 9 states, and about 90 per cent of the total number operate in 12 states." In his annual report for 1949 the Commissioner of Public Roads said that, when the federal secondary road program was undertaken, "the complete absence of engineering personnel in over two-thirds of the counties made it necessary for many states to provide engineering assistance." [7] If engineering control is not widespread in the counties, the situation is worse in the townships. In about half of these, control is in the hands of the elected members of the governing body, and road supervisors are elected by the people in approximately another 2,200 units.

It is doubtful, however, whether the majority of small districts could attract sufficient talent even if they could be brought to insist on engineers as road officials. For example, the state planning commission in Pennsylvania in 1946 reported that 45 per cent of the townships in that state had fewer than 1,000 inhabitants, that 12 per cent had fewer than 10 miles of roads, and that 55 per cent spent less than $5,000 annually on road work. The commission recommended defining the minimum highway work unit as one having either a population of 5,000 or the equivalent of 80 miles of unimproved or stabilized surfacing, and it estimated that if this definition were adopted, only 17 per cent of the state's second class townships could qualify.[8]

It has long been the contention of the engineering profession and of federal and state administrators that engineering supervision should replace that which in small units more often than not rests with elective or politically appointed amateurs. Nearly every aspect of local highway administration reflects the absence of expert management. Engineering control should be required in every state, and means should be devised to make expert advice and direction available to all local units. The fact that few small units engage in systematic planning and programming may be traced to the rapid turnover of politically chosen supervisors and the resulting lack of continuity of policy. In any event, sound management theory would suggest the desirability of taking road work out of the hands of members of the governing bodies, restricting them to policy formulation, and leaving technical work to trained personnel. Statutes might be more widely enacted permitting joint em-

---

[7] *The Local Rural Road Problem*, p. 42; *Annual Report of the Bureau of Public Roads*, 1949, p. 28.

[8] See editorial comment in *Better Roads*, vol. 21, no. 2, p. 60 (Feb. 1950).

ployment of such personnel by adjacent units as well as requiring approval of their appointment by the state highway department.[9]

At the level of the township, however, it seems unlikely that these suggestions will be generally accepted voluntarily. What is rather to be expected is the withdrawal of the township from highway work within the fairly near future. Actually this is even now well under way. It is being accomplished in various ways. In Iowa, Indiana, and Michigan within recent years, the township road systems have been turned over to the county departments by legislative act. In Minnesota and Wisconsin and in a good many other states, individual townships are arranging with the counties to do their road work. In Kansas a statute of 1917 provides that the transfer of township road responsibilities to the county may be initiated either by the county board or by popular petition. Half the counties of the state are now operating, apparently with general approval, under the county unit system.[10]

THE FEDERAL GOVERNMENT AND LOCAL ROADS

Great impetus towards better administration at the local level has been provided by the Federal-Aid Secondary Highway program authorized by Congress in 1944. This program provides that 30 per cent of federal-aid funds shall be allocated to the states for the maintenance of secondary or feeder roads. During 1950 and 1951 federal expenditures under the program amounted to about $150 million and similar amounts are to be made available for 1952 and 1953. As this is written the plan is in effect in about 2,800 counties and about 400,000 miles of roads are covered. The progress of the program has been spotty, since in many instances the lack of competent engineering talent in small areas and the absence of close state-local relations between staffs have been obstacles to the prompt planning and execution of projects.

Since so much is said about state and federal influence in local road building and maintenance, it is well to point out that this influence is not altogether centralizing in its effect. There is nothing arbitrary about the federal government's participation in the secondary road program. The roads in the system are carefully selected in each state and county so as to provide for the maximum commu-

[9] There is a complete summary of present local administrative practices in *The Local Rural Road Problem*, pp. 38-46; see also *Highway Practice*, pp. 26-27.

[10] See Walter Johnson, "Steady Trend in Kansas to County-Unit Plan," *Better Roads*, vol. 21, no. 7, pp. 19-20, 33-34 (July 1951).

nity service possible within the limits of foreseeable revenue. The selection of the roads to be improved is made in cooperation with the state and local officials concerned, the federal Bureau of Public Roads being required by law to consult the latter. Where state and local authorities work closely together, the county officials are active in planning; where such cooperation does not exist, the state departments are necessarily more active. In the overall administration of the federal law the Commissioner of Public Roads is assisted by a Board of County Engineer Consultants consisting of one county engineer or other county official from each of the ten geographical divisions through which the federal bureau conducts its field operations. This board was established in 1946 to assist the federal commissioner and has proved so valuable that it has been continued.

Most observers are of the opinion that this program has strengthened local administration and, in a sense, local autonomy. "Some of the accomplishments of the federal-state-local partnerships established for the improvement of secondary roads under the federal-aid highway act of 1944 are now clearly visible. Such partnerships, it should be noted, exist as actual working relationships in a minority of the states. Generally speaking, county highway units have become active participants in states where county road work has had the benefit of progressive engineering management and where, through the operation of law or tradition, or both, state-local relations have been cordial and close. Elsewhere the federal-aid secondary programs have been largely state undertakings, whether state or county mileage has been involved . . . (but) the secondary program is clearly well out of the experimental stage." [11]

HIGHWAY FINANCE

If small local units are inadequate as administrative areas still less can be said for them as units for financing road work. No uniformity exists among them as to valuation, mileage, or topography. For that reason both the costs of highway construction and maintenance and the local ability to meet those costs will vary widely. So long as the property tax remains the mainstay of local finance, roads either will vary in quality or taxes will be many times heavier in poor districts than in those better off. Lack of uniformity in the char-

---

[11] Editorial comment in *Better Roads*, vol. 18, no. 11, p. 56 (Nov. 1948). Frequent articles dealing with the progress of the program in individual states have appeared in successive issues of *Better Roads* since 1947; see, for example, J. G. Schaub, "Secondary Program Is Joint Effort," *Better Roads*, vol. 18, no. 9, pp. 23-4, 30 (Sept. 1948).

acter of rural roads would perhaps be of no great general importance if the traffic on such roads were purely local. Actually about 18 per cent of all rural road travel occurs on distinctly minor roads and, although this is not a large proportion of total highway travel, it is large enough to indicate that few roads are entirely matters of local concern. Still more important, it furnishes the rural population with an argument for financial aid which it has not been slow to use.

The rural population finds itself in a difficult situation. To maintain good roads for even local use under generally accepted standards of construction and maintenance means, in hundreds of units, almost confiscatory tax rates on tangible property. On the other hand, if local roads are to be financed by state aids some control from above seems bound to follow. The prosaic matter of road building and maintenance thus comes to involve the important question of centralization and local self-government. This problem has arisen in every state, but nowhere, in the nature of the case, has complete success been reached in allocating financial support on the one hand and fixing administrative responsibility on the other.

As a matter of theory it may well be that rural inhabitants prefer poor roads under local control to better roads planned and built by a distant authority which may not prove amenable to local influence; as a matter of fact they have tried to get better roads at state and federal expense and avoid the control that normally goes with such largesse. These attempts to shift financial burdens to the state and national government are not confined, of course, to the field of highway expenditures. The public, or at least powerful groups of the public, have been making steadily increasing demands for schools, hospitals, public safety, and public health facilities, and these demands have constituted a steady pressure on the inelastic local tax base. In short, demands for state and federal aid in the case of highways is only a part of a general reallocation of functions now going on at a quickened pace.

Financial aid for local roads comes for the most part from the state governments. Fifty years ago the states derived more than half of their revenue from the property tax. By 1950, however, the proportion of total *state* revenue from this source was less than 3 per cent. The bulk of state revenue is now derived from new sources hitherto unexploited. Of primary importance in connection with highway costs are taxes on motor vehicles. These are of three principal sorts: registration fees, operators' license fees, and the tax on

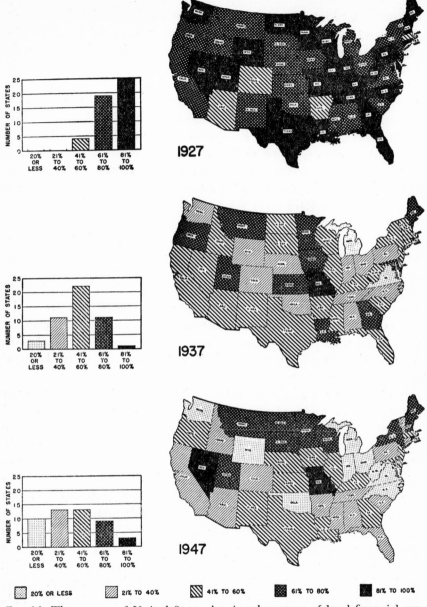

FIG. 14. Three maps of United States showing the extent of local financial support for local roads in 1927, 1937, and 1947.

motor fuel. The first registration fees were imposed primarily for regulatory purposes and the amount was nominal. Thus the first New York registration fee was one dollar and produced $954 in 1910. Within a few years, however, the revenue possibilities of such a levy were seen, and in 1950 it produced more than $700 million. Operators' license fees brought in $50 million. But by far the most lucrative levy is that on motor fuel which produced $1.5 billion. The automobile, then, provides the state treasuries with something over two and a quarter billion dollars a year, or about one-fourth of all state revenues excluding unemployment compensation taxes.

State aid for local roads was initiated by New Jersey as long ago as 1891, and by 1917 every state was participating in local highway construction and maintenance, either by grants of money or by the direct construction of roads which were then turned over to local units. A very substantial type of assistance to local governments consisted in the assumption by the states of responsibility for the building and maintenance of a system of primary roads. Since such highways are the most traveled and the most costly, their transfer to the state relieved the local governments of a heavy burden. The mileage which has thus passed under state control now totals 400,000. But even these changes represent only a part of the success of the local units in lightening their road costs.

The presence in the state treasuries of steadily increasing sums derived from highway-user taxes was an open invitation to local groups to demand that larger sums be allocated to local roads. The success of this demand in the various states is shown by the maps in Figure 14. In 1927 local taxes constituted more than 80 per cent of the support of local highways; by 1947 these sources amounted to only 39 per cent. State support increased correspondingly so that more than half of the total costs of local roads is defrayed by state aid. Moreover, a little more than 4 per cent of all road revenue is now contributed by the federal government under the secondary highway program inaugurated in 1944. The percentage distribution of local highway revenues in 1947 is shown on the next page.

This is truly an amazingly successful record. The Bureau of Public Roads points out that "in 1927 there was no state in which less than 40 per cent of the revenue came from local sources. In 1937 there were 14 states, and in 1947 there were 23 states in which the locally raised proportion of revenue available for road purposes had dropped below this percentage. In more than half the states there

Source of revenue	Percentage
Federal aid	4.2
State:	
Highway-user imposts	52.9
Other	3.5
County:	
Property taxes	19.6
Other	7.3
Town, township, district:	
Property taxes	7.4
Other	5.1
Total	100.0

has been an almost unbroken decline from 1927 to 1947 in the percentage of total revenue for local roads obtained from local sources, while in every instance there has been a corresponding increase in the percentage obtained from state sources. In some instances these trends reflect the avowed policy of certain state legislatures of providing additional state support to increase the total available for local roads. In some instances local units have utilized the additional state revenues merely as a substitute for local funds. This latter practice effectively defeats the intention of those state legislatures which may have supplied the state revenues in the expectation of expediting the improvement of the local roads. . . . It is popular grass-roots politics to promise relief from the local tax burden by promoting the shift of that burden to superior levels of government. This practice, which has been successful to a considerable degree, frequently generates a reluctance on the part of local units to continue their financial support." [12]

Local units vary enormously, of course, in their ability to raise revenue for governmental purposes, and many of them would need help from the state even if they did their very best. For example, revenues per mile of town road vary from $312 in Maine to $1,182 in Massachusetts, and of county roads in California from $211 to $3,570. Even so, it seems doubtful if local units generally are doing their share. The Board of County Engineer Consultants asserts that local units in 1947, a year of great agricultural prosperity, were contributing to the support of local roads less than half of what they were paying in 1927. "Based upon past evidence of effort it appears,

---

[12] *The Local Rural Road Problem*, pp. 31, 37.

therefore, that local units have a capacity to make greater contributions than they now make to the financing of local road needs. An additional annual contribution from local sources ranging in amount from $100,000,000 to $250,000,000 appears both reasonable and proper." The smaller of these two figures represents almost one-third of the sum now being raised from local sources.

STATE ADMINISTRATIVE CONTROL

There is a growing mass of evidence that the state governments are now insisting not only on a more efficient use of state grants but also upon greater local support of local roads. This new attitude is a result in part of the policy of federal aid for secondary highways. This policy has practically compelled state highway departments to become better acquainted with local administrative practices and policies and to bring pressure for their improvement. A few examples will illustrate this development.

In Michigan, by an act passed in 1951, the state highway commissioner is made responsible for the approval of all road projects in the state, by whatever authority proposed. He is also charged with reports on construction progress and with the accounting for the expenditure of road funds at every governmental level. In 1950 New York entered upon a ten-year town road improvement plan under which all town projects require the approval of both the county superintendent of highways and the state director of public works before state assistance is forthcoming. Moreover, assistance is not available unless the town gives evidence of having made an equitable contribution from its own funds. In Illinois, all county road projects and all awards of contracts must be concurred in by the state department of public works. In Iowa, the annual construction program of each county is required to have prior approval of the state highway commission. Present New Hampshire law provides for direct state expenditure of all funds, town as well as state, on state-aided highways.[13]

On the other hand, it is reported that there is no state technical or supervisory assistance for county roads in North Dakota, the county authorities being wholly responsible for building and maintaining all highways outside the state system. In Arkansas the state

---

[13] See Charles M. Ziegler, "Commissioner in Michigan Correlating Head," *Better Roads,* vol. 21, no. 8, pp. 32-3 (Aug. 1951) and Wells M. Allred, "New York Takes Steps to Improve Its Town Highway System," *Ibid.,* vol. 20, no. 7, pp. 23-4, 36 (July 1950).

exercises no supervision over county roads except those that are a part of the federal-aid secondary system, even though state financial aid is distributed to the counties. Colorado requires no state supervision, although state technical assistance is available to counties requesting it. A recent survey of highway needs, however, contains suggestions for improving state-local relations. Generally speaking, state administrative supervision seems to proceed less rapidly in the more rural states but, taking the country as a whole, the units of highway work tend to grow larger and a steadily increasing proportion of rural road mileage is passing from completely local control.

In the developing pattern of federal-state-local participation in highway administration it seems clear that leadership is passing to the higher governmental levels. A growing influence will be exerted by the federal authorities. It will be influence, however, as distinct from direct administration, for the federal officials recognize that the service characteristics of local roads and the day-to-day operations involved in their maintenance are matters which require maximum autonomy of local governmental units.

The higher standards of performance required by federal regulations may be expected to find their way into local highway work as state laws more definitely recognize and enforce them. There is reason to believe that a good deal of the inefficiency and irresponsibility of local governments may be fairly attributed to outmoded state laws and to the absence of machinery for state-local cooperation in road work. The administrative practices of local units proceed in many instances from statutory requirements which are inapplicable under modern conditions but which have undergone only infrequent and minor revision. State highway departments have generally been so preoccupied with the vast job of managing the primary road system that regular and effective administrative relationships with local agencies have not developed. It is only through such relationships that technical and financial improvements can be brought about.

Impetus toward changes of this sort was provided by the federal-aid secondary highway act of 1944 and its amendments, since this act almost compelled the states to obtain the needed cooperation of their local units. One way to regularize this cooperation is to create within the state department a division responsible for the coordination of state-local plans and activities in the execution of secondary and local road programs. The establishment of such a division was recommended by the Board of County Engineer Consultants and a majority of the states have taken steps to comply.[14]

STATE CENTRALIZATION OF HIGHWAY ADMINISTRATION

It was because of the defects of decentralized administration, the inequality of taxpaying ability among counties, and the ineffectiveness of the system of apportioning state-collected revenues among the counties, plus depression conditions, that the legislature of North Carolina in 1931 took the revolutionary step of turning over all highway work to the state. The action was preceded by an exhaustive study of the highways of the state by the federal Bureau of Public Roads, the State Highway Commission, and the State Tax Commission. The road survey found that not many of the counties had any very clear information about their actual mileage; that only a few had any recent maps of their roads; that the conditions of county maintenance varied all the way from hopelessly inadequate to very satisfactory; that maintenance expenditures varied from $14 per mile in one county to $658 in another; that in many counties no satisfactory records of costs were kept; and that there was little or no attempt on the part of county authorities to integrate the state and county systems.

The North Carolina survey discovered that nine-tenths of the three million dollars distributed as state aid had not been devoted to road work, but had been used to service the debt for local roads, a debt which was said to be in excess of the worth of all the county roads. Summing up the economic and physical difficulties in the way of efficient administration by the counties, the survey said, first, that the county unit was not large enough to include areas of rich and poor development, and, second, that the area of the county and its road mileage were not sufficient to permit full utilization of the force and equipment necessary for efficient operation.

Since state assumption of the care of all roads took place, testimony of those in touch with developments is to the effect that the

---

[14] Valuable brief articles on the federal-aid secondary highway program appear from time to time in the quarterly issues of *American Highways*, the official organ of the American Association of State Highway Officials (Washington). Among these may be cited: Otto S. Hess, "State-County Cooperation on Federal-aid Secondary Roads," vol. XXIII, no. 4, pp. 7-8, 21 (Oct. 1944); Wilfred Owen, "The Highway Finance Program from the National Viewpoint," vol. XXVIII, no. 2, pp. 16-18 (Apr. 1949); and two by T. H. MacDonald, federal Commissioner of Public Roads. "Highway Development under the New Federal Legislation," vol. XXV, no. 2, pp. 8-9, 22-3 (Apr. 1946) and "A National Program for Secondary Road Development," vol. XXV, no. 3, pp. 8-9, 18 (Jul. 1946).

experiment has been successful, not only in giving very substantial relief to property taxpayers but in providing very much better secondary and local roads. The protests of home rule advocates were scattered, and in the main the transfer of functions from the county to the state was recognized as an economy which did no serious violence to local interests. Within a year substantially the same reform was adopted by all but three counties in Virginia, and it is believed by observers that better roads are now provided by the state at considerably less cost. In 1934 Pennsylvania assumed the responsibility for some 20,000 miles of township roads. Highway centralization has since taken place also in Delaware and West Virginia.

In both North Carolina and Virginia state assumption of all highway functions was admittedly a crisis development. Local residents wanted above all relief from heavy direct taxes, and for this relief they were willing to exchange whatever values they normally associated with local self-government. Yet the return to normal conditions brought no demand for a reversal of policy. If we take a broad view of the subject of state-local relationships, state centralization in the field of highway administration may be simply one of many experiments which will be made in our search for an area more suitable for administration in the Great Society than the small groups within which the practice and tradition of self-rule grew to maturity. Whether it is possible to find any accommodation between the demands for a large area and a wide tax base which modern administration seems to involve, and the dependence upon primary contacts which is implicit in the notion of self-government, depends upon our fertility of political and administrative invention and upon our willingness to attempt what may appear to be dangerous experiments.

In reality we do not yet know enough to say that the value of local self-government can be realized only in certain traditional areas. In New England it is the town which is looked upon as the cradle of self-government. In the South it is the county, and in parts of the Middle West it was at one time the township. In the technical sense, home rule has reference primarily to the legal status of incorporated municipalities. That men can associate the sentiment with territorial areas of such different sizes and characters leads one to believe that perhaps other areas may be equally serviceable in preserving the values of local autonomy. It is certainly true that under modern conditions and for some purposes the nation itself may have its affairs so skillfully dramatized as to weld the people together in a self-governing unit.

Within the individual states the figures seem to show that citizens devote more attention to state issues than to local ones. Nor is this all. There are Western counties which are greater in area than such Eastern states as Connecticut, New Jersey, and Massachusetts, and many Eastern counties are far more populous than such states as Nevada, Utah, and the Dakotas. In view of these facts, is it possible to say at what point self-government is being threatened? Until we know more than we do about the relations between governmental areas and the requirements of both efficient and democratic government, it is the part of wisdom to suspend judgment on the whole question.[15]

---

[15] On this question the writer has found very suggestive Baker Brownell's *The Human Community* (1950) and John Dewey's *The Public and Its Problems* (1926). The narrower question of the allocation of functions should be considered in the light of such discussions.

CHAPTER 11

Public Education

The most costly and important function administered by local governments in the United States is the provision of instruction to the nation's youth. One-sixth of our entire population, or more than 80 per cent of all persons between the ages of five and seventeen, attend publicly supported elementary and secondary schools. This means an army of over 23,000,000 children, slightly more than half of whom live on farms or in rural non-farm territory. The teachers in charge of these pupils number about 850,000, more than 480,000 of them in the "country" where are found about four-fifths of the grade schools and three-fourths of the high schools. The United States Office of Education estimates that school enrollment will reach more than 27,000,000 by 1960, and the Bureau of the Census predicted in 1949 that elementary school enrollment would be 50 per cent higher in 1960 than in 1947. The support of these schools costs the huge sum of $2,900,000,000 annually, while the value of school property is about eight billion dollars, or $400 for each pupil enrolled. The total school debt is well over two billion dollars, requiring an annual interest and amortization payment of more than $209,000,000, or more than a million dollars for each day that school "keeps." No matter how we view it, instruction is the most important peacetime public enterprise of the nation.[1]

No other nation in the western world exhibits the same degree of decentralization in the control of education as the United States. "The autonomous school district, organized separately from the ordinary system of local administration, is essentially an American device. England had some such units at one time, and there are examples in Canada and elsewhere, but it is primarily in the United States that the district system is now to be found. Nowhere else is it

---

[1] Much of the factual and statistical material in this chapter is drawn from *The Forty-Eight State School Systems*, published in 1949 by the Council of State Governments, and from the *Biennial Survey of Education in the United States*, published by the United States Office of Education.

so extensive or so deeply intrenched." [2] Though there is plenty of statutory and judicial assertion of the paramount authority of the state in this field, in practice each local community goes very much its own way, at least so far as actual administration is concerned. While the central state authorities may prescribe rather minutely with regard to standards and curriculum, only a little observation is required to show that those on the spot may, by their administration, insensibly but vitally nullify the policy of the state.[3] Hence, while nearly every other function has yielded to the necessities of an industrialized society and passed, in fact as well as in law, under the more or less complete control of the state, the work of education, on the lower levels at least, still remains very largely under the control of local people. Because of our almost pathetic belief that education offers us a solution for all our problems, and our tendency to be sentimental about our children, the "little red schoolhouse" has come to be the symbol of local democracy and indeed the very epitome of local self-government itself. In fact, numberless romantic legends, embodied in poem and song and story, have been instrumental in keeping alive the mores of the pioneering era among thousands whose own instruction was received in the marble palaces of a more expansive epoch. Thus the rural school has exerted strong though subtle influences throughout modern American society.[4]

THE DISTRICT UNIT

Elementary education in rural districts is at present administered through four different units—the independent school district, the township (town in New England), the consolidated district, and the county. The typical unit is the independent district which is retained in all, or a portion, of more than half the states.[5] The district system originated in Massachusetts and, under early conditions, was the only feasible plan of organization. If instruction was to be

---

[2] William Anderson, *The Units of Government in the United States* (Public Administration Service, No. 83, 1945), p. 21.

[3] A good general study for a single state system is George W. Campbell, "The Influence of Court Decisions in Shaping the Policies of School Administration in Kentucky," *Bulletin of the Bureau of School Service,* College of Education, University of Kentucky, Vol. IX, No. 4 (Lexington, June 1937). The most comprehensive account is Newton Edwards, *The Courts and the Public Schools* (Chicago, 1933).

[4] The "little red schoolhouse" is actually the one-room, one-teacher, ungraded rural school. In April 1950, the Office of Education reported that there were still 75,000 such schools.

[5] The district unit is used in all or part of twenty-six states; the county unit is found in eleven states; and the town or township in nine states. The Delaware system is almost completely centralized in the state. Consolidated districts are widely scattered. See *The Forty-Eight State School Systems,* pp. 52-55, 192, 196.

made available to all children, the area supporting a school had to be small enough to make it possible for pupils to get to and from school afoot or by the conveyances then in use. As a matter of fact, the school district may be looked upon as the political organization of the rural neighborhood in an even more intimate sense than the town or township or other local area with general governmental powers. The one-room, one-teacher schoolhouse served the needs of ten or a dozen families and furnished instruction to half a dozen to twenty or thirty children.[6] But the school itself was far more than an educational center. Under primitive conditions of travel, when men lived their whole lives within the boundaries of a single county, when hard work for long hours was the rule, when leisure was scanty, the schoolhouse was the social center of the neighborhood. Spelling "bees," singing contests, "lyceums," and "sociables" were held in the schoolhouse, and the district which supported it loomed larger in the consciousness of local citizens than any other unit to which they belonged. Only the highway district could pretend to rival it in the concreteness of the services rendered, and since the children's welfare was bound up with the school district, even good roads were of secondary importance.[7] It is these services, or the lingering nostalgic memory of them, which brings it about that the small district continues to flourish after the conditions which called it forth have largely disappeared. It is not possible to be completely accurate, but there are at this time about 100,000 such districts in the country as a whole. These maintain a total of 141,318 schools (exclusive of high schools) of which more than 75,000 are one-teacher schools.[8]

---

[6] The average area of the district in the states classed as district unit states was about eighteen square miles in 1935. In the township unit states, the average area was twenty-seven square miles; in the county unit states it was 378 square miles. The area of the typical rural district was considerably smaller, probably not much greater than five square miles. It is worth pointing out here that pioneer families were larger than modern families, and that, for that reason, district schools with small school populations were relatively fewer in number than they are today. Since the first edition of this book, consolidations have caused an increase in these average figures.

[7] "The land was dotted, before the nineteenth century was very old, with thousands of these districts, each with its school, consisting usually of only one room. . . . Although the small school district and its one-room, ungraded school are now largely outmoded . . . it is well to pay tribute to the pioneers who succeeded in placing such an institution within walking distance of almost every six year old child." J. H. Kolb and E. de S. Brunner, *A Study of Rural Society* (3rd ed., 1946), p. 433. Quoted with permission of the authors and the publishers, Houghton, Mifflin Company. The same authors point out that it does not seem possible in the foreseeable future to reduce the number of school districts much below 75,000.

[8] Many districts exist legally but do not operate a school. In these cases, they levy a tax to pay the tuition of children sent to a school maintained by a neighboring district. In 1947-48, 99,713 districts of all sorts—county, independent, etc.—were reported. *The Forty-Eight State School Systems*, p. 192.

INEQUALITY OF DISTRICT RESOURCES

The existence of such a large number of petty districts gives rise, in the case of education, to all the evils associated with a multiplicity of governing areas with respect to other functions. There must always have been inequalities of wealth between districts, but these have been greatly accentuated with the progressive decline of agriculture, the change in the character of wealth, and the increasing cost of meeting modern educational standards.[9] Since practically the sole source of local revenue is the general property tax, and since at best the productive value of property may vary widely even between neighboring districts, all degrees of inequality arise when it comes to meeting the modest minimum requirements imposed by state authorities. Shifts in crop areas or the depletion of the soil due to poor farming, erosion, or unwise removal of forest covering, or changes in demand due to the vagaries of public taste, may make much of the land submarginal for agriculture and lead to a steady decline of population, heavy tax delinquency, and excessive burdens upon the remaining property. Other accidental factors often play a part in rendering the small district inefficient. Though not generally known, a very large proportion of the cost of maintaining local schools is derived from taxes laid upon railroad and other public utility property. The property upon which these taxes are laid does not, of course, touch by any means all of the thousands of school districts which may exist within a single state. Districts within which there is extensive trackage and valuable terminal property have a rich source of revenue near at hand and are able to finance an adequate program without laying a heavy burden upon local owners of real estate. Less fortunate districts can maintain respectable schools only by levying taxes at almost confiscatory rates or by accepting the bounty of the state in the form of grants or subventions. One of the most difficult problems facing state educational authorities within the present generation has been to find ways of equalizing educational opportunities between districts of such very unequal local resources.

---

[9] The only way to make this completely clear would be for the student to study such comparative figures as may be available for his own state. In the United States as a whole, per capita income varies from $659 in Mississippi to $1,781 in New York, and $1,842 in Nevada. In eight states, per capita income exceeds $1,600, and in ten it is less than $1,000. Equally striking differences must exist within the limits of almost every individual state.

SMALL DISTRICTS AS ADMINISTRATIVE UNITS

One of the unfortunate results of clinging to the traditional district system was the preservation of a large number of local schools in which the enrollment was so small as to make the per capita cost very high. An investigation by the Office of Education in 1933 disclosed that there were more than seven thousand one-teacher schools enrolling five or fewer students each, and several times that number with fewer than ten pupils.[10] In the same year more than one-third of the 7,059 one-teacher schools in the state of New York enrolled not more than ten pupils. Under the law, as it stood in that year, the state contributed $1,000 annually to each of these schools. Eight districts actually had but one pupil each; the total cost to the state in these cases was $1,166.51 for all purposes in each district, while the total local contribution was only a little more than $2,000. The state planning commission estimated late in 1934 that for $95,-000 the state could buy the entire land areas of these districts.[11] Although these are, of course, extreme cases, they illustrate the unreasonable cost of maintaining very small schools. A comparison of data from the several states fifteen years ago led to the generalization that "when schools enroll between one and five pupils the cost per pupil per year averages between $250 and $300 depending in part upon the salaries paid and in part upon the length of the term maintained; in schools with an attendance of from six to ten pupils the cost averages between $150 and $200; and in those with as many as twenty to twenty-five pupils the average falls to between $40 and $100. The smallest elementary schools are, therefore, from three to six times as expensive as the larger schools. . . . The average cost per pupil attending elementary schools was about $75 for the United States as a whole in 1930."[12] In all such discussions, the important

---

[10] See W. H. Gaumnitz, *Economies through the Elimination of Very Small Schools,* U. S. Office of Education, Bulletin No. 3, 1934.

[11] *Summary Report of Progress of the New York State Planning Board,* Jan. 1935, pp. 35, 38, 39. The extent of consolidation in New York State since this date is indicated by the fact that there were in 1948-49 only 2,900 districts of all types actually operating schools. There were in the same year only 1,322 one-teacher schools, about 180 of which had fewer than ten pupils. This information was supplied by Dr. Theodore C. Wenzl, Chief of the Bureau of Apportionment of the State Education Department, in a letter of March 5, 1950.

[12] W. H. Gaumnitz, *op. cit.,* p. 25. The state planning board in New York concluded that the cost of a one-teacher school in that state was about $1,500 per year regardless of the number of pupils in attendance, and that the cost per pupil was four times the average when the school had five or fewer pupils, and twice the average when there were from six to ten in attendance. The Illinois Tax Commission reported in 1932 that nearly 4,000 of the 9,601 one-room schools in that state operated with twelve or fewer pupils. See *The Rural Schools of Illinois,* pp. 7, 8.

figure to keep in mind is, of course, the optimum teacher-pupil ratio, that is, the number of pupils which one teacher can instruct with the maximum efficiency, other factors being equal. It is obviously impossible to be dogmatic in setting such a figure, but in those schools which, by the standards that we have, are regarded as most efficient, each teacher normally instructs from twenty to thirty pupils at a per capita cost certainly not in excess of $100 per year. Though, as will be pointed out later, experience with the consolidated district and other larger areas has made it possible to question the extreme claims of economy made for such reforms, it still is true that very real savings would result in most cases. The district organization, however, stands squarely in the way of this kind of reform. "Tradition, sentiment, personal prejudice, and convenience stand in the way. Nevertheless, the citizens of these districts cannot 'have their cake and eat it.' They cannot have a little inadequate and antiquated school within sight of the old home place, however glorious and wonderful it may seem to them, without paying in many instances excessive taxes." [13]

EXCESSIVE NUMBER OF BOARD MEMBERS

Clinging to the small rural district also requires the choice of a very large number of school directors or trustees, to say nothing of such petty administrative officers as school tax collectors and district treasurers. Thus, in Illinois, where something like 12,000 school districts were still operating in 1945, the election of more than 36,000 directors was required. Since the typical rural district is little, if any, larger than four miles square, this means that three directors must be found among the local residents.[14] It is obviously absurd to expect to find anything like that number of persons competent to frame and supervise a sound educational policy, which is precisely what they attempt to do, no matter how much of this responsibility may *legally* rest with state authorities. At present, the nearly 100,000 rural school districts of the country are managed by 382,000 school board members. Since the total number of rural teaching positions is about 480,000, this means that there are even now nearly as many board members as there are teachers. In fact in twelve

---

[13] Quoted from a manuscript by Frank B. Bachman in Gaumnitz, *op. cit.,* pp. 32-33.

[14] The average population of school districts in Nebraska was about 250 in 1932, in South Dakota 200. See W. S. Deffenbaugh and T. Covert, *School Administrative Units* (Office of Education, Pamphlet No. 34, Jan. 1933).

states only a few years ago, the board members outnumbered the teachers.[15]

If we look at the facts in a majority of the rural school districts of the nation, it is silly to suppose that first-, or even second-rate, talent can be found to this extent; and the quality of the local personnel from which such officials must be drawn would seem to be declining rather than improving as the position of agriculture becomes more and more precarious. As the soil grows less productive, tenancy increases and a type of farmer appears who is not interested in maintaining the same educational standards that were in vogue in more prosperous days. In any event, there is ample evidence that supervisory talent was not distributed evenly by Providence among the small school districts. In many cases even the business management of the schools, where one might expect at least frugality to prevail, leaves much to be desired. The keeping of records is neglected and the physical plant and equipment of the school are allowed to fall into a condition that can often be described only as scandalous.

When districts had few pupils and the school program was not extensive, perhaps no great harm was done by this sort of laxness. In view of the much greater school population and the greater variety of educational offerings today, even small districts would profit from the adoption of efficient business practices. It is true that "most states now require some form of school budget for all districts. In a number of states, however, the requirement is still rather superficial, as no plan has been developed for giving competent guidance or for assuring that budgets will be properly prepared and carried out." [16] Students of school finance attribute the absence of sound business methods to the fact that the basic administrative units are too small to attract the necessary leadership in education and business management.[17]

In any event, it is far too generally true that, under the district

---

[15] E. P. Cubberley, *State School Administration*, pp. 163, 165; *12th Yearbook,* Department of Superintendence, National Education Association, pp. 39, 41. These states were Arkansas, Idaho, Kansas, Minnesota, Mississippi, Missouri, Montana, Nebraska, Oregon, Nevada, South Dakota, and Wisconsin. Indeed there must, even now, be a good many districts in which the board members outnumber the pupils!

[16] *The Forty-Eight State School Systems,* pp. 154, 238.

[17] See Paul R. Mort and Walter C. Reusser, *Public School Finance*, 2d ed. (1951), p. 156. This book contains selected references to the literature of school finances and management.

system, the elementary schools are in the hands of an excessive number of unimaginative, tight-fisted, and uninspired board members to whom the possession of wide legal powers is not a challenge to constructive effort in a great social enterprise, but rather a temptation to penny-pinching and the pettier forms of tyranny over those so unfortunate as to have to deal officially with them. Not the least valuable results of using a larger administrative unit would be the widening of the area from which board members would be chosen and the creation of an opportunity to select somewhat abler people for this service.

Because of its concrete nature, one might expect the physical plant of the school to receive reasonable attention from the governing board. But "facts available from a variety of sources show that there are many communities in practically every state today where a large proportion of the children do not have adequate school plant facilities. In some communities the situation is critical. In others there is no special problem. In some states the situation is much more severe than in others, but in general school plant needs are more acute today than they have been for many years." [18] In spite of the fact that school enrollment is expected to increase by several million in the next ten years, little has been done over large areas of the country to plan for the 250,000 additional classrooms that will be needed. At the same time a very large number of school structures are obsolete, non-fire-resistant, or otherwise unsuitable for efficient work, and little has been accomplished in correcting such situations.

In a very large number of small districts little improvement can be recorded over the past generation with respect to such matters as contracts and purchases. It must be admitted, of course, that these failings are not in all instances the fault of the directors. Inequality of district resources, restrictive tax and bonding laws, and the absence in small districts of facilities for preparing contract and purchase specifications, all combine to supply explanations of the general inefficiency encountered. Financial and technical assistance is furnished by a few state governments with respect to school plant construction and improvement, as well as bus transportation, but, except in the case of the last-named, the sums involved are not yet large enough to be significant in view of the magnitude of the needs.[19]

---

[18] *The Forty-Eight State School Systems*, p. 88.
[19] For details see Ch. VI of *The Forty-Eight State School Systems*.

THE SMALL DISTRICT AND CENTRAL SUPERVISION

The excessive number of small districts is open to the further objection that it violates what might be called the principle of economy of supervision. In nearly every state, some machinery exists by which local conduct of the schools may be watched by central authorities, either from the state capital itself or through county or other regional supervisors. It is clear that when a county, for example, contains a hundred or more school districts, such supervision is bound to be of the most perfunctory character. It can consist, at best, of brief and casual visits by agents of the state department, and the collection of statistics whose accuracy and fullness can scarcely be checked. Hence, any contribution in the way of educational leadership and advice which the state may theoretically be in a position to make is, in practice, not realized because of the sheer multiplicity of local agencies with which contact must be maintained.

THE SMALL DISTRICT AND EDUCATIONAL PHILOSOPHY

It may further be suggested that the maintenance of the small independent district perpetuates certain imponderable, but none the less significant, attributes of the enterprise of public education. Some of these deserve examination, although it is admittedly difficult to deal with them in any concrete fashion. In a social democracy like the United States, all institutions are under constant pressure from equalitarian forces intent upon compelling these institutions to serve the prejudices and cater to the vagaries of the community.[20] Such pressure is never wholly absent on any level of government, and no governmental device is exempt from the danger of being diverted from its rational ends. When the unit is small, the rank and file of the population find few obstacles to overcome in compelling action in accordance with their prejudices and assumed needs. The democracy of the small school district exhibits in miniature all the typical weaknesses of democracy elsewhere. And the schools have met the fate of all other institutions in a society where the urge is towards equality—they have become "service" institutions. What does this mean?

As actually managed, the public schools are concerned not so much with the strictly intellectual progress of the children com-

---

[20] It is a matter of amazement to foreigners to find the public, on the one hand, waxing sentimental over teachers as "moulders of our youth" and, on the other, in moments of hysteria, imposing the final indignity of a special loyalty oath.

mitted to their care, as with the nebulous objective often described as "fitting them for life." [21] Time was when instruction was largely confined to the "three R's" and when the graduate was left with this equipment to find his own niche in society. This narrow curriculum dealt with matters as to the value of which there could be little argument in the school's constituency at a time when aristocratic ideals dominated society. All were fundamental tools in the acquiring of professional skills and, as actually taught, did often make some valuable contributions toward sharpening the wits and disciplining the mind. Pupils were prepared for the trades through an established apprentice system. In the pre-industrial age, this educational system met adequately the needs of individuals destined, for the most part, for farming or petty business enterprise. The coming of the machine destroyed the value of the skills formerly gained by laborious effort as an apprentice and threw upon the schools the task of teaching dozens of new subjects of assumed value to a highly organized industrial system. In this the rural school was bound to share, since many, if not most, of its graduates no longer returned to the "old home place," but joined the workers in the cities, or in other ways found places for themselves in a complicated social order.[22]

This revolution in the curriculum was assisted by the naive American faith in education (or at any rate, in instruction), a popular conviction that everything can be taught in school. The results of this faith or conviction have been manifold. The original intellectual content of the common school curriculum has been greatly diluted by the addition of a large number of subjects of a severely practical nature.[23] This has served to depress the level of intellec-

---

[21] As one commentator puts it: "The objective of education also changed from that of equipping the individual with intellectual tools to that of training for participation in society; the school, both in its curriculum and in its methods, is becoming socialized, and is endeavoring to serve the community as an educational and social center for both young and old." E. D. Sanderson, *The Rural Community*, pp. 557-58.

[22] In recent years, many educators frankly view their task as keeping adolescents off the labor market. With respect to this, a distinguished critic of modern society remarks: "One motive, for instance, for raising the age-limit of compulsory schooling is the laudable desire to protect the adolescent and fortify him against the more degrading influences to which he is exposed on entering the ranks of industry. We should be candid about such a motive; and instead of affirming what is to be doubted, that everyone will profit by as many years of tuition as we can give him, admit that the conditions of life in modern industrial society are so deplorable, and the moral restraints so weak, that we must prolong the schooling of young people simply because we are at our wits' ends to know what to do to save them." T. S. Eliot, *Notes toward the Definition of Culture* (1949), p. 107. Quoted with the permission of the publishers, Harcourt, Brace and Co.

[23] See Mortimer Smith, *And Madly Teach* (Henry Regnery, Chicago, 1949).

tual achievement of the pupils, for the simple reason that a democratic system is bound to neglect those with a capacity for abstract and original thinking in favor of the many who are capable of doing the "practical" thing.[24] Thus, cooking and sewing, printing, carpentry, typing, drafting, "dramatic art," and so on—things once learned in the home or through apprenticeship or "on the job," where, doubtless, they may best be learned—have been turned over to the schools, which therefore tend to settle to the level of intellectual attainment found in the community which supports them, and to reproduce on a small scale the social institutions surrounding them.[25] The school therefore becomes the one institution which various groups in the community attempt to control to the end that it may turn out products attuned to the interests of the dominant set.

Those who are concerned with emphasizing the more purely scholastic work of the schools are faced with this dilemma: The American people, having embarked on the enterprise of educating everyone, are in the end bound to call the tune. In publicly supported institutions, at any rate, it would seem useless to stand against this pressure. This is scarcely less true in private schools, so pervasive is the force of democratic standards in a society such as ours. The content of education was long defined by an untitled aristocracy of "gentlemen"; we are now witnessing its redefinition by the democracy.[26]

All this, of course, is perfectly normal, for education is by its very nature conservative, only a degree less so than the church itself.[27]

---

[24] Some indication of where officialdom places the emphasis may be derived from the fact that in most state departments there is a pronounced understaffing of non-vocational phases. This may possibly be due, of course, to the fact that federal funds are not available for the employment of such personnel.

[25] Early in 1935, the attorney-general of Kentucky was asked by a local school authority whether the district could legally spend public funds for instruction in ballroom dancing and bridge. The assistant attorney-general, in holding such an expenditure legal, said that these amusements "have become so integral a part of American life and are indulged in by so many persons, that they should not only be permitted to be taught, but should be encouraged to be taught." *N. Y. Times*, March 7, 1935, p. 25.

[26] The writer is aware, of course, that there is implicit in this discussion a point of view hopelessly out of date. It is at least not the view held by the educational theorists responsible for the training and, incidentally, the placement of the vast majority of the teaching and administrative personnel. There is some reason to be encouraged, however, by evidence here and there that thoughtful people are beginning to be critical of the educational "experts" now so firmly in the saddle. See Albert Lynd, "Quackery in the Public Schools," 185 *Atlantic Monthly* 33-38 (Mar. 1950).

[27] Thus, Aristotle: "No one will doubt that the legislator should direct his attention above all to the education of youth, for the neglect of education does harm to the

It is the inescapable business of the public schools to preserve and hand on what the race and the community have found of value in the business of getting on with each other and with the impersonal forces of nature and society. It is expecting too much to look for a very critical attitude toward things as they are from those who occupy positions of authority because they agree with the prevailing system of values. Difficulties arise, however, from the fact that the democracy exemplified by the small district passes very easily from the preservation of values to the encouragement of all sorts of popular vagaries. The possession of power by those who have legal control creates a constant temptation to substitute force for reflection and to confuse what is of transient interest with the permanently useful and valuable. That this temptation is only feebly resisted is evidenced by the steady growth in the bulk of legislation drawn so as to control the content of the curriculum.[28] "All told, schools have been directed to do more than fifty different things. One or more states require special observance of twenty-one different days such as Washington's Birthday, Arbor Day, Armistice Day, Good Roads Day, etc. In one Eastern state . . . the legislature has made it mandatory upon each school to do, at least once a week, twenty-one different things, varying from a daily salute to the flag and a daily reading of not fewer than five verses of the Bible, to the weekly fire drill, etc., etc. In all, the forty-eight states have placed on the statute books nearly 1,000 enactments relating to the way time is spent in the schools. School boards or teachers are faced with the alternative of ignoring the law or of handicapping the conduct of more essential work if the law is complied with. In hundreds of small communities, therefore, the law becomes a dead letter, a solution to the problem which is admittedly the less of the evils." [29]

---

constitution. The citizen should be moulded to suit the form of government under which he lives. For each government has a peculiar character which originally formed and which continues to preserve it. The character of democracy creates democracy and the character of oligarchy creates oligarchy; and always the better the character the better the government." *Politics,* Book VIII, Ch. 1. But when Aristotle used the word "legislator" he did *not* have in mind American school board members or even state legislators.

[28] It should be said that a good deal of this legislation is not demanded by local authorities or by local school patrons. Much of it is suggested by enthusiastic experimenters and educational evangelists connected either with the central administration or with the state teachers' association, or "civic" and patriotic organizations.

[29] E. de S. Brunner and J. H. Kolb, *Rural Social Trends,* pp. 191, 196. A complete review of legislative prescriptions may be found in the *12th Yearbook,* Department of Superintendence, National Education Association (1934), pp. 94-96. The latter source says that when the general prescriptions are broken down, they reveal thirty-nine sub-

THE QUALITY OF TEACHING

Ultimately, of course, the schools exist for the pupils, and any judgment as to their effectiveness must be based upon the results of instruction. Measuring these results is admittedly difficult. Doubtless many children still receive a sound education in the one-room ungraded district school, while many others profit little from the expensive outlay provided by wealthy cities. On the whole, however, it seems clear that the small rural school is inefficient not only from the point of view of its cost in dollars and cents, but also in the provision of instruction. For, when one teacher must instruct students in eight grades, she is compelled to teach from twenty to forty classes each day, devoting ten minutes or less to each; and she is obliged to teach perhaps as many as a dozen subjects. Under such conditions work is likely to be superficial, and little attention to individual pupils is possible. Furthermore, it is probable that the small enrollment in many rural schools deprives the pupils of the stimulus offered by competition where the numbers are larger. The poverty of many small districts not only compels the employment of untrained and immature teachers and makes impossible an adequate school year, but it also enforces economies at the expense of equipment sorely needed for good teaching. Finally, it is the universal testimony of observers and students of education that the petty neighborhood jealousies fostered and kept alive by the retention of the small district create a situation in which it is next to impossible to maintain rigorous standards or to secure the benefits of professional teaching.

There are no reasons in strict theory why the small school district should not serve as an acceptable administrative unit in the work of education. If people were in fact as much interested in learning as they pretend to be, the country would be full of educational enterprises conducted on the principle of bringing together Mark Hopkins and the eager student.[30] We have to take things as

---

jects about which instruction is ordered to be given, "varying from 'dictionary' and 'metric system,' through 'thrift,' effect of tobacco, oratory, manners, fire prevention, importance of animals, cotton grading, and 'social and ethical outcomes' "—whatever they are! This record does not, of course, include matters inserted at the fiat of local boards.

[30] "After all, it is very little that a teacher can do by direct teaching. He can certainly look after the preliminary drill, but beyond that it is mainly by being himself that he can do any good. If he cares for great things and if his pupils are capable of caring for them too, there is every chance that they will learn to do so." John Burnett, an essay on "Ignorance," printed in his *Essays and Addresses* (1930), p. 250.

they are, however, and, when we do, the use of the small district is condemned. Most of the conditions which made it acceptable have passed away and, so far as one can measure such things, education has progressed in rough proportion to the abandonment of the district plan of organization. The gross inequalities of wealth, traceable ultimately to the industrialization of the country, and the decline of agriculture have made it impossible for many small districts to meet the needs of a modern program of instruction. In many sections the drift of population to the cities has drained off the more energetic individuals and weakened local interest in the schools. Its very "democracy" in many cases has meant the perpetuation and intensification of petty local and personal jealousies which, in reality, sacrifice the standards of the school to the grudges and ambitions of local potentates. Persistence of the small district leads directly to the lowering of standards of personnel by requiring the choice of an absurdly large number of board members and by making almost impossible the adoption of sound business methods. Here and there, in district schools throughout the nation, there are doubtless teachers who do not suffer by comparison with the masters of a most difficult art; on the whole, however, so long as men and women are faced with the fundamental human problem of getting an adequate living and are endowed with normal ambition for professional achievement, the small district will stand as an obstacle to effective work.

THE CONSOLIDATED SCHOOL DISTRICT

These judgments as to the efficiency of the small district have been widely accepted, and for a generation this type of organization has been giving way to one in which the unit is much larger.[31] The simplest type used to replace it is the consolidated district. The essential features of the consolidation idea are the abandonment of a selected group of neighborhood one-room schools and their replacement by a modern school building at a convenient point. Such a school should contain a sufficient number of grades to accommodate the elementary pupils of the consolidated district and might even include a high school if the number of pupils warrants it. As a mat-

---

[31] The extent of consolidation in recent years is indicated by the fact that, whereas in 1931 there were 151,000 one-room schools (*Recent Social Trends*, p. 527), there were in 1947-48 just half that number of one-teacher schools. In the latter year, there were eight states in which more than 75 per cent of the elementary schools were one-teacher schools, while in fourteen states, one-teacher schools were less than 25 per cent of the total. Figures are from *The Forty-Eight State School Systems*.

ter of fact, it is the opinion of most students that only under exceptional circumstances can a district be justified unless it offers a high school course. Under favorable conditions, instruction in such special subjects as manual training, art, and domestic science may prove feasible, while the school building may house a branch of the county library, if one exists, and contain also an assembly hall. Arrangements for transporting pupils at public expense are, of course, necessary. Ideally, therefore, the pupil is carried to a much more efficient school, which reverses the procedure in the district system where a more or less successful attempt is made to carry the school to the pupil. Under the most favorable conditions, since the consolidated district is larger and wealthier than the single small district, the new school is well graded and well taught by trained and better paid teachers and is supplied with special physical equipment beyond the narrow means of the typical small district. In short, the consolidation movement aims at securing a better school plant, a better teaching personnel, and a better course of study.

Massachusetts seems to have been the first state to provide by law (in 1867) for this type of school. Since that date, the growth of the movement has been steady until today some consolidated schools are found in every state. The chief factors favoring the movement have been the improvement of roads and the greater ease of transporting children, and the growing belief that, if the tax base were widened, inequalities of the tax burden might be remedied. The heyday of the consolidation movement was in the fifteen-year period which coincided with the upward swing of prices following 1913. During these years more than 1,000 consolidations took place annually. With the coming of economic depression, which affected agriculture some years before it reached industry, the movement grew much less rapidly, but during the past few years, it has been resumed at a quickened pace.[32] In many parts of the country, its results have not always been happy. The directors of the large districts, impressed by the enlarged tax base at their disposal, were not always able to keep themselves free from the vice of attempting to "keep up with Joneses." Elaborate buildings were erected in many districts only to be reflected later in embarrassing fixed charges when public revenue sharply declined. In these and many other cases, sharp controversies arose between the villages in which the schools were fre-

---

[32] Kolb and Brunner report that, between 1920 and 1946, the number of consolidated schools increased from 9,752 to more than 22,000. *A Study of Rural Society*, p. 452.

quently located and the surrounding local population which felt itself unduly burdened to support an institution whose policies it could not sufficiently influence. In some extreme cases, the financial position of the consolidated district was fatally weakened by special legislation permitting the withdrawal of rural territory from the district. If, as seems likely, American villages come to be the centers of harmonious rural communities, the consolidation movement will have an assured future. There will, however, always be many sections of the country where it will be impracticable. Where population is sparse and distances great, the costs involved in such items as transportation of pupils would seem to be insuperable. In areas of this description, the one-room ungraded school will continue indefinitely.

These developments do not warrant the conclusion that the consolidation of schools has been a mistake. On the contrary, there is plenty of evidence that they are greatly superior from every point of view to the average district school, even when no account is taken of the important fact that they bring secondary education within reach of many rural children who previously could secure it with great difficulty, if at all. What experience does indicate most strikingly is that few local districts in rural areas can hope to supply a high type of educational service so long as they are restricted to the general property tax as a source of revenue. Some way must be found by which, constructively at least, the whole state shall be the unit of support for such districts. Consolidation embodies a sound theory of educational administration, but it cannot of itself create the values from which bills must be paid.

THE TOWN OR TOWNSHIP UNIT

In about a dozen states, including all of those in New England, and parts of Pennsylvania, New Jersey, Indiana, Michigan, Iowa, and North and South Dakota, the town or township is the accepted unit of school administration. In New England the town was the original governmental unit for the performance of all public functions delegated to localities. The small school district grew out of the town as its population spread from the immediate center to the periphery. The educational administration was reintegrated beginning in 1882, when Massachusetts provided for unified management under the control of the town. Thus it comes about that, in the New England states, town and school district are coterminous, and that education is one of the functions of the municipal government, though under the immediate supervision of a town school committee. This unification of authority in the town does not mean that outlying schools are abolished, as is the case with the consolidated district. The one-room, one-teacher school may, and does, linger on where, for any reason, actual physical consolidation has not been brought about. What the town unit does mean, however, is that the resources of the whole town are pooled, and proportional shares may be made available to individual neighborhoods which still have schools. It means further that better secondary schools are possible and that centralized and professional supervision is practicable. "The effect of the system is a pooling of effort by the people of the entire town. This results in an equalization of both tax rates and educational advantages throughout the entire town. Other beneficial results are an equally long term for all children; better teachers and at better wages; better and more sanitary buildings; a uniform course of instruction for all the schools of the town with high school advantages for all; free transportation to and free tuition in a central high school; special instruction (in music, art, etc.) for the outlying schools as well as the central town school; good professional supervision; and a systematic organization of the town's educational resources under a single small board responsible to the people for results." [33]

These results seem to have been largely realized in the New England states where the town is still to a considerable degree a "natural" unit and where the population is relatively dense. Farther west, however, the township has not proved in all cases a satisfactory unit. This has been attributable, for the most part, to the fact that the township lines were drawn in advance of settlement and, therefore, do not always include unified communities. In certain other cases, the sparseness of the population has caused popular interest to shift to a larger unit such, for example, as the county.

THE COUNTY UNIT

There are at present eleven states in which the county is the mandatory or optional unit for school administration.[34] It should be

[33] E. P. Cubberley, *State School Administration*, pp. 187-88. It may be added that, in most of the New England states, towns are grouped into districts for supervisory purposes.

[34] These states are: Alabama, Florida, Georgia, Kentucky, Louisiana, Maryland, North Carolina, Tennessee, Utah, Virginia, and West Virginia.

pointed out that there is not complete agreement among educational authorities as to what constitutes a true county unit. The principal question seems to be the extent of the power conferred on the county authorities, and the amount of authority left to the local districts which, it should be noted, may continue to exist with certain powers. If a definition is required, it might be said that the county unit exists when the county is the area chosen for the support and the administration of elementary and secondary schools. It does not mean that all the district schools shall be abolished and the work of instruction centralized in one building. It does not necessarily involve the abolition of the local districts as legal entities, for in some states they apparently still retain a shadowy existence. It does mean, however, that the tax base from which the schools draw their support is the entire county, and that a single elective or appointive board is responsible for the allocation of the revenue among the local schools and for the general supervision of all the schools in the county. Thus, the wealth of the county is pooled, as is its experience. The enterprise may be planned with larger objectives in view than the pleasing of some cross-roads tribune of the people or self-appointed censor of community manners. It is well to keep in mind, however, the following caution by Engelhardt: "A county school system has many limitations. It cannot be universally applied to any state without creating other inequalities. The mere fact that counties were not created or laid out with any specific reference to their adaptability to school district organization is sufficient to make one skeptical of the county unit as the ultimate solution of the school problem." [35]

It would be misleading, however, to give the impression that all of the advantages of this sort are actually being realized in many of the counties of the United States. The supporters of the district system, and traditionalists generally, have bitterly fought the extension of the county unit system, and at present it may be regarded as firmly established in only a few states. Even in most of these states, it would perhaps not be correct to say that the county unit is realizing all of its theoretical potentialities. As to the remainder of the country, there is a distinct tendency in the direction of increasing the importance of the county as an educational unit. In a few states, the evidence for this is found in a rather rudimentary development of more important powers in a county school board or in the office of

---

[35] Blakey, *Taxation in Minnesota*, p. 464.

the county superintendent; in others, this development has gone considerably farther; while, in still others, a number of individual counties have availed themselves of permissive statutes to accomplish a higher degree of unification and centralization.

While the true county unit system involves the abolition of the district system and the use of the whole county as a single district, there is nothing to be gained by a dogmatic insistence on a stereotyped plan. Under some circumstances, as, for example, in the South where the county is often a small area, two or three counties may be combined into one unit. On the other hand, there may be good reasons in some states for regarding the county as too large and, thus, for dividing it into districts designed to represent real rural communities. The Rural School Survey of New York State reported that "the county is too large in most cases for the administration and supervision of so intimate an institution as a school" for "it is in no sense of the word a community. . . . Its lines often run through a village or divide a district which is in local interests a closely united community. The county serves well for political administration where interests are under consideration which are purely material and impersonal—but county boundaries are in no way related to the growth of church centers and grange centers and lines of travel to the store or railroad station. The life of a community is determined in all these personal interests by the possibilities of easy transportation and communication." [36]

This is a cogent argument when applied to a settled and well-populated area where community lines are already established and where shifts of population are not frequent or great. In such cases, more might well be gained by using an intimate community as a unit than by purchasing a hypothetical efficiency at the expense of more subtle values. If the use of such a community be criticized, as it has been, as little more than a concession to a conservative sentiment favoring the old district, it should be said that there are circumstances under which even the district renders good service, and these should not be jeopardized out of deference to the dogmas of the experts. There are few sure-fire ways of handling any of these matters.[37]

---

[36] *Rural School Survey of New York State,* p. 197.

[37] The community unit plan recommended by the Survey Commission is now under way in New York State. In Illinois in 1949 there were operating 222 community districts with 1,819 attendance centers.

Administrative and Teaching Personnel

Obviously, the most important factor in the enterprise of public education is the people who are engaged in it. These may be conveniently divided into those who direct the school system, such as school board members, inspectors, supervisors and superintendents;[38] and the teacher who comes into direct contact with the pupils. These groups are primarily responsible for the accomplishments of our scheme of instruction, and it is essential that their competence be analyzed.

The State Superintendent

The administrative head of the state school system is nearly everywhere a state official known variously as the Commissioner of Education or the Superintendent of Public Instruction or, popularly, simply as the State Superintendent. In thirty-one states he is chosen by popular vote, while in others he is elected by a state board of education appointed by the governor or chosen in some other manner calculated to secure representation of various interests and sections within the state.[39] From the point of view of the stability of the office and the professional competence of its occupant, better results are normally secured by appointment. Where popular election is used, choice is, in some states, made by the use of a non-party ballot in the hope that the office will not become involved in partisan politics. While the device does seem to have done something to minimize the direct influence of the organized parties, it has not, by any means, taken the superintendency "out of politics." The candidate has still to seek office before the people, and, democratic politics being what they are in the typical American commonwealth, his tactics on the stump may at least skirt the edges of demagoguery.

It is not surprising, therefore, to discover that the office does not normally attract men of genuine eminence or outstanding professional attainments. In fact, it is too often filled by a type of educational politician less able consistently to apologize for his ma-

---

[38] According to the Biennial Survey of Education for 1945-46, the administrative officers and assistants in the state, county, city, and district systems of the country numbered 35,911.

[39] Appointment of the superintendent is made by the Governor in Maine, New Jersey, Ohio, Pennsylvania, Rhode Island, Tennessee, and Virginia, and by a state board in Arkansas, Connecticut, Delaware, Maryland, Massachusetts, Minnesota, Missouri, New Hampshire, New York, and Vermont. The salaries ranged (in 1947-48) from $3,300 in North Dakota to $20,000 in New York. In only eight states was it $10,000 or more.

neuverings prior to election, than his partisan colleagues in the state executive departments who, running frankly as machine men, have no illusions as to the nature of the tactics required for victory. Moreover, so long as continuance in office depends upon a fickle electorate, it is not likely to appeal to men interested in making a career of educational administration.[40] Nor is this all. Once in office, the superintendent too often finds himself with much less opportunity for service than he might have supposed while seeking votes. While it is true that his duties are primarily concerned with the improvement of rural schools, he too often finds himself without real power to achieve this object. A good deal of his time is consumed in the routine of managing his office, in making addresses to various groups, in collecting and interpreting statistics, in serving on certain official and semi-official committees, and in playing the intricate game involved in securing his re-election or reappointment. Ideally, a man in the position of state superintendent should be primarily concerned to afford vigorous leadership in education and to tell people what they should be thinking about and what their aspirations should be. In reality, however, the office does not attract such men and if, by happy accident, such a one is chosen, he finds his opportunities for service seriously restricted.

What needs to be done to make the office attractive to men of high calibre is suggested in a bulletin of the Office of Education where the objections to popular election are thus summarized:

"This method of selection limits the field from which to choose, as the superintendent must be a citizen of the given state. In states where the superintendent is appointed by the state board of education or by the governor, this official may be selected from the country at large. Such freedom of selection is clearly in the interest of better service.

"Where the state superintendent is selected by popular vote the salary is fixed by law. The salary cannot be adjusted to fit the person desired; but a person must be found to fit the salary.

"Where the state superintendent is elected by popular vote, the term of office is short—two to four years—and re-election is uncertain. This lack of continuity in the service is a serious handicap to the superintendent, however capable.

---

[40] Four years is the most frequent term; in six states the superintendent serves at the pleasure of the appointing authority. Twenty-six states report no legal requirements as to the educational qualifications of the superintendent.

"This method of appointment makes the office political and subjects it to all the fluctuations of party and factional politics."

Certainly, if the larger usefulness of the office is to be attained, some such changes as are here suggested should be adopted.

THE COUNTY SUPERINTENDENT

The county superintendent is the principal link between the local school organization and the state administration. The office exists in all but two states.[41] In fifteen states he is appointed by a local board or by certain state and local officials acting together. In twenty-five states he is chosen by the people of the county. The two-year term is most frequently found, although there are a few cases of three, four, or five-year terms. Salaries range from as little as $100 a year in a few poor and sparsely settled counties to as much as $12,000 in a few counties in the South. In eleven states, salaries of $5,000 or more are reported, while in ten others, the average does not exceed $3,000.

It is easy enough to demonstrate that in theory the county superintendent should occupy a key position in the educational system. His purely professional duties make an imposing list. "His work is to correlate and unify the educational work of his county; to act as educational adviser to the district or township authorities; and to stimulate an interest in education and in the improvement of educational conditions in the districts or townships of his county." [42] An official who would fill in this role with even tolerable success would be a person of real importance in his community. But the office is seldom filled by such persons, and the local schools are usually left to develop under whatever leadership may exist in their own constituencies. There are men and women capable of performing these functions, but they are found almost entirely in the urban school systems where the opportunities for a career are much more nearly a reality.

As things now stand in the rural sections of the country, every circumstance works against the possibility of professionalizing the office. As a result, it is too often filled by petty educational politicians, "joiners," and "backslappers," little interested in the professional aspects of their work, and often gifted with neither wisdom

---

[41] The exceptions are Delaware and Nevada. In Delaware school administration is centralized in the state government; in Nevada supervision is exercised in six areas comprising from one to six counties each.

[42] Cubberley, *State School Administration*, pp. 211-212.

nor skill nor vision. Where candidates for the office are required by
the rules of the democratic political game to engage in peddling
themselves from the stump, it is not surprising that men and women
seriously interested in education refuse to submit themselves to such
indignities, and that the office is normally filled by persons of quite
a different stamp.[43] Further obstacles exist in the short and insecure
tenure of office, the low salary, the requirement of local residence,
the dull grind of merely clerical duties imposed upon the incumbent,
and the frequent vagueness in the legal qualifications which has the
effect of putting the able and the stupid on a par and thus discourag-
ing the former—if such were not a work of supererogation! In view
of these difficulties, it is fair to say that the office is normally a blind
alley occupied by a succession of mediocre men and women who,
when not engaged in mending their political fences, are immersed
in a stultifying routine of "inspecting" rural schools, collecting statistics, auditing local accounts, smoothing over parochial quarrels, dealing out blank forms to local officials, and running errands for the
state department. In the typical county, it would be naive to look
to the superintendent for light and leading.[44]

If the preceding remarks seem to paint too dark a picture of the
supervising personnel of the schools, it is important to point out
that this personnel may be evaluated realistically only in connection
with an understanding of the growing responsibilities of state authorities in the field of popular education. More and more as time
has gone on, the state has found itself in a position of legal primacy
with respect to local schools. It now finds itself called upon to assume leadership in developing the work of education. The gains
to be achieved by a complete centralization of educational authority
are probably illusory, since there is clearly no way to compel local
people to prefer higher to lower standards; but the power of persuasion in the hands of earnest and competent men in conspicuous posi-

---

[43] The Indiana State Committee on Governmental Economy recommended in 1935
that the county should be the school unit under a board of five members. "This board
should have the power to name the county superintendent subject to the approval of
the State Director of Education. All employees in the county schools should be responsible to the superintendent and the county board of education should act upon appointments, transfers and dismissals only on recommendation of the superintendent."
It was also recommended that "the board should have power to consolidate schools.
If this power were used so as to reduce greatly the number of schools, a superintendent
so chosen might well become an educational leader in the community." See *Report of
the Committee,* pp. 24-25.

[44] There is a good discussion of the office in W. A. Cook, *Federal and State School
Administration,* pp. 177 ff. Details may be found in Table 25 of *The Forty-Eight State
School Systems,* p. 198.

tions can do much to inculcate an appreciation of, and insistence upon, a better quality of work. Until fairly recent years, the city school systems have had almost a monopoly of men and women of this type, and the rural schools have suffered from the lack of that sort of leadership which might be effective in the promotion of state policies in education and in the supervision of both local administrative practice and methods of instruction. Studies of developments within the states covering the last generation indicate clearly that state supervision no longer means the sort of haphazard and cursory "visiting" of schools which was formerly almost the total content of the term, but that the "tendency is decidedly to emphasize the professional leadership and instructional supervisory phases of the work of the rural school officers. Less and less emphasis is placed on inspection, more and more on systematic supervision." [45]

In view of these developments, unless some method of professionalizing the office of the state or regional supervisors is worked out, the power which such officials possess will continue to be exercised without the sense of responsibility which a truly professional staff might be expected to exhibit. To accomplish this, it is desirable that the residence requirement for both state and county superintendents be abolished, that appointment be substituted for popular election, that the qualifications for holding these offices be made more definite, and that they be guaranteed a greater security of tenure than they now normally enjoy. It is doubtful, of course, whether any method of choice or system of tenure will be successful in protecting these officials from the pressure of popular prejudices in a democracy like ours; but it is urgent that every likely means be adopted to secure and make effective the leadership and authority of persons disposed to resist such pressures.

LOCAL SCHOOL AUTHORITIES

The strategic position in school administration is occupied by the local school authorities, known variously as the trustees, the directors, or simply as the board. Under our decentralized administrative system, the local board has almost complete authority over the routine conduct of the schools, including the power to levy taxes, borrow money, employ and dismiss teachers, erect and maintain buildings and buy supplies, and, in some degree, to control the curriculum. To some extent, their powers of control are limited by the

---

[45] F. G. Crawford, *State Government*, p. 372.

necessity of meeting certain standards set by the state or by unofficial accrediting agencies, with regard, for example, to the training and experience of teachers, the length of the school term, and the character of the school plant. It is further true that, where the state contributes to the support of the local schools, it may be able by that fact to "buy" a compliance with certain rules which might not otherwise be observed. These possible controls, however, should not be taken too seriously. It is important to remember that the local board is everywhere elective, that the typical rural district is very small and the board members thus very close to the people, and, therefore, that local management of the schools becomes a branch of party, factional, or even personal politics. Hence, where there is the will to evade restrictions, local ingenuity is normally not strained to find popular ways of doing so. Taking the country as a whole, state and county supervision is neither vigorous nor alert, and information as to good practices is not widespread nor generally accepted, so that it remains true that the local board maintains its dominant position.

The local board might be considered from the point of view of its legal powers, but these are relatively unimportant in a study of this sort. The important question will always be, what kind of persons are chosen? In this field, an examination of the product of universal suffrage is not heartening. There is no way to deal with such a question statistically, and, if there were, it would be almost valueless. Reliance must be had upon observation, "on the ground," as it were. In open country districts the board members are necessarily farmers or the wives of farmers. Since there are few if any qualifications beyond residence in the district, tenants with large families may dispose of the property of their landlords through the device of ad valorem taxation; mortgage-holders may, in their turn in the place of power, draw tight the district purse strings and deny educational opportunities to the children of others; while bachelors, spinsters, and the childless, with a fanatic belief in frugality and the uselessness of everything beyond the "three R's," may be, and often are, chosen with results which may be imagined. And all may be depended upon to finance the district by "soaking" the railroad or other public utility corporation unfortunate enough to be required to pass through its boundaries.

If the district contains a hamlet or a village, the composition of the board is likely to be more variegated, for in these cases there will be found upon it representatives of local businesses and professions.

Such a board will probably contain not only active but retired farmers resident in the village, small businessmen such as bankers and merchants, and usually the local physician or dentist or lawyer. Since there are no qualifications, these persons are frequently chosen with no reference to their competence in the field of education, or even their own education. Board members who themselves are practically illiterate are by no means rare.[46] In fact, elections almost normally turn upon inconceivably petty or irrelevant "issues." The superintendent's policy toward interscholastic athletics may divide the community, and board members not shrewd enough to gauge the majority drift find themselves retired to private life. Interdenominational religious quarrels frequently determine the personnel of the board. Questions of discipline within the schools often enliven elections, especially if the pupils involved chance to be related to board members or important local personages. Petty business and professional quarrels, if, as is often the case, they are circulated by the door-to-door canvassing of disgruntled patrons, often determine the popular choice when vacancies are to be filled. Often the local banker, because of his position as the largest creditor in the district, uses his vantage-point to dictate the choice of his colleagues. Merchants who do not like the way in which the superintendent and teachers spend their salary checks have a very good reason for manipulating elections and are usually not slow to avail themselves of it.[47]

---

[46] So far as the author knows, there have been no comprehensive studies of the social and occupational composition of rural school boards. G. S. Counts, however, makes this summary statement concerning the personnel of county boards: "The typical county board of education in the United States is composed of six members. These members are elected by the people for a term of four years. One of the six members is a woman who follows the occupation of a housewife. Of the five men, three are farmers, one is a merchant and one is a physician. Four of the members have children attending the public schools of the county. From the standpoint of formal education they reflect somewhat favorably the attainments of the citizens of the community. Three of the members are products of the elementary school only; one has attended the secondary school; and two have enjoyed college or university privileges." George S. Counts, *The Social Composition of Boards of Education* (University of Chicago Press, 1927), pp. 78-79. A statistical study of district and village boards would probably reveal a somewhat similar situation, though open country boards would doubtless contain fewer members having college or university training.

[47] Counts complains, in the work cited, that "the dominant classes in our society dominate the board of education" and remarks mournfully that "in times past the school has certainly with monotonous frequency been the tool of dominant classes and has been made to guard the special interests of these classes." But is there anything very surprising in this? After all, the people who now control local schools would seem to have attained the kind of success deemed most desirable by a majority of our citizens. And a long view of history would seem to indicate that changes in ideals and revolts against established standards are almost always accomplished by persons not the products of the official system of education. Socrates, Jesus, Voltaire, and the English Philosophic Radicals of the early 19th century stand out as examples. In no social order can the public schools be expected to produce rebels.

The product of such petty maneuverings is bound to be anything but inspiring. Men and women capable of being influenced by such childish considerations can scarcely be expected to take a large view of affairs. It is a curious but well-authenticated fact that the management of what we loudly proclaim as the first care of the community is commonly placed in the hands of persons the choice of whom depends upon qualifications and tactics which go far to unfit them to discharge their trust. It must be admitted, however, that it is hard to suggest ways to improve this situation. If a larger area were adopted, it might aid to a degree in protecting the schools from the meaner forms of board interference and thus free superintendents from restrictions which must be galling to self-respecting individuals, and which are certainly inimical to the cultivation and perpetuation of professional standards. But those who advocate such a change need perhaps to be reminded that a larger district may well mean increased temptation to other types of tyranny and skulduggery. Moreover, it is only fair to point out that any board in a typical rural district normally finds its representative function hard to discharge. The theory of democracy demands that men and women in such positions carry out the mandate of the electorate even though it be irrational or contrary to sound practice. So long as the position of a board member is regarded as conferring an honor or affording opportunity for personal advancement, those who hold it will be under a strong temptation to act so as to retain public favor. Here, as elsewhere, the device of representation is not at fault so much as the character and competence of those being represented. Mere machinery offers no easy cure for this.[48]

The Rural Teacher

While administration of the educational system is of genuine importance, it is distinctly secondary to the teaching personnel. A good school is first of all a good teacher, and ultimately administrative devices must be judged by their effectiveness in securing and retaining such teachers. It must be admitted that a survey of the present situation with this thought in mind gives little reason for optimism. First of all, much remains to be done in nearly every state to insure even reasonably well prepared teachers. Traditionally we have spoken of teachers as members of a profession, by which we presumably mean a class of public servants adequately trained to dis-

---

[48] The novel *The Hickory Stick* by Howard Scott (1948), while often guilty of exaggeration and of bad taste, gives a not unfair picture of unenlightened school management.

charge an important function, assured of a career by the conditions of their appointment, and remunerated on a scale at least fairly comparable to that found in other callings where something like the same degree of preparation is required. If this has been our theory about teachers, it may as well be bluntly admitted that we have made no serious effort to make it the practice.

It is admittedly difficult to find, except in terms of formal training and instruction, any generally accepted standard of adequate preparation. Persons with little formal education may be successful, while others with a full complement of academic degrees may be failures, in the classroom. But it may be assumed that training beyond high school means that a teacher has both maturity and some promise. In the case of high school teachers, forty-two states now require at least four years of college work plus varying amounts of professional training in "education." In thirty-two states, the requirements for certification as elementary teachers are lower than they are for teaching in high schools. It is true that local school boards may add to these requirements, but this is presumably done, if at all, largely in city systems, with the result that in rural areas, where the elementary teacher is a front-line soldier, requirements normally do not exceed the legal minimum. In many rural areas where the one-teacher school is still the typical one, preparation should be, if anything, more thorough than in schools where fewer subjects are taught and where teachers have the advantage of better equipment and more adequate professional supervision. In short, although somewhat fewer than half the teachers in the country hold bachelors' degrees, the percentage in rural schools is undoubtedly very noticeably smaller.[49] Where, as is the case in a considerable number of states, no college preparation, or less than two years, is required (there are 110,000 teachers or one-eighth of the total in this category), it is certain to be true that a very large proportion of elementary country school teachers will be very young and immature women.[50] In one-teacher schools, probably not far from one-quarter are less than twenty years of age. Age may not necessarily bring wisdom, but it may help.

[49] The details may be found conveniently in *The Forty-Eight State School Systems,* Ch. V and the statistical tables there referred to. Data as to salaries are presented at the same place as well as in the *Biennial Survey of Education in the United States.* This chapter relies heavily upon these sources. For permission to lay the first under contribution, the writer wishes to thank Mr. Frank Bane, the Executive Director of the Council of State Governments.

[50] Only about 17 per cent of all teachers in the country are men.

For a variety of reasons implicit in the discussion that follows, the supply of teachers within recent years has fallen very considerably behind the demand. In not one of the forty-two states reporting to the Council of State Governments in 1948, were enough teachers being prepared to meet the normal needs occasioned by the withdrawal of teachers from the profession. And this takes no account of the very substantial needs which will appear with the enrollment, before 1960, of some eight million additional pupils. Nor do the figures supplied include teachers needed to replace those now holding sub-standard emergency certificates. Even if the surplus of teachers preparing for high school work could be persuaded to take elementary school positions, there would still be a rather alarming shortage at the latter level.

There can be little doubt that the obvious reluctance of men and women to enter teaching as a career is related to the economic status of the profession. In terms of dollars, teachers have been somewhat better off since the outbreak of the Second World War, for the plight of the profession has had a good press, and it has been able to win the support of some influential sections of the public to whom it, at any rate, has been clear that teaching at a median country-wide salary of $1,073 (in 1937-38) could hardly seem attractive, in a period of rising prices, in comparison with the financial returns available in industrial employment. As this is written the median salary for all teachers stands at $2,440. With respect to this latter figure, however, a number of things must be said. In the first place, when account is taken of the rise in the cost of consumers goods, the median figure turns out to be only $1,448, certainly not a munificent one by any standard. Next, it must be pointed out that the majority of teachers in the lower salary brackets are those in the country, many of them in the smaller districts. Finally, it must be remembered that "horrible examples" of completely inadequate salaries still exist over wide areas. Thus in Alabama, 83 per cent of all teachers received less than $2,400 in 1947-48, in Arkansas, 90 per cent, in Kansas, 86 per cent, in Nebraska, 75 per cent, and in North Carolina, 97 per cent. There are ten states in which at least 25 per cent of all teachers received less than $1,500, and eighteen in which more than the same percentage received less than $1,800.

While it is true, of course, that even teachers must eat and be housed and be attired—if not exactly like the lilies of the field!—one may with justice ask whether the emphasis on salaries in all the recent popular literature has not been, in some degree, misplaced. Newspaper columnists and other shrill defenders of our culture have been suggesting in reality a standard which teachers have tradition- ally repudiated. Let us suppose that, in some access of generosity, the public should hold out to prospective teachers salaries equal to those, say, of successful radio announcers. This might well have the effect of attracting to the profession those pontiffs whose feverish and clangorous pronunciamentos now fill the air waves—a consuma- tion surely not to be wished even by those most careless of the public good.

Teachers were originally priests. The leaders of the oldest reli- gious community in the western world are called by a title which originally meant teacher. Poverty has normally been the portion of this class, and reverence its compensation. Teachers are still, when at their best, monks and nuns, and it were best that they aspire not to a dubious economic equality with the local captains of industry. No one wants teachers to starve, but it may well be questioned whether, even in a community where the ruling standards are pecu- niary, status can be assured solely by higher compensation. It is doubtful whether the local merchant would feel for a teacher, sud- denly elevated to the same income status, quite the same envy and respect which he now has, grudging though he may be in admitting it. The teacher's standing, as an intellectual leader, depends upon what the trade unions call the conditions of employment, more even than it does on his or her salary. A community civilized enough to set a proper value on things of the mind will not be too niggardly in the end in providing a sufficient material basis for intellectual lead- ership. It is suggested that, in securing this change of emphasis, higher salaries will be only one factor.

If rural teaching were a real profession, it would afford a life- long career to those entering it. Hence the annual turnover would be small and, at any given moment, a large percentage of its mem- bers would be experienced in the craft. What are the facts? If teachers, like lawyers and physicians, could with assurance look for- ward to steady employment from, say, the age of twenty-five to re- tirement at sixty-five, the new members entering every year, making allowance for deaths, premature retirement and other changes, should not exceed three or four per cent of the number in service. At present the percentage of new teachers added annually is seldom less than six per cent, and in many states it is several times this figure. "In short, the length of service of elementary teachers in the country as a whole is so brief that the equivalent of the entire force must be recruited anew every five or ten years, varying with the state." [51] Bachman's study shows that, as concerns the rural one-teacher schools of the country, 24.3 per cent of the teachers have had one year or less experience, 17 per cent over two years' experience, and only 45 per cent four years or more. When it is remembered that in the strictly rural states a large proportion of all elementary school children know no other school, the significance of this short professional life of the teacher is apparent. To the intangible losses to the community caused by the absence of a permanent teaching personnel must be added the fact that, during eight years of schooling, children are instructed by as many as half a dozen fledgling teachers.

Most of these shortcomings are theoretically curable by law or by better administration. Behind the law and current administrative practices, however, are found a number of factors beyond the reach of legislature or bureaucrat. What are the conditions under which the teacher does her work? Regardless of what the law says, no calling can attain true professional status unless the environment in which it operates encourages the professional attitude. There is no point in being merely polite about the matter. The fact that some millions of our rural children are instructed by immature, poorly prepared, inexperienced female nomads, uninterested in their work or in the communities which they serve, is directly traceable to the attitude of the public which employs them and which exacts from them a stultifying conformity to a set of mores admirably calculated to drive from the work the ambitious, the energetic, the intellectually honest, in fact any who care to preserve a sense of personal dignity.

The actual status of the rural teacher cannot be grasped unless one recalls that he or she is typically the hired servant of a school district, with a population of a few score or a few hundred, and that this district is presided over by a board of directors popularly chosen and constantly aware of their representative, not to say menial, char-

---

[51] Bachman, *Education and Certification of Elementary Teachers* (Field Study No. 5, George Peabody College for Teachers, 1933), pp. 8-12. The writer has been unable to find any more recent statistical compilation with respect to teacher turnover, but, in view of what was said above with reference to the supply and demand of teachers, the figures of this earlier study certainly do not overstate the case.

acter. The fact that the teacher is frequently a stranger, and usually the only educational "expert" in the community, gives her a high degree of visibility, especially since her daily doings are reported, quite often in garbled form, by that large share of the population committed to her care. Not only, therefore, does she live under the constant espionage of her charges, but she is seldom free from the feeling of utter dependence upon the community which controls her "job" through its power to control her immediate masters, the board. From the moment she arrives in the district, her goings and comings become matters of general interest, and in every real sense her life ceases to be her own. Where she shall "board and room," do her banking, attend church, seek diversion and recreation, the charities she supports, the books she reads, where she will make her personal purchases, the choice of her associates, and her clothes, the use of her week-ends—all of these are topics for gossip or comment in the village which has "hired" her and which pushes its proprietary interest to the limit. A rigid conformity to the lowest common denominator of village mores is normally exacted under pain of dismissal by the superintendent who, in his turn, is scarcely more free himself. Considering what the typical rural school district compels its teachers to suffer in the way of personal indignities, it must be asserted that it gets more than it deserves in the way of devotion and industry.[52]

It is not easy to be moderate in one's condemnation of the folkways exhibited by the average rural community, even though mere indignation is sure to be futile. So long as teachers in the abstract are the subject of maudlin sentimentalism, and actual teachers are dealt with as if they were menial servants, the public cannot expect, unless by accident, to secure honorable intellectual leadership.

The Financing of Education

Public education is defined as a function of the state government in each of the forty-eight states. It would seem to follow, therefore, that its support would devolve upon the states. This, however, has

---

[52] Politely, the matter is thus put by Bachman: "The public does not look upon teaching in the elementary school as a man-sized job, calling for ability, prolonged preparation, and experience. In the popular mind, almost anyone with a modicum of intelligence and learning, with the 'proper connections' can teach elementary school children." Cf. A. C. Blumenthal, *Small Town Stuff*, pp. 327-329. Professional educators would find the task of destroying these popular savageries far more valuable to society than the monotonous efforts to make teaching a "science."

not been the case, and for the most part, until very recently, the central governments have considered their obligation discharged when they authorized or required their local subdivisions to levy local taxes for the support of the schools. Generally speaking, little support from the state treasury has been forthcoming. The reason for this is to be found in the American dogma that local self-government is one of the chief guarantees of individual liberty. Local self-government would, it was thought, "permit each community to work out untrammeled the ideas and objectives in which it believed with only the minimum of supervision from state authorities." [53] State as well as local officials believed in this dogma, and their belief in it made the latter willing to forego state support if it meant state supervision, and made the former hesitate to interpret the state's legal responsibility as one involving financial support.

When education was very largely a local matter and when wealth was distributed fairly equally among localities, the offering of the schools was reasonably uniform in quantity and quality, and its cost did not exceed the resources of these communities. A small annual appropriation by the legislature, together with the income of the permanent school fund, served adequately to supplement local revenue. This division of the responsibility for support became unsatisfactory when taxable wealth took forms beyond the reach of small local units, when the educational program expanded to include far more than the traditional subjects, and when the school enrollment increased many times. In many cases today the cost of the standard program is too great for local revenue sources to pay for. For this reason, the demand has arisen in every section of the nation that the state contribute more substantially to the support of the local schools. What this really amounts to is a demand that local real property be relieved of a part of its tax burden by shifting a portion of the cost of schools to tax revenues administered by the state. This demand is now being heeded by the state governments. In 1900, slightly over 20 per cent of public school revenue was derived from state sources; by 1947-48, it was estimated that 39.8 per cent came from such sources. The proportion of total school revenues supplied by the states is indicated in the following table:

---

[53] Harlan Updegraff, "Financial Implications of the Principles Underlying American Education," *Research Problems in School Finance* (Report of the National Survey of School Finance, 1933), p. 18.

Revenue Derived from State (%)	No. of States
More than 50	15
40 to 49.9	7
30 to 39.9	8
20 to 29.9	6
10 to 19.9	10
0 to 9.9	2

If the figures are analyzed further, it is found that the percentage contributed varies from 3.9 per cent in Nebraska to 87 per cent in Delaware. Stated in dollars, the sums contributed by the states in 1950 were reported as totaling slightly under $2,000,000,000. The smallest amount was $728,000 distributed by New Hampshire, while at the other extreme stood New York with contributions amounting to more than $233,000,000. While it is true that every state now makes some grants from its funds, it is significant that almost half of the total amount is accounted for by the states of New York, California, Texas, Pennsylvania, Michigan, and Ohio. The movement to subsidize the local schools has thus progressed very unevenly, taking the country as a whole. Nevertheless, something like a revolution in school financing has occurred. Fifteen years ago, 70 per cent of the burden of supporting the schools fell upon local units of government; today the corresponding figure is 53.2 per cent.[54] State funds are derived from the income of permanent school funds and lands, the proceeds of certain earmarked taxes, and appropriations from the general fund, the last-named tending to grow in importance.

The main object of apportioning state funds to local districts is to bring about equalization of educational opportunity among the various parts of the state, something impossible to achieve when each district is dependent entirely upon the tax on general property. The only way this could be done completely would be to make the state the sole unit of school support. This, of course, is not likely to be done. But a good deal can be accomplished in the direction of equalization if even a small fund is scientifically and equitably apportioned.[55] Working out such an equitable system is a difficult

---

[54] Small sums of money are contributed by the counties and by the federal government—5.7 and 1.3 per cent respectively in 1947-48.

[55] The committee of the Council of State Governments reported in 1949 in *The Forty-Eight State School Systems* that "it is important to recognize that school finance programs need no longer be left to chance or guesswork. Techniques are now available which make it possible to work out in every state a defensible program which will assure that the major objectives of a sound school finance plan will be attained," p. 122.

technical problem which no two states have attempted to solve in quite the same way. The variety of solutions is so great that it is impossible to generalize, and we can set down only briefly as illustrations the essential features of a few representative states. In New York, the state government contributed $193,000,000 in 1948-49 to the support of the public schools—about 40 per cent of the total cost. The state appropriations are principally from the General Fund. Although various special types of aid are provided for by the statutes, 95 per cent of the total is for the support of the "foundation program," that is to say, the acceptable minimum program in which the state will participate. The state's contribution is designed to bring about equalization of educational opportunities among the local school districts, and its size in any given case depends upon the local ability to finance the approved minimum program. This ability is measured by the actual valuation of real property behind each pupil in average daily attendance. As the formula was applied in 1949, high valuation districts ($40,000 assessed valuation per pupil) received $103 per pupil; middle valuation districts ($10,000 valuation) $169 per pupil; and low valuation districts ($4,000 valuation) $203 per pupil.[56]

In Illinois, state aid for 1949-50 amounted to about 23 per cent of total local school costs. Although aid is available for nine special purposes (vocational education, handicapped children, transportation, and so forth) about three-quarters of the total is for general and equalization aid. The first category involves flat grant payments of $22 per elementary school pupil, and $7 per high school pupil. Beginning in 1950-51, equalization aid guaranteed $160 per pupil in attendance, provided the local district levies a tax of four mills per $100 of the full equalized valuation. An interesting provision of the Illinois law is that, after 1953, no elementary or high school with an average daily attendance of fewer than fifteen pupils may, without the special permission of both county and state superintendents, receive state aid.[57] In Pennsylvania, legislation now distributes aid in accordance with a formula which provides for flat grants

---

[56] I record my thanks here for a memorandum on state aid furnished me by Dr. Theodore C. Wenzl, Chief of the Bureau of Apportionment of the State Education Department.

[57] Data are from *State Aid for Common Schools in Illinois,* prepared by the Research Department of the Illinois Education Association, Springfield (Dec. 1949), and *Financial Aid for Local Governments,* Publication 92 of the Illinois Legislative Council (Oct. 1948).

per teaching unit, establishes minimum salaries for the holders of various types of certificates, and takes account of "average daily membership," and local effort as measured by a minimum mill rate on taxable real property—the latter figure being subject to revision by the State Council of Education if, in its judgment, the locally determined value is below fair market value.[58]

In Connecticut, state aid for general educational purposes is computed on the basis of the number of pupils in average daily membership in schools of various sizes, with the proviso that the grant may be reduced if the local district fails to expend $140 per pupil for net current expenses, or otherwise fails to maintain schools according to law.[59]

In the examples given above, the principal emphasis has been placed upon the use of state aid in supporting an equalized or "foundation" program, some type of which exists in about forty states, although there is considerable variation in the efficiency of the measures used to determine local need. To complete the picture, it must be noted that aid is also given for a wide variety of special purposes and programs, for transportation of pupils, and, in some cases, for plant construction and repairs. A study of the systems now in effect makes clear a number of things. A carefully constructed plan at the state level may contribute greatly to the recognized objectives of public instruction; at the other extreme, the plan may make only a slight contribution or even have a negative result by condoning undesirable practices or not insisting on proper standards. In view of what has been demonstrated as to feasible devices for administering state aid, there would seem to be little excuse for the persistence of such situations—except perhaps lethargy or lack of power at the state level and political pressure from the districts. It is also clear that state aid may be a powerful instrument in compelling the employment of better-trained teachers, the payment of better salaries, the improvement of school buildings and equipment, and the elimination of schools of uneconomic size. By the same token, it is clear that the local units, in accepting state funds, are compelled to surrender a certain amount of their autonomy. They can seldom qualify for

---

[58] Act No. 515, Session of 1947 and No. 536, Session of 1949. In addition to $92,-000,000 disbursed for general education purposes, $3,500,000 were expended through the Commonwealth Department of Public Health for school health services.

[59] The data for Connecticut were furnished through the kindness of Mr. Roger M. Thompson, Chief of Federal-State-Local Relations of the State Department of Education, February 1950.

substantial grants without modifying their budgets, with all that this means in terms of the quantity and quality of the service rendered.

On the other hand, the rather dramatic increase in the size of grants in recent years has not led to the development of as much administrative supervision as one might expect. Central officials are normally not given wide discretion in allotting money, the general practice being to incorporate the formulae used directly in the statute. Legislatures have been loath either to increase the discretionary powers of educational administrators or to add to their staffs. Local pressure seems to have been strong enough to secure considerable help from the state treasury and also to prevent the growth of an extensive bureaucracy at the state capital.

CHAPTER 12

Public Welfare

Within the past generation, something like a revolution has occurred in public welfare administration. This revolution has involved vast changes in machinery and new intergovernmental arrangements; but, more fundamental than these, it has meant a change in theory. The full significance of this revolution in ideas cannot be understood without an excursion into history.

CHANGING ATTITUDES TOWARD THE UNFORTUNATE

Most of our traditional machinery for the "relief" of dependency is the outgrowth of a point of view toward poverty and misfortune which is now rather generally abandoned, and it is difficult to discuss the methods and contribution of modern social work without knowing something of the newer theories. According to the older notion of charity, born in the Middle Ages and persisting far into the modern period, the poor, the sick, the crippled, and the afflicted generally were proper objects of the benevolence of the more fortunate. The State could scarcely be said to exist prior to the seventeenth century and, for that reason, the Church—to which all were presumed to belong—was most active in good works. The object of almsgiving, when it was not merely to aid in the salvation of the giver's own soul, was only to relieve suffering, never to get at the causes of distress. As a matter of fact, few rational explanations were offered for poverty and other social ills, such being attributed to the inscrutable will of God, to chance, or to human wickedness. In any event, Christian ethics and practice looked upon poverty and suffering as unconnected with what we now call "social" conditions. The expression "maladjustment," now so frequently applied to the handicapped, could not possibly have been coined until the relative importance of environment as opposed to personal factors was greatly emphasized.

While it is true that the Elizabethan Poor Law of 1601 acknowledged the responsibility of the state for the poor, both the beliefs and the interests of the dominant classes in the early modern period had the effect of holding charity or assistance of any sort to a minimum.[1] The indigent were compelled to work for their support, and their children were apprenticed at the earliest possible age. There was the high authority of Malthus and others for the widely held belief that the poor and the afflicted were simply the victims of their own wickedness or imprudence, and that their infirmities were the castigations of a righteously angry Creator. The pauper, said Malthus, "should be taught that the laws of nature, which are the laws of God, had doomed him and his family to suffer . . . that he had no claim of *right* on society for the smallest portion of food, beyond that which his labor will fairly purchase; and that if he and his family were saved from feeling the natural consequence of his imprudence, he would owe it to the pity of some kind benefactor, to whom, therefore, he ought to be bound by the strongest ties of gratitude."[2] So long as something of this sort remained the accepted view, there could be no question as to what we now call the "social" causes of dependency, no examination of the working of the productive and distributing machinery of society as it might bear upon individual fortunes, and little or no attempt to do more than grudgingly afford a squalid living to those in need.[3]

Now an agricultural and village society seems to afford fertile soil for the propagation of such notions.[4] Toil has traditionally been

---

[1] A. D. Lindsay quotes a "notorious eighteenth century catechism" as saying that "the purpose of laws is to confirm the rich in their possessions and to restrain the vicious poor." *The Modern Democratic State*, I: 206. The reader of W. E. H. Lecky's *England in the Eighteenth Century* or of Louis Kronenberger's *Kings and Desperate Men*, especially Part III, Chs. III and IV, can judge for himself whether the rich or the poor in that century were the more vicious.

[2] *Essay on Population* (Everyman Edition), II: 201. A far cry indeed from modern discussions of the "right to work" and the assurance that government will allow no one to starve!

[3] Though the doctrine of individualism to which Malthus was giving expression has been the source of much callousness in modern civilization, it may not be out of place here to remind ourselves of the comment of Leslie Stephen: "Energy, self-reliance, and independence, a strong conviction that a man's fate should depend upon his own character and conduct, are qualities without which no nation can be great." *The English Utilitarians* I:131. A humanitarianism prone to attribute every misfortune to "social" causes needs to be reminded of the truth contained in this statement.

[4] Millspaugh says that, in the agricultural era of American history, "the socially unfortunate were viewed with feelings ranging from fear and hatred to scorn and contempt." *Public Welfare Organization*, p. 15.

a grim necessity which even moderate material success too often has exalted into a positive virtue. Free land was the chief capital of men, and those who being so blest, still failed, were not unreasonably looked upon as incompetent if not vicious. Certainly their fellows could not be fairly held responsible for their plight, and a secluded, barren, and cheerless almshouse was all such unfortunates could expect from the community. Since all should, if possible, pay their way, the almshouse was on a farm, and its inmates were required, when able, to perform farm labor. Likewise, the superintendent was normally a farmer with little knowledge other than farming.

~ Local Administration of "Relief"

So long as the market was largely local, it was natural to regard the "relief" of the poor as a local responsibility. Where the town was the important unit, as in New England, the obligation rested upon it to make proper provision for paupers having a legal "settlement" within it; elsewhere the task fell upon the township or the county government. When paupers could not prove a "settlement" in the jurisdiction in which their condition was discovered, the officials upon whom demands for "relief" were made usually lost no time in unceremoniously bundling them off to the unit legally responsible for their care.[5] In any event, "relief" for the indigent was originally of two sorts—outdoor and indoor. By the former was meant the care of the poor at their own homes—usually by supplying them with the minimum creature comforts of food, clothing, and fuel. Indoor relief signified their care in such institutions as the county "poor farm," "infirmary," "county home," or almshouse. Where the town was the important unit of local government, each town supported its own almshouse or boarded its paupers in private homes or contracted with a neighboring town for the care of its indigent in the latter's almshouse. Where the township was used as a unit for relief it seldom or never maintained an almshouse, committing its helpless poor to the county "home" and dispensing outdoor

---

[5] The English law of settlement dates from 1662. Relief of the poor was in the hands of the parish authorities who made the law a pretext for oppressive action. "The overseer was often a petty tyrant; his aim was to depopulate his parish; to prevent the poor from obtaining a settlement; to make the workhouse a terror by placing it under the management of a bully; and by all kinds of chicanery to keep down the rates at whatever cost to the comfort and morality of the poor." Leslie Stephen, *The English Utilitarians*, I:91-92. In parts of New England the overseer is still referred to as the "poormaster."

relief to those still able physically to care for themselves at home.[6]

While local boards of one sort or another were long in charge of the relief of the poor and unfortunate, they did not come near to covering the entire field of welfare work as that term is now defined. The administration of such forms of assistance as blind pensions, the care of delinquent children and indigent widows, veterans' relief, and the handling of cases of desertion and nonsupport was generally assigned to commissions or other special bodies more or less independent of the general governing board of the local area. The function of this latter board was normally confined to financial control and the general supervision of the newer welfare functions, and members of the board spent the bulk of their time in the direct administration of outdoor relief. The absence of "rhyme or reason" characterized, of course, the administration of most local functions. The able student who stated that "the outstanding features of local administrative organization . . . are complicated, intertwined, and deeply rooted, as a general rule ill-adapted to the purposes of modern administration, but extremely difficult to change" was well advised when he added that "the problem of public welfare organization cannot be effectively dealt with unless the problem of local administration as a whole is comprehended." [7]

There was little or nothing of which one could be proud in the traditional system of poor relief as managed by local governments. There were, of course, notable exceptions to the rule, but taking the country as a whole, neither outdoor nor indoor relief was well managed; nor did the system make any contribution at all toward the economic rehabilitation of its beneficiaries. In other words, most administrators did not think of their problems in terms of the better adjustment of individuals to society. Outdoor relief almost universally resolved itself into a matter of issuing "grocery orders" to the poor, with no prior investigation of real needs or, at best, but a perfunctory one. In those sections where the responsible local governing board was chosen from districts, it was common practice to permit each commissioner or supervisor to act as a petty sovereign

---

[6] Persons may enter a county poorhouse only as a result of being committed by a competent court which has adjudged them destitute, or on the authority of some other local official such as a county commissioner, township trustee, or justice of the peace. Those in immediate charge of the institution have no alternative but to provide for all sent to them by such officers.

[7] A. C. Millspaugh, *Public Welfare Organization* (1935), p. 204.

within his district, in authorizing the delivery of food or other necessities to the unfortunate families subject to his ministrations.[8]

On the whole, the impression one gets after reading the reports
of various investigations is that poor relief methods constituted one
of the darkest pictures in the whole field of rural administration.
This is perhaps to be expected. In a society long taught to measure
every value in terms of money, the unforgivable crime was not to
have accumulated money. Traditionally, the ownership of property
has been most widely distributed in agricultural areas, and it is not
surprising to find that the pauper was normally regarded as a nuisance to be disposed of at the least possible cost to the public treasury. Thus, an investigation a generation ago in Kentucky presented
evidence that, in some counties, the poorhouse was being maintained
"primarily as a threat with which to drive off applicants for alms." [9]
Some years later, the New York Commission on Old Age Security
reported that relief in the rural areas of that state "gets down pretty
nearly to the level of the old English poor law administration; the
able-bodied get nothing except by going to the almshouse, or if they
do, it is in the form of groceries whose cost is limited to what it might
cost the town for the food that the dependent would consume if he
were at the county almshouse." [10] Generally speaking, local officials
proceeded on the theory that immediate relief in the form of minimum essentials was the only need. This, of course, left untouched
the basic problem which was that the persons or families relieved
had reached dependency because of the operation of causes which
were unaffected by extending material relief. It was, of course, grotesque to call this a policy.[11]

But the ineffectiveness of the traditional methods of outdoor
relief is not summed up by saying that it was lacking in any rational
theory. In practice, it was a frequent source of petty graft and political jobbery. Thus, in Virginia, where overseers of the poor were

---

[8] Thirty years ago Porter reported one Pennsylvania county in which 139 persons
were legally competent to carry on outdoor relief! See Kirk H. Porter, *County and
Township Government*, p. 247.

[9] *County Government in Kentucky*, Report by the Efficiency Committee of Kentucky (Advance Pamphlet VIII, 1923), pp. 64-65.

[10] *Old Age Security*, Report of the Commission on Old Age Security (Leg. Doc. No.
67, 1930), pp. 533-534.

[11] "Relief is to be given to respectable persons. . . . The chief question to decide
is whether to aid or not to aid. When aid is granted seldom is the official's concern
to avoid giving aid if possible, and it usually means a small amount of fuel or groceries. When the decision is not to aid, the responsibility of the official is at an end."
F. W. Hoffer, *Counties in Transition*, p. 55.

elected one from each magisterial district in the county and paid but forty dollars a year, it was reported that the position was eagerly sought by local storekeepers seeking the profits to be had from the sale of supplies to the poor.[12] And the New York Commission on Old Age Security said that, in the rural sections of that state, the fact that people were in need was "taken *ipso facto* to mean that they are neither worthy nor trustworthy. The overseer decides just what they may have for food or fuel or clothing, if any, and orders it from the grocery or country store if he does not actually bring it himself and charge the time to his *per diem*."[13] In 1933, a state department welfare official reported that, in one county of the state, a local official had publicly said that "we have enough trouble relieving the Republicans, we can't bother with the Democrats."[14] That party organization should thus traffic in human misery may seem shocking, yet there is ample evidence that it has always been influential in the administration of relief. Even the petty post of overseer of the poor was not to be overlooked in building up the machine!

Even if the business of outdoor relief were conducted in an honest, efficient, and non-partisan manner, it would be an extremely ineffective way of meeting the real problem. This would be apparent on any close investigation of the causes of indigence. A study some years ago of 580 families seeking outdoor relief in six Virginia counties showed that the following conditions were responsible for dependency in a varying percentage of cases: old age, 37.4 per cent; sickness, 20.8 per cent; dependent children, 9.8 per cent; tuberculosis, 6.0 per cent; desertion and nonsupport, 6.5 per cent; blindness, 3.3 per cent; feeblemindedness, 3.1 per cent; crippled persons in the family, 2.0 per cent.[15] Thus, nearly ninety per cent of these cases were accounted for by the various mischances listed; and while this may not be a fair sample, it is certainly true that a large proportion

---

[12] *Report of the Commission on County Government* (Sen. Doc. No. 3, 1931), p. 43. "Sixty-four per cent of the town welfare officers are employed on a part-time basis and the salaries of these officials range from $15 to $1,800 a year. Eighteen per cent of all town welfare officials receive less than $100 annually and the average salary for all towns is approximately $525. Thirty-three per cent of the towns pay their welfare officers on a fee or a part-time basis. The actual rate of pay is often absurdly small; yet in terms of the volume of work actually done, many of these officials seem to be overpaid." *State and Local Welfare Organization in the State of New York,* a report of the Governor's Commission on Unemployment Relief (Leg. Doc. No. 56, 1936), p. 73.

[13] *Old Age Security,* p. 534.

[14] *N. Y. Times,* June 10, 1933.

[15] F. W. Hoffer, *op. cit.,* p. 58.

of all families seeking relief came to their situation through some such circumstances. Let us see what would happen to outdoor relief if rational attempts were made to strike at the real causes of dependency. Old persons, no longer capable of paying their own way, might well be pensioned and kept in their own homes, thus preserving to them some shreds of that self-respect, the deprivation of which profits the community not at all. The chronically ill, especially if also past their productive years, should be in hospitals or, at any rate, have made available to them adequate medical attention; and the same may be said of those suffering with tuberculosis. Mothers cast off by their husbands might well be assisted in their own homes, under proper supervision, while the blind, the crippled, and the feebleminded should, in most cases at least, be given institutional care by the state. If these deductions were made, few persons indeed in the average rural community would be left to the ministrations of the local relief officials. This is the policy which, as we shall see later, has now been generally adopted.

INDOOR RELIEF

Indoor relief for the poor was normally furnished by local governments in institutions known variously as the county home, the infirmary, the poorhouse, the poor farm, or the almshouse. In units too small to make such an institution feasible, the local poor might be boarded out with resident families or in the institution maintained by a neighboring local government.[16]

By whatever name it was called, the local institution had little to recommend it, though there were, of course, notable exceptions where there was little to criticize. In the first place, the county "home," in perhaps a majority of cases, had become a mere catchall for "cases" which local official ingenuity could devise no better way of handling. Into it was crowded every conceivable type of individual defect and social misfit, until the variety of problems would have

---

[16] Prior to the adoption of the federal social security program in 1935, the practice of "boarding out" paupers was apparently on the wane. In a somewhat different form it seems now on its way back. In the writer's own state in 1950, while only three of the 93 counties were still operating poor farms, five others leased them to private persons who ran them as boarding homes for the aged and infirm, and three others used the proceeds of the sale of their farms to buy town properties then leased as boarding homes. All such homes must meet the specifications of the Federal Social Security Board and the State Department of Assistance, and their operators receive their compensation directly from the inmates who receive aid from federal, state, or county funds. I am indebted to my colleague, Dr. Roger V. Shumate, Director of Research for the Legislative Council of Nebraska, for this information.

taxed the capacities of the most expert staff.[17] Thus, in 1931 the county infirmaries of Michigan cared for 21,670 inmates. Of these, 3,156 were insane or feebleminded—roughly one out of seven, or 15 per cent. There was also a small group of blind, deaf, and crippled.[18] In 1932, in the poor asylums of Indiana, of 5,833 inmates only 617 were reported as able-bodied. Among the remainder were found the senile, the mentally feeble, the very "untidy," and men and women afflicted with infectious diseases. It is little wonder that the State Board of Charities reported that "the providing for suitable custodial facilities at the county poor asylums is one of the most perplexing problems the officials of these institutions face today." [19]

When local administration had not been brought into contact with modern developments in the care of dependency, the local almshouse was likely to be a place where were gathered such classes as the aged and helpless poor, the chronically ill, those suffering from incurable diseases, the feebleminded, the indigent blind, broken prostitutes, tramps and hoboes seeking shelter for the winter, and the crippled. Cases were once not unknown in which children were born and spent a good part of their lives in such institutions. Even if the institution were staffed by specialists, the task of managing it efficiently would be a staggering one. Yet it seldom had any adequate supervision.

In the second place, the typical American county is too small to supply an institutional population large enough to warrant a proper expert organization. The bulk of our county "homes" had an average population of fewer than ten.[20] Under these conditions, it was futile to expect such places to be much more than shelter for their inmates who were by necessity subjected to any treatment which occurred to the lay persons in charge.

---

[17] The shelter of the poorhouse "is the guarantee against starvation which the state offers to all, no matter how unfortunate or degraded. Consequently the inmates of the almshouse are often the most sodden driftwood from the social wreckage of the time." Amos G. Warner, Stuart A. Queen, and Edward B. Harper, *American Charities and Social Work*, p. 90.

[18] Opal V. Matson, *Local Poor Relief to Dependents* (Michigan Local Government Series, 1933), pp. 29-31.

[19] *Report of the State Board of Charities for the Biennium Ending June 30, 1932.*

[20] See the article "Almshouses" in the *Encyclopedia of the Social Sciences*. An investigation by the Ohio Institute in 1927 showed that "in a majority of counties the population of the home was less than fifty, and in several it fell below twenty-five. There can be no question but that in many counties the number of inmates was too small to permit the most efficient operation of the institution." *County Welfare Organization in Ohio*, p. 14. For the country as a whole, the population was fewer than ten in about 40 per cent of all local almshouses.

What we find upon examining the actual conditions in the county homes still existing is as grotesque as one might imagine. Though under the general supervision of the local governing board, the "home" is under the immediate care of an appointed superintendent. Since it is in our tradition that those "on the county" should pay their way if possible, the home is normally located on a farm. For this reason the superintendent is chosen with reference to his experience and skill as a farmer, though sometimes the position is handed out as a reward for party services, or given to the person willing to assume it for the smallest compensation. Where such conditions are operative, it is not surprising to find almshouse administration of low quality. Even if the superintendent were a person combining the skills of merchant, physician, social worker, sociologist, dietician, and general executive—which he, of course, never is —most of his time is naturally consumed in overseeing his farming operations, and very little is left in which to look after his charges. The results of this part-time and ignorant attention are everywhere deplorable. Official reports teem with references to the bad physical condition of the institution. In many places the fire hazard is great, and fire escapes are either inaccessible or require more agility than the aged and infirm inmates possess; there are usually inadequate bathing and toilet facilities, insufficient segregation of the sexes, and lack of space for personal belongings; dining and living rooms are dark and cheerless, medical care is haphazard and nursing is of the most rudimentary kind, the superintendent and his wife dosing the sick inmates with nostrums and "home remedies." Add to this the fact that the almshouse is frequently in an out-of-the-way part of the county, and that its inmates have largely cut themselves off from the attention of the public by having been guilty of the crime of financial failure, and the situation affords us little reason to feel hopeful. In short, "the inmates for the most part are housed in old, dilapidated, ill-kept buildings, surrounded by dirt and squalor, afflicted by disease, and left to themselves in despair, loneliness, and hopelessness." [21]

Theory and Practice of Social Work

Paradoxically, the same set of economic factors which produced the doctrine of laissez-faire also made many doubt the soundness of

---

[21] F. W. Hoffer, *op. cit.,* p. 77. Ernest P. Boas, "The Care of the Aged Sick," **IV** *Social Service Review* 197 (June 1930).

the same doctrine when applied to the causes of poverty. The savage, not to say superstitious, code which stigmatized as paupers those who failed yielded slowly before the analysis and criticism of those 19th century humanitarians who themselves were the products of the Industrial Revolution, since most of them came from the class which the factory system had rapidly enriched. The coming of political democracy widened the sympathies of men and, in the end, forced home the belief that the weakness or ineffectiveness of any individual or class, regardless of the origin of that weakness, is a matter of direct concern to society as a whole. Thus the economic system, now felt to be so largely instrumental in producing individual delinquency and dependency, provided itself a principle of cure.

This reversal of ideas on the subject of dependency, in proportion as it has changed from emphasis on "charity" to a more extensive set of arrangements for combating social maladjustments, has altered most of the conditions of the old problem of "relief." While there still linger among us, especially perhaps in rural regions, large numbers of people who attribute economic dependency to defects of individual character, there is a growing conviction that social insecurity (aside, of course, from congenital illness) is due to the faulty working of an economic system for which no one person may justly be held responsible. And it is plain to most that it is distribution and not production that is at fault. Nature is not niggardly, nor has man's genius faltered in producing; we have not learned how to exchange the goods which these forces have given us.

These changes in the attitude toward the unfortunate are full of significance for welfare work by local units. So long as the efforts of both public bodies and private persons were directed to the alleviation of the sufferings of the individual, the emphasis on the technique of relief, administrative and otherwise, was at a minimum. As soon, however, as the view was accepted that true relief involved an attempt to get at and remove more fundamental causes of misfortune and poverty, much of the old apparatus was doomed. This changed concept has introduced into the administration of welfare programs the theory and practice of social case work. This involves a "scientific" study of the causes operating in each individual case to produce dependency, the careful keeping of case records, and the close supervision over plans for individual and family rehabilitation, which are worked out by the case worker on the basis of his or her findings. Here "relief," as commonly understood, is secondary; the first objective of social work is to restore the dependent person to economic sufficiency.[22] The procedure is theoretically unsentimental and hard-headed and, in any event, one which requires painstaking and long continued work of an unexciting character. It therefore may be conjectured that it will not be congenial to the rule-of-thumb methods of neighborly charity as commonly practiced in rural areas.

The technique of social case work was elaborated in urban areas with urban situations in mind. The very existence of large numbers of people in close contact with one another not only alters the nature of the problem of relief, but also its methods. The very fact that the population is divorced from the land and dependent for its elementary needs upon the smooth working of a complicated industrial and economic machine means that there is a constant problem of dependency which has called into being a permanent staff of social workers. The vast number of "cases" in a relatively small area makes possible a degree of specialization which can scarcely exist in more sparsely populated areas. The very impersonality of city life no doubt has aided in the development of case work, whereas the neighborliness of the countryside assures a detailed knowledge of social conditions which is, in fact, common property. Moreover, funds for social work have never been sufficient in rural areas, while nearly always forthcoming in more or less adequate amounts in populous centers. In short, scientific social work is the product of urban conditions, and both its point of view and its procedure are alien to the tradition and spirit of rural people. The bearing of scientific discovery upon such matters as stock-breeding and the cultivation of crops is apprehended without great difficulty, once the ancient rural superstitions are destroyed, but the case is different with the imponderables involved in social work. "In the average rural community the name 'social worker' has little meaning. It does not mean that the person has completed a course of training which makes him eligible to membership in the American Association of Social Workers. Any kindly person willing to help his fellows is considered qualified to undertake the social services needed by the community." It should be said, however, that this willingness to help, which is wide-

[22] The point of view of modern case work was expressed many years ago by Professor C. H. Cooley when he wrote: "No matter how mean and hideous a man's life is, the first thing is to understand him; to make out just how it is that our common humanity has come to work out in this way. This method calls for patience, insight, firmness, and confidence in men, leaving little room for the denunciatory egotism of a certain kind of reformers." *Social Organization* (1908), p. 15.

spread in the country, is a resource which should be carefully husbanded, no matter what administrative changes may be thought desirable. Voluntary work by well-disposed people, if properly supervised by trained persons, should certainly be encouraged. The "professional" may easily overdo the business of pooh-poohing good intentions.[23]

The National Social Security Program

The changing attitude toward the causes of individual distress and the newer theories of welfare administration received definitive and nation-wide recognition in the federal Social Security Act of 1935. This act established the present pattern of public welfare work into which previous local arrangements have fitted themselves. What the act did was to guarantee, through federal, state, and local financial support and cooperative administration, a national minimum of well-being—at least with respect to the conditions covered —below which no person is to fall. It recognizes the fact that, in a very large measure, the causes of misfortune are national and not local in their origin and, at the same time, preserves a degree of autonomy of administration on the state and local levels. Public welfare administration in rural areas is now a part of a nation-wide program.

Although the Social Security Act was revolutionary in its implications, it would be a mistake to assume that it was, in all respects, an innovation. The way had been prepared for its acceptance by years of experimentation, and essentially what it did was to make uniform throughout the United States ideas and devices tested in many places. It may be worth while to summarize the influences and experiments upon which the act is based.

In the first place, so far as the federal program makes use of the principles of insurance,[24] there had been extensive experimentation

---

[23] In 1932 it was reported that fewer than one-fifth of the 1,537 counties with a county welfare plan employed one or more full-time trained social workers. Current progress in social work in rural areas may be followed in the numbers of the *Social Service Review*. There is some good material in the chapters on social work and public welfare in *Recent Social Trends*, but the picture has changed considerably since the data there discussed were gathered, for the entrance of the federal government into the field of relief has given a powerful stimulus to the use of scientific methods. One of the best current sources is the *Social Security Bulletin*, published monthly by the Social Security Board.

[24] This would be true with respect to the Old Age and Survivors' Insurance scheme and, in a sense, of Unemployment Compensation. The first of these is administered solely by the national government; the second is administered by the states, the federal government paying the administration expenses.

for many years, especially in Europe, but also in some American industrial enterprises. As one distinguished American social welfare
expert writes: "There had been an accelerating use of the principle
of insurance both in commercial enterprises and as a means by which
workers could pool their resources in dealing with the economic
consequences of old age, invalidity, sickness, and death. On the Continent there had been a considerable development of mutual benefit
societies of various kinds, trade union insurance funds, and special
provisions for certain occupational groups." [25] Widespread familiarity with schemes of these sorts was a part of the background of the
German social legislation of Bismarck's age and of the first British
unemployment, old age, and health insurance a generation later.

In the second place, prior to 1935 there had been many signs of
progress in the individual states. Here and there states had enacted
statutes providing for assistance to the aged, dependent children,
the blind, and other special classes, so that later comprehensive legislation was not a novelty. There had also been encouraging improvements in administration. Beginning about 1915, there occurred on
the state level a rather general movement toward a greater consolidation of state agencies in charge of functions previously administered by separate boards and commissions. At about the same time
occurred a very considerable extension of state supervisory power
over local administrative agencies. Typical fruits of this "centralization" were seen in the permissive and mandatory legislation as to
county welfare departments, stricter supervision of the choice of personnel with a view to replacing amateurs by experts, and the use of
state grants to assist localities either to support traditional services
or to care for special problems. State legislation during the same
period indicates a widening of the conception of welfare to include
many classes of the unfortunate formerly ignored or treated indiscriminately with paupers.

A further development of great significance was the adoption of
the county as a unit in welfare work. Even when the states had
adopted the policy of caring for the tuberculous, the crippled, the
insane, and the feebleminded in central institutions, it was recognized that a great deal of welfare work remained which could only
be performed by decentralized machinery. After all, with minor
exceptions, dependent persons have to be cared for where they live.

---

[25] Karl de Schweinitz, *People and Process in Social Security* (Washington: American
Council on Education, 1948), p. 7.

The administration of such policies as old age assistance, soldiers' relief, aid to the blind, the care of dependent children, the management of almshouses where they existed, and the administration of outdoor relief and medical care—all of these had to be looked after by local machinery. But the traditional machinery was decentralized beyond all reason. Pennsylvania presented a picture of local organization for poor relief that "forms a patchwork quilt quite as strange as the amazing complex of laws under which poor relief operates. There are sixty-seven counties in Pennsylvania, but poor relief is administered not in sixty-seven districts but in 425 poor districts, with eighty-five almshouses and with 966 directors of the poor. In twenty-two counties of the state, the county commissioners serve as directors of the poor in addition to all their other duties. In twenty-seven counties there are separate county-wide boards of directors of the poor elected by the people to serve in that capacity. In fifteen additional counties there is a special poor district for every separate township or borough, or for aggregations of two or more townships or boroughs. . . . In three remaining counties special forms of poor relief organization are found." [26] An investigation in Ohio in 1928 reported that "the responsibility for the conduct of charitable and correctional activities is divided among at least five separate bodies. . . . A more scrambled up administrative system would be difficult to find." [27]

Beginning in 1917 attempts were made in almost half the states to centralize local welfare activities under county welfare boards. Two ideas were involved in the use of these boards. First is the notion that the various social services such as mothers' aid, blind pensions, and old age assistance should be placed under the oversight of a small committee of laymen capable of expressing the general point of view of the public toward these services. The function of the board was primarily representative and advisory rather than administrative. In the second place, it was expected that the county board would employ a trained welfare director and whatever assistants were needed and hold them responsible for the actual administration of relief. Since the statutes are not always reliable guides to what is actually being done, it may be surmised that a welfare program existed in many states largely on paper; however, the county

---

[26] A. Dunham, "A County Welfare Plan for Pennsylvania," I *Pennsylvania Social Work* 16, 23, quoted in W. S. Carpenter and P. T. Stafford, *State and Local Government in the United States*, p. 219.

[27] *County Welfare Organization in Ohio* (The Ohio Institute, 1928).

unit in welfare was an important forward step, since it prepared many local governments for ready assimilation to the federal security program. It did this by providing an administrative organization through which that program could be smoothly implemented on the county level; and it was important as a means of habituating rural people and their officials to the practice of scientific social work.

While the national government performs a number of services popularly designated as "social security," the only ones with which local units are at present concerned are old age assistance, aid to dependent children, aid to the blind, and aid to the totally and permanently disabled. The Old Age and Survivors' Insurance program is administered solely by the national government; and the unemployment insurance program is managed by the state governments which receive grants from the national treasury sufficient to pay the expenses of administration. The so-called "categorical" aids—to the aged, dependent children, the blind, and the totally and permanently disabled—have no insurance features, but are assistance pure and simple or, if one likes, "charity." The support which the national government gives to these classes is based upon the generally accepted view that their situation is of *national* concern, and that the ability of the states to supply aid varies so widely as to make national assistance both desirable and just.[28]

No national funds are yet available to assist the states and the local communities in caring for indigent or dependent persons not in any of the four categories. What is called "general assistance" is still the financial responsibility of the states and their subdivisions. For those groups comprised in the national program, the pattern of financial support and administration is essentially that found in the older federal-aid programs.

OLD AGE ASSISTANCE

Fifty years ago about 4 per cent of our total population consisted of persons of sixty-five years of age or over. Today probably between 7 and 8 per cent fall in that class. Population experts predict that in another forty years the figure will reach 13 per cent. It seems likely

---

[28] The per capita annual income in the richest state is about three and a half times as large as in the poorest; average payments for the categorical aids vary in about the same proportion.

that, over the years, at least three-quarters of those over sixty-five are in varying degrees dependent on others for their support. When their number was small, and traditional laissez-faire attitudes were well-nigh universal, these persons presented no public problem. Those who had no relatives probably lived in almshouses where they were conveniently forgotten. In any case, the meager support furnished them did not appear to be a serious burden on the economy. The conviction has grown, however, that both the money and the social costs of the traditional care (or neglect) of the aged were unreasonably high. It also came to be believed that the problem was national in its scope and that the local units had a fair claim to national assistance in solving it.

Under the national old age assistance program, the federal government gives to each state and territory three-quarters of any payment made to an indigent person over sixty-five years of age up to $20 per month, and half of any additional payment up to $50. This means that the maximum federal payment is $30, and that this must be matched by at least $20 paid by the state. The states may go as far beyond this maximum figure as they wish and, in fact, they vary greatly in the sums paid. Some pay as much as $80 or $90 per month. There is also considerable variety in the conditions which the states impose, some giving assistance to those who own property or have relatives capable of helping, others insisting on almost complete destitution as a condition for assistance. By 1950, about two and three-quarter million persons, or 231 of every 1,000 over sixty-five years of age, were receiving old age assistance under the social security program. The average monthly payment was about $45. The total cost was $1,372,000,000, of which federal funds amounted to $759,-000,000; state, $561,000,000; and local, $52,000,000.

The number of recipients of old age assistance may be expected to decline as the federally administered program of old age and survivors' insurance extends its coverage. In 1950, in fact, the number of those receiving benefits under the latter program slightly exceeded those receiving old age assistance, and its cost was about the same. About two-thirds of the beneficiaries of the insurance program were 65 years of age or older. The persons now receiving old age assistance are for the most part those who had missed out on the protection extended by the insurance program, that is, persons who had worked in non-covered employment, men who had already been disabled or retired or their wives, and widows whose husbands had died too soon to earn insured status after the insurance program went into effect.

As new categories of workers are added by statute to the insured class, it is likely that more persons will retire on *pensions* and thus be dropped from the old age assistance rolls. The same result may follow the extension of the program of assistance to the permanently and totally disabled referred to below. For the present the Social Security Board reports that the old age and survivors' insurance program "has already taken over the major role in providing income for orphans and their widowed mothers. About 630,000 orphans (with one or both parents dead) were receiving benefits under old age and survivors' insurance in June 1950." [29]

AID TO DEPENDENT CHILDREN

The second category of persons eligible for federal aid comprises those children under 18 years of age who have lost one or both parents through death, disability, or desertion. Heretofore, such children have lived in orphanages or boarding "homes." It is now generally believed that, if the mother survives, it is better that the home should be preserved by assisting her. The federal law now provides for a payment to the state of three-quarters of the amount paid up to $12 for each eligible child, and half of any additional amount up to $27. The states are free, of course, to pay additional sums from their own funds. As this is written, about 1,500,000 children in about half a million families are recipients of this aid. The total cost of the program in the calendar year 1949 was $472,000,000, of which the federal treasury contributed $205,000,000, the remainder being furnished by the states and their local subdivisions, most of it by the state governments.[30]

AID TO THE BLIND

Before the inauguration of the federal social security program, the blind who were not cared for by relatives were either inmates of

---

[29] *Report of the Federal Security Agency for 1950,* p. 26.

[30] Many orphaned children, of course, still live in orphanges or "children's homes," or are boarded out in selected homes or placed with foster parents. Publicly supported orphanages are subject to supervision by the appropriate state or local authorities, as are the homes in which children are placed. Federal funds are available for the support of such children. The federal law was amended in 1950 to include children living with relatives other than parents.

special state institutions where they were taught certain handicrafts as a means of partial support or were simply recipients of "general assistance" from local governments. Under the Social Security Act, the federal government pays to the state three-fourths of the first twenty dollars of the average monthly payment per recipient, and one-half the remaining amount that is subject to federal matching. Under this scheme, about 77,000 blind persons, or one in three of the estimated total blind population, were being assisted in 1950. The average monthly payment was $47.52 and the total cost was somewhat over $42,000,000. Of this total about 40 per cent was contributed by the federal government, something over 50 per cent by the states, and less than 8 per cent by local governments, although in 29 states no local contributions at all were made.

AID TO THE PERMANENTLY AND TOTALLY DISABLED

A fourth category of persons eligible for assistance through federal grants was added by an amendment to the Social Security Act in 1950—the permanently and totally disabled. The scheme of payments is the same as that for old age assistance. By the autumn of 1951 this program was in operation in 29 states, the District of Columbia, and three territories. Recipients numbered slightly over 100,000, or roughly one-tenth of those receiving "general assistance." Average monthly payments were about $44. The Social Security Board predicted in its report for 1950 that the new category will "take care of many persons now on general assistance rolls and reduce still further the demands upon general assistance as a 'catchall' in caring for persons who cannot qualify for insurance benefits or other types of assistance."

LOCAL ADMINISTRATION OF SOCIAL SECURITY

The federal social security program is administered by agencies of the several states acting under rules and regulations promulgated by the Social Security Board in Washington. The act itself simply provides that federal aid shall be paid to every state which meets certain requirements which it sets forth, and it leaves it to the Board to determine whether these requirements have been met. In addition to the financial arrangements, which have already been described, each state is required to prepare a plan for administering the provisions of the act within its borders, and to designate or create an administrative agency acceptable to the Social Security Board.

Beyond this, the Board has required each state to choose its welfare personnel, upon both the state and local levels, by a merit system satisfactory to the Board. It should be pointed out, finally, that the Hatch Acts forbid political activity by all state and local employees whose salaries are wholly or partly paid from federal funds.

Within these very general conditions, the states themselves determine who shall receive assistance and in what amounts. Very naturally, the states vary greatly in the requirements which they impose as to eligibility, in accordance with their traditions, policies, and resources. In all but five of them, however, a single agency—a department or a board of public welfare—is the responsible state agency, with authority to implement the policy of the state legislature and to supervise county and other local welfare officials.[31] Although the Social Security Board insists on adequate standards, there has been little or no tendency on its part, or on the part of the central state departments, to usurp local prerogatives. It has been recognized by the supervisory authorities that "local responsibility in such an intimate phase of government work is . . . exceedingly important. The prevention of waste and the elimination of unworthy recipients of public relief are, in the long run, greatly accelerated by a local organization responsive to local sentiment."[32] As might be expected, local officials vary in their efficiency and vigilance, some being liberal in their attitude toward those requesting aid, others tight-fisted and exacting doubtless beyond the requisites of efficiency. It is well to remember, however, that local budgets everywhere are under heavy pressure from organized groups interested in good roads, better schools, and a score of other services besides welfare. Those disposed to be critical of the authorities would do well to ask themselves what *they* would do if placed at the center of such converging forces.

Although there are differences in detail from state to state, local assistance machinery conforms to a general plan. There is commonly a county welfare or assistance director named by the governing board and approved by the state department. Subject to rules promulgated by his superiors, this official is responsible for the routine supervision of assistance to the aged, the blind, and dependent chil-

---

[31] This refers primarily to the "categorical aids," but it is also true with respect to general assistance, at least in those states which make grants to local subdivisions.

[32] L. D. White, *Introduction to the Study of Public Administration* (3rd ed. 1948), p. 162.

dren. His staff of workers must possess qualifications acceptable to the state department and to the Social Security Board. Persons requiring aid are investigated by staff workers who make recommendations to the director and the governing body and supervise assistance clients continuously. Local departments are inspected periodically by state agents and are required to file periodical reports with the state. The state department, in turn, reports to the Social Security Board.

This discussion, it must be emphasized, concerns only the "categorical aids." Persons not eligible for any of these types of assistance may still be in need. If so, their support is a charge solely on state and local funds. The Federal Security Administrator has, for several years, urged national grants for "general assistance," but Congress has not responded. Expenditures for "general assistance" in 1949 totaled nearly $300,000,000, about two-thirds of which was contributed by the state governments in the form of grants to their local units, about 10,000 of which were engaged in this type of "relief." In about one-third of the states in 1950, the general assistance burden was borne entirely by the local governments; and in thirty states, more than half the funds for this purpose was raised from local sources. At the other extreme were those states in which the entire cost of general assistance was paid by the state treasury. Local funds for aid of this sort are derived almost entirely from the general property tax and are usually insufficient. As a result, local agencies feel compelled to exclude whole groups from eligibility, so that those unable to qualify for the categorical aids are, to all intents and purposes, victims of the poor laws of the 17th century.

Some reflections may not be out of place in concluding this chapter. It has attempted to deal with matters with which large numbers of people are deeply preoccupied. To a new interest in adequate care of the ill, the aged, the blind, and the indigent must be added a widespread conviction that government should guarantee a minimum of security to all citizens who have not been able to acquire it through their own efforts. For the time being at least, the traditional willingness to take arms against a sea of troubles and abide the consequences has been abandoned. Even though it be admitted that the incidence of the contingent has grown sharper and less predictable, the question is a fair one whether a population centering its attention upon security has not lost some of its virtue. If policies directed to this end have in mind, as may be suspected, greater national efficiency, they may be in the end self-defeating. Life, to have zest, must have in it some elements of danger.

The historian Gibbon believed that, beyond doubt, the happiest and most prosperous epoch in human history was the second century of the Christian era, when the universal empire of the Romans was under the benevolent autocracy of the Antonines. But there is something wrong here, even from the point of view of social efficiency. "The long peace and the uniform governments of the Romans," says Gibbon, "introduced a slow poison into the vitals of the empire. The minds of men were gradually reduced to the same level, the fire of genius was extinguished, and even the military spirit evaporated," and finally, "the rich and polite Italians, who had almost universally embraced the philosophy of Epicurus, enjoyed the present blessings of ease and tranquillity, and suffered not the pleasant dream to be interrupted by the memory of their old tumultuous freedom." [33]

Social security on a national scale must necessarily proceed in accordance with a plan, formulated and executed by a bureaucracy. To a considerable degree, such a plan is imposed upon those who are to administer it in direct contact with its beneficiaries. It therefore runs the danger of being found commendable if it seems to its authors a model of symmetry and order. But life is not orderly, and society does not exist to conform to those standards that please top administrators. The facts and the figures in this chapter are taken, largely of necessity, from official sources. As one reads them, and the enthusiastic recommendations of those who draw conclusions from statistics, he detects a note of evangelism which raises doubts as to the validity of these conclusions. Although we wish our officials to be zealous and enthusiastic about their work, we may legitimately wonder whether they do not sometimes labor to amplify their jurisdiction to a point beyond what sober reflection would justify. Much is said about the lack of imagination, the inefficiency, and even the hard-heartedness of local welfare officials, but it is possible to say something *for* them. Men and women who, in the intimacy of the rural neighborhood, know something about the deserts of their fellow-citizens, may judge better than a distant bureau chief when benevolence is justified.

---

[33] Edward Gibbon, *Decline and Fall of the Roman Empire* (Modern Library), I:50-1, 53.

CHAPTER 13

Public Health

There is a persistent tradition in the United States to the effect that the country is a more healthful place than the city. This has no doubt been fostered by literature of the Old Oaken Bucket school expressing a point of view not even yet eradicated from an urbanized society. It has always been assumed by country people that being well is the normal thing and that, in any event, if one were ill the responsibility for that misfortune was a personal and family, and not a community, one. In spite of this belief, however, there is a rural health problem. It consists not only in the fact that people in the country get sick just as they do in the city, but also that the rural population clings to certain attitudes now generally abandoned by city-dwellers, which make it difficult to organize for an attack on disease. "Promotion of sanitation and control of disease through public measures, such as immunization and quarantine, had to justify themselves in rural society. Public health nurses have had to win their way in country communities just as professionally trained agriculturalists, home economists, and social welfare workers have had to do." [1] These factors are reflected in the types of organization for health work which do not square with modern knowledge of disease and which are serious obstacles to progress. Discussing rural health administration means examining the relation between these factors.

RURAL HEALTH CONDITIONS

It is hard to make any very positive general statements about the health of the rural population. The gross figures for the urban and rural death rates for the country as a whole show that the advantage is with the rural portion of the population. But it should be pointed

---

[1] J. H. Kolb and E. de S. Brunner, *A Study of Rural Society* (1946), p. 574. Quoted with the permission of the authors and the publishers, Houghton Mifflin Co.

out that, although these figures seem to favor the rural population, the urban rate has decreased more rapidly than that for the country. Thus, in 1900 the rural death rate was 50 per cent under the urban, while in 1940 it was only 10 per cent lower.[2] If the figures for infant mortality be taken as better indicating rural health conditions, a somewhat different story may be told. There are many states in which the infant mortality rate in the country is much lower than either the national average or than the rate in cities. On the other hand, in the rural parts of Kentucky, Louisiana, Maine, Maryland, Mississippi, Missouri, North Carolina, and other states, the rate in the rural sections exceeds both the national average and the average in cities of over 2,500 population. And it is today true that children born in any one of the ten largest cities within the past ten years have had on the average a better chance of living beyond their first birthday than children born in the rural parts of the country. No sweeping generalizations as to rates seem possible except that, in spite of some apparently very healthful rural states, there are many "black spots" on the map. As to the causes of infant deaths, it is significant that measles, whooping cough, diphtheria, influenza, lobar pneumonia, diarrhea and enteritis account for a greater proportion of deaths in rural areas than in the cities. This relatively poor showing may very possibly be due to the absence of preventive and educational work and community sanitation in rural districts. Certainly, the death rate from preventable diseases tends to be higher in rural than in urban areas.

As to the incidence of disease and the nature of physical defects of the rural population generally, we have a mass of data from which it is possible to draw fairly reliable conclusions. It is well established that hookworm disease and malaria are almost exclusively rural in their incidence, that there is far more dysentery and typhoid in the country, and that tuberculosis of the respiratory tract is surprisingly prevalent in spite of the abundance of fresh air. With the exception of tuberculosis these diseases are all traceable to polluted water,

---

[2] "Regardless of how it is measured, the health of rural residents still is better than that of urban residents but the difference is much less than forty years ago. Indeed, for certain causes of death against which medical and public health activities have been especially successful, the death rate is now lower in urban than in rural areas. If present trends continue, mortality rates among urban residents may become less than those for rural residents for an increasing list of diseases." Harold F. Dorn, Senior Economist, United States Public Health Service, 7 *Rural Sociology* 27 (Mar. 1942).

food, or soil and are eradicable by routine sanitary measures. Studies exist in large number indicating that rural school children have poor health habits and numerous preventable or remediable physical defects, and that they go to schools which are frequently in a scandalously insanitary condition. Examinations of entering college students seem to show that those from large cities not only have fewer preventable and remediable defects such as enlarged tonsils, adenoids, spinal curvature, decayed teeth, and defective vision, but also that they generally have fewer previous histories of the preventable infectious diseases of childhood.

During the years 1928-1931, the Committee on the Cost of Medical Care, in cooperation with state and local health departments, studied 9,000 families living in rural, urban, and metropolitan areas. It was found that children between one and ten years of age and adults over 65 in the country were ill less often than such persons living in large cities, but that the morbidity rate of all other age groups was higher in the country than in the city. For the country as a whole it was said in 1931 that "in our rural communities there are about 1,000,000 persons incapacitated all the time by illness, much of which is preventable; about 70 per cent of the school children are handicapped by physical defects most of which are preventable or remediable; about 30 per cent of the persons of military age are incapacitated for arduous productive labor or for general military duty, largely from preventable causes; and over 60 per cent of the men and women between 40 and 60 years of age are in serious need of physical reparation, largely as a result of preventable causes." [3]

Data collected during more recent years do not greatly change the picture. In 1943, for example, the selective service boards found with respect to eighteen- and nineteen-year-old registrants that 41.1 per cent who were classed as farmers were unfit for service because of physical defects, as contrasted with 25.4 per cent of registrants in general. Infant and maternal mortality rates are considerably higher in the country than in the cities, and those for typhoid, paratyphoid, diphtheria, malaria, pellagra, and influenza very much higher. Local studies in widely separated sections of the country show not only a heavy incidence of preventable diseases, but con-

---

[3] L. L. Lumsden, "Cooperative Rural Health Work of the Public Health Service in the Fiscal Year 1930," *Reprint No. 1421, Public Health Reports* (1931); death rates are found in the annual volumes of *Mortality Statistics* issued by the Bureau of the Census and in the mimeographed special reports issued from time to time by the same agency.

siderable chronic illness and a surprisingly high rate of mental disorders in the rural population.[4]

These figures seem to indicate that life in the country is not particularly healthful. The death rate may indeed be lower on the average, but physical defects of a debilitating kind seem even more frequent than they are in the cities, and it may well be doubted whether the population as a whole is as fit. On examination it is clear that most of the defects reported are definitely preventable, either by such routine procedures as the protection of food and water supplies, by minor surgery, or simply by systematic education in good health habits. In other words, the rural health problem is largely one of social organization. Fresh air and sunshine have apparently done their best, and driving the rural death and morbidity rates still lower depends upon willingness of rural people to overcome the lag which separates them from modern health standards.

If the country is less active than the city in the care of the health of its citizens, it is not necessarily because of any perverseness on the part of the rural inhabitants. It may be true that newer ideas about nutrition, personal hygiene, preventive medicine, and environmental sanitation make their way more slowly in the country; but this explains the situation only in part. Preventive and curative measures cost money—private money or public money. A study of the mortality and morbidity figures shows immediately that, for the most part, those areas where the incidence of disease is highest are those in which per capita income is lowest. This means not only that fewer people can afford to pay for medical care from their own resources, but also that the tax base is too narrow to permit large public expenditures for public health. The optimum standards of the experts are quite beyond the reach of such communities.

Moreover, medical, hospital, and nursing care is simply not readily available to people, even if they can afford it. Many rural areas have no physicians or dentists at all, members of these professions preferring to practice in cities, where the financial rewards are higher and hospitals and clinic facilities better. "Physicians trained in modern medical schools to utilize elaborate diagnostic and treatment facilities find it difficult to practice in communities where these facilities are not easily available." In 1940 there was, in the United States as a whole, one physician for every 935 persons. In the opin-

---

[4] A vast amount of data is summarized by Kolb and Brunner in *A Study of Rural Society,* pp. 573-581.

ion of the American Medical Association a danger point is reached when the ratio falls below 1 to 1500. The situation of the rural areas is indicated by the fact that the ratio in such urban states as New York, Massachusetts, and California is 1 to 597, 696, and 747 respectively. It is 1 to 1784 in Mississippi, 1684 in Alabama, 1657 in South Dakota, and 1565 in South Carolina. The most rural states in 1940 had only one active physician for each 1295 persons, while in the most urban states the ratio was 1 to 613. In 1944, in the nation as a whole, there were no active physicians in 81 counties; 20 counties had more than 10,000 persons per physician and two had more than 22,000 persons per doctor. The general shortage of dentists and nurses is even more serious and, with respect to both, the country is relatively worse off than in the case of physicians.[5]

WHAT IS PUBLIC HEALTH WORK?

A leading American authority, Dr. C. E.-A. Winslow defines public health as "the science and art of preventing disease, prolonging life, and promoting physical health and efficiency through community efforts for the sanitation of the environment, the control of communicable diseases, the education of the individual in the principles of personal hygiene, the organization of medical and nursing services for the early diagnosis and preventive treatment of disease, and the development of the social machinery which will insure to every individual a standard of living adequate to the maintenance of health; organizing these benefits in such a way as to enable every citizen to realize his birthright of health and longevity." Whatever else may be said of this definition, no one can say that it lacks comprehensiveness. If anything in the whole field of social service or social reform is left out it escapes our attention. It was evidently evolved in an urban environment. As Hiscock remarks: "The forces which

---

[5] Data as to the number and distribution of medical, dental, and nursing personnel may be found in the annual reports of the Federal Security Agency and in a memorandum prepared by the Bureau of Research and Statistics of the Social Security Board for the Senate Committee on Education and Labor and printed for the committee as *Senate Committee Print No. 4,* 79th Congress, 2d Session (1946). The medical profession, however, does not accept the standards used by the Federal Security Agency in determining the present adequacy of medical service. Thus, the economist of the American Medical Association in 1951 argued that, because of better communication facilities in rural areas and improvements in medical technology, medical service is constantly growing more, rather than less, accessible to the rural population, and that the facts point to "a surplus or potential surplus of physicians rather than a deficit." See Frank G. Dickinson, "Supply of Physicians' Services," *Bulletin 81,* Bureau of Medical Economic Research, American Medical Association, April 21, 1951. In this battle between governmental and medical bureaucrats, the layman is sure to be puzzled!

have built the modern city have given us the means to protect us
against the ravages of disease and inefficiency." [6] Chief among the
factors which created and helped to solve health problems are: (1)
the crowding into cities, which created almost overnight such problems as water supply, waste disposal, food protection, housing, and
occupational diseases, problems which occur not at all or only on a
small scale in rural districts; (2) the development of communication
agencies which, although they made easier the spread of disease,
also aided greatly in the dissemination of knowledge about it; (3)
an increase in the speed and pressure of living under competitive
conditions, and a resulting emphasis upon personal efficiency; and
(4) the discoveries of modern science and their application to the
control of disease as well as the improvement of industrial processes.

Most of these developments are foreign to rural life, in which
few of the conditions exist favoring the same sort of attack upon disease which are now commonplace in cities. There is little of the
overcrowding that occurs in tenements, offices and factories, and thus
less obvious need for meeting the dangers involved in such contacts.[7]
There is also much less familiarity even today with socialized action
in any field, for the difficulty of organizing farmers has long been
notorious. In spite of the telephone, radio, and improved highways,
social isolation is not yet completely broken down and there is too
often a lack of a lively sense of community. In line with the tradition of individualism each family is expected to look after its own
physical well-being. Practices long ago accepted by the regimented
population of cities are looked upon as coddling and pampering in
rural areas.

Finally, it is generally agreed among students of rural life that
ignorance of the nature of disease is widespread in the population.
The belief dies hard that fresh air and sunshine are sovereign reme-

---

[6] Both quotations are from Ira V. Hiscock, *Community Health Organization*, pp.
13-15. In short, public health consists of all facilities and procedures with respect to
physical fitness for which the public is willing to pay, for "the division between preventive and curative medicine no longer exists as a practical factor," J. R. McGibony
and Louis Block, "Better Patient Care Through Coordination," *Public Health Reports*,
Vol. 64, No. 47 (Nov. 25, 1949), p. 1514.

[7] On the other hand there is a rural housing problem. A survey of rural housing
conducted by the Federal Emergency Administration of Public Works in 1934 arrived
at the conclusion that 730,000 farm houses required complete demolition and replacement. This is more than one-tenth of the total number. *Slums and Blighted Areas in
the United States*, Housing Division, Bulletin No. 1, Federal Emergency Administration
of Public Works, p. 96. A sampling reported in the Census Bureau's Current Population Survey of 1947 indicated that 15.5 per cent of all rural farm dwellings were in need
of major repairs. Overcrowding was markedly higher in all of the rural census areas.

dies for all ailments. Dietary knowledge is not general, due partly to poverty, partly to ignorance and lack of access to information. It is doubtful if the germ theory of disease causation and transmission is at all generally accepted. "The old oaken bucket" may be romantic in the Third Reader, but it may also have all the shortcomings of the now forgotten common drinking cup. The farmer may believe in sunshine and fresh air, but there is ample evidence in the studies of the health habits of school children that he is afraid of the "night air" and sleeps with his windows closed. The rural states are the home of anti-evolution legislation, anti-vaccination sentiment, armed resistance to bovine tuberculosis inoculation, self-dosing with proprietary nostrums, and of irregular practitioners and cultists of undemonstrated efficiency. Where such things are possible, it is not surprising to find provisions for protecting water supplies extremely primitive or entirely lacking. Illinois is a rich state, and yet its planning board reported in 1935 that over 300,000 persons lived in places having no recognized safe water supply and over half a million were without systems for the disposal of sewage which met the standards of the state. Some years ago the federal Department of Agriculture found three out of four farm water supplies sufficiently polluted to be unsafe. As to waste disposal in rural regions, the fact that in 1936 a state could publicly celebrate the erection of the 100,000th sanitary privy suggests faintly what conditions must be in the rural portions of those commonwealths not yet blessed with so many of these monuments to hygienic progress.

Because the cities perforce first discovered that disease could be conquered by measures of community hygiene and individual education, they have set the pace in public health organization. The country has lagged far behind until the city is in a fair way to establish itself as a more healthful place than the countryside. While this slowness of the country is in part attributable to ignorance of the nature of disease, a good deal of it must be set down to the lack of financial resources and to the persistence of faulty administrative organization. These latter factors are, as a matter of fact, closely connected.

RURAL HEALTH ORGANIZATION

Rural health machinery was set up in the day when the filth theory of disease was generally held and when there was no accurate knowledge of the method of disease transmission. Health procedure consisted largely in the abatement of nuisances and the quarantine of those ill with clearly contagious diseases. It was thought that small areas could serve as health districts as readily as they could for assessment, electoral, or highway purposes. For this reason such familiar areas as the county, town and township were made health authorities in rural sections. This meant, of course, a very large number of small health districts in the average state. Thus there are even today in Minnesota 2700 local units—cities, counties, villages, and townships—with responsibility for direct health service. In Iowa there are 1600 township boards of health plus those of some 900 incorporated municipalities. New Jersey has 567 municipalities responsible for public health work, and Ohio nearly 170.

Whatever the unit employed, the enforcement of the health laws is usually entrusted to a local board of health. These are constituted in a great variety of ways. In some states the board of county commissioners is the county board of health; in others certain county officers serve *ex officio,* as in Nebraska where the sheriff and the county superintendent act with a county physician named by the county board, or in North Dakota where the county health board is composed of the state's attorney, county superintendent, and a superintendent of public health whom they choose. In a number of states, the state department of public health has a hand in appointing members of the county board. Thus, three of the five members of the county board of health in Virginia are named by the state board, and a similar plan is followed in Kentucky and South Dakota. Where the township exists there may also be township boards as well as those acting for incorporated municipalities within the county.[8]

These legal and structural details are, however, of relatively little significance. Not all counties and practically no townships under modern conditions are proper units for public health administration. From the point of view of administration they exhibit to an exaggerated degree all the defects of small areas in relation to other public functions.[9] Especially is the township an irrelevant

---

[8] The most recent comprehensive study is Haven Emerson and Martha Luginbuhl, *Local Health Units for the Nation* (Commonwealth Fund, 1945).

[9] A sub-committee on local health units of the American Public Health Association in 1945 gave as its opinion that "no population unit of much below fifty thousand can either afford or justify the services of a highly trained full-time public health officer and associated professional and other personnel." See Martha Luginbuhl, "Local Responsibility for Health Service," **VI** *Public Administration Review* 30-41 (Winter 1946), and Haven Emerson and Martha Luginbuhl, *Local Health Units for the Nation* (Commonwealth Fund, 1945). It may be pointed out here that about 85 per cent of the counties of the United States have fewer than 50,000 inhabitants.

nuisance. The Michigan township was made a health authority in 1846 when, as one investigator puts it, "diseases were thought to arise from smells and cemeteries, and when anyone able to detect an odor or manage a cemetery could have qualified as a health officer." Such tiny areas, many of them too poor to perform their other functions without state assistance, are unable to afford the personnel or the equipment needed to carry out a health program of any sort —and a health program is commonly regarded as of much less importance than, for example, education or roads. The health officers employed are more often than not untrained, serve in their spare time, are paid only nominal salaries, and are quite unconvinced of the value of the scientific measures recommended by the state department which exercises a nominal supervision over them. Of the 1,160 township health officers in Michigan, 660 are not physicians, while in Indiana townships many of them are paid as little as ten dollars a year. The post is a minor avocation of its holder and the work consists in most places of "an occasional quarantine, an abatement of a nuisance, and a lighting of fumigators following quarantine." [10]

The truth of the matter is that over much of the rural areas of the United States there exists no public health service worthy of the name. This is partly because the population is not yet conscious of any health needs, and partly because of the poverty of the small districts. There are literally hundreds of townships which report no expenditures at all for public health, and many counties in which the health officer confines his activities to the care of the county poor and an occasional quarantine. In Minnesota, Anderson found that the average per capita expenditure for public health in 265 places under 1,000 population was nine cents, and in those under 500 population it was three cents, with many showing no outlays at all. Even making allowance for the lack of interest in public health in rural areas, it is quite likely true that these pitiable sums represent the limit of financial ability in many small rural districts. A health program covering the minimum of preventive and educational work would cost at least $12,000 a year or more, or nearly one dollar per capita in a county of the median population. Anderson admits that most of the 87 counties in Minnesota are probably unprepared at

---

[10] N. F. Sinai, *Organization and Administration of Public Health* (Michigan Local Government Series, 1933); *A Study of Rural Health Service,* published in 1933 by the Commonwealth Fund; *Indiana State Commission on Economy in Government Expenditures,* 1935.

present to assume such a burden, and this inadequacy would be even greater in the case of smaller areas.[11]

A sub-committee of the American Public Health Association, on the assumption that an expenditure of one dollar per capita will provide the minimum basic framework of local health service, and that county and multi-county health districts were organized, concluded that fewer than 1200 units could serve the entire United States. A study of present health activity in 1157 of these suggested areas disclosed an average per capita expenditure of sixty-one cents. However, for 63 units no expenditures were reported, in 300 units expenditures averaged less than thirty cents, and in 639 units less than fifty cents. Only ten per cent of the units spent ninety cents or more and comprised between one-sixth and one-fifth of the nation's total population. "Not only can it be said, therefore, that one-third of the nation lives in communities without a full-time health officer, but it can also be said that only one-sixth of the nation lives in communities spending even the minimum per capita desirable for local health service. The deficiencies of administrative organization inevitably result in a large measure of wasteful expenditure of even the meager funds currently devoted to local health protective facilities."[12]

RURAL HEALTH UNITS

Even if it wished to do so, then, the typical rural political subdivision cannot supply itself with health services which measure up to the standards worked out by the cities. Is there any way by which the undoubted needs may be met? The problem is to find an area populous and wealthy enough to finance preventive and educational work. While there is no area ideally suited for health work in all states, it is generally agreed that the county is the smallest feasible unit from the standpoint of efficiency of service and administration. In most sections the use of the county makes it possible to abandon the large number of ineffective organizations found in villages and townships, as well as place behind the local health program the resources of the entire county. If the state does its part in guiding and assisting the

---

[11] William Anderson, *Local Government and Finance in Minnesota* (1935), pp. 260-3. It was asserted in 1931 that a study of per capita personal income in various rural counties indicated that 70 per cent of the counties fall in the class in which incomes were less than $500 per year. See R. M. Atwater, "The Organization and Functions of the County Department of Health," in *Rural Government* (Proceedings of the 14th National Country Life Conference), p. 102.

[12] Martha Luginbuhl, *op. cit.*, p. 32.

local organization, a county health department could render those services of which the rural population stands most in need and which the smaller areas are simply incapable of supplying to any degree— namely, milk and water sanitation and farm sanitation, as well as a more adequate educational program through such agencies as the schools and maternal and infant clinics.

The county, therefore, has been the area through which health experts have attacked the rural health problem. The approved device has been the county health unit. By this is meant a full-time, permanent organization able to furnish the accepted public health services to the entire population of a county. The minimum personnel of such a unit consists of a full-time medical health officer, a nurse or sanitary inspector, and an office clerk. A more efficient organization is secured if both nurse and inspector are provided; and still larger units would include additional nurses and inspectors and such specialized employees as a sanitary engineer, a dentist, nutrition expert, and bacteriologist. Thus the American Public Health Association, which regards 50,000 inhabitants as the optimum size for a health unit, recommends the following personnel: (1) One full-time medically trained administrative health officer; (2) one public health nurse per five thousand population; (3) two workers in environmental sanitation per fifty thousand population, one to be professionally trained, preferably as a sanitary engineer; (4) one clerk per fifteen thousand population; (5) part-time clinicians and dentists, and laboratory workers, dental hygienists, health educators, and others as local conditions require.[13]

In terms of duties, a county or larger unit would be able to render at least the following services: (1) Recording of vital statistics and data on communicable diseases; (2) the control of communicable diseases; (3) the safeguarding of water, milk, and food supplies through the inspection of premises and the enforcement of well-understood requirements as to hygiene; and (4) the provision of nursing service in connection with mothers and infants. Professional students of public health needs estimate that the per capita cost of a program, administered in about 1200 districts of optimum size, would be 97 cents, as compared with 61 cents expended in 1942.

---

[13] The United States Public Health Service reported that in 1947 only 5.6 per cent of the population residing in areas with a full-time health officer had sufficient personnel to meet the minimum requirements for public health service. See *Public Health Personnel, Facilities, and Services in Areas Having a Full-time Health Officer* (June 1949).

The adoption of such a program would increase total local health expenditures from $77,000,000 to $127,000,000.

The minimum of staff and functions here outlined seems very modest in comparison with the extensive organizations and services maintained by large cities. And yet almost no rural county has organized such a unit of its own free will. The impetus for any progress that has been made in rural health work has come from state departments of health, the federal Public Health Service, from private foundations such as the Commonwealth Fund, the Rockefeller Foundation, the Milbank Fund, and the Rosenwald Fund, or from local philanthropic and social service groups. It is significant that local self-government has not generated enough interest in such an enterprise as public health work to lead local initiative to attack the problem. The primary job in almost every case has been to educate the local population to want health work undertaken at all in any serious or comprehensive way. Even relatively enlightened local officials have not been willing to appropriate funds in the face of the obvious indifference or hostility of their constituents. To win popular support the first step has usually been to set up a demonstration unit in a county, financed by state, federal, and private funds, in the hope that its accomplishments will lead the local government to assume a larger share of its support as a permanent function. The county unit movement began in Washington, North Carolina, and New York in 1911, and has since spread to other states until at its peak there were 616 units in every section of the country.

Although county health units are widespread, a map showing them is deceptive in terms of the adequacy of their staffs. There were in the United States in 1948, 1,319 health organizations employing full-time personnel. Of these 653 were single county units, 261 local health districts, 124 state health districts, and 281 city health departments. Almost all of these received state or federal aid. The population served was 83.2 per cent of the total of the nation. This sounds impressive until the figures are more closely examined. Such an examination reveals that less than 5 per cent of the population lives in units having sufficient personnel of each category to meet minimum standards. There are enough nurses for only 12.6 per cent, physicians for only 28.9 per cent, sanitation personnel for 55.6 per cent, and clerical workers for only 40 per cent of the work required. To put it another way, the Federal Security Administrator alleges that only seven million persons in 1948 lived in areas where the local health units could be considered as adequately staffed, and adds that "notwithstanding the steady development of local public health services over the past decade, an aggregate population of 40 million is living in areas which, at best, employ only a part-time health officer, who may or may not be a qualified physician.[14] There is, in fact, nearly everywhere a dearth of trained personnel, and the money available is usually not enough to attract and retain the most competent workers. About all that can even yet be said is that tools have been found to attack the rural health problem, and that these tools are precarious hostages to the good will of the local population and the patience of private sponsors.

THE STATE GOVERNMENT AND RURAL HEALTH

The state governments entered public health work by direct expenditures for such special services as the maintenance of tuberculosis sanatoria and orthopedic hospitals, the detection and prevention of venereal diseases, and the provision of laboratory services to medical practitioners and local health officers. Most of these functions had little direct relation to the local health programs already in existence, and their cost made up only a small part of total state expenditures. Modern knowledge of disease causation, however, rendered obviously inadequate the traditional local health organization, so that the state became more deeply involved. State health departments assumed advisory functions with respect to such local problems as sewage disposal, rural sanitation, stream pollution, protection of water and milk supplies, and the collection of vital statistics. For many years, however, very little work was done by the state departments at the "grass roots." The conviction has grown in recent years that the public health is a state and national problem, and that a closer relationship between the state and local levels must be created if the problem is to be attacked successfully. This new understanding of the nature of the problem has resulted in three developments in state government: (1) the strengthening of the authority of the central state agency; (2) the working out of a system of state grants-in-aid; and (3) the acceptance by the state of important duties in the expanding public health program of the national

[14] See *Public Health Personnel . . . in Local Areas Having a Full-time Health Officer* (1949), pp. 2, 10; *Annual Report of the Federal Security Agency* (1948), The Administrator's Summary, p. 29; Joseph W. Mountin and Evelyn Flook, *Guide to Health Organization in the United States,* United States Public Health Service, Miscellaneous Publication No. 35 (1948), p. 33.

government. The last of these is discussed below; the first two may be dealt with briefly here.

The state's part in the organization of public health services has involved extensive activity in both legislation and administration. During the past twenty years, nearly every state has enacted laws, usually of a permissive character, under which local units may approach more closely to the goal of full coverage of the state by modern health departments. Lack of trained personnel for such departments and, in many cases, local apathy have caused many of these acts to be non-operative, but they are evidence of growing state concern. A better indication of this interest is found in the fact that state appropriations have steadily increased.[15] On the administrative side, it can be said that the range of the state departments' activities is very wide. "The states have wide authority (1) to issue binding orders and regulations for local health officers; (2) to provide a wide range of services for local agencies; (3) to review local acts; (4) to control local functions, frequently through specifications attached to grants-in-aid; (5) to appoint or remove local officials in some states; and (6) to take direct action in the event that local authorities fail to perform." [16] In addition to these supervisory duties, state departments in various states administer certain functions directly, such as the venereal disease and industrial hygiene programs and the sanitary inspection of public camps. The departments have also shown increasing activity in developing health education programs, directly and in cooperation with local agencies and private associations.

State aid to local units for public health work is as yet not highly developed, amounting in 1948 to only about $20 million, exclusive of grants earmarked for hospitals and institutions for the handicapped. This figure is to be contrasted with about half a billion dollars for highway aids, more than $600 million for public welfare, and about a billion and a half for schools. On the other hand, state aid for public health amounts to about one-fifth of all public health expenditures made from the state treasuries and to about one-third of local costs for the same function. Actually, health grants are so little developed that it is impossible to speak of them in any detail. So far as can be determined, little use of "equalization" grants has been made; much of the money expended is apparently for specific

---

[15] The details may be found in the successive issues of *The Book of the States.*
[16] *State-Local Relations,* p. 40.

purposes. State health authorities seem generally to be aware of the desirability of developing a rational system of state aid, but legislatures have been loath to appropriate adequate sums. In 1948, only fourteen states are reported as making any grants at all. As a result, the principal fiscal connection between the states and their local units is as go-betweens in carrying out federal specialized health programs.

THE FEDERAL GOVERNMENT AND PUBLIC HEALTH

While the inadequacy of local health work in the past may justly be attributed to the ignorance and apathy of the local inhabitants, the plain truth in many cases is that local resources are insufficient to finance an adequate program. If small local units cannot afford such programs, the states themselves have done little better. The enthusiasts for better public health administration have not been nearly so successful in securing state appropriations as those interested in schools, highways, and conventional "social security." As in the cases of these other functions, however, we are witnessing the rapid development of a program involving national support and having as its objective nothing less than a comprehensive program of rural health improvement. The intervention of the federal government in this field has not been abrupt. For many years, cooperative relationships have existed between the United States Public Health Service and the state and territorial health authorities. The principal results of these relationships, however, have been the collection of statistics, the encouragement of local health efforts, the conduct of special local studies, the training of some local personnel, and special services with respect to venereal disease detection and treatment. The recent expansion in the role of the federal government in this field may be explained not only as the result of steady pressure by reformers, but also by a widening of the conception of social security to include more than the categories contemplated in the original Social Security Act.[17]

At the present time, federal participation in local health activities takes place principally in two ways. There has been, first, an expansion of the more or less traditional services to the states under the supervision of the United States Public Health Service, now,

---

[17] According to the report of the Federal Security Agency, federal funds for general health work, including industrial hygiene, amounted to $11,200,000 in 1948. Of this sum 45 per cent was allocated by the state health departments directly to local health units.

significantly, a unit within the Federal Security Agency. A consoli- .
dation of the laws relating to the Public Health Service, approved in
1944, provided considerably larger sums for cooperative work with
the states and their subordinate health districts, not only to attack
such old problems as venereal diseases and tuberculosis, but also to
assist the "states, counties, and health districts, and other political
subdivisions of the States in establishing and maintaining adequate
public health services." [18]

Potentially more important than this Act is the Hospital Survey
and Construction Act of 1946, enacted to assist the states in providing
"adequate hospital, clinic and similar services to all their peo-
ples." [19] The significance of this act can be appreciated when it is
remembered that the absence of adequate medical care in rural areas
is frequently explained by the lack of hospital and clinical facilities
in these districts. Where such facilities are not available, competent
and ambitious physicians are not likely to remain long. It is the
long-range purpose of the act to bring about a more even distribution of physicians, dentists, and nurses by giving the country opportunities of this sort which are now found almost entirely in the
larger towns and cities. After authorizing the expenditure of
$3,000,000 for surveys (under state auspices) of local hospital and
health facilities and needs, the Act provides for the annual expenditure for five years of $75,000,000 for the construction of "hospitals,
health centers, and related facilities." Every state is participating
in the program. The first project received initial approval late in
1947. By June 30, 1950, approval had been given to a total of 1367
projects involving total construction costs of $952,299,000, of which
the national government contributed $344,059,000. The Federal
Security Agency reported as of the same date that these projects provided for the addition of 65,542 hospital beds: 51,651 in general
hospitals, and 6,555, 4,527 and 2,809 beds respectively in hospitals
for the care of mental diseases, tuberculosis, and chronic illnesses.
Health centers to the number of 244 were added in 32 states and

---

[18] *Public Law 410,* 78th Congress, 2d Session. Under this act each state is required
to spend from its own funds such amounts as may be determined by regulations of the
Surgeon General. Actually, of a total federal, state and local expenditure for public
health in 1945, of $149,000,000, the federal share was less than $22,000,000. See *The
Book of the States* (1948-49), p. 349-351.

[19] Generally referred to as the Hill-Burton Act. It should be pointed out that the
money made available under this Act may be used to assist only non-profit private or
publicly owned hospitals. The general hospital projects so far authorized are about
equally divided between those sponsored by public agencies and those sponsored by
private groups.

territories. Most of the new hospitals being built with federal assistance are small ones—68 per cent will have fewer than fifty beds and 89 per cent fewer than a hundred. Of the new hospitals, 71.3 per cent are in places of less than 5,000 population and only 12.1 per cent are in towns and cities of more than 10,000. In terms of funds expended, almost one-third of the federal contribution is in small country towns. "Compared with our present distribution of hospitals, the program is tending to place hospitals in the smaller population centers where they will serve predominantly rural people. This is precisely the purpose for which the program was designed. . . ." [20] The vast majority of the approved projects are in areas of less than average income, but "the program is not developing facilities in the very poorest areas," probably because such communities simply do not have the funds to build or maintain hospitals even with federal aid.

It is too early to predict the possible results of federal aid under the terms of this Act. Perhaps it is overoptimistic to say that "for the first time a policy has been established whereby hospitals and health centers are to be planned, located and operated in relation to the overall health requirements of the people. If full advantage is taken by the states of the aid which the Act authorizes, it will be possible to bring essential health services within the geographic reach of all individuals throughout the nation for the first time in our history." [21] There are two reasons why one may question this statement. In the first place, it seems likely that many areas will always remain too poor to afford the kind and degree of health service envisioned by the Act, even though their inhabitants should be aroused to the need of such a service. In the second place, the success of the Act will depend in considerable measure upon the attitude of the medical profession. The hospital act assumes that the provision of hospital and clinical facilities will keep competent medical men in the country and even attract them there. The difficulty here is that doctors seem to be much like businessmen in preferring high to low incomes. Probably a community too poor to support a hospital from its own resources is too poor to pay the sort of fees which are to be had in larger and richer centers of population. However, a beginning has been made—a beginning without which little improvement is possible.

---

[20] *Hospital Construction under the Hill-Burton Program*, Reprint No. 3025, Public Health Reports, Vol. 65, No. 23, June 9, 1950.
[21] *The Book of the States* (1948-49), p. 344.

This review of recent developments leads straight to the conclusion that public health work today includes every type of public activity devoted to the physical improvement of individuals which taxpayers can be made to finance. Public health work in the past was restricted to the prevention of the spread of infectious and communicable diseases. Curative procedures were regarded as being the responsibility of the individual, except when he was a public charge. It is no longer possible to define public health work in such terms, if attention is directed to what is actually being done. There are clinics everywhere devoted to the removal of tonsils, the care of the teeth, the treatment of heart ailments, the feeding of babies, even the care of arthritis. Only by very devious reasoning can such types of work be called preventive in the older sense of that term. Advancing medical knowledge has itself led to a blurring of the old distinction between prevention and cure. This difficulty has been seized upon by public health enthusiasts, welfare workers, and humanitarians generally as a basis for a redefinition of public health work. The regimented populations of large cities, divorced from the soil, dependent utterly upon money wages, and plagued by the spectre of insecurity and periodic want, have accepted as a matter of course a variety of services certainly going far beyond anything justified by previous views of public responsibility. These services seem destined to be extended throughout the nation no matter what such a development does to theories about the sphere of the state.

Some final reflections may not be out of place. A conception of the general welfare which includes the provision by the state of a national minimum of medical care and social security below which no one is to fall, is undoubtedly in part the result of the growth of humanitarian sentiment and a widening of human sympathy. But when full allowance has been made for these factors, it still remains true that such a policy is an aspect of our growing nationalism, evidences of which are found in every part of our community life. It is a commonplace to say that we live in a dangerous world, in which genuine internationalism has a precarious existence. The difficulties that beset us are currently described in terms of new and conflicting "ideologies"—individualism or "the American way" on the one hand, and strange collectivist creeds on the other. This is, I venture to think, a superficial view if it is held to state a new situation. The real protagonists in current international politics are the characters long familiar to us, nations, not creeds, except as creeds serve the usual purpose of strengthening the sinews of a nation. In such a struggle, little argument is needed to prove that victory will go to the more efficient. One of the things that will contribute to this victory is an efficient labor force and a population convinced, by the promise of security, of the beneficence of its rulers' purposes. And in truth nationalism everywhere seems to eventuate in collectivism. Humanitarian sentiment and a livelier sense of fellow-feeling are thus harnessed to the ends of the state—ends which may or may not be consistent with the highest human goals. Universal provision of those social services that are described here and elsewhere in this book requires a powerful state, and it may well be that such a state has ends hostile to the citizens' deeper aspirations.

CHAPTER 14

Local Units and a New Governmental Pattern

One of the ideas which we have sought to emphasize throughout this book is that rural institutions are inadequate because they have not been adjusted smoothly into a social and economic pattern which is very largely the product of urban and industrial forces. This is, of course, only to state in rather specific terms a fact frequently observed, namely, that social and political devices tend to remain stationary after the conditions under which they were developed have changed. Examples of this disharmony will readily occur to any serious student. With particular reference to rural government, we observe that political devices suitable to a sparse population of isolated farmers continue to exist and to work, after a fashion, in an environment which bears no resemblance to that in which they were first developed. It is difficult to exaggerate the importance of the shift in industry from an economy of hand tools to one based on the use of power-driven machinery. The more obvious result, of course, was to increase productivity, and thus to make it possible, with the same outlay of energy and time, to support a much larger population.

The results, however, did not stop there, but spilled over into fields normally referred to as "social" and "political." The massing of the people about the centers of available power, the changing use of land, the greater mobility of population, the growing number of wants with a corresponding increase in the facilities for supplying them, the changing forms of wealth, and the heightened inequalities produced by these changes—all these and many other elements introduced by technology have altered the face of society and have thrown out of gear the relationships between politics and economics, upon which the original forms of American government were based. Thus we see appearing even in rural districts such new problems as the provision of recreation, old age dependency, delinquency, new forms of crime such as bank robberies, which are literally machine-made, to say nothing of new techniques for handling such matters as the assessment of property, the managing of institutions, and the keeping of records.

The original structure of American government envisaged the town as a collection of more or less discrete units known as families; a loose collection of towns and counties was the state; and the nation was simply a loose confederation of states. The Constitution of the United States and the actual government of the various states were simply statements in legal phraseology of the way in which people had grouped themselves from time immemorial.[1] The framers of the Federal Constitution and the architects of our original state governments could do no better than institutionalize these forms of social organization and make some more or less satisfactory arrangement for future amendment. No matter how much the sentimental patriot of today may wish to endow them with the competence of supermen, such they were not.

Precisely because they were so successful in adjusting government to the actual forms of social organization, their handiwork came to be prized beyond its true worth, and to have attributed to it a sanctity which belongs to no human devices. Local self-government and states' rights became fetishes before which men habitually and unthinkingly bowed, their very devotion making them blind to the vast and rapid changes going on about them. "We have inherited town meeting practices and ideas. But we live and act and have our being in a continental national state. We are held together by non-political bonds and the political forms are stretched and legal institutions patched in an *ad hoc* and improvised manner to do the work they have to do. Political structures fix the channels in which non-political, industrialized currents flow. . . . Political and legal forms have only piecemeal and haltingly, with great lag, accommodated themselves to the industrial transformation."[2]

Examples may be taken almost at random to illustrate the lag to which Dewey refers. The typical school district was not only an area for administering the common schools—it was also the political as-

---

[1] On this interpretation of the constitutional distribution of powers between state and nation, see the essay entitled "The American Commonwealth" by John W. Burgess, **I** *Pol. Sci. Quar.* 1-35 (Mar. 1886), reprinted in part in J. Mark Jacobson's *The Development of American Political Thought*, pp. 489-496.

[2] John Dewey, *The Public and Its Problems*, pp. 111, 113-114. Quoted with the permission of the publishers, Henry Holt & Co.

pect of the rural neighborhood and the center of such group life as was possible in a day when travel was difficult. Travel is no longer difficult, but we still have more than 75,000 one-room schools, not because we are not acquainted with a better practice, but because ease of travel has not yet, in our thinking, come to be sufficiently relevant to matters of school administration to force a change. Much of our health organization, with its scores of local health officers, is reminiscent of the days when men were cupped and bled for diseases now recognized as being caused by bacterial infection, to which county and town lines are equally irrelevant. The rural tax system, whether we consider it from the point of view of its base or its machinery of administration, harks back to the day when property was mainly in the form of land or chattels (cattle!), ignoring the enormous growth of what we call intangibles. In fact the whole rural ideology, centered as it is upon the small unit, the isolated individual, seems pathetically beside the point in a world which moves daily toward an organization which leaves little room for the self-sufficing units of a primitive agricultural community.

CENTRALIZATION AND DECENTRALIZATION

It is with some of these considerations in mind that we may best approach the question of the relationships between local and central government. Now the necessity for giving names to things has given rise to such words as "centralization" and "decentralization," and for a hundred and fifty years this question has been discussed with a liberal use of these words. It must be confessed that it is hard for anyone who sees what is actually going on in the world to attribute any special significance to these words as they are commonly used. Our thinking is undoubtedly simplified if we can bring ourselves to do it in terms of dichotomies such as "centralization" and "decentralization." But it is also deprived of all realism. Constant use of the expressions "centralization" and "decentralization" subtly persuades us that the problem of relationship is to be solved either by a unified bureaucracy operating from the state capital or by a well-nigh complete "anarchy of local autonomy." Either solution is absurd.

As a matter of law, the state in the United States has always been free, as we have seen, to manage as it would all the public business within its borders. Courts have left no doubt that local units exist at the pleasure of the state which may alter or abolish them at its sovereign will. Local officers, in the contemplation of the law, are state officers, the state as a mere matter of convenience to itself preferring to use them rather than others sent directly from the seat of government. But the spirit of our people has never in practice supported the legal view. The local election of officers has been sufficient to effect an almost complete decentralization of administration. Long freedom from external control, with the consequent building up of a class of local politicians intent upon preserving a monopoly of local offices and spoils, has erected "local self-government" and "home rule" into dogmas, accepted by local inhabitants as unthinkingly as most other dogmas are accepted.[3] The molders of local opinion have been, for the most part, ignorant of or indifferent to those social changes that have made "home rule" almost ludicrous, and they have commonly resisted with an almost religious fierceness all attempts to organize political power so as to make it able to cope with social and economic realities. The man-mountain of the state has regularly been reduced to impotence by the swarms of the Lilliputians from township, village, and school district. Hence, whether rational or not, belief in "home rule" is a political reality the significance of which cannot be passed over in any discussion of state-local relations.

Beginning with the premise that ultimate legal power resides in the state we have, broadly speaking, dealt with our local governments in two ways. In the first place, we have attempted what is usually called "legislative supervision." This consists essentially in conferring powers and liabilites upon local governments or local officials, and relying upon what is vaguely known as responsibility to the law for the enforcement of the state policy as declared by the statute. Thus, a statute may require a local governing body to embark upon a new function. If that body is opposed to the policy of the statute, there is normally no way to compel it to act except a suit by an eligible person to secure a judicial decree compelling such body to act as specified by statute. Or, contrariwise, a taxpayer who for one reason or another thinks the proposed action illegal may attempt to enjoin it. In fact, a good deal of the law dealing with local powers and procedure has been developed by the courts in passing

---

[3] The existence of local "machines" was clearly recognized by the founders of the Republic. Thus, Hamilton in No. 1 of *The Federalist* wrote: "Among the most formidable of the obstacles which the new Constitution will have to encounter may readily be distinguished the obvious interest of a certain class of men in every State to resist all changes which may hazard a diminution of the power, emolument, and consequence of the offices they hold under the State establishments."

upon such requests. And, in effect, under legislative supervision we have what may be called government by lawsuit. Stated bluntly, the system means that the state puts upon each taxpayer or other party in interest the burden of calling to account each official about to perform an unpopular or legally dubious act.

Such a scheme, of course, affords no guarantee that the standard imposed by the state will be followed locally. It may be described as centralization in the statute books and local option in the counties. For under American conditions, it is often true that a policy which can command a majority of the state legislature represents at best only a vague aspiration of the membership, or is the price exacted in return for the support of a more immediately practicable proposal.[4] Legislative supervision under such circumstances is very likely to mean defeat in detail of the state policy in communities where opinion is indifferent to the standards set by the state. One is at times tempted to believe that the ultimate justification for local self-government lies in this opportunity for informal nullification! In any event, so far as the realizing of a uniform public policy or adequate standards of performance is concerned, experience under the regime of legislative supervision has demonstrated the essential sterility of the notion of state supremacy, however much we may be disposed to grant its validity as a merely legal principle.

The weakness of legislative supervision has not passed unnoticed even by the legislators themselves, and various devices have been created to make state oversight more effective without depriving the localities of all control over their affairs. For a generation it was widely believed that, in municipal home rule, the secret of combining these two objectives had been found. Municipal home rule may be briefly defined as the right of the local unit to the independent control of all purely local and municipal affairs. The difficulty here lies in determining what *are* purely local and municipal matters. Municipal home rule was heralded as a specific for legislative tampering and domination by rural legislators. On the whole, however,

---

[4] "Legislation, in legal contemplation, emanates from the entire legislative machinery and speaks the will of the sovereign state. The reality is rather different. In the case of a small city represented by a single legislator in each house, what passes for the will of the entire house is actually the will of the particular member. His party colleagues stand ready not only to accept his judgment as to all matters relating solely to his district, but to enact it into law. If the matter has no partisan significance he can expect the same courteous latitude from his colleagues on the other side of the house." J. D. McGoldrick, *The Law and Practice of Municipal Home Rule*, p. 2. Quoted with permission of the author and the Columbia University Press.

its results have been disappointing, though it must be granted that
it has made possible a variety of experiments which could scarcely
have taken place while cities were in legislative strait jackets.

Home Rule for Counties

When it comes to home rule for counties, the outlook is even less
promising. A generation ago, reformers were disposed to see in
county home rule a means of allowing fruitful experimentation with
governmental and administrative devices on the local level. It was
widely believed that home rule would give counties greater freedom
in meeting the growing number of problems facing even rural areas.
It is significant, however, that "even the most enthusiastic advocates
of home rule . . . admit that it must be even more limited for
counties than for cities. Thus the *Model State Constitution* of the
National Municipal League provides an elaborate series of safeguards for cities exercising home rule but, while making county
home rule also available, the model constitution provides that home
rule powers shall be directly subject to legislative definition. The
State of New York, which has perhaps seen the highest development
of county home rule, similarly vests the state legislature with greater
authority in county, than city, affairs." [5] It is fair to say today that
few persons, aside from those living in areas with quite special problems, and mostly in urbanized counties, are very optimistic about
the probable results of county home rule, and that the interest of
even academic students is no longer great.

If provisions respecting county government were removed from
the state constitutions and their affairs left as responsibilities of the
legislature, it might be possible to reconstruct county machinery
along modern lines. This change would amount, of course, to admitting that county functions are really state activities and therefore
is not likely to be introduced—at least not overtly. But something
like it is being tacitly admitted in those counties and other rural
units too poor to pay their own way. In such cases, something similar
to central administration of the aided functions, or at least cooperative arrangements, with the state the "senior partner," is actually in
force. For, in areas too poor to support necessary public functions,
home rule is both unnecessary and unworkable. The situation is
different, however, in wealthy—and urban or suburban—counties
where functions are as numerous and as varied as in a large city.

---

[5] *State-Local Relations*, p. 177.

Here, a good case can be made for a considerable measure of home rule. Most of our counties fall in the former category. With respect to them, the legislature is likely to exercise greater and greater control and, if they have technical home rule, it is pretty certain to be limited to matters of machinery.

County home rule is now provided for in the constitutions of six states—California, Maryland, Texas, Ohio, Missouri, and Washington. Constitutional provisions vary considerably as to the extent of local powers made available to counties but, generally speaking, they do not go beyond a grant of the power to frame and adopt a charter thought desirable by the local population. Ordinarily few additional substantive powers are granted to home rule counties and, in any case, the power of the state legislature over matters held by the courts to be of general interest remains unimpaired. A county may secure a home rule charter either by petition of a certain percentage of the voters or on the initiative of the governing board. The charter itself is drawn up by a local charter commission whose members are either appointive or elective. In some cases the charter, to become effective, must be approved by the governor or state legislature, but this is apparently routine.

At present about a dozen counties are operating under home rule charters. Ten of these are in California, one in Maryland (Montgomery County, suburban to Washington, D. C.), and one in Missouri (St. Louis County). In some of the other home rule states, while there seems to be some sentiment in favor of locally drawn charters, the constitutional provisions are so difficult to comply with that there have been no adoptions. Qualified observers report that counties now operating under their own charters are among the best governed in the country. In a few other states, a degree of flexibility in county organization is made possible by statutes permitting counties to adopt alternative forms of government. This falls short of home rule, of course, but it is a desirable development. It should be emphasized, however, that home rule has meant very small additions to the discretion of counties with respect to new powers and functions and that where additional powers are granted, as seems to be the case in California, the courts construe these very strictly.[6]

---

[6] See William Anderson and Edward W. Weidner, *State and Local Government* (1951), pp. 137-42 and the remarks of Wager in the chapters dealing with the county home rule states in his *County Government across the Nation.*

Administrative Supervision

Reformers have not been without a remedy for the evils of legislative supervision. It has been found, or at least thought to be found, in what is called *administrative* supervision of local government. The notion is simplicity itself. Let the state set the standards of performance in those fields that clearly involve general as distinct from local interests and then enforce compliance with these standards by a system of inspection, reports, the withholding of state aid, and perhaps even the removal of inefficient local officials. Such a scheme has the theoretic merit of flexibility and comparative ease in operation and is compatible with a large degree of what is called home rule. It is clear that this is a device produced by the impact of technology on government. It is superficially consistent with our social and economic order, resting, as that order does, upon the sciences, since it transfers the task of enforcing state-adopted standards from the hands of inexpert legislators to those who are assumed to have special competence and to be in a position to take a professional and impersonal attitude towards their official duties. Since there exists, or appears to exist, such a pat consistency between the device and the social environment in which it is to operate, administrative supervision is favored no doubt by the great majority of academic students of administration.

In any governmental system as decentralized as ours has been, there is doubtless always present a tendency towards concentration. In spite of the tenacity with which we have retained our belief in local self-government, that policy has not been able successfully to resist centripetal forces. As a result, in every state some progress has been made towards endowing central officials with authority over local functions. In discussing this matter, it is important to keep in mind that what is found in the statutes is not always a safe guide to what actually happens in day-by-day administration. What seems on paper to be a very imposing and thoroughgoing system of central supervision may actually amount to very little, either because of inadequate central staff agencies, insufficient appropriations, or political interference with the work of the central authorities. With these reservations in mind, it is worth while to pass in review the devices now provided by law for the supervision of local government.

The machinery of modern scientific administration was first developed in France, and the system and technique there worked out have been widely copied in other Continental countries. In all these nations, the fear of aggression from other states, and the necessity of building up at home a unity of spirit, have operated in most cases to halt the development of any strong local feeling and have therefore made relatively easy the concentration of political and administrative power and competence at the national capital. In France, central control of local government is very largely in the hands of the Minister of the Interior through whom the will of the national legislature is transmitted to the prefects who are the local agents of the central power, holding office at the pleasure of their superiors at Paris.[7] This system has never been copied exactly in any of the English-speaking countries. On both sides of the Atlantic, the legislative body has traditionally been looked upon as the source of such direction as was thought necessary by the central government. This theory of relationship is the basis of what we have above referred to as "legislative supervision." [8] In England, it is still exercised generally by private and general statutes of Parliament; in the United States, by special acts of the state legislatures or by general codes of law intended to apply to all local areas of a valid classification. Both in England and the United States, the courts are used as agencies for enforcing the will of the legislature in the event that local authorities refuse to act or act beyond their powers, although this is now much less frequently the case in England, with the growth of administrative discretion in the central departments.

When governmental functions were relatively few and simple, and no particular objection could be raised to a high degree of local autonomy, no special harm resulted from the use of this rather spasmodic type of control. As soon, however, as administrative problems became intricate, and society so well knit as to make local anarchy a threat to the general welfare, the device of legislative control rapidly grew inadequate as a means of enforcing state policy. Furthermore,

---

[7] Under the Fourth Republic, some tentative moves were made in the direction of widening the powers of the departments, but the position of the prefect as an agent of the national administration has not yet been seriously weakened. See Chapter 7 of Part 2, of John C. Ranney and Gwendolen M. Carter, *The Major Foreign Powers* (1949).

[8] "We made laws . . . and bade the courts to see to their enforcement, but we did not subordinate one official to another. No man was commanded from the capital as if he were the servant of officials rather than of the people. Authority was put into commission and distributed piecemeal, nowhere gathered into a single commanding force. Oversight and concentration were omitted from the system . . . we printed SELF large and *government* small in almost every administrative arrangement we made." Woodrow Wilson, "Democracy and Efficiency," 87 *Atlantic Monthly*, 295-96.

such a scheme necessarily involved an excessive rigidity, since the rule announced in a general statute would have to be applied to widely differing local conditions; or, if reliance were placed upon special legislation, the central law-making body was overwhelmed by a mass of proposals with which it was unfitted to deal intelligently, and which in the United States, at least, opened the way to purely partisan attacks in local governments.

ADMINISTRATIVE SUPERVISION IN ENGLAND

For all of these reasons, there has developed in England during the past century a system of control and supervision through the central administrative departments. Legislation by private bill has by no means disappeared, but in the vast majority of cases local authorities have found it cheaper and more satisfactory to seek additional powers when needed by appealing to the appropriate central department.[9] This procedure allows the central authority to deal with local matters as seems wise in each case, as against the method of legislative supervision, under which, even when local units are classified, a certain undesirable inflexibility is to be found. If the central authority finds, after inquiry, that the desired local action ought to be taken, the requisite order is issued. This order may or may not be subject to subsequent parliamentary action. In any event, the supervisory powers possessed by the central departments have been conferred by Act of Parliament.[10]

The possession of authority of this kind over local government has led naturally to the building up of both a rather extensive staff of inspectors, auditors, and other such officials, and also a more or less complicated system of controls. In some cases, the supervision of the central government extends scarcely beyond the provision of information and the offering of advice to the local units. In other cases, it may involve such matters as the requirement of periodical reports, the prescribing of forms for records and accounts, the audit (and the

---

[9] Even in those cases where local authorities proceed by private bill, the opinion of the officials of the appropriate central department is given great weight by the Private Bill Committee. See Sir C. P. Ilbert, *Parliament*, pp. 85-89; F. A. Ogg, *English Government and Politics* (Rev. ed. 1936), pp. 646-655. In the 18th century, legislation by private bill was regarded as a way of keeping matters in local hands, since it was believed that a general law would require a central commission, a development frowned upon as likely to increase the power of the government and lead to jobbery. See Part III of Leslie Stephen's *The English Utilitarians*.

[10] An extensive treatment of the system of orders will be found in C. T. Carr, *Delegated Legislation*, and in B. M. Laing, "The Legislative Functions of Government Departments," in *Public Administration*, **VIII**: 335-348 (1930).

allowance or disallowance) of expenditures, and the enforcing of prescribed standards of performance through inspections and reports to
the central office and, in some cases, the withholding of financial support where local performance falls below the standard set by the
national authorities. It would be fair to say that until fairly recently
the mechanism of central control in England rested largely on the basis of encouragement and assistance, with a minimum of coercion. It
is only within the past generation that such devices as review, appeal,
and direct appointment and removal of local officials have figured at
all prominently in official reports and unofficial comment.[11] Hence,
it is still correct to say that the English system of central supervision
is one which allows more scope for local initiative and experiment
than is true in the more "centralized" systems of the Continent. It
will be noted further that no single central department in England
is vested with the same powers of "general supervision" which the
Ministry of the Interior has in France. While the bulk of the work
is done by the Ministry of Local Government, certain other agencies
share it, notably the Board of Trade, the Ministry of Transport, the
Home Office, and the Electricity Commissioners.[12]

ADMINISTRATIVE SUPERVISION IN THE UNITED STATES

In the United States, development within the individual states
has followed substantially the same course as in England, although it
has not yet gone so far with regard to most governmental functions.
Beginning about fifty years ago, however, the movement in the direc-

---

[11] Consult W. A. Robson, *The Development of Local Government*, Part V, for comment on the powers of the district auditor, and Ch. IX of H. J. Laski's *Studies in Law
and Politics*. A complete discussion will be found in Herman Finer's *English Local
Government;* there is a brief discussion in the chapter on England in William Anderson
(Ed.), *Local Government in Europe* (1939).

[12] It is estimated in England that scarcely 1 per cent of the orders issued by the executive departments are disallowed by Parliament. These orders are framed by the
experts of the permanent staff but usually, it appears, with adequate safeguards for
the interests affected. This influence exercised by the permanent civil service has, of
course, raised the old cry against bureaucracy, a criticism eloquently voiced by Baron
Hewart, Lord Chief Justice, in his book, *The New Despotism* (1932). For a more tem-
perate discussion, see F. J. Port, *Administrative Law* (1929). On the whole subject of
delegated legislation, reference may be made to C. T. Carr, *Concerning Administrative
Law* (1942) and C. K. Allen, *Law and Orders* (1947). By an order in council effective
in January 1951, the functions of the Ministry of Health with respect to the supervision of local government were transferred to the Ministry of Local Government, which
was the new name given by the same order to the former Ministry of Town and
Country Planning. The chief responsibilities of the Ministry of Health are now those
related to the national health service. See *Parliamentary Affairs*, Vol. IV, No. 4, pp.
476-480 (Autumn 1951).

tion of central administrative control has been more rapid, although the germ of it may be found in the legislation concerning local finance of more than a century ago.

The reasons for the trend toward this type of supervision are thus summarized by the Committee on State-Local Relations of the Council of State Governments: "1. Technological developments in transport and communications have pushed in the direction of centralization. . . . In the absence of rapid means of communication, decisions can be made and executed only by officials physically within local areas. Modern developments in ground and air transportation and in communication by phone, telegraph, and radio have greatly decreased the necessity of this local decision making, [and] basic decisions can be made from central points. 2. Experience has made clear that full efficiency and economy in certain governmental operations depend upon a large area of administration. The demand for more adequate services and for their economical administration has thus resulted in the imposition of supervision. . . . 3. Large numbers of people have developed the conviction that no justification exists for any part of the country to fall below a minimum standard of governmental service. If minimum services are not maintained, it is widely believed that some central agency must raise sub-standard conditions to an acceptable level of performance. 4. Finally, and most immediately pertinent, the trend toward state centralization is due to the fact that there is no correlation between the tax-raising capacity of local governments and the cost of the services they must perform."

When forty-eight separate authorities are involved it is, of course, possible to find a score of subjects which, to a greater or less degree, are supervised by state administrative officials somewhere. The supervision that we now have, however, is most widespread and thoroughgoing in the fields of finance, public health, education, and highways. In addition, examples of the same type of control may be found in public utilities, housing, fire prevention, civil service, libraries, port and harbor development, and dependency and delinquency.

) Control of Local Finance

State administrative supervision over finance exists with reference to such matters as assessment procedure, local accounts, indebtedness, and budgets. It is most thorough with regard to the first of these, and least developed in the case of the last. As to assessment practices, it is well within the truth to say that if the state tax commissions exercised fully their power to prescribe forms for reports, to inspect and review local assessments, equalize local valuations, and, in a few cases, appoint and remove local assessors, a very high degree of unified control would be established. However, because of political pressure, lack of appropriations and an adequate central staff, to say nothing of the magnitude of the task of efficient supervision, these powers are nowhere fully used. In some states, a good deal has been done in the way of collecting information and statistics concerning local methods of assessment,[13] and something has been accomplished in the direction of toning up local administration and introducing modern methods, but, beyond this, central control has existed very largely on paper.

Some degree of control over local accounting and auditing exists in more than forty states. In most of these, supervision is applied to all accounts of the governmental units involved, whereas in others only general funds of such units are supervised. Detailed exposition of the various schemes would be wearisome, but it may be said that in only thirteen states does supervision extend to all local governments.[14] There is, of course, considerable variation as to the type, extent, and thoroughness in this field. Forty-five states make or supervise audits for local governments—some for all units and some for only certain classes. Since real inspection and thoroughgoing audits over perhaps several thousand local units would place a heavy burden on the state department, it is perhaps true that state supervision in this and other fields is in many cases nominal. Closely related to supervision of accounting and auditing is the requirement of reports of local financial transactions, which exists to some degree in about forty states.

In the matter of local indebtedness, the primary method of control is through legal debt limits, prescribed either in the State Constitution or in general or special statutes. Recently, however, there has appeared a tendency to make greater use of administrative devices.

---

[13] For example, the excellent annual publication of the State Tax Commissioner of Connecticut, entitled *Information Relating to the Assessment and Collecting of Taxes,* the biennial reports of the State Tax Commissioner of the same state; the *Statistics of Municipal Finance,* published annually by the Director of Accounts of the Massachusetts Department of Taxation and Corporations; *Comparative Financial Statistics,* published annually by the State Auditor of Ohio as Supervisor of Public Offices; the *Reports on Municipal Accounts,* and the annual reports of the New York State Tax Commission; and the *Reports of the State Controller* of California.

[14] The details as to this and other types of central supervision are set forth in *State-Local Relations,* pp. 14-41.

Quite generally, local units are required to report bond issues to a state office. In thirty-eight states, at least some units must receive state approval before bonds are issued. Usually, central review extends no further than to test the legality of the proposed issue. In a number of states, however, central supervision may concern itself with the wisdom of proposed bonded indebtedness, and some state authorities exercise the power to reject local government proposals. Finally, in six states, designated state agencies act as receivers for local units in default on debt service.[15]

SUPERVISION OF LOCAL HEALTH AUTHORITIES

State administrative control over public health matters is at least as extensive as over finances, and in practice public health organization is perhaps more closely knit. Not only does the state collect information from the localities with regard to births, deaths, and disease; its central authorities usually have some power to issue ordinances binding upon local health officers; it may participate in the selection of local personnel; it may exercise the power of removal in cases of gross inefficiency in local administration; and in nearly every state the central authority may step in and entirely supersede the local organization in times of epidemic or a serious breakdown in the local service. In addition to these functions, it is quite common to find statutes giving the state health authority varying degrees of supervisory power over local water supplies and sewage disposal. This supervision ranges from mere advice to local officials to a rather strict control over projects initiated by them. There is reason to believe that the standards of equipment and personnel in state departments have grown steadily higher, with a corresponding improvement in the character of the service rendered to local units.

SUPERVISION IN OTHER FIELDS

It would be merely repetitious to discuss central supervision in other fields, and what needs to be said about it is best said in connection with the discussion of specific functions of rural government. It is sufficient, perhaps, to note here that such central supervision as we have in all fields involves substantially the same sorts of mechanism. The various devices now used run all the way from the furnishing of

[15] See Wylie Kilpatrick, *State Supervision of Local Finance*, Publication No. 79, Public Administration Service (1941); *State-Local Relations*, pp. 27-38; Dale Pontius, *State Supervision of Local Government: Its Development in Massachusetts* (1942); *Annual Reports* of the New Jersey Local Government Board.

advice and the collection and publication of information, the choice of local personnel, removal of local officials, and the withholding of state aids, to complete assumption of the function by the central government.[16] The extent and vigor of state control vary from place to place and are subject to numerous vicissitudes. In general, "centralization" of this sort has proceeded further in the more thickly populated urban and industrial states, but there is a definite tendency nearly everywhere for administrative supervision to replace that provided by detailed legislative enactment and enforced by judicial decree.

Although its exact future pattern cannot now be predicted, it seems certain that some type of administrative supervision of local government will, within a generation, be well established in nearly every American state. Social and technological developments point clearly in that direction. These developments will accelerate this kind of centralization more rapidly in urban and industrialized states than in rural areas, but no section will escape the tendency with respect to that growing number of functions which are everywhere regarded as of more than local interest. For it must be remembered that even rural regions are by no means untouched by the forces of urbanism and industrialism. Since the value of state supervision is to be judged by its contribution to the improvement of local administration, almost everything depends upon how successful the states are in creating the conditions under which supervision may be effective. Even though the quality of local management should greatly improve, the case for state administrative supervision will still be strong, since it assumes the inadequacy of the isolated and unguided local unit. It is important, then, to examine the shortcomings and the requirements of sound supervision at the state level.

PRINCIPLES OF SUPERVISION

A fundamental need, met in few, if any, states, is the collection and regular publication of the *facts* about local government. Some states, as has been noted, collect and publish financial statistics, and many publish data concerning supervised activities, but nowhere near enough of this is done, and probably there is no state where the data

---

[16] It is interesting to follow the development of some of these relationships culminating in complete state assumption of highway construction in North Carolina. See Paul V. Betters, *State Centralization in North Carolina* (1932). Strictly speaking, the removal of local officials and the withholding of state aid are sanctions useful in making good the authority to supervise, rather than methods of supervision.

collected are comprehensive. The value of extending and improving this sort of service needs no extensive justification. The prompt and regular publication of facts and figures about local performance would obviously be of great help to supervising officials of the state governments. Moreover, once such a service were established it would have important results in stimulating interunit competition. The United States Bureau of the Census has issued some valuable reports, but they cover only a part of the field and are not detailed enough to be of great use to administrators.[17]

In the second place, there is urgent need in most, if not all, states for a codification of the statutes dealing with state-local relations. In almost all states, provisions with reference to these matters are a mass of constitutional requirements and general and special statutes. There has been over the years a multiplication of rigid and petty specifications which put in doubt local powers and confuse state supervisory officers. Closely connected with such a codification is the desirability of revising the constitutional and statutory provisions regulating the relations between the state legislatures and local units. It goes without saying that special legislation should be abandoned, or allowed only in unusual cases and with adequate safeguards. Detailed local legislation should be replaced by broad grants of authority to local governments through general laws and constitutional home rule, or both. As it has come to be interpreted by the courts, home rule is completely compatible with a large measure of administrative supervision. Finally, there would seem to be no good argument against broad and flexible grants of authority to supervisory agencies, as contrasted with the frequent detailed prescriptions found in legislation creating these agencies. Unless administrators are given reasonable leeway they are thwarted at the outset.

Beyond doubt the most important need, if administrative super-

---

[17] "The relation of the states to the federal government is given continuous study at no single point in the federal government. Nor in any state will there be found a point at which the problems of local areas are considered in a methodical, comprehensive fashion. In fact, the disorderly manner in which higher levels of government have handled their responsibilities towards the lesser areas accounts for much of the difficulty in which the lesser areas find themselves." James W. Fesler, *Area and Administration* (1949), p. 127. Since this was written, the Hoover Commission, after making certain general recommendations concerning federal-state relations, added the following: "We recommend, in order to accomplish all of these things in an adequate and orderly manner, that a continuing agency on Federal-state relations be created with the primary responsibility for study, information, and guidance in the field of Federal-state relations." *The Hoover Commission Report* (1949), pp. 476-7. Bills to accomplish this have since been introduced into Congress.

vision is to succeed, is that the state's supervisory personnel be qualified for its duties. This means, at a minimum, that state employees
be selected in accordance with the merit principle. There is reason
to believe that some improvement is being made in this respect. In
1935, only nine states had merit system laws, and probably in none
of these did the law cover a majority of civil servants. In 1950, all
employees paid in whole or in part from federal funds were required
by federal regulations to be chosen by a merit system acceptable to the
federal authorities. This means that, in all states, some state employees have security of tenure, and that they meet at least minimum
standards of competence. Aside from these employees, however, it
was reported in 1949 that only twenty-two states had merit laws covering more than half of their civil servants. In addition to these, however, it may be assumed that there are, even where the spoils system
survives, considerable numbers of employees who have in fact security
against removal for partisan reasons, and some degree of skill and experience. The requirements of steady and skillful administration in
services growing rapidly more technical have probably convinced
even partisan legislators of the necessity of improving the quality of
the supervisory personnel. Nevertheless, much remains to be done
before the line agencies of the state are adequate to the task of supervision and, if administrative oversight is to realize its potentialities,
the personnel of these agencies must be further strengthened.[18]

Even though administrative supervision may be the typical device
of the future in state-local relationships, it is well not to expect too
much of it. There will still be local units and local loyalties, and these
will have their effects. It will not do to assume that, the state being a
larger unit, its officials, even though endowed by statute with great
authority, will be much less beholden to private and local interests.
No merely mechanical change can cause such officials to take a completely detached and impersonal attitude in the enforcement of any
state policy that impinges on the interests regarded as local by the
voters of a rural area. To a limited degree, such a change of attitude
may take place, but one must not count on it. Few states are so large
as to be able to avoid having their official policy warped and twisted
by a thousand local compromises, for the formal structure is in fact at
the center of a host of personal, partisan, and local influences. What-

---

[18] See *State-Local Relations*, pp. 46-51; James W. Fesler, *Area and Administration*
(University, Alabama, 1949), pp. 42-43; Robert Parks, "Trends in Rural Local Government," Ch. XI of J. B. Shannon (ed.), *The Study of Comparative Government* (1949).

ever law and theory may say, every state officer, appointive or elective, is himself the product of the same pushes and pressures that operate to improve or degrade the standards of local administration.[19]

These things seem to be true, even on the scale of a large state, because politics is in essence an intensely personal matter. Any close observation will supply proofs of this fact. The typical state central committee is essentially an aggregation of county and community bosses and leaders; the typical legislator is a local mogul who has served his turn in various local posts and quite often continues a member of the "courthouse gang" at home; while the device of the "balanced ticket," not entirely outmoded by the direct primary, points to the fundamental basis of state politics and administration. It is possible, of course, that service in the state legislature in time may widen the mental horizon of the member and make him familiar with the concept of the *general* welfare; the short terms of office and the use of the small legislative districts, however, tend to emphasize dependence upon local influences.

Mere widening of the area for the choice of administrative officials is no guarantee of equal and impartial enforcement of the law, unless, of course, competent officers, once chosen, are more effectively shielded from partisan and popular influences than has ever been the case in the past. Under present conditions, the crude notions of the electorate work their way into the central administration through the machinery of the party; indeed, in a representative democracy that is what politicians are for. In short, the state is not a different thing from its component parts; in its performance of those functions of interest to localities, it tends, in fact, to accept as a goal the least common denominator of local performance. In an area with the variety of interests, population, background, and traditions presented by the typical American state, it is an obvious impossibility to get general agreement on anything more than a very modest standard of administrative competence. Such standards as are locally understood and supported will, of necessity, set the pace to be followed by state administrators, and it is futile, at any rate within the forms of democracy, to attempt to enforce compliance with higher ones. The theories of political scientists and the dicta of judges must reckon in

---

[19] These forces were powerful enough to bring about significant changes in the personnel and procedure of the North Carolina Local Government Commission created in 1931 to exercise administrative supervision over the finances of local units. See B. U. Ratchford, "The Work of the North Carolina Local Government Commission," **XXV** *National Municipal Review* 323-27, 368 (June 1936).

the end with the realities of a gossipy local democracy, intent upon keeping its affairs in its own hands and very largely indifferent to such recondite matters as efficiency, unit costs, and standardization.

Finally, the very magnitude of the task involved in thoroughgoing administrative supervision carries certain important implications. If the function were education, it would mean maintaining close relationships and rather constant contact with anywhere from two to five thousand local school districts. If inspection, advice, auditing, and the other devices of supervision were to mean anything, efficiency would involve a staggering amount of detailed work and a correspondingly large central staff to accomplish it. In the case of the other functions, the units to be supervised would not be so numerous, but in all cases, scores and even hundreds would have to be given attention. One conclusion is clear: if supervision is to be anything but the most cursory sort, it depends on a very sharp reduction in the number of units now engaged in performing governmental duties on the local level. The only alternative would seem to be the creation of a massive and complicated bureaucracy, a development which no one seriously expects to take place.

The more one reflects upon the issues raised by the general question of the proper relationship between the state and its local units, the more one is driven to the conclusion that our difficulties result from the influence of the legal concept of the supremacy of the state over its local subdivisions. The practical effect of our literal interpretation of this theory has been to set the state and the locality in distinct spheres. But the problems in the solution of which they cooperate are units. The literal interpretation of state supremacy on the one hand, and the stubborn insistence on the local control of policy on the other, have produced a state of affairs out of which sound administration can be secured only by the use of a new technique for which a strict application of the legal formula of state "sovereignty" leaves no room.[20]

It gets us nowhere, for example, to repeat that education, or public health, or taxation, is a subject of state concern, when common ob-

---

[20] "Static control is always marked by the endeavor of the state to superimpose its purposes upon local communities. Dynamic state supervision recognizes that changing local communities themselves must participate in the process if the effort is to be fruitful and not a sterile paper reorganization. Supervision must be viewed not as an end for law enforcement but as a means to the end of a responsible government placed under public control. Supervision is or can be made a means to implement the healthy functioning of financial and civic life." Wylie Kilpatrick, "An Inventory of State Supervision of Local Finance," **183** *Annals* 170 (Jan. 1936).

servation tells us that under some circumstances the state, as a matter of fact, abdicates in the actual conduct of the function. It is easy, in theory, to demonstrate that the state has an interest in an increasing number of functions hitherto largely local in their implications, and that it should take measures to protect and further that interest. And it is, of course, equally easy to show that the state, if it wishes, has the legal authority to take such measures as it likes for these objects. But political life, like all other aspects of life, refuses to be compressed within the narrow limits of theories and legal formulae. It was a wise man who reminded us that "nothing is easier than to simplify life and make a philosophy about it. The trouble is that the resulting philosophy is true only of that simplified life." Something like this mistake has been made in much of our thinking about state and local relationships. On the one hand, observers, impatient and perhaps a little supercilious towards the clumsy methods of local officials, call loudly for a more rigid central control. On the other hand, the mystical devotees of "home rule" and "local self-government," anxious to prevent the building up of a state administrative hierarchy, would apparently go to the other extreme of almost complete local autonomy.[21]

But we are not driven to such a hard alternative. The problem of government is a single one, and it is due almost entirely to historical accident that various territorial organs have arisen to handle it. Processes of "subterfuge, indirection and fertile adaptation" are going on all about us. For it is in fact possible to begin with the assumption that there is no serious divergence in most cases between the standards desired by the better opinion in a state and the willingness of local officials, once they are informed, to attempt to reach those standards. As the world shrinks, we must elaborate a technique based upon this assumption, a technique which will recognize the unity of the problem of government, while leaving room for the infinite variety of forms of solution demanded by differing local conditions.

----

[21] In writing of federalism, Arthur W. Macmahon uses language which is relevant to the problem we are discussing here: "It is increasingly unrealistic to conceive of a federal division of functions in terms of subjects as wholes. Each has phases appropriate to central and to local attention. Federal constitutions which disregard this fact are brought into conformance with it in the end, although tardily and imperfectly, by subterfuge, indirection and fertile adaptation." *Encycl. Soc. Sci.*, article, "Federation." For evidence of the truth of this, we need look no further than to the interesting intergovernmental relationships being worked out in connection with the administration of all the federally aided services.

STATE-LOCAL ADMINISTRATIVE COOPERATION

Actually, political life has gone its way only slightly disturbed by the warfare in the legal contingency, and such a technique is even now being created. This is being accomplished through a number of devices which deserve to be noticed. For example, there is going on between state and local officials a good deal of informal cooperation in the solving of problems of interest to both units of government. Some of this takes place through more or less formal meetings of local and state officers as, for example, the periodical meetings of local tax officials for the receiving of instructions and the discussion of common problems. A good deal of it arises quite naturally out of the ordinary contacts between local officials and sympathetic state officers. In a few states, the advisory function of state departments has been formalized by statute, but it may be suspected that in most of them it goes on quite without legal recognition. The value of such contacts is, of course, difficult to measure, but there is evidence in many quarters that it is very great. This value is increased, if anything, by the fact that it is not always a matter of law, but arises out of the necessary relations between the two levels of officials. It is thus a product of practice and experience and not of mere legal theory, and practice and experience are a better foundation than theory.[22]

Some very hopeful evidence of the importance of the two-way relationship between the states and their local units may be found in nearly every area of public administration. The full extent of state-local cooperation could be understood only if detailed studies were made in every state and the results assembled. Although this has not been done, a search of the statutes and wide observation of actual administrative practice would reveal many examples of such cooperation. These may be found in the field of personnel selection and management; in the joint use of state purchasing facilities; in the exchange of data and personnel in highway administration; in public health activities; and in welfare work. As one writer put it more than twenty years ago: "We have state officers who are local citizens admin-

---

[22] An able student, after studying three governmental activities in Minnesota, has this to say: "With the possible exception of regulations made necessary by grants-in-aid and, to a lesser degree, certain regulations about technical matters, the extent of the state's administrative supervision of local governments is largely determined by a meeting of minds of state and local officials. This is not to deny state supervision but to point out that it is much more of a two-way process than is usually believed." Edward W. Weidner, "State Supervision of Local Government in Minnesota," **IV** *Public Administration Review* 233 (Summer 1944).

istering state policies by adaptation to the county, either in exact application or in collaboration by local programs. The purpose of the county use and adaptation of state policies can be achieved only by integration of the state government that formulates the policies and the county mechanism charged with responsibility for cooperative execution of common functions." [23] It is important to distinguish here between direct state appointment of local officials and what might better be called the *influence* of the state departments in the choosing of such officials. The former indicates a reliance upon a legal *right;* the latter points to a more subtle relationship. The state can indeed do much to assist localities in securing better administrative talent, and this is already recognized by the laws of some of our commonwealths. For example, in New Jersey, all local health officers are required to hold a license which is issued only after they have passed an examination set by the state board of health. In the same state, private accountants may not audit local accounts unless they hold licenses issued by the state Commissioner of Municipal Accounts. In several states, county engineers, though named by the county boards, must have their appointments ratified by the state highway department; while in Illinois, the same official is named from a list of eligibles compiled after an examination conducted by the state department of public works. It is obvious that where the will to do so exists, ways will be found to circumvent such requirements, but the fact remains that this device is superior both to uncontrolled local discretion and direct state appointment of local officers. Substantial progress towards efficient administration is more likely to lie along this line than in any other direction, and it might profitably be extended to other officials.

It seems quite probable that other developments are contributing to the technique of state-local cooperation. Such organizations as our state leagues of municipalities serve through their annual conventions as meeting places for the exchange of ideas between state and local officials. Similar in nature and possible influence are the various associations of local government officials such as assessors, tax collectors, attorneys, and recording officers. The formal meetings of these groups are usually attended by interested state administrators, and it is certain that more or less constant contacts are maintained between the two levels of officialdom. From one point of view, of course, such organizations may be considered as decentralizing in their influence.

[23] Wylie Kilpatrick, *County Management*, pp. 36-41.

However, they do not seem to have been able to accomplish a great deal in this direction. But they may have possibilities in the conduct of research and the accumulation of the sort of data on which sound administration ultimately depends. And there can be no doubt of the close tie-up existing in some states between the league and responsible state administrators.[24]

LOCAL REFORM AND ADMINISTRATIVE EFFICIENCY

Any fruitful use of most of these developing techniques depends upon the realization of certain conditions which do not exist at present in local government. In the first place, a sharp reduction in the number of local authorities is greatly to be desired. Unless this happens, there is little or no possibility of creating meaningful relationships between the two levels of government. Next, it is essential that local officeholders be chosen for longer terms or that the tradition of re-election be more firmly established, that the short ballot be introduced and the administration more closely integrated, and that the merit system be more widely applied in the local services than is the case today. It is only by the adoption of some such changes in governmental structure and practice that we can hope to redeem local democracy from its present weakness and general inefficiency. And it is not too much to say that the preservation of free government in this country depends upon our success within the next generation in accomplishing this redemption. Changes of this sort would so stabilize conditions in localities as to enable sound relationships to be set up and maintained with the central authorities for periods long enough to make cooperation productive of much real benefit.[25] There is,

---

[24] "A significant possibility in organization that already has passed from the realm of theory to that of demonstration consists in the unofficial organizations of state and local governments or of public officers' associations. . . . The associations have demonstrated capacity in fostering improved administrative techniques, especially in budgeting, city planning, and personnel training. As service agencies they can lighten the task of state supervision and reduce the degree of detail imposed upon state agencies, if a harmonious and complementary relation is established between the public and the private organizations. By inviting the participation of the associations in drafting regulations and procedures, the states will more nearly approach a cooperative mechanism than by imposing their own methods without consultation." Kilpatrick, *Annals* (Jan. 1936). This development is, indeed, of more than purely local interest at a time when traditional ideas of federalism are being tested, for, as Kilpatrick adds, "Federalism may take a new form. If guided into a cooperative pattern of administration, American government will demonstrate its adaptability."

[25] "Control is presumed to correct the deficiencies in local organization and maladjustments in local areas to make up for incompetence in local personnel and to protect taxpayers from extravagance after they have failed to protect themselves. Neither supervision nor control can accomplish these ends without the local reordering of

finally, an absence in many communities of any regular channels through which interested groups may be kept informed as to the best practice. For this reason, there are in the average rural area few centers of independent and intelligent criticism of official conduct as distinct from village gossip. Improvement with respect to these shortcomings may perhaps be expected through the steady progress of the merit system, the simplification of the machinery of local government, and the more ample support being given to scientific research through local bureaus of municipal research and the better-financed tax-payers' leagues.

ᵧ CENTRALIZATION AND LIBERTY

Whether we like it or not, we live in a world in which all the powerful tendencies in social organization are centripetal. There is ample evidence that the small business unit, to take one example, belongs to the past, and that man's producing and trading activities pay little attention to state or even national lines. The world over, the "little man" fights a losing battle against the trust, the cartel, and the international monopoly. The once independent corner merchant is now the hired employee of an absentee corporate manager, who in turn represents an ownership so diffuse as to deprive the relationship of all personal or intimate characteristics. Even professional men like lawyers, teachers, and physicians find it desirable to associate themselves on a national scale.[26] These are facts within the knowledge of us all and it is not, or ought not to be, surprising that government responds to the same forces. Haltingly, but bending to an inexorable pressure, the township gives way to the county, the county to the state, and the state to the nation, with regard to one function after another, while there are in existence at least the rudiments of international government and administration.

structure and administration. Deficiencies in local structure complicate the task of state supervision. In state after state the most formidable obstacle to efficient performance of supervisory duties arises from faulty local organization and the multiplicity of local units. Supervision can best be effective when the state deals with adequately organized and capably managed communities." W. Kilpatrick, *Annals* (Jan. 1936), p. 172.

[26] "The fact is that our whole social organization and existence is tending toward a wider and wider base. Not business alone, but the professions, labor, philanthropy, reformers, social organizations, civic organizations are reaching toward or have in fact already attained a nation-wide structure with varying authority vested in a central governing body." L. D. White, *Trends in Public Administration*, pp. 139-140. Some obvious examples: The *American* Federation of Labor, The *American* Medical Association, The *National* Conference of Social Work, the *National* Civil Service League, the *National* Association of Highway Officials, the *American* Political Science Association.

It is useless to charge these changes to the perversity of politicians and the shortsightedness of rulers. Government must be commensurate in its magnitude with the tasks it is called on to undertake. No doubt its primary responsibility has always been to protect life and property. But the notion that this protection could best be supplied through police, armies, and courts was fitted only to an era in which men dealt largely face to face and could be relied on, barring exceptions (which brought in the police and the courts!), to look after their own interests. In an age in which business relationships have reached the last stage of impersonalism, the protection of persons and property involves a positive, interventionist government with administrative experts at the controls. It seems to some that such a government can be created only on the ruins of what we have traditionally called local self-government.[27]

What has been lost by these developments is not easy to compute. There are many who are pleased to jeer at the "mere parochialism" which they see in the small unit, whether it be in the political or in the industrial field. These do not mourn the passing of the township or the corner grocer; they are, on the contrary, fascinated by the rise of the far-flung omnipotent state. But the transfer of power to the larger unit is a solution as delusive as it is apparently easy. For while it shifts the problem of government it does not solve it. In a society which values liberty, the ultimate justification of local self-government is that it affords a direct and easy channel through which public opinion can function. The larger the increment of power, the greater the temptation to abuse it; and the greater the distance between those who rule and those who obey, the easier it will be to evade responsibility. It would be an unusual official who did not regard his daily task as important and did not wish to magnify it by enlarging his jurisdiction—as good judges are said to do. This is true even though no considerations of patronage are present, and they are seldom wholly absent. When present, the pressure to lengthen the payroll is intense unless the most powerful traditions operate to offset it. And a swollen payroll must meet the attacks of partisan critics by finding work to occupy its hands. The modern world has found no way by which these attributes of official status may be altered. In short our salvation is not by machinery, for it is individuals, not organizations, who

---

[27] In modern liberal thought, man is considered "precious but not perfect. He is intoxicated by power and hence most humane in a society which distributes power widely." A. M. Schlesinger, Jr., *The Vital Center*, p. 156.

govern. Few are those who are so gifted with imagination or insight as to enable them to grasp in any meaningful fashion such an abstraction as the imperial national state; and those who are momentarily carried away by the illusion of sharing in such an enterprise are more than likely, by that very experience, to be duped into a passive surrender of any effective part in its conduct.[28]

Free government, if it is to be maintained at all under the conditions of the future, must solve the paradox of preserving, on the one hand, the conditions favoring intimate human cooperation in public affairs and, on the other, of creating organs of government capable of acting upon problems long since grown beyond the limits of the petty areas within which popular political processes were first developed.[29] A possible key to the solution of this difficulty may be found in the structure of society as it has taken shape in modern times. For the territorial centralization of the state has only followed the progressive weakening of the geographical tie in other human interests. In scarcely any field of endeavor is the village, the county, or even the state *as such,* of importance in binding men together in their social, professional, or commercial enterprises. In the country, to be sure, the institutions of local government may be looked upon, in a sense, as the political organization of the neighborhood. Even this, however, is nowhere near as true as it once was, as the rural population finds itself exposed, through the radio, the metropolitan press, national advertising, banking and credit connections, and rapid transportation, to the same set of influences as play upon those in the cities. More and more it becomes true that it is the tie of occupational and economic interest which counts, rather than residence in the same artificial area of local government. And, as government becomes increasingly involved in the economic and social life of the people, it may well be that we can most hopefully look for the preservation of

---

[28] "As in the relation between the social classes and as in the relation of the several regions of a country to each other, it would seem that a constant struggle between the centripetal and centrifugal forces is desirable. For without the struggle no balance can be maintained; and if either force won the result would be deplorable." T. S. Eliot, *Notes towards a Definition of Culture* (1949), p. 83. Quoted with the permission of the publishers, Harcourt, Brace & Co.

[29] Cf. Alfred E. Zimmern: ". . . in all societies in all ages the law of the larger unit tends to be held in less esteem than that of the smaller, and progress consists in making the spirit of the smaller, with its appropriate ideas and customs, transmute and inspire the larger." *The Greek Commonwealth,* 5th ed., p. 100, quoted in Charles H. McIlwain, *The Growth of Political Thought in the West,* p. 7. The student could not do better than read the first chapter of Professor McIlwain's study to get an understanding of the importance of the small local unit in the preservation of liberty.

the technique of popular government to the elaboration of organizations of business and professional groups alongside the formal organs of local government.[30]

It must be admitted that there have been counter-currents in the long contest between localism and centralization. In France these are illustrated by the long (and as yet largely fruitless) discussion of regionalism; in England by various projected schemes for devolution; and in the United States by the municipal and county home-rule movements. In this country such movements have had at least a limited success, but they have usually accomplished little beyond giving local units a certain freedom of choice as to governing machinery.[31] This, of course, has normally had very little to do with either the efficiency or the genuinely popular character of government. And ultimately it will be found that the surest guarantee of both efficient and popular government will involve the adoption of the changes which will make that government more competent and more comprehensible to citizens. For the trend toward centralization is chargeable in large degree to the demonstrated feebleness and incompetence of local authorities in the face of new functions. While centralization may indeed not remedy these defects, men may be regarded as not unreasonable in acting as if they thought it might have that effect. Far from threatening local liberties therefore, structural changes such as the short ballot, improvements in personnel, longer official terms, and heightened responsibility are the surest guarantees that local government will command that popular respect without which it cannot much longer retain even the outward insignia of authority.

If such formal legal devices as municipal and county home rule

---

[30] "A vital continuing interest in politics can be secured only by developing alongside the institutions of local self-government, a network of institutions and agencies based upon the economic and occupational relationships of individuals." W. J. Shepard, article "Centralization" in the *Encycl. Soc. Sci.* Commenting upon the "functional" organization, Dewey, while admitting that "ties formed by sharing in common work . . . have now a force which formerly they did not possess" goes on to say: "But these ties can be counted upon for an enduring and stable organization, which at the same time is flexible and moving, only as they grow out of immediate intercourse and attachment. . . . There is no substitute for the vitality and depth of close and direct intercourse and attachment." For "the local is the ultimate universal, and as near an absolute as exists." *The Public and Its Problems,* pp. 212-13, 215.

[31] The summary contained in Joseph D. McGoldrick's *Law and Practice of Municipal Home Rule* (1933) shows how pitiably small are the segments of power which the courts, in their interpretation of home-rule grants, have been willing to allow local areas. No comprehensive study has appeared since McGoldrick's, but it is safe to say that the courts have not grown more liberal.

have proved disappointing in the preservation of local self-government, some measure of the latter has paradoxically been achieved by
developments commonly regarded as centralizing. One of our ablest
students of public administration, after calling attention to the stag-
nation of the home-rule plan, suggests that "it is more likely that a
new network of administrative relationships will make home rule
more and more an anachronism in our administrative system." [32]
This new network consists not only in the cooperative arrangements
between state and local officials already referred to; federal programs
have also impinged upon local governments with results quite the
opposite from what might have been abstractly predicted. A situation in which the national government works with local government
is a legal anomaly. Cities, counties, and other local units are ignored
in the constitution of the United States and in federal law generally.
Any contacts between the two should legally take place through the
state governments, which are the creators of the local governments
and co-sovereigns, as it were, with the national government. Economic facts, however, are at variance with legal theory. For just as
local units have proved financially unable to support a governmental
standard of living demanded by local residents, so have the state governments for much the same reasons proved inadequate in many
fields of modern public service. [33] The relative poverty of all but a
handful of states, the greater financial strength of the national government, the desirability of stimulating local units to perform certain
functions, and the necessity of cooperation in the twilight zone between national and state power—all these have created certain more
or less direct relationships between the federal and the local governments which are sure to be permanent, whatever their strictly legal
nature may be.

Contacts between the federal and the local governments—sometimes through the state governments, sometimes by-passing the latter
—are numerous and growing and assume many forms. Federal highway grants extend now to secondary roads and involve direct contacts
with local officials and a general tightening of administration all
along the line. Local health administration has been deeply affected
by such developments as surveys and demonstrations conducted by
the United States Public Health Service and, latterly, by work done

[32] Leonard D. White, *Introduction to the Study of Public Administration* (3rd
ed., 1948), p. 163.
[33] See Part Three of *State-Local Relations* for an excellent exposition of the
relative fiscal strength of states and localities.

under the Federal Hospital Construction Act. Numerous federal agencies are the developers and custodians of standards of materials and processes and administrative procedures widely adopted by local units. The ubiquitous county agent and soil conservation worker, supported by federal, as well as by state and local, funds in many instances have been powerful forces in bringing to individual farmers the latest scientific practices in soil and crop management. And finally, although this does not exhaust the list, federal funds, federal direction and suggestion, and federal stimulation in the field of social security are at work in every county in the land.

To those accustomed to thinking in legal categories, these contacts between "higher" and "lower" levels of government may seem inevitably to involve centralization and threats to local self-government. On the contrary, and paradoxically, there is evidence that these devices of assistance, persuasion, and supervision have in many instances had just the opposite result. A good case can be made for the proposition that the observed apathy of many electorates is to be explained by the inability of their local governments to provide services in which popular interest may be enlisted.[34] It is the opinion of the committee on state-local relations of the Council of State Governments that state aid, "to which administrative supervision is an inevitable hand-maiden," is "an important instrument for the preservation of local self-government. Financial aid gives localities the means to maintain activities demanded of them. In the absence of aid, localities would have to follow one or more undesirable courses of action. For one thing, localities might be forced to leave important services without sufficient support: this would inevitably damage their prestige and popular support. A second important consequence might force localities to widen their revenue systems to include taxes obviously ill suited for local collection: this would result in great inequities and an economically unsound tax structure. A third unwholesome course might lead state governments to assume functions which could be administered more effectively on the local level." [35]

---

[34] How much of this apathy really exists is, of course, hard to determine. It is certainly risky to generalize. Two contrasting views as to the capabilities of ordinary people in managing public affairs may be found in David Lilienthal's *TVA: Democracy on the March* (1944) and Granville Hicks, *Small Town* (1946).

[35] See *State-Local Relations*, p. 52. These conclusions are adapted from the excellent work by Alvin H. Hansen and Harvey S. Perloff, *State and Local Finance in the National Economy* (1944).

When we examine the influence of the national government, it is by no means clear that the results of its activities have been hostile to the preservation of local self-government. Actually, the effect of federal grants in connection with such programs as social security in many cases has been to touch into new life local agencies long considered moribund. Even though these agencies are subject to a supervision often resented, they do have the wherewithal to administer substantial programs in their own communities. The possibility of rendering these services has given the traditional units of local government a new importance in the eyes of local voters, and has brought to many of them for the first time a familiarity with improved methods of administration which they probably would have been long in accepting otherwise. Of perhaps more significance in stimulating local self-government is the program of the Soil Conservation Service in which, in the words of A. W. Griswold, "we find government ending in 'the administration of every man's farm by himself' in an almost literal fulfillment of Jefferson's prescription." [36]

Although it has always been tacitly assumed, it is by no means self-evident, that local self-government is democratic, and that centralization means a derogation from democracy. There is, of course, a very seamy side to decentralization and a hollowness about many of the stock arguments favoring local self-rule. As a matter of fact, the transfer of administrative responsibilities to larger areas is often a recognition of the fact that local units tend to escape genuine popular control. As one able student puts it, Americans "have wisely preferred the assumed imperfections of democracy to the supposed efficiency of monocratic regimes. But the allegedly necessary evil of inefficiency should not be apotheosized into a glowing virtue. Government, like any other provider of goods and services, must yield a product that satisfies the customer. The movement of functions to higher levels of government with their greater areas is a genuine response to the need for consumer satisfaction." [37] There is, moreover, some reason to be suspicious of some of the arguments of those who, in order to prevent the effective performance of certain regulatory or service functions, raise the cry that "home rule" is being threatened by their transfer to central authorities. When the area charged with

---

[36] A. Whitney Griswold, "Jefferson's Republic—the Rediscovery of Democratic Philosophy," 41 *Fortune*, pp. 111-12, 125-26, 129-42, at pp. 140, 142 (1950).

[37] James W. Fesler, *op. cit.*, pp. 41-42.

such functions is smaller than the optimum one, there is no regulation, which is precisely what is wanted by those devoted to a spurious self-government. It may be added that there are probably few oligarchies more brazen than the cliques of local officeholders and special local interests of all sorts who, time and again, in the name of local self-government, have blocked sensible proposals for the consolidation of inefficient local areas. The victims of such unctuous selfishness may well discover that more distant governments are actually more democratic than those under their own noses.

These conclusions are in considerable measure borne out by an important study conducted in 1946 in five counties by a national council on intergovernmental relations. It is, incidentally, significant that the national council acted in cooperation with the federal Bureau of the Budget. Individual local studies were made by committees representing not only the governmental units (federal, state, etc.) operating within the county, but the "general public." These local council members went into their work with "the complete conviction that all state aid and practically all federal functions should be turned over, with their corresponding assets, to local units; in the main, they have stayed to discover that there are fairly good grounds for the prevailing pattern of functional distribution, that their local units are in fact saddled with many functions which demand larger administrative areas, and that in many cases federal administration operating at the local level is actually more responsive to the local will than their own 'local' government." [38] As a matter of fact, it seems clear that all attempts to discuss liberty and centralization as antithetical suffer from oversimplification. We are still under the spell of the unpretentious eloquence of De Tocqueville's explanation of American liberty in terms of the independence of the primitive townships of more than a century ago.[39] Nearly all defenses of local self-government since he wrote *Democracy in America* have been in terms set by him. It is probably true that the burden of proof should be upon those who would transfer functions from lower

---

[38] This appraisal by Rowland Egger is printed in *Grass Roots: A Report and an Evaluation,* published by the Council on Intergovernmental Relations (1947). There is a good summary of these studies in Fesler, *op. cit.,* pp. 115 ff. The counties studied were Blue Earth (Minn.), Henry (Ind.), Colquitt (Ga.), Santa Clara (Cal.), and Skagit (Wash.). The project was financed by the Spelman Fund.

[39] And perhaps the young French aristocrat himself was under the spell of the gracious people who entertained him!

to higher levels, since there is no substitute for local knowledge. But this does not deny the possibility that liberty may find defenders beyond as well as within the boundaries of local units.[40]

---

[40] "All virtue does not lie in the states, nor all good government and true economy in the grass-roots and villages. Grass-roots and sidewalk taxpayers may be able to watch carefully and perhaps intelligently the dimes that go into local school taxes, but they are no authorities on atomic research. Nor can we safely assume that crossroads wiseacres know all the answers to other international and scientific riddles. The concept of weak Federal Government supported by strong States has no more validity than that of a gigantic national bureaucracy undermining the States and subjugating the municipalities. Our native common sense will dictate the compromises which will preserve our American system and still meet changing world conditions." Robert Moses in the Task Force Report on Public Works of the *Commission on the Organization of the Executive Branch of the Government* (Hoover Commission), Jan. 1949, p. 19.

CHAPTER 15

Reconstruction and Reform

THE POLITICAL MAP AND ECONOMIC REALITIES

The areas traditionally used in the work of local government were laid out when economic and social conditions were very different from what they are today. Trade was local, wealth was mainly in real estate or in other types of tangible property, functions were few in number and concerned for the most part the local population, and administration was so simple that laymen had no difficulty in discharging the duties of local offices. All this, of course, has changed fundamentally. Functions have multiplied beyond what would have appeared possible to our ancestors, and some of them have grown complex beyond belief. There are very few today which do not in some way have ramifications extending far beyond the boundaries of the "pure and elementary republics" of which Jefferson spoke in such glowing terms. We have come to believe, for example, that the state and even the nation have an interest in the quality of the educational offering of the smallest and most remote township, and we know, when it comes to such a thing as an epidemic, that county and town lines are simply irrelevant.

The administrative talent needed to supervise modern public services is, of course, not evenly distributed among the 155,000 units of government and could not be paid for by most of them if it were. Property which was once in farms, farm animals, and farm implements has taken myriad forms with the growth of the corporate form of business and the prolific creation of new types of "securities." The economic activity which gives value to these indices of income and taxpaying ability ignores local and even national political boundaries. Organizations such as our great manufacturing, trading, and financial corporations are, in reality, economic states, rivaling in power, as they do in extent, the political state which in legal theory endows them with life and supervises their activities. Determining what they shall pay for the support of government is surely not a matter for township assessors or county boards. It is not necessary to multiply proofs that political organization as exemplified in towns, townships, and counties is separated from the economic realities of our day by a gulf which can be bridged, if at all, only by a far-reaching reconstruction of local institutions. Such local areas cannot pay for what they need from their own local resources; they cannot supply from their own inhabitants the skills needed; there are some functions which they ought not to be carrying on at all; and they are generally unsuitably organized for doing even those things which might fairly be regarded as belonging to them.

This is a summary statement of the fundamental problem of local government in the twentieth century—the inadequacy of its traditional units from the points of view of their area, population, taxable resources, and internal organization for their work. Any plan to reorganize local government must give consideration to *all* these aspects of the problem. Area and population, as we have seen elsewhere, bear directly upon the question of the sufficiency of the government with relation to various functions; but neither can be discussed apart from the question of taxable resources. Nor can reform of the internal machinery of a county, for example, be discussed as if it stood alone and without intimate relations to such matters as functions, taxable wealth, area, and population. And even if one's wisdom were sufficient to assign each of these factors to its proper place in a scheme of reconstruction, the pattern would be incomplete if it did not include the relationships between local units and the state, as well as those between the state and the national government. If these matters are considered here one by one, it is only in the interest of clear thinking, not with the idea that each problem can be solved independently of the others. Further than this, it should be said that no plan can be of equal validity for all sections, for the character of change, as well as the speed of its adoption, will depend upon the nature of local problems, legal and constitutional situations, popular attitudes, and the state of the administrative arts. Reformers ought to be humble.[1]

---

[1] "The conclusions and recommendations of students in different states have naturally been affected by differences in regional conditions, in points of view, in emphases, in objectives, and in methods of study. In each state the student has been confronted by the intrenched forces of tradition, prejudice, inertia, and self-interest. These imponderable but stubborn facts have to be reckoned with; and the method of reckoning in one region cannot be precisely the same as in another. Thus, suggestions

No better diagnosis of the ills of local government and no better statement of the remedies commonly proposed can be found than that supplied by the New York Commission for the Revision of the Tax Laws. The report of this commission said: "Every study of local government in New York State from that which anticipated the constitutional convention of 1915 to that made by this commission, has exposed its incapacity generally to deal with the problems of a modern civilization. Every legislative commission which has had to deal with the problem, whether its purpose was a complete readjustment of local government and its relation to the state through constitutional revision, or merely by legislation here and there throughout the statutes to minimize the ill effects of an ancient and outworn system of government and administration, has inevitably reached the same conclusion. Local government in the state of New York with its multiplicity of administrative units, poorly defined distribution of powers and duties as between the state, the counties, the cities, villages, towns and special districts, its non-articulated, irresponsible system of assessment and tax collection, and its increasing incompetence to deal economically and efficiently with the needs of a modern civilization, is still a major problem before the people." [2] This diagnosis is followed by prescriptions for treatment which agree quite closely with those developed by surveys in other states. These may be summarily stated as follows:

1. The units of rural local government should be enlarged.
2. All overlapping of local jurisdictions should be abolished.
3. As functions now performed by local authorities become of more than local concern, the state should take over increasing responsibility for their accomplishment and support. [3]

To these must be added the suggestion that the internal structure of local units should be so modified as to provide for a definite and responsible head presiding over a hierarchy of officials and employees. We may generalize and describe these as demands for consolida-

---

for reorganization are characterized not only by variety but also by experimentalism, tentativeness, and approximation." A. C. Millspaugh, *Local Democracy and Crime Control,* pp. 4-5. The present discussion leans very heavily upon this excellent study. The quotations from it are made with the permission of the author.

[2] *Third Report of the Commission* (Leg. Doc., 1933, No. 56), p. 94.

[3] *Report of the Commission* (Leg. Doc., 1932, No. 77, Memorandum No. 10), p. 67. To these recommendations the Commission added one to the effect that all local governments should be abolished in certain very sparsely settled districts.

tion of areas, internal reorganization, and reallocation of functions. Each of these needs to be examined.

THE CONSOLIDATION OF LOCAL AREAS

The notion of consolidation is simplicity itself. Many persons interested in making local areas more serviceable, and appalled at their prodigious number and tangled relationships, jump to the conclusion that consolidating adjacent ones is a quick way out of our difficulties. It is the county especially that has been studied from this point of view. The average number of counties in a state is something over sixty. The average county can be crossed in an hour. The average population is about 50,000, and the median a good deal less than this figure. The per capita wealth of many hundreds of these units is so small that they cannot be expected to support effective governments. If, so the reasoning goes, proper combinations of counties were made, nearly every state could get along with a fifth or a fourth as many. The more enthusiastic of these political cartographers then skip lightly to the conclusion that the remaining areas would not only be vigorous units of local government, but that we could at once save millions, or even hundreds of millions each year, by discharging more than half of our elective officials and closing hundreds of county institutions. Not all students, of course, have been as optimistic, but the idea has been an attractive one. The possibilities of county consolidation have been studied during the past twenty or thirty years in more than three-fourths of the states, and, in a number of these, statutes exist by which consolidation may be brought about. It is proposed, for example, that the fifty-eight counties of California be reduced to fifteen; that in North Dakota the number be reduced from fifty-three to as few as thirteen; in Wyoming from twenty-three to six; in Kentucky from 120 to twenty; in Tennessee from ninety-seven to twelve; in Oregon from thirty-six to seven; and in Nebraska from ninety-three to fifteen or even six. The more striking reductions, it is true, are proposed without presenting evidence of much serious reflection; on the other hand, careful students, on the basis of thorough investigation, suggest quite radical changes. Consolidation, therefore, cannot be dismissed as entirely chimerical.

The movement for county consolidation has for its object the creation of units which will have area, population, and wealth enough to support effective government. This means, theoretically, finding areas with populations of 20,000 at least, covering not over 6,400 square miles.[4] A population of this size, it is assumed, would have enough wealth to support a considerable number of functions, would be convenient from the standpoint of administration, and would be small enough to permit the existence of real self-government. What are the possibilities of finding such areas? And, if they are found, do they offer a way out?

Even a cursory investigation will disclose that neighboring counties which, if consolidated, would fit the theoretical specifications occur only rarely on the political map of the United States. In the thinly populated sections of the Western and Mountain states, for example, consolidations including the minimum of 20,000 population would be larger in area than many Eastern states. Thus Cherry County, Nebraska, has a population of about 11,000 covering a territory of nearly 6,000 square miles, which is greater than that of Connecticut. An examination of the area and population of the counties to the east, west and south shows very clearly that no new area with as many as 20,000 inhabitants can be created which will be smaller than 8,000 square miles in extent. This is larger than any one of half a dozen Eastern states and violates the criterion of convenience examined earlier in this study. On the other hand, in the states to the east where the population is denser and where a larger area might be more convenient from some points of view, it is not at all clear that economies would result from consolidation, since there is evidence that beyond a certain population point economies disappear. As a matter of fact, feasible consolidations of counties seem to depend upon an evenness of population density which seldom occurs in real counties. This may account for the fact that the only two consolidations that have so far been made have involved only five of the more than three thousand counties in the country. It is the judgment of an able investigator that "consolidation is probably not theoretically applicable to more than a quarter of the counties in the United States" and that "in most regions, an effort to consolidate would merely waste time and energy." [5]

Theoretically, county consolidation would reduce the costs of local government in two ways: (1) by doing away with duplication in overhead costs, such as salaries; and (2) by providing a volume of work large enough to realize the economies possible when an admin-

---

[4] See the discussion of these criteria in Chapter 3.
[5] Millspaugh, *op. cit.*, p. 141.

istrative staff is fully occupied with tasks heretofore apportioned among two, three, or four organizations. But it does not follow that these results would occur. It is true that one supervisory board would take the place of several, but everything depends upon the method used in paying such officials. If they are to be paid by the day and if they should continue the same sort of direct and constant personal supervision of county affairs now customary, the cost might well be higher than at present. Or, if a salary is provided, the greater responsibilities involved may be successfully urged as an argument for a larger compensation. Nor will it do to assume that the cost of maintaining county buildings will be entirely eliminated. If courthouses are already too small, as many are, a new one may have to be built for the much larger area. And what use can readily be made of an abandoned courthouse or county jail? It is hard to say what might be saved through concentrating a larger volume of work in a single organization, but certain things here are likely to make one skeptical. The "experts" who will presumably manage the functions of the new area are likely to be expensive in comparison with the present part-time officials who are paid almost nominal salaries or are compensated by fees. Finally, it may be assumed that the rulers of the new district, perhaps precisely because they have higher administrative standards, will be somewhat more expansive in their plans. In any event, it is not by any means clear that large economies would follow county consolidation.

Two other reflections seem in order at this point. The government of an area such as the county is not only a rectangle on the map, it is an affair of human beings, with all that implies in the way of interests, prejudices, passions, jealousies, and distrusts. "One of the first difficulties," says Anderson, "arises out of the fact that units of local government are human organizations. We shall, therefore, not expect to determine their size with the precision insisted upon by physicists, engineers, and others who have more control of their material." To be more specific, how would county consolidation appear to the present "courthouse gang"? Or to the business group in the county or town? Or to the lawyers? Or to the Main Street "social set" which fondly looks upon itself as setting the pace for the hinterland? Just to ask these questions is to suggest innumerable difficulties.[6]

---

[6] "The interlocking of local-state politics which gives undue weight in state legislatures to the opposition of local officeholding politicians to the abolition of local units,

In the second place, even assuming that these obstacles could be overcome, are county consolidations under local auspices likely to be wise ones? If equalization of the tax burden and the quality of the public services is an objective of consolidation, are these likely to be secured through the efforts of local people acting under permissive statutes? The isolated consolidations which might occur under such conditions would probably prevent the extension of financial help to many counties needing it most. Unless some authority exists with power to deal with the local government problem of the whole state, piecemeal consolidation would probably do more harm than good. It is for this reason that the Committee on Administrative Areas of the Minnesota State Planning Board, after suggesting the formation of a state commission to report upon a systematic revision of county boundaries, recommended that, after such a commission had reported, the legislature should exercise its power to determine the boundaries of all local units, instead of leaving the matter to local choice on the basis of purely local feelings and desires.[7] We must keep steadily in mind the fact that many so-called county functions are really of state-wide importance. It would seem wiser to explore the implications of that fact than to further a movement which denies it. For to the extent that these are state responsibilities, no county or combination of counties is the proper area of support or administration.

Cooperation among Administrative Units

Although much talked about at various times, the movement for county consolidation has actually made little progress. There have been, in fact, only two consolidations in recent history. James County, Tennessee, in 1919 voted to join with its neighbor, Hamilton (Chattanooga). In 1932, Campbell and Milton Counties, Georgia, were merged with Fulton County (Atlanta). Both cases were exceptional in that they involved metropolitan districts. In predom-

---

re-enforced by the loyalties to existing units of the local publics, has been the chief obstacle to the consolidation and enlargement of local units." Robert Parks, "Trends in Rural Local Government," in Jasper B. Shannon (ed.), *The Study of Comparative Government* (1949), p. 201.

[7] See the *Report of the Committee,* pp. 4-5, 29. In speaking of the perhaps rather special case of counties in the Ozark region of Missouri, Clarenbach concludes that "county consolidation alone is an inadequate remedy for the ills of local government in the Ozarks; and the more nearly adequate remedy of improved state supervision could be applied to reorganized county governments within existing county boundaries." Fred A. Clarenbach, *Needed Local Government Reorganization in Ozark Land-Use Adjustment Areas,* Mo. Agr. Exp. Sta. Research Bull. 331, pp. 65-66 (1941).

inantly rural sections, consolidation would involve the difficult
problem of working out combinations of counties for all of the functions now performed by these units. Actual administrators, conscious of these difficulties, have avoided them by seeking larger areas
for one function at a time. There are, therefore, numerous examples of inter-county cooperation in such fields as health, welfare,
hospitals and sanatoria, and crime control, while the prosecuting
function is in some states discharged on a district basis. There are
examples also of city-county cooperation in more thickly populated
areas. This method of procedure has obvious advantages. It makes
possible a practicable administrative area for each function without
seriously disturbing the vested interests of officeholders. County
boards do not have to be abolished nor county seats removed. An
area may be chosen more exactly suited to the functions concerned
than would be the case if all of the services had to accommodate
themselves to the same enlarged area of two or three adjoining counties. Moreover, new vested interests are not so likely to grow up
about such an area as about a county, and it may be more readily
altered when conditions require change.[8]

On the other hand, such a device has some very distinct disad-
vantages. If all the usual "county" functions—roads, welfare,
health, and so on—could agree upon the same districts, there might
then be created a prospect for more general consolidation of areas.
But this is not at all likely to happen, since the same area is seldom
regarded as suitable for more than one function. Moreover, in view
of the usual disintegrated character of county administration, it is
probable that each *ad hoc* district would be planned without reference to other functions.[9] Such a development on any large scale
would simply further complicate the administrative map. Nor is
this all: The control of these special districts would necessarily be
divided between the authorities of the cooperating counties, thus
further weakening a responsibility which is even now too indefinite.
Finally, if the functions thus dealt with are to any great degree of
interest to the state at large—and this is implied—and if larger areas
are desirable, they should be arranged, not at the option of local

---

[8] The virtues of the intergovernmental contract as a substitute for consolidation
of local areas are pointed out in Frank M. Stewart and Ronald M. Ketcham, "Intergovernmental Contracts in California," **I** *Public Administration Review* 242-48 (Spring
1941).

[9] See Conrad H. Hammer, "Functional Realignment vs. County Consolidation,"
XXI *National Municipal Review* 515-518 (Aug. 1932).

bodies, but in accordance with a state-wide plan. Otherwise there is no assurance that they will be set up where there is the greatest need. We may conclude, then, that while the plan of interdistrict cooperation has real merits, its adoption is only a way of sidestepping the fundamental question as to the more rational assignment of functions between the state and local levels.

INTERNAL REORGANIZATION

In many of the current schemes for the reconstruction of local government, great stress is laid upon the need of introducing centralized responsibility into the management of public affairs. The reformers usually begin with an analysis of the existing system designed to point out the illogical grouping of functions and division of powers and the opportunities for the evasion of responsibility. The general impression conveyed is that our present system was devised by a long succession of absent-minded legislatures, each ignorant of the work of its predecessors, and that stupidity, if nothing worse, presided over its evolution. The remedy usually suggested is to centralize responsibility by a regrouping of functions under heads of departments, each answerable to a manager or other strong executive. It is assumed that, if state administrative reorganization and the city manager plan have been successful, the same device would work in other areas. And, as a matter of fact, there are examples of this type of organization in a few counties. Thus the supervisor in certain New Jersey counties approaches the status of a county executive, as do probate judges in Alabama counties, and the chancery clerk in Mississippi. Elsewhere over the country, the county clerk or auditor has some integrating functions, especially in the field of finance. Moreover, officials known as "manager," "executive," or "director" exist in a number of counties.

Believers in this process of dealing with county administration expect great things of it. It will, it is urged, not only bring about substantial savings in money but, by centralizing responsibility, will make for vigorous administration and restore popular interest, thus realizing the values attributed to local self-government. Before attempting any evaluation of this plan, it should be pointed out that no orthodox manager has anywhere been introduced into county administration. In no county has it been found possible or desirable to bring about complete unification of the administration under either a manager or an executive. Some officers everywhere continue to be chosen by the people or appointed by some authority other than the manager.[10] In a good many cases, the exceptions are due to constitutional requirements; in others they may be traceable to local situations. In any event, it is worth noting that in practically all cases the officials excepted from control by the manager are those responsible for *state-county* functions—the school superintendent, the state's attorney, the sheriff, the clerk of the court, and so on. Whatever the reasons may be for these deviations from the orthodox pattern, it is clear that the exclusion of these officers prevents the complete unification of responsibility which the manager plan envisages and which has been more nearly achieved in cities.

It does not seem, however, that the difficulties involved in introducing the manager plan into county government are due entirely to constitutional obstacles or even to peculiar local conditions requiring compromises. Looked upon as a means of revitalizing county government and fostering local interest in it, it is open to the objection that this end could be attained in fullest measure only by turning over to the refurbished county administration the functions now shared with the state. In any case, such a large degree of local control would have to be set up as to interfere very seriously with the control and supervision now in the hands of state administrative officers. It is scarcely reasonable to think that such a reversal of developments can take place. Most rural counties would be swamped by the financial burden. On the other hand, if the existing integration of functions between the county and the state levels is left undisturbed, we should have a situation in which state officers now sustaining relations of supervision and cooperation with various local officials would presumably have to establish new ones with the manager. It is felt by many that the adoption of the manager plan would be a gratuitous disturbing of these relations, not justified by the "unification" which the plan is supposed to bring about on the county level. Since locally chosen officers could not be directed at one and the same time both by the local manager and by state officials, it would become increasingly difficult to coordinate state and county policy with regard to the functions now shared. It would likewise be hard to conserve those standards of service which have been built up by cooperation between the two sets of officials. In

---

[10] "In at least twenty-five states . . . the constitutions specify that necessary county officers be elected (as in Nebraska and Wyoming) or actually name long lists of elective officials. . . ." *State-Local Relations,* pp. 175-76.

short, it is believed that as long as the county acts so largely as an agent of the state, attempts to strengthen its organization in this way are contrary to well-established tendencies towards state-county functional integration—tendencies which ought not to be blocked since they represent a "natural" development.

Other critics of the manager plan point out that even today, when the county acts with the state in performing many state-county functions, there is too little to do in the typical rural county to justify the employment of a skilled manager. These critics admit that there is room for improvement in the conduct of the business of the county, but they contend that this is already taking place through the introduction of better business methods and the centralizing of financial responsibility in the hands of such officials as the county clerk or auditor. In view of these developments, it is believed that a manager would be a supernumerary, since the only field in which he could be useful is already being occupied by other officials.

Finally, and closely allied to these objections, is the argument

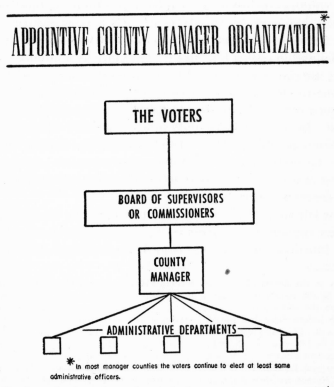

APPOINTIVE COUNTY MANAGER ORGANIZATION*

THE VOTERS

BOARD OF SUPERVISORS
OR COMMISSIONERS

COUNTY
MANAGER

ADMINISTRATIVE DEPARTMENTS

*In most manager counties the voters continue to elect at least some administrative officers.

Fig. 15. Organization chart of appointive county manager organization.

that while the manager plan may be successfully adopted by cities, it has no logical place in the administration of rural counties. The contention here is that a city is a "natural" area whereas the county is an "artificial" one. In support of this, it is asserted that the mere fact of incorporation is evidence of a community consciousness which does not exist in an area such as a county, which normally comes into existence without the request or consent of the local inhabitants who are forced willy-nilly within the boundaries determined arbitrarily by the official surveyor. It is further asserted that the functions performed within a city have reference to the needs of a self-conscious community and therefore, taken together, have a unity about them not possessed by the scattered functions performed by the county as a mere agent of the state. These critics do not object to the manager plan in urban counties, for these, they say, differ in no essential respect from true municipal corporations.

The evidence from the record is not absolutely conclusive as to this argument. In 1951 there were about twenty manager counties in the country—five each in California and Virginia, three in North Carolina, two each in Maryland and Tennessee, and one each in South Carolina, Montana, and New York. Most of these are urban counties and in only a few does the manager have anything like the powers associated with the office in cities. In most cases the voters continue to elect a considerable number of county officers and the manager's executive powers are therefore more or less severely restricted. In completely rural Petroleum County, Montana, with a population of about 1,200, the plan has been notably successful. There, however, it grew out of a crisis situation and experience under it may not justify any conclusion as to the plan's feasibility in rural counties generally.[11]

It is fair to say that the arguments against the manager plan for counties contain an unexpressed presumption in favor of what is called functional integration. In ordinary language this means that

---

[11] As to the fitness of the plan for counties generally, Kilpatrick remarks: "Confronted by the county in operation, the proponents of the county manager have never placed on the ballot a county charter incorporating an orthodox manager. The mold has been broken each time by the necessity of a concrete situation." *County Management*, p. 10. The experience of Petroleum County is described in R. R. Renne, "Too Small to Be Efficient?" in **XXXVI** *National Municipal Review* 78-82 (Feb. 1947). There is an excellent summary of the arguments for and against county executives in William Anderson and Edward W. Weidner, *State and Local Government* (1951), pp. 478-86. In 1951 Nevada authorized the county manager plan for counties of more than 10,000 population.

the movement to bring state and county functions closer together is approved by the critics, because they regard it either as simply inevitable or as in itself desirable. It is clear, however, that if "centralization" should proceed to the point where all functions in which the general interest is dominant are transferred to the state, there would be very little left for the county to do. Certainly in most rural counties there would be too little left to keep a manager busy. No judgment as to the soundness of these criticisms is possible until we examine a third suggestion for overcoming the inadequacy of the county—the reallocation of functions.[12]

THE REALLOCATION OF FUNCTIONS

Whatever may have been the nature of the functions originally performed by such areas as the county and the township, it is clear that they have long since come to be *state-local* rather than purely local ones. This is recognized by the long-established trend toward a quasi-partnership between the state and the local unit, both in their management and in their financing.[13] This arrangement is not an entirely satisfactory one, since it involves at best divided responsibility and, in cases where money grants are made, encourages a reckless local spending of money supplied from the state treasury. Most of the plans for the reconstruction of local government, since they ignore the dual character of these functions and the progress already made toward their integration, turn out on examination either to be inconsistent with their professed aim of securing functional integration or to halt this development. The time has come to recognize the fact that the vast majority, at least, of rural counties cannot continue to lead a double life. They cannot act as units of local government on the one hand, and as agents of the state on the other. The rural county "cannot win the undivided attention of its

---

[12] It is Millspaugh's belief, after a very able analysis, that "the manager plan would be financially impossible, unnecessary, or undesirable in from one-half to three-fourths of the counties in the United States." *Local Democracy and Crime Control*, p. 170. The feasibility of the manager plan for counties is discussed in the *Report of the (Virginia) Commission on County Government* (1934); "County Government in California," *Final Report of the California Commission on County Home Rule* (1930); Wylie Kilpatrick, *County Management* (1929), and in numerous articles in the *National Municipal Review*. The experience of Virginia counties with the manager plan is examined in George W. Spicer, *Ten Years of County Manager Government in Virginia*, University of Virginia Extension, Vol. XXIII (Sept. 1945).

[13] For example, take the provisions found in many states for cooperation of state supervisory departments and local authorities in the choice of local personnel, or joint action of state and local highway authorities in planning and executing local road improvements.

citizenry so long as it remains a pauperized agent of the state parading in the raiment of self-government." [14] But pauperization is the price for acting as an agent at all, and extinction the result of a refusal to be pauperized! For this is the ultimate dilemma of the rural county—the almost complete impossibility that it can serve as a unit both for genuine self-government and for supporting and administering state-local functions.[15]

If this dilemma is not to be resolved either by the consolidation of local areas or by schemes of internal reorganization, the remaining possibility is to attempt a more satisfactory distribution of functions between the two levels of government. Upon what basis may such a distribution be made? There is no general principle better than that suggested by the able New York Commission for the Revision of the Tax Laws: "It seems hardly open to question that the desirable objective is to have each unit of local government . . . perform those functions which it can perform most efficiently and economically." [16] Although this may seem vague, there is abundant evidence that a number of functions not only belong logically to the state, but are also too costly to be effectively administered by the typical rural county. Certainly in most sections, and with respect to the resources of a great majority of the counties, the following functions are suitable for transfer to the state: roads, public health, relief and welfare (at least with regard to their main features), schools, tax assessment, election administration, judicial administration, and crime control. It is, of course, not likely that any such wholesale transfer of functions will take place at once, even in a single state. Nor is it necessary that it be so. It is, however, wise to keep some such reallocation in mind as a desirable ultimate objective. And it should be observed that roads, schools, and welfare to-

---

[14] Millspaugh, *op. cit.*, p. 173. The number of these "paupers" is very large. Thus, in New York state in 1934, of the sixty-seven counties, thirty-three received from the state in the form of aids more than was collected by the state within their boundaries. In Minnesota, highway grants are derived very largely from a state-wide property tax. In fifty-nine of the eighty-seven counties, more money was handed back by the state than was collected through this tax in the counties. See *Report of the (N. Y.) State Tax Commission* (1934), p. 338; William Anderson, *Local Government and Finance in Minnesota,* pp. 213-15.

[15] "The simple fact is that the American people have desired two things which seem to be incompatible. One is complete local self-government in a system of small units coming down from earlier days; the other is a standard of services higher than ever before and a distribution of expenses over wide areas, so that no local area, especially not a poor one, will be unduly burdened." William Anderson, *op. cit.,* p. 327.

[16] *Sixth Report* (1935), p. 30.

day make up the bulk of the expenditures made within local units, and that their transfer might be expected to relieve the pressure upon the general property tax, thus aiding in that equalization of the burdens of government which is supposedly one of the aims of various consolidation schemes.

Such a reallocation of functions might be expected to go far toward solving that part of the local government problem which has to do with its financial inadequacy. What does it do, however, to local self-government? It may as well be admitted at once that such a development would destroy the substance of local self-government as that dogma has hitherto been understood. It is well enough to argue that the functions enumerated above *are* of interest to the state, and it may easily be demonstrated that many local areas are now financially unable to manage them efficiently; the fact remains that all of these functions originated as *local* needs and that the theory of local self-government grew up about their maintenance. If transferring these functions to the state means that their management as well as their financing is to be taken away from the local electorate, it is idle to pretend that much worthy of the name of local self-government is left, at least as that term has traditionally been understood.

There would seem, moreover, to be little force in the argument often advanced to the effect that a county, for example, is not a fit area for home rule, since it is a mere agent for carrying out state policy. Apparently county residents do not believe this. On the contrary, the opportunity to participate even in the "mere administration" of functions is one for which local political groups at least will vigorously contend. These groups evidently do not make the distinction in their own minds between policy and administration which has occupied so large a place in treatises on political science. To local people, self-government apparently means an opportunity to preserve contacts with those who make decisions of interest to the local community, whether those decisions be political or administrative in the academic sense of those terms. In the typical county, administration is the stuff of policy.

But if a redistribution of functions involving an enlargement of state power and responsibility is fatal to the preservation of local self-government, it may still be a desirable development if it can be shown that it is worth the price to be paid. Whether it would be or not depends upon a more accurate assessment of the values of local self-government than we are now able to make. For it is clear that these values can scarcely be measured by any research tools yet devised. Until we have such tools, all we can suggest is that the consciousness of personal significance or power or influence or security which may arise from sharing in the work of relatively small groups may not necessarily be connected with the traditional areas of local government. Certainly it would be hard to demonstrate that these subjective values are necessarily connected with townships or counties or other areas of government in rural sections, whatever may have been the case a century ago. Associational life is extremely rich in the United States, and there is an imposing body of opinion to the effect that other groupings beside territorial ones are significant in affecting the temper and operations of government. Our difficulty, then, may be simply one of understanding what is involved in local self-government, for it may well be that group life is able to make its contribution to the political process, even though there should be a serious reduction in the strictly governmental importance of the areas to which we have grown accustomed.

Nor does it follow either that the functions best suited to central administration should be everywhere transferred to the state, or that a rather general shift of this sort would leave local communities with nothing to do. In nearly every state there are, no doubt, some counties competent to manage such functions as welfare, highway maintenance, and assessment as well as, or better than, they would be managed by the state itself. Under these circumstances it may be satisfactory to make the transfer optional. Under other conditions, improvement may be made by permitting local units to contract with state departments for the furnishing of certain services, such as police protection, choice of personnel, and purchasing, at cost. In view of these possibilities, any suggestion of a wholesale shifting of state-local functions to the state smacks of the dogmatic, even though it be agreed that such a shift may be a desirable ultimate objective of reform.

If the burden of what are regarded as truly state functions were transferred to the state, is it true that local areas like townships and counties would be completely denuded of vital functions? With regard to townships, this might well be the result, and few could be found to mourn that fact. As to counties, however, the case may be different. There is no good reason why the county should not continue to serve as the unit for recording such legal documents as wills, mortgages, and deeds. The functions of maintaining parks, forests, community halls, libraries, playgrounds and theaters, and rural zoning are purely local and, once they have emerged as full-fledged public purposes, are eminently proper for local administration.[17] If local inhabitants can pay for such functions and manage them well without supervision from above, then nothing need be done about the situation. But certainly it is vain to argue that saddling these units with functions only partially local is a good way to revitalize them.

A high degree of "centralization" would not necessarily involve the obliteration of all local units. A state legislature, setting out today to redraw the political map of the state, would be compelled to retain at least some units like the traditional ones, even though a rather complete transfer of functions to the state government had taken place. Within these areas, there is no reason why the state should not avail itself of the counsel of local groups as to the incidence of administrative programs upon the local community. Experience shows few, if any, examples of a central power setting at naught local opinion even though that opinion had no strictly legal claim to be heard; and there is ample reason to believe that local groups would find ways to make themselves heard. Whether such a contact with state administration would be an adequate substitute for the time-honored local self-government is, of course, open to question, but, in view of the large number of organizations now active in watching the administration of such functions as welfare, education, agriculture, highways, and tax administration, it is at least arguable that they would be satisfactory and influential channels for the expression of community opinion. Indeed a local area with truly local functions might well be a sharper challenge to the democratic urge for self-rule than one such as the county with its divided allegiance and complicated machinery.[18]

---

[17] The optional functions of counties and other rural areas are being increased at every legislative session, although it is difficult to say how extensively rural governments actually embark on such new enterprises. Probably a good many do, in view of the general weakening of the traditional bias against an active government. It is also true, as was pointed out in the preceding chapter, that the effect of such centralizing devices as grants-in-aid and state supervision has, in many cases, been to strengthen local government simply by giving it the wherewithal to discharge significant functions.

[18] In a valuable article, Professor Edward W. Weidner presents some cogent arguments in favor of the county-manager and county-executive plans as against the somewhat skeptical views taken by the present writer. He points out quite correctly that the number of functions suitable for local control is increasing steadily, that the growing interdependence of federal, state, and local governments does not mean that

THE TACTICS AND STRATEGY OF REFORM

The movement for the reconstruction of local institutions has encountered other obstacles beside the inertia of local populations and the strength of vested interests. Although these obstacles are met with everywhere, their existence is often lost sight of by zealous reformers. One of these is the difficulty of dramatizing "efficiency" in a rural population prone to personalize all political issues. An out-and-out contest between Jack Brown and Jim Jones for the county clerkship takes on the character of a horse race and may convulse the whole electorate. On the other hand, it is hard to make colorful the budget system, or central purchasing, or the merit system. Yet there is no escape in a democracy from carrying these causes to the people. Everyone takes a proprietary interest in the local government and wants to be "shown." While people may rather generally be expected to give at least lip-service to the idea of efficiency and economy, the mass of men find the vital details of such things so dull or so complicated to master that interest in the general policy is likely to evaporate very rapidly. As a matter of fact, the rural electorate has proved itself time and time again to be adept at preventing the realizing of reforms of this sort. Some nauseous scandal or a widespread and long-continued abuse is needed to furnish the emotional drive behind all revolutions.

The really significant reforms in administrative methods have been made in our cities, perhaps because the problems met with in supplying public service are obviously complex to a degree which even the dullest must recognize, and because of the greater familiarity with a minute division of labor in every field. These things have not been a part of the traditional background of our rural population, and this fact for a long time placed reform movements in rural areas under a heavy handicap at the outset. There is reason to believe, however, that this is much less true than it was a generation

counties should not have unified executives, that the chief obstacle to local unification has not been the state officials but local "politics," tradition, and vested interests, and that even in some small counties the manager has found plenty to do and has operated successfully. Edward W. Weidner, "A Review of the Controversy over County Executives," VIII *Public Administration Review* 18-28 (Winter 1948). While admitting that the county has shared in the overall growth of governmental functions, and that the executive or manager plan has had its victories and ought to be tried in other places, I am of the opinion that what I have written is still true of the great majority of our local units and will continue to be true. It should be pointed out that Mr. Weidner's article is extremely valuable as a summary of the periodical and monographic literature on the subject.

ago. The pressure of mounting costs has been a powerful argument in favor of modernization of methods and equipment. It has grown increasingly easy to draw the obvious analogy between the results of rationalization in industry and rationalization in government. Local businessmen, who count so heavily in county, township, and village government, have perforce become acquainted with modern accounting as income taxpayers and have thus become habituated to it in public affairs. Federal aid programs have insisted on up-to-date administrative practices. Finally, the steady pressure of the suppliers of equipment and services has been effective in many a courthouse and village hall. Silently and without fanfare, these and other results of urbanism and industrialism have worked, in dozens of local governments, an undramatic but real revolution. It is still true, as Aristotle remarked more than twenty centuries ago, that men prefer disorderly to orderly living, but they can be persuaded to *some* measure of the latter.

In all formal schemes for the reform of local government, great stress is laid upon the need of introducing centralized responsibility into the conduct of the public business. This is normally held to require the shortening of the ballot and the conferring of greater power upon some directing official. Although there may be a good deal to the contention that the short ballot would actually increase popular control, it is doubtful if this argument is very forceful with respect to rural conditions. The typical rural county is small in population and everyone is acquainted with everyone else. In such situations, the personal character of the "race" for many offices may actually heighten the interest of the voters, and there is surely no reason why they should not be familiar with the qualifications of the candidates. Whether or not this is true, the fact may be that the rural population is suspicious of the implications of power which are involved in the demand for increased responsibility. There is no concealing the single powerful official, and his possession of power is likely to make a deeper impression on the public than his alleged responsibility. After all, humanity has probably lost more than it has gained from the doings of the possessors of political power, and the common man may be forgiven if he interprets such power in terms of evil rather than of good.

It ought also to be pointed out that every reform threatens some vested interest, and that realized reforms almost always represent

simply some realignment of interests.[19] This is true not wholly because men are incapable of disinterestedness (though most men
are), but rather because each is likely to confuse his own good with
that of the public. Reformers in the past have been rather generally
preoccupied with the machinery of government. This is in line with
the contemporary tendency to seek the causes of our ills in "society," or "institutions," or almost everywhere except in the character
of the persons who make up "society," who support "institutions,"
or who work the machinery of government. Most of the structural
changes urged upon us could be made without producing any special
improvement in the actual functioning of local government. The
ultimate problem of government which consists in reconciling power
and responsibility, if it is soluble at all, cannot be dealt with on the
assumption that when men are given the facts they will act ration-
ally with an eye to the public good. In a democracy, at least, that
good is defined in terms of the scarcely reconcilable objectives of
warring groups. Under such conditions, getting good government
—or any government at all, for that matter—is only partly a question
of man's equipment for rational effort; it is more largely a question
of his ethical bent.

Ideally, government ought to be conducted for the welfare of
the governed, and it ought constantly to aim to advance their virtue.
But this is only to say that all who hold power of any sort, hold it as
trustees for those who must resort to them for service. If all human
institutions are measured by this standard, it is doubtful if government will be found more deeply cursed than any other. For every
breach of trust by public officials, at least another can be laid at the
door of the holders of economic power; for every extortion by officeholders, there can surely be found another chargeable to those prom-
inent in the marketplace; and the business world generally is no
stranger to bribery, collusion, misrepresentation, fraud, and sharp
practice. Men holding political power in a society dominated by
a materialistic philosophy can scarcely escape the influence of that

---

[19] "And it ought to be remembered that there is nothing more difficult to take
in hand, more perilous to conduct, or more uncertain in its success, than to take the
lead in the introduction of a new order of things. Because the innovator has for
enemies all those who have done well under the old conditions, and lukewarm
defenders in those who may do well under the new. This coolness arises partly from
fear of the opponents, who have the law on their side, and partly from the incredulity
of men, who do not readily believe in new things until they have had a long experience in them." Niccolò Machiavelli, *The Prince*, Ch. 6.

philosophy. The wonder is not that government is corrupt, but that it is as good as we actually find it. For, on the balance, the ethics of government are higher than those of the market. After all, the much criticized politician must at least go through the motions of consulting his supporters and obeying their will. Even though he may himself manufacture that consent by virtue of which he rules, his methods are certainly no more reprehensible than those used by some of our business organizations in selling their wonder-working nostrums to the public.[20] Local governments, it is true, have occasionally fallen into the hands of pirates, but even these have usually given *something* in return for the votes which elected them. Can as much be said for those who peddled worthless South American bonds to Kansas country bankers or saddled unconscionable debts upon cities to improve now vacant subdivisions?

This discussion is not without point in connection with schemes for structural reform. Someone has wittily said that we shall not have pure and efficient government until our economic future is behind us! So long as we live under the influence of an expansionist and gambler psychology, with each year bringing its quota of roads to be extended, subdivisions to be improved, and additional offices to be filled, we may confidently expect the temptation to corruption to be too great to be resisted. If this is so, there may be something to be said for preserving a rather elaborate system of checks and balances even in local government, the resulting inefficiencies being endured in order to prevent wrongdoers from using the processes of government for their own ends. In any event, it is by no means clear that the formula "centralization of responsibility" is an adequate substitute for the traditional semi-automatic machinery.

The Personnel of Reform

The reform of institutions has notoriously almost never come from within. There is no deep mystery about this. However badly an institution may now serve the end for which it was created, it is almost always found to do surprisingly well for those who work it. The interest of reformers never has about it the cohesiveness which

---

[20] If *noblesse* obliges, so does power and, further, so does skill. Those who practice a skill, as well as those who wield power or enjoy privileges, bear a responsibility to those who deal with them. And it may therefore be argued that the growth of political power is often to be explained by the failure of business and the professions to discharge their responsibilities to those who must resort to them, rather than by "usurpation" by "scheming politicians."

a material stake in the *status quo* can give. Nor is the personnel of reform always such as to command the confidence of "practical" men. Much of the impulse to reform has come from the academic community. While the American people have been generous in their support of education, they have generally regarded with suspicion the intrusion of the scholar into the field of practical affairs. The fundamental shrewdness of this judgment cannot be doubted. The scholar's attitude towards his own speciality is one of detachment, and this is a necessary implication from the scientific approach. While it constitutes the peculiar strength of the investigator, it is a great disadvantage to the man of action. For the latter's stock in trade is not the patient amassing of facts and their unimpassioned interpretation, but rather a subtle faculty by which *certain* facts are implemented into a plan of action likely to secure popular support. Such men we call politicians and, "good" or "bad," they must be regarded as the natural flowering of a system based upon free public discussion and popular consent. The world of actual politics goes whirling on in its accustomed grooves, while the reformer with his paraphernalia of good will, research, and the scientific spirit works valiantly to change its speed, its direction, and its orbit. The man of affairs knows that the material with which he works is not categorized into those sharply separated compartments which characterize much of what is called "scientific reform," and that the mass of men are interested in the short and not in the long run. John Bright is credited with having said that, during his memory, Parliament had done many good things, but that it had not done any of them *because* it was good. Academic reformers would do well to keep this in mind, for it illustrates clearly the fact that their appeal has to be made, not to the patriotism or the public spirit, but to the interests of those able to realize the reforms. And this is the work not of academic reformers but of practical men. Our real task is to improve the quality of the latter.[21]

The force and effectiveness of reform movements in most states suffer at present from a lack of cohesiveness and a unity of purpose.

---

[21] From the point of view of the hypersensitive and the esthete, it may as well be admitted that much of the rude work of the world, including governing, is accomplished by quite "ordinary" people. "For politics, we know, is a second-rate form of human activity, neither an art nor a science, at once corrupting to the soul and fatiguing to the mind, the activity either of those who cannot live without the illusion of affairs, or those so fearful of being ruled by others that they will pay away their lives to prevent it." Michael Oakeshott (ed.), Thomas Hobbes' *Leviathan*, Introduction, p. lxiv.

Those who seek efficiency, those who seek democracy, those who want "good government," and those who emphasize tax reduction are very often asking for things which are irreconcilable. They cannot all be attained at the same time or by the same tactics. Nor are there many states in which a frontal attack on the problem of local government is at present at all feasible. Constitutional and legal obstacles make many changes impossible except as distant objectives. More time and energy needs to be expended on the formulation of a strategy directed at what can be done here and now. While reformers should avoid the quackery of politicians, they might do well to learn something of their facility at compromise. Whether this can be done in a setting of free discussion and in spite of the traditional individualism of reformers is problematical, but progress is sure to be slow until emphasis shifts to the feasible.

Reform and Local Leadership

No reform of local government is likely to be permanent unless it is accepted and defended by local interests. The lack of political inventiveness and the generally low standards of performance in rural areas may very well be due to the absence in many of them of any capable leadership among the residents. Historically this leadership in the United States has been supplied by the clergy and the teachers, and in the 18th and early 19th centuries, members of these callings discharged their responsibilities on the whole admirably. The population movements of the last century, however, broke up the community of the older towns of the East by draining off to the West or to the growing cities some of the ablest of the former leaders. As the successive waves of migration swept westward, they left nothing that compared in permanence with the settled communities of the seaboard, but rather a succession of boom towns, each of which in turn lost the more energetic of its population as opportunity beckoned from the next frontier. Today the rural pastor and teacher are both on the lookout for a promotion or a "call"—usually to a city where the rewards are greater, both in cash and in independence. The most pronounced effect of these population movements has been to produce a general disorganization of rural life fatal to the growth of a true community spirit and to the production of leaders devoted to the building of the community. For not even the notion of a community can arise in the minds of people who, far from wishing to put down roots, are merely stopping off between two adventures.

The urbanization of the country has also had direct effects in preventing the rise of a class of rural leaders. As the city comes more and more to set the standard of living, rural life becomes less and less satisfactory to the educated portion of the local community, and the city thus takes its toll of the more energetic members of the population. Nor can the rural districts successfully compete with the cities in providing their inhabitants with the necessities and amenities of modern life without widespread changes in rural organization for which the population is not yet prepared. To some extent, the loss of potential leaders to the city has been made up by the coming of such persons as the county agent and extension workers, but these are also likely to be non-residents with ambitions for a career on a wider stage.

In a very real sense, the growth of farm tenancy in some parts of the country, and the increase in the size of the agricultural unit also work against the development of a desirable type of rural leadership. The former introduces into the community a social stratification based upon wealth with all the disruptive results of such a change; while the industrial organization of large units may well reproduce in the country the attributes of feudalism found in many industrial centers, and thus create a class of masters rather than leaders.

The cause of reform has also had to contend with a very lukewarm support of the press in rural regions. The country newspaper is probably no more servile than the city press; but it is, for a variety of reasons, less critical in its outlook and less outspoken in its opinions. The city newspaper draws its support, financial and otherwise, from a wide variety of sources and is able, at least on occasion, to take an attitude of independence towards political questions. On the other hand, the typical country newspaper has a small circulation confined strictly to the county, a small capital supplied normally by a single person or a partnership, few resources in the way of lucrative advertising, and is likely to depend for a large part of its support upon the legal advertising and "job" printing of the local offices. In short, it is in no position to take up the cudgels for reform and make vocal the criticism of the more intelligent section of the rural community.

The outlook for the creation of local leadership is perhaps not hopeless, but improvement is bound to be slow. For all signs indicate that we are still in the midst of a period when population is shifting from one economic field to another, and history is witness to the fact that such movements require long periods for their completion. With the disappearance of the frontier, there is a possibility that the population will grow less migratory, and that the identification of a few generations with the same area may breed in time a consciousness of community. There may also be some reason to expect the creation of an attractive village civilization in the country to take the place of the rather shabby thing we now have. The spread of good roads and the greater ease with which electric power can be distributed may lead to a decentralization of industry and the spread of the amenities of life, the absence of which has driven many persons to the city. A society centered around a village with a stable means of support and a citizenship whose fortunes were bound up with the locality would show no dearth of leaders. To the extent that such a development takes place, it may be possible for local leaders to look favorably upon standards of administration foreign to the experience of the present rural population. All this, however, is largely speculation; we certainly do not know enough to predict.

Appendix

In writing and revising this book, I have tried to draw my material so far as possible from the "sources." There are, of course, a number of excellent textbooks whose authors have followed the same procedure, and I acknowledge my indebtedness to these, not only for facts which have eluded my own search, but also for ideas and points of view. Candor, however, compels even a mature student to confess that he learns as he goes along, and to admit that his subject has reality to him in direct proportion to his reliance on basic data. The sources which have been most useful are obviously those cited in the footnotes. No apology is offered either for the number of these, or for the fact that they appear in immediate proximity to the text, instead of being collected at the end of the book. The serious reader has a right to know the author's sources, and he will find them most useful if he does not have to search too far for them.

This arrangement seems to me to have the advantage of encouraging the student to go with the writer in the latter's search for an adequate understanding of the subject. The plan adopted in the first edition of having references at the end of each chapter, without intending to do so, may have had the effect of creating an illusion of finality, an illusion which, in any case, the printed page produces for the unwary. It is for these reasons that I have concluded to ask the reader to find his bibliography in the footnotes. I use this brief essay as a means of collecting in one place certain aids to study of a more general nature.

BIBLIOGRAPHIC AIDS

Laverne Burchfield, *Our Rural Communities,* published by the Public Administration Clearing House, 1313 East 60th Street, Chicago, 1947. This is an excellent collection, arranged by functions, of periodical and monographic materials in print at the time of publication.

Public Administration Organizations: A Directory, published also by the Public Administration Clearing House. This lists a large number of organizations, public and private, interested in various aspects of public administration, with their addresses, officers, type of publications, and so forth. An indispensable guide to materials available from organizations which, in many cases, specialize in studies of state and local government.

The National Municipal Review lists each month the more important current research reports, some of which deal with rural affairs.

Reports issued by both public authorities and private research groups are in most cases listed in *Public Affairs Information Service*. More popular articles may be found by consulting the *Readers' Guide to Periodical Literature,* which is issued each month. Articles appearing in law reviews may be found listed in the *Index to Legal Periodicals,* published by the H. W. Wilson Company, New York City, for the American Association of Law Libraries.

Although no longer up-to-date, the articles in the *Encyclopedia of the Social Sciences* contain good bibliographies.

A bibliographical essay by the present writer, "Local Government in the United States," which appeared in the spring of 1951 in *Contemporary Political Science,* Publication No. 426 of the United Nations Educational, Scientific, and Cultural Organization, reviews recent and contemporary literature in the field.

STATISTICAL COMPILATIONS

The publications of the federal Bureau of the Census are, of course, very voluminous, and only government depository libraries can be expected to have all of them. Of the general census reports, students of local government will find most useful the series on Population and Agriculture. It is to be noted that these series are divided into separate compilations for each state. The latter are inexpensive and, in some cases, are available for free distribution, so that, where the entire set is not readily accessible, the student may be able to find at little cost basic data as to population and agricultural and industrial production for his own state. Special reports are also issued by the Bureau on such subjects as mortality statistics, revenue and expenditures, housing, public debt, and so forth.

Many valuable compilations are issued by the Government Division of the Bureau. Among these may be mentioned Governmental Revenue, Governmental Debt, Public Employment in the United States, and occasional special reports on County Government Finances, State Aid to Local Governments, Election Statistics, and Governmental Units. Anyone may get his name on the Bureau's mailing list to receive notices of forthcoming publications in any of the many categories. The cost of most individual publications is nominal.

The Statistical Abstract of the United States, published annually by the Department of Commerce (cloth $3.00, paper $2.00) contains in summary form most of the material collected by the Bureau of the Census with respect to governmental operations and the private economy of the nation.

All of the states issue statistical publications in considerable variety. The comprehensiveness of these depends upon the extent of state supervision of local affairs and their value upon the skill of the state officials concerned. The present writer has found specially valuable the reports of the Massachusetts Department of Corporations and Taxation, the State Tax Commissioner of Connecticut, the State Tax Commissions of New York and Illinois, and the Local Government Commissions of New Jersey and North Carolina; but excellent and informative reports appear from time to time in nearly all the states. The best way to keep abreast of developments is to consult the bibliographical aids referred to above, or to write for information directly to the proper state office.

PERIODICALS

The following journals should be accessible to serious students of rural institutions. Few of them are devoted solely to local government, but all will publish from time to time valuable articles, reviews, and research reports, and all are useful in building up a bibliography.

The American Political Science Review, official quarterly journal of the American Political Science Association, published at 1785 Massachusetts Avenue, Washington, D. C.

The American Journal of Sociology, published quarterly for the American Sociological Society by the University of Chicago Press.

The Journal of Criminal Law and Criminology, published quarterly by the Northwestern University School of Law, Chicago.

The Journal of Politics, published quarterly by the Southern Political Science Association in cooperation with the University of Florida, at Gainesville, Florida.

The National Municipal Review, monthly organ of the National Municipal League, 299 Broadway, New York City. Devoted largely to city government, but contains occasional articles as well as a section in each issue on county and township government.

The Public Administration Review, the quarterly journal of the American Society for Public Administration, 1313 East 60th Street, Chicago. Contains scholarly articles on the organization and operation of government departments and the administration of specific functions, and valuable reviews of significant books and research reports.

Public Management, the monthly journal of the International City Managers' Association, also at 1313 East 60th Street, Chicago. Contains informed technical articles on many phases of local administration.

State Government, monthly magazine of the Council of State Governments, at same address as preceding. Prints brief, readable articles on administrative problems facing state and local governments, many of them by working officials.

The National Tax Journal, published quarterly in Boston; formerly appeared as *Bulletins of the National Tax Association;* contains occasional excellent articles on local revenue and financial administration.

Rural Sociology, the official journal of the Rural Sociological Society; published quarterly by the North Carolina State College of Agriculture and Engineering of the University of North Carolina, at Raleigh, N. C.

PUBLICATIONS OF RESEARCH AGENCIES

The principal change that has occurred in the study of local government in the last generation has been the institutionalization of research. The task of even describing the machinery and operation of local governments has exceeded for a long time the resources of the independent, solitary worker. It is true, of course, that books still appear in considerable numbers under the names of individuals, but these are generally either textbooks summarizing the work done by various cooperative groups, private or governmental, or monographs devoted to special local situations or to a small segment of the total field.

Since there are literally hundreds of privately financed bureaus or institutes devoted to cooperative research, it is clearly impossible to name them here, much less to list their publications. The student may follow the latter in the bibliographies printed in the various journals listed elsewhere in this note. Reference will be made only to those organizations whose published work has been found most useful to the author.

A very large body of fundamental research is done under the auspices of various associations of local government officers. A considerable number of these have their secretariats under one roof at 1313 East 60th Street, Chicago. The Public Administration Clearing House, at the same address, will furnish those interested with lists of the publications of these associations: the American Municipal Association, the Council of State Governments, the Civil Service Assembly of the United States and Canada, the Municipal Finance Officers' Association, the National Association of Assessing Officers, the Federation of Tax Administrators, the International City Managers' Association, the American Society of Planning Officials, the American Public Welfare Association, the National Association of Housing Officials, the American Public Works Association, Public Administration Service, and the American Society for Public Administration. Most of these organizations publish regular "house organs," periodical news letters, and special reports of interest to their members, make special studies when requested by local governments, and render consultative services to local authorities. Of particular value to students are *The Book of the States,* published biennially by the Council of State Governments, and the *Municipal Yearbook,* issued by the International City Managers' Association. The Council of State Governments has been responsible for such excellent monographs as *State-Local Relations* and *The Forty-eight State School Systems.* The publications of the Council have been of particular value in the field of state-local and federal-state relations.

Another type of research organization which has performed valuable service is exemplified by the Institute of Public Administration (684 Park Avenue, New York City) and the Brookings Institution (722 Jackson Place, Washington). Both of these have been active in field surveys of state and local government and in the developing of high standards of public administration. Many of the administrative reorganizations carried out during the past thirty years by state and local governments were preceded by detailed surveys made by experts attached to these organizations. Their publications can usually be procured inexpensively.

Valuable studies on various questions of interest to students of local administration are published by such privately supported agencies as the National Industrial Conference Board, the Twentieth Century Fund, The Russell Sage Foundation, the Commonwealth Fund, and the Milbank Fund, all in New York City. The executive directors or secretaries of these foundations will supply lists of publications in print upon request. A good deal of material is published by industrial corporations and trade associations interested either directly in selling their products to governmental units or indirectly in keeping down costs. For example, highway revenue figures are collected and published, with appropriate conclusions drawn, by the American Petroleum Institute, 50 West 50th Street, New York. In the field of the professions, such organizations as the American Medical Association, through its Bureau of Medical Economics and Statistics, is active in issuing bulletins bearing upon the supply and quality of medical service, while the American Public Health Association, through its monthly *Journal*, keeps its members informed about public health and hospital services. Nearly all public officials have organized professional societies, many of them with periodical journals. Since most of these are, in a sense, lobbying organizations, it is usually not hard to get on their mailing lists.

In recent years, bureaus of public administration established in some of the larger state universities have devoted considerable energy to investigating local government problems in their respective states, either on their own motion or as agencies of their state governments. Research in matters of importance to local government has only recently become a function of state administrations, but the growth of this sort of service has been rapid. With the development of national and state financial support of such functions as public welfare, highways, education, and public health, careful analysis of local needs and the local use of funds has become of vital importance to the state governments. It is, therefore, common to find divisions of research in the state supervisory offices, and from some of these proceed studies of value. In a few states, legislative councils, set up as aids to the legislature, have produced creditable studies of local governmental problems. Finally, in a number of the more wealthy states, investigations of very high quality have been produced by staffs attached to the regular standing or special committees of the legislature. It is often possible to secure reports from all such agencies, either by writing directly to the agency concerned or to the secretary of state.

Of particular interest and value in the study of rural problems are the bulletins produced by the agricultural experiment stations attached to the land-grant universities. These are likely to be concerned with purely local situations, but in the aggregate they give a fairly comprehensive view of the local scene throughout the country. These publications, as well as other official state reports, are listed in the *Monthly Checklist of State Documents,* issued by the Library of Congress. Most of them are available to responsible persons gratis or at nominal cost. The formal reports of the established state administrative departments are, for the most part, rather unrewarding, many of them being only perfunctory attempts to meet the statutory requirements of publication. There are many exceptions, however, where reports are both informative and imaginative. Only rather extensive experience will enable one to find nuggets in the rubble.

A great deal of important research is done by almost every agency of the national government. The student of local government will find particularly valuable that done by those departments involved in the various grants-in-aid programs. A vast mass of information, for example, will be found in the annual reports of the Federal Security Agency. For current statistics on the welfare, education, insurance, and public health programs, as well as technical articles, the student should become acquainted with the *Social Security Bulletin,* published monthly by the Office of Publications and Reports of the Federal Security Agency, at $2.00 a year. Public health statistics and articles on health administration may be found in *Public Health Reports,* issued weekly by the United States Public Health Service. The Bureau of Public Roads in the Department of Commerce publishes not only annual reports, but also such special studies as *Highway Practice* and the annual *Highway Statistics,* and monthly releases dealing with the sources of highway revenue, the objects of expenditure, and the distribution of federal grants. The *Agricultural Yearbook* and the annual *Agricultural Finance Review,* published by the Department of Agriculture, contain much information with respect to most of the matters touched on in Chapter 1. The Office of Education in the Federal Security Agency issues not only its *Biennial Survey of Education in the United States,* but also a very large number of special studies and the monthly journal *School Life.* The easiest way to keep in touch with federal publications is to request the Superintendent of Documents, Government Printing Office, to send as they are published the price lists of documents in one's fields of interest. The various agencies are permitted to distribute a certain number of their publications gratis; others are sold at nominal cost by the Superintendent of Documents. Brief descriptions of the organization, activities, and regular publications of the executive departments of the federal government may be found in the *United States Government Manual,* issued annually by the National Archives and Records Service ($1.00), and in the *Congressional Directory,* usually published twice a year.

Books on Rural Sociology

The rural sociologists have assembled and discussed a bewildering mass of data bearing upon rural life and rural social organization. We are indebted to them for many suggestive insights on all sorts of rural problems. The list of books which follows is not meant to be complete. It contains simply the books which the writer has found most useful or are most recent.

John H. Kolb and Edmund de S. Brunner, *A Study of Rural Society,* 3rd ed., 1946.
Paul H. Landis, *Rural Life in Process,* 1942.
Lowry Nelson, *Rural Sociology,* 1948.
Dwight Sanderson, *Rural Sociology and Rural Social Organization,* 1942.
N. L. Sims, *Elements of Rural Sociology,* 1944.
T. Lynn Smith, *The Sociology of Rural Life,* rev. ed., 1947.

It should finally be noted that local government is still *government,* and that no one can fruitfully study it unless he brings to it the sort of background that can be acquired only through wide reading and reflection. Since, even in an age of specialization, there is a sense in which all knowledge is a unit, it is obviously impossible to list all the books valuable in giving one perspective and insight. Good books are still being written, of course, and fresh analyses of political ideas and administrative procedures are constantly appearing. These should not be ignored. On the other hand, it is easy to fall victim to the enthusiasm of publishers and reviewers in claiming novelty and penetration for works which, on reflection, are seen to be something less than revolutionary, something less than profound.

There is still a great deal to be said for reading the old books, the "classics," if one dare the risk of being called "behind the times." The important questions of government and politics are perennial and have for centuries challenged the best minds of the race. It is no accident that new editions of the masters of political thought still find a ready sale; the world will not let them die. If this is true, why should we prefer the up-to-date when examination shows that it is, perhaps unknown even to its author, a crisp and clever rehash of ideas that were old before Columbus left behind him the Gates of Hercules. It is surprising, once one gets acquainted with *The Republic* of Plato, to see that Socrates was aware of precisely the same problems that today plague presidents, senators, and county commissioners. Why not begin with Plato's account of the irritating conversation of the Athenian gadfly? The same questions were discussed and different answers suggested by Plato's distinguished pupil, Aristotle. Machiavelli wrote about them, as did Hobbes and Locke and Mill and the fathers of the American Republic.

The young student cannot, of course, be expected to have read all of these writers; but he can keep them by him and work them into his own thinking. He may be safe, I think, in cherishing a faith that what they have had to say will, as he reflects on it, illuminate a subject which, superficially, seems so little "theoretical." In the end, it is only the possession of such equipment that will enable him to deal with local government in something like the grand manner. All this is only to say, of course, that even so apparently pedestrian a subject has no position of its own, apart from the general movement of political ideas. It is not the private preserve of the technical researcher, the expositor, and the constructor of organization charts. At any given epoch, it is the result of the interaction of men's ideas, ideals, passions, and inertias, and these can be understood only in their historical setting.

Every teacher who shares this view will implicitly acknowledge his indebtedness to other scholars in advising his students as to their reading. In my own case, among modern writers I have found the following suggestive:

J. H. Randall, *The Making of the Modern Mind,* rev. ed., 1940.
Crane Brinton, *Ideas and Men,* 1950.
Frederick M. Watkins, *The Political Tradition of the West,* 1948.
R. M. MacIver, *The Web of Government,* 1947.
Bertrand de Jouvenel, *On Power,* 1949.
Graham Wallas, *Human Nature in Politics,* 1908.
E. Pendleton Herring, *The Politics of Democracy,* 1940.
Ralph H. Gabriel, *The Course of American Democratic Thought,* 1940.
A. D. Lindsay, *The Modern Democratic State,* 1947.
Carl Becker, *The Heavenly City of the Eighteenth Century Philosophers,* 1932.
Vernon L. Parrington, *Main Currents in American Thought,* 1927-30.
Alfred N. Whitehead, *Science and the Modern World,* 1925.

Index